The Excellent Board II

The Excellent Board II

New, Practical Solutions
for Health Care Trustees and CEOs

Karen Gardner
Editor

Health Forum, Inc.
An American Hospital Association Company
CHICAGO press

This publication is designed to provide accurate and authoritative information in regard to the subject matter covered. It is sold with the understanding that neither the authors nor the publisher are engaged in rendering legal, accounting, or other professional services. If legal advice or other expert assistance is required, the services of a competent professional should be sought.

The views expressed in this publication are strictly those of the authors and do not represent the official positions of the American Hospital Association. AHA is a service mark of the American Hospital Association used under license by Health Forum, Inc.

Printed in the United States of America—02/08

Cover design by Cheri Kusek

Library of Congress Cataloging-in-Publication Data

The excellent board II : new, practical solutions for health care trustees and CEOs / Karen Gardner, editor.—2nd ed.
   p. ; cm.
Articles originally published in Trustee.
Includes bibliographical references and index.
ISBN-13: 978-1-55648-350-9 (alk. paper)
   1. Hospital trustees.   2. Hospitals—Administration.   3. Health facilities—Administration.   4. Chief executive officers.   I. Gardner, Karen.
II. Title: Excellent board 2.   III. Title: Excellent board two.
   [DNLM: 1. Hospital Administration—Collected Works.   2. Chief Executive Officers, Hospital—organization & administration—Collected Works.   3. Trustees—organization & administration—Collected Works.   WX 150 E96 2008]
   RA971.E9865 2008
   362.11068'3--dc22
                              2007045116

ISBN: 978-1-55648-350-9   Item Number: 196126

Contents

About the Editor

Karen Gardner has been a health care editor for more than 25 years—as editor of *Trustee* magazine since 1989 and, prior to that, as executive editor of periodicals for the Joint Commission. Before entering the health care field, Gardner edited several legal publications.

Gardner writes a monthly column in *Trustee*, has published numerous articles in the magazine, and is the editor of a book on quality in hospice care published by the Joint Commission, as well as the first edition of *The Excellent Board* (AHA Press, 2003). She is also the editor of *Better CEO-Board Relations: Practical Advice for a Successful Partnership* (AHA Press, 2007).

Gardner shepherded a major redesign of *Trustee* in 1995, and under her editorial direction, the magazine has won a number of editorial and graphic awards—from the Society of National Association Publications (including a Gold Award for General Excellence), from the American Society of Business Publication Editors, and from the American Society of Healthcare Publication Editors.

Gardner received a master of arts in teaching (M.A.T.) English from the University of Chicago and, before entering the editorial field, taught English at the high school and middle school levels in Chicago.

Foreword

Over the past year, I have spent countless hours in hospital and health system boardrooms, working with trustees on their self-assessments, sharing governance best practices, discussing their roles around quality and helping them to develop board improvement plans. What has most impressed me is the desire of these motivated volunteers to perfect their craft in order to deliver on the promises made by their health care organizations to their communities.

This desire becomes even more impressive when we realize that being a trustee is not their primary vocation. Trustees are a group of diverse people, from diverse professional backgrounds and with diverse interests who come together in an attempt to make sense out of a very complex and confusing enterprise in order for it to serve a greater good for those entrusted to its care. Achieving this understanding is not an easy task, even for those who are involved in delivering health care every day, let alone for trustees who take on the responsibility for guiding and holding our hospitals accountable to their very public mission.

How can we assist trustees and boards to achieve perfection in their craft? We clearly have an obligation to take their experience and insight and develop effective tools for them to improve the health care system. Boards are only valuable when they help our organizations make sense out of our circumstances, provide input and ensure we are grounded in our mission. We must provide them with those resources that assist them in making the connection between their perspectives gathered over a lifetime and their organization's current situation.

The American Hospital Association (AHA) is committed to being the source for trustees to achieve exceptional governance. Through its Center for Healthcare Governance, the Health Research and Educational Trust and Health Forum, the AHA has developed a portfolio of tools, educational programming and publications to assist trustees on their journey of providing outstanding leadership to our health care institutions and to their communities. Delivering this high level of support is one important way to recognize the contributions of trustees and increase the professionalism of their role.

The Excellent Board II compiles some of the most important resources for trustees to develop to their full potential. Culled from the pages of *Trustee* magazine, the AHA's premier governance journal for trustees and executives, are articles and workbooks that cover almost every aspect of hospital trusteeship. There are few other reliable sources that trustees can access to find an almost perfect guide to honing their skills.

As you read these pages—as a trustee, executive or student of health care governance—consider the great debt we owe to our trustees. Use this information to strengthen the trustees' role and to help our health care institutions fulfill the promise they have made to their patients and communities.

John R. Combes, M.D.
President and COO
Center for Healthcare Governance

Preface

Don't you sometimes wish you had the opportunity to remake yourself? Keep the parts that work really well and eliminate what's out of date or never worked that well in the beginning? I'm sure the second edition Karen Gardner would be better than the first. Only my parents would disagree.

With the revised edition of *The Excellent Board,* we've had the chance to improve upon the original—added the best and most up-to-date material from *Trustee* and eliminated what might have gotten a little stale.

Over the years, trustees have told us that the topics we've included in this book are the ones they find most compelling. In the editorial field, we use the word *evergreen* to describe articles on issues that have always been important to readers and will continue to be, at least in the foreseeable future. These are the articles we can accept and hold for longer than usual before publishing, if necessary, confident that they won't go out of date—in other words, the kinds of articles we've collected for this book.

For example, every health care board has to identify and recruit new members, ensure quality of care and patient safety, and maintain its organization's financial viability. *The Excellent Board II* addresses these issues and more in the ways you've come to expect of *Trustee*—articles that are straightforward, with the needs and interests of the health care board member a top priority; practical, highlighting the ways boards can make a positive impact on their health care organizations and communities; and stimulating, presenting current issues and concerns in a highly readable style with a fresh perspective.

These articles will give both new and experienced trustees, as well as board and committee chairs, a firm grounding in what it takes to be a productive board member and how to reach the level of excellence health care organizations must achieve. Not only has the learning curve for boards contracted significantly in the past decade, but with more attention being paid to public governance, the not-for-profit sector is feeling the deflected heat.

Articles are organized into eight parts, which begin with the fundamentals of governance and board composition to give trustees a meaningful context within which to understand their job. Learning about the complexities of ensuring quality of care and patient safety and the board's role in effecting change will only be confusing and confounding unless trustees have a firm grasp of what it means to be on a health care board. In the same way, trying to understand the board's roles and responsibilities won't make a lot of sense if you don't first know who should be sitting on your board and why.

There's nothing about directing or managing a hospital or health care system that's easy. And, as regulations become stiffer and operating margins slimmer, those jobs become increasingly more difficult. That's why *The Excellent Board II* is such a valuable resource today—and will be tomorrow. It's evergreen.

Acknowledgments: First, I would like to thank all the authors of the articles included in *The Excellent Board II,* both professional and volunteer. Their articles were great when they were originally published, and they have stood the test of time.

A major thank you is due to Richard Hill, editor of *Hospitals & Health Networks OnLine* and director of editorial for Health Forum's AHA Press. Rick not only guided the process of putting this book together but also lent his considerable expertise to the final product.

And finally, Peggy DuMais, assistant manager for production at Health Forum, was responsible for shaping this book into its present format.

Karen Gardner

PART ONE

Board Composition

Nurturing a Precious Commodity: Trustee Recruits

By Laurie Larson

Rather than "a feather in one's cap," today's hospital trustees are more likely to describe their work as a much weightier mantle of responsibility.

Besides the need to digest a growing encyclopedia of regulatory, clinical, technological, financial and business information, trustees face heightened scrutiny and potential liability. In short, serving on a board has become harder work that needs to be done by smart, busy people at greater personal risk.

"The most complex organization in the United States is the hospital," says James E. Orlikoff, president of Orlikoff & Associates, Chicago. "You need a good board just to get by, but you need a great board to really succeed."

"Trustees can no longer simply be familiar in a casual way with the issues affecting hospitals," says Larry Walker, principal at The Walker Company, a health care consulting company in Lake Oswego, Oregon. "They have to know [those issues] from a strategic standpoint."

And that means that asking only those you already know to join the board may not be enough—and neither will a passive approach to meetings.

Laurie Larson is *Trustee*'s senior editor.

"Governance culture has changed," says Larry Bass, member of the American Hospital Association's Committee on Governance (COG) and trustee with Sparrow Health System in Lansing, Michigan. "You can't operate with all the CEO's friends on the board, and you can't hand trustees a packet with all the information for the meeting as they walk in."

Given all of this, who would volunteer to be a trustee today? How can someone who already has a demanding career possibly act intelligently on all the complicated information that must be absorbed and analyzed? How do trustees get that information? And how can they know they're doing their best to meet their fiduciary responsibilities? One thing is for certain—such questions have made health care trustee recruitment much more challenging.

"We are discussing these questions every day," says Donald Wegmiller, chair of Clark Bardes Consulting Group, Minneapolis. The group works with search firms to find board members, in addition to work with health care executive compensation.

"We advise boards to develop a process to identify the major [national] issues as well as the locally important ones and then plan comprehensive and clear educational sessions," Walker says. "Boards should ask themselves, 'What are the biggest challenges to the whole industry? What do we need to do to understand their effect, their relevancy to us? How might they impact us in the future?' Next, they should look at what barriers exist to dealing with those issues and what their implications will be on the way the board governs and what it discusses."

These same questions and types of analyses are helpful in orienting new trustees, as well as in anticipating who those new trustees should be, Walker adds. For example, trustees might ask themselves, "Who has had workforce issues in their own business? Who has a reason to study insurance trends?"

Walker calls the board the hospital's "strategic lightning rod" for setting policy and defining organizational vision.

"Boards should ask themselves, 'Is what we're working on and discussing the most critical work that is going to define the success of our organization next month, and over the next five years?' Do an audit of [the board's] time to see if you are being strategic enough."

What Do Trustees Need to Know?

Walker's "top six" list of what trustees most need to know include: Medicare and Medicaid reimbursement trends and proposals; understanding how hospitals get paid, including an understanding of contractual allowances and bad debt; emerging trends in health insurance—and how those trends could emerge in the local market and affect the uninsured and underinsured; niche providers; government regulations; and finally, emerging medical technologies such as gene therapy, realizing that "the pace of change has the potential to dramatically change service lines, and capital purchases may get outdated too quickly," he says.

Wegmiller adds, "As margins have become squeezed, there is equal demand for new facilities and new technology. [Hospital leadership] put off new building 10 years ago because margins were not great, and now they have to rebuild—facilities are falling apart. The magnitude of capital issues has grown, and it's availability has shrunk."

Bottom line, "there is more demand for technology than any organization could possibly afford," Wegmiller says. "Trustees need to understand how technology works [well enough] to link it to long-term strategy." In other words, since "you can't have it all," purchasing decisions must be tied to where a hospital sees itself five years down the road.

In addition to this "big-picture thinking" as he calls it, Orlikoff targets understanding quality improvement/patient safety and "financial literacy" as his top three areas for governance acumen.

Quality-of-care oversight and improvement and patient safety are "the equivalent of financial transparency in the for-profit world," Orlikoff says. Quality transparency means that not only must boards understand and be able to monitor quality and safety, they "must be the conduit of information about quality to the community," he says.

As far as financial literacy goes, Orlikoff says board nominating committees need to "kick into overdrive," and work harder to find top financial candidates, as they will be competing with a multitude of for-profit boards seeking the same expertise.

"Many [health systems] are trying to upgrade the financial expertise and literacy of their boards," Orlikoff says. "There are very few who meet the Securities and Exchange Commission's (SEC) financial expertise requirements, and there is hot demand among the Fortune 1,000 [corporations] for people who meet those requirements."

There may be a "run," as Orlikoff describes it, on the major financial experts under the SEC's definition of the term, but financial literacy can be taught to trustees, he believes. In-service continuing education or outside conferences can explain Sarbanes-Oxley and other emerging rulings. And all types of financial institution professionals, such as certified public accountants or anyone who has had previous external oversight audit experience, would be acceptable additions to the board to lend their insight and financial analytical skills, Orlikoff says. But will they want to?

Too Tough to Serve?

"There is an anticipation of Sarbanes-Oxley creep into the not-for-profit health care world," Orlikoff asserts. "There is significant potential with these [added] requirements and accountability that there will be a chilling effect on getting new trustees and a strong possibility there will be a diminishing pool [of trustees to draw from]."

Michael Peregrine, partner at Gardner, Carton & Douglas law offices, Chicago, agrees with Orlikoff but is more optimistic.

"I think we are on the cusp of having a problem recruiting and retaining directors, but the job is not harder than before," Peregrine says. "Sarbanes-Oxley should not frighten people away. Board work is not more risky, it just requires more self-reflection on the qualities of a good board and a better job of managing those duties. Liability is not greater than before, it's just the prism of how the board is looked at that has changed."

The solution? Staying on top of fiduciary responsibilities in the first place and being "aggressively responsive" to state authority questions about how those duties are being covered.

"You have to be in a position to regularly be able to explain your fiduciary responsibilities," Peregrine says. "If you do your homework and are informed and alert, you should have no problem." He also thinks trustees should be naturally skeptical.

"You are looking for people who have fundamental analytical skills, who recognize red flags and will have the gumption to ask questions when they see issues that arouse suspicion," Peregrine says. "Every board needs a bulldog."

Wegmiller maintains that most trustees are adequately indemnified by the hospital, and their greater worry lies in seeing their name in the paper in connection with some alleged administrative impropriety.

"They're embarrassed, even if they're not sued—that's the big concern," Wegmiller says. Orlikoff advises trustee candidates to ask the board during their interview for assurances that their personal risk will be minimized. He says board leaders should not "gloss over or placate" candidates. Board strategies and policies for compliance should be fully explained, as well as how the board is anticipating risk and upcoming standards.

"Tell new trustees, 'We will help you,'" Peregrine says. "'We will have the governance policies that will tell you how to act, the maximum directors and officers' (D&O) liability insurance and statutory protection. We will tell you what questions to ask, what the oversight of senior management guidelines are, what confidentiality rules are.'"

Peregrine further recommends that the hospital's general counsel give an annual report on the status of the board's D&O coverage, explaining where the "soft spots" may be, where boards should be exceptionally careful.

Wegmiller believes that the SEC and the New York Stock Exchange rules are the places to watch for new not-for-profit board expectations and scrutiny.

"It's all coming from the New York Stock Exchange rules," Wegmiller says. "[Eventually, there will be] the same expectations for health care boards as [there are] for corporate boards."

Orlikoff adds, "It's most important that not-for-profit health care boards pay attention to what's happening in the for-profit world. For-profit companies are the bellwether now."

Wegmiller explains, "You need to act like a corporate board, balanced with an understanding of the local community."

Acting like a corporate board also means both being frank about the time commitment expected of incoming trustees and respecting that time.

"Be honest about the time [commitment] up front," Orlikoff advises. "Don't be vague and don't underestimate what is required.

That [honesty] goes a long way. It doesn't scare people away. It shows a thoughtful, deliberate board."

To make the best use of trustees' time, particularly if they are coming from out of town, board materials and reports should be mailed well ahead of board meetings, should be succinct and pertinent, and the discussion agenda should "pull the board to the future, not the past," Orlikoff says.

"Make board service meaningful, don't review the past . . . and don't expect trustees to be on three committees in addition to the main board," Wegmiller says.

Targeting Recruits

To make the best recruitment choices for the board, Orlikoff recommends beginning with a profile or "snapshot" of the current board by age, gender, professional experience and years on the board, including whose terms will be ending and other considerations. Simultaneously, on a yearly basis, the board nominating committee should develop "ideal profiles" of trustees they need, based on upcoming hospital strategic issues.

Next, Orlikoff recommends doing a "gap analysis" between the current board composition and the ideal profile list.

Walker suggests putting together a long-term vision task force comprising the CEO, several trustees, and others in the community, to research the trends and risks that will affect the hospital over the next five years, including studies from public accounting firms and an "environmental scan," as he calls it, for the effects of significant health care trends on the community.

The task force should then brainstorm what to do to ensure the hospital's future success—including a "top 12" list of potential board members to best take on those challenges.

This task force could serve several purposes, Walker suggests, since not only would it help the hospital look to the future, but those serving on it could be future trustees themselves, using the task force as a trial run of their fit with the existing board. In fact, assisting on any hospital committee might be useful for a potential trustee and the board to openly test the waters for future board membership, Walker says.

So who's finding the trustees they need?

Case Study: Sparrow Health System

As the fourth-largest employer in the state, Sparrow Health System's three-hospital, 900-bed, not-for-profit system has its own HMO, physician-hospital and pharmacy/lab networks, as well as hospice and home care services. COG member and chairman emeritus Bass says area residents "feel it's an honor to be part of the organization." As such, they have little trouble recruiting trustees.

Still, Sparrow actively maintains an ongoing pool of potential candidates by sending out questionnaires to interested community members or those who are recommended by someone within the system. Bass emphasizes that these names are not controlled or determined by administration.

Questionnaire respondents rate their interest among seven possible Sparrow subsidiaries, including its foundation, home care services and physician health network, in addition to the hospital and system boards. Respondents are also asked to circle their various areas of expertise among several options.

If they become candidates, potential trustees fill out a more detailed demographic and skills profile, listing other boards on which they serve and board committee preferences. Space is left for essay-type suggestions on how applicants might suggest improving Sparrow Health's governance.

Lastly, if a candidate is nearing acceptance on one of the system's boards, he or she fills out a conflict-of-interest questionnaire as well. Bass says the system currently has 100 people on a waiting list for appointment consideration.

"This [method] works because we're a great organization," Bass says. "Our service area has 900,000 people, and we're very visible in the community."

Local or Beyond?

Although questionnaires are working for Sparrow, the growing complexity of health system governance raises the question of whether or not a hospital's "own back yard" is big enough to find needed talent. There is no consensus among the experts.

"You need to go beyond the local options to find trustees," Orlikoff asserts. "Governance shouldn't just be local people. Effective boards go outside the community to find [people with] needed skill sets, to get an objective perspective."

Wegmiller agrees, advising that boards keep a smaller size and not just recruit locally, but look statewide and nationwide for candidates. "We see a distinct difference in successful organizations and their board makeup and those that aren't successful," Wegmiller says. He advises looking for candidates with specific expertise versus "community leaders." Examples might include an investment banker who understands the importance of raising capital for needed improvements, or a technology or quality executive from a corporation like General Electric.

"Board members should reflect the strategic issues facing a health care system," Wegmiller says. "You need people from large-scale organizations who understand the scope of issues."

On the other hand, although Walker "doesn't object" to going outside the local community, he says, "I am a firm believer that there are people who can lead locally, if they are developed. It's a 'grow your own' strategy. If there are people who are not yet ready to be on the board, you look at how you can grow their capacity now to be ready in a few years."

Board development committees could take this on, he suggests, looking for a larger pool of candidates to join the board in two to four years, keeping them current over time by giving them the same educational materials the current board receives.

Smaller hospitals may not have the same needs as large systems, but they should still seek the best possible diversity they can, Wegmiller believes. To do so, they could, for example, look for board candidates in a larger city in their region. "The problem is that we don't ask or look strategically enough. See what you need, and ask [in the larger community]," he says.

Case Study: Cambridge Health Alliance

One board that seems to have mastered getting a sophisticated, professional, diverse, but still local, board(s) is the Cambridge (MA) Health Alliance (CHA). As a unique independent public health authority partnership between the cities of Cambridge and Somerville, Massachusetts, the alliance's supervisory board must comprise 10 Cambridge residents and five Somerville residents. The

CEO must be ex-officio, there must be at least one physician on the parent board and a city employee from each of the two towns appointed by the city manager. Rick de Filippi, an AHA Committee on Governance member, is the alliance's chair.

"We have tried to get a blend of business expertise, those who have ties to the health community and prominent public people," de Filippi says. This has not been a problem, he says, given CHA's elaborate public service, academic and political network. Among the trustees who sit on the 19-member parent board are the former mayors of both cities, an economist, a public health lobbyist, a chief of pathology at one of the hospitals and other "professionals of clout and heft," de Filippi says. However, he thinks that the board could still use more financial and biotechnology expertise.

De Filippi admits they are in an admirable position for drawing on a wider network of connections than the average health system. "We are a university town and a high-tech town—we do have a broader group," he concedes.

Two subordinate boards report to the alliance board: a hospital board, comprising three community hospitals and 20 area health centers; and a public health board, which advises the parent alliance board on community needs. Various community organization and human service agency leaders form this board. At least half its 16 members are non-native English speakers, and include members of the area's Hispanic resident organization, mental and substance abuse center representatives and youth group leaders. Although this board has no statutory functions, its trustees must also represent the two cities equally.

CHA's mission also demands great diversity on all three of its boards, reflecting both the majority of the area's patients and its employees, de Filippi says. Law firms in Boston have been a good place to inquire about minority leaders, not only among the attorneys themselves but through their connections to leaders in the community at large. The chair of the Massachusetts Immigrant and Refugee Board is on the CHA system board, and de Filippi says the board has also gone to other cultural organizations in both cities, as well as professional vendors, seeking trustee candidates.

Whether a board is local or bicoastal, homogenous or eclectic in its makeup, however, the most basic requirements remain the same, governance experts agree.

De Filippi believes that what a board most needs is a collective sense of responsibility among individuals of strong character.

"You see who's at the table and how seriously they take it," he says. "You establish a board culture in recruitment. Having someone who's the head of a corporation doesn't mean anything if [he or she] doesn't show up [to meetings]. . . . The board is a group of total equals—there should be a 'collectivity' of how it works . . . that's the point. You want someone who says, 'I owe something to my community and I will take responsibility.'" And the trustees doing the recruiting have to have that same conviction about the importance of bringing in the best new recruits.

"You need to have a good case for yourself as a health care system," Orlikoff says. "The reputation of the organization is not enough. Talk to candidates about the value and importance of the organization to the community. Talk about the risks we are facing in health care. Tell them, 'You can make a major contribution to the community and to the redesign of the American health care system. You can shape policy.' This is an effective approach for those whose antennae are up on what matters."

And that's precisely the type of candidates boards are seeking, isn't it?

Finding the Perfect Fit

By Karen Sandrick

*Is your board chair
the right person
in the right place?*

Bruce Stickler learned in a hurry how it feels to be a board chair in the line of fire. In his first month as chair back in 1999, the Illinois Department of Public Health (IDPH) threatened to close the 80-plus-year-old Mount Sinai Medical Center in Chicago because of its antiquated sprinkler system. Stickler, a local attorney, mobilized into action. He met with members of IDPH, the governor's office, state legislators and lobbyists, and worked with the hospital CEO and the governor to secure $8 million in capital financing from the state to make the needed improvements.

"It can be quite overwhelming," Stickler says understatedly, "when you don't know if you're going to be able to keep your organization open." Of course, most board chairs don't assume the gavel under such tumultuous conditions. All do, however, face extremely complex issues, and have especially in the last couple of decades.

Board consultant Michael Annison, president of The Westrend Group, Denver, acknowledges that it was hard for board chairs not to do well when health care was purely a cost-reimbursed business.

Karen Sandrick is a health care writer based in Chicago.

"If I send you a bill and everything is marked up 10 percent, and you [don't have to think twice about] paying it, the job of the board chair is pretty straightforward in terms of overseeing the organization," he says.

But expectations for boards and their chairs have changed dramatically. "Now it takes a far wider range of skills to deal with the changes in medical technology, financing, public policy, collaborative arrangements, and community services," Annison says. These days, he says, board chairmanship "is not a training-wheels job."

Stickler agrees. "Board chairs have to be much more active today in every arena, including policy. They can't leave the work to staff; they have to provide direction and leadership, and [be] involved; they must stand up and speak out for, and on behalf of, their organizations."

A Profile

Board chairs must possess a unique blend of characteristics, advises Dan Vitale, chair of Community Medical Center, Toms River, New Jersey. Chairs must be involved in their community and committed to health care; they must be able to cooperate, show compassion, support the organization's strategic plan, and work with lay and physician board members as well as senior management. "A board chair needs to be an effective communicator and consensus builder who encourages open dialogue and participation among board members, respects other people's opinions, and has an open ear for listening to their concerns," Vitale says.

Chairs must also have respect for their colleagues, a clear sense about the values that motivate their behavior and the organization, curiosity, a willingness to learn and integrity. "They are not too tightly connected with management, keep issues open to discussion, are intellectually honest, and ask for help through personal education or outside resources when they don't have good answers," Annison says.

Very large shoes to fill, indeed. So what if a board can't find someone with the right shoe size? What if it tries to place a 9 AA into 11 EEEs? How bad can it be?

Without a knowledgeable and skillful board chair, upstart or splinter groups may vie for board control, particularly when there is a shift in strategic focus or an issue that is dividing board members. Without a steady hand on the board tiller, "boards can develop a sense of hubris and begin to think there is nothing quite like them; they can become narrow-minded, unwilling to see others' points of view, and substitute the part for the whole," Annison adds. Then, at best, disciplined two- to-three-hour board meetings turn into free-for-alls, says Carl Thieme, president of Cambridge (MA) Research Institute. At worst, a full-blown board coup erupts.

And when boards disintegrate, they can take their organizations with them. The most dramatic cases involve mismanagement, corruption and bankruptcy. More common are lost opportunities and lack of control. Annison knows of one board and its chair that became so obsessed with management's fixation on debt income that it lost sight of the fact that the hospital was losing market share and thus missed chance after chance to prevent the organization from growing financially weaker.

Another board failed to insist on rejuvenating the medical staff and, as a result, was held hostage by one of its physicians. "The hospital was run by one hospital-based doctor who chose which contracts he would and wouldn't sign," Annison explains. "Since neither the CEO nor the board would deal with him, I told them all to go home. [I said] 'Why waste your time? Just turn over the place to the guy who's running it anyway.'"

What causes board and board chair failures? Simple, says Annison; it's poor choice in leaders—the breakdown comes because of personal foibles or failures. In other words, a board selects a flawed individual in the first place, or it chooses someone who doesn't understand what governance means and how to exercise it.

What Does the Job Entail?

The selection of a board chair comes down to finding someone who understands the job, which, Annison stresses, is not operational. Because board members typically are community leaders who have been successful in the private sector, they may believe the chair of a community organization such as a hospital is the same as that of a corporation. Although chairs of boards in the private sector tend to be extensions of the executive offices, board chairs in the voluntary sector are not. "Chairs of hospital boards need to be clear that they are not the chief executives of the organization; they are responsible for governance," Annison notes.

Chairs, therefore, must be familiar with, and willing to ensure that their boards follow, the basic rules of governance and meet expectations for fulfilling their duties. "The board chair must distinguish between the issues that matter and the fads of the moment," says Annison. The most fundamental issue for hospital boards is monitoring how their organization treats patients, which includes not only the practice of medicine but patient satisfaction. Next is service to the community, which takes many forms, including health screenings, education, and programs for the underserved.

The financial health of the organization is, of course, a core board chair focus, but it is not an end in itself. "If there's a mistake in health care, it's becoming too preoccupied with money," Annison says. He explains that a hospital's net income is nothing more than a reflection of the organization's ability to select services that meet the needs of the community, maintain a streamlined organizational structure, and foster good working relationships between staff and physicians. "If an organization is providing services that people in the community don't think matter or won't use, if it has become inordinately complex or if its employees don't help each other, its income will go down," Annison explains.

Thieme recommends that boards prepare a job description that clearly defines the roles and responsibilities of the chair. One potentially overlooked duty is remembering the link between the hospital and its ownership, the community. Boards need to be sure their chairs are aware of the concerns of all segments of the population. "Boards need to have input through surveys and focus groups about where their communities and key constituencies are coming from. We can't assume anymore that because [board chairs] are members of an ethnic group or a strata of society that they speak for those groups," he says.

Another major board chair responsibility is to decide who will be assigned to individual board committees, who will become committee chairs, and what the committees' charge will be. "Good board chairs will demand a work plan from their committees that identifies the issues they will tackle and that presents their agenda for the year," says Thieme.

Particularly important is creating boundaries between the board, its chair and the CEO. "Who makes what decisions? What does the board reserve for itself? What does the board want to know before the CEO makes a decision? This whole area of policy development is where boards most often get into trouble," Thieme says.

Finding the Right Person

How do boards choose the right leader? The most common method is through advancement, a process that follows members of the board as they serve on committees, chair key committees, such as finance and nominations, assume the role of vice chair, and eventually rise to the chair position. "It's not an out-of-the-blue kind of thing, but an organized method of board chair selection, the theory being that if board members are exposed to enough different pieces of board operation, they eventually will be good board chairs," Thieme says.

The process of advancement through the board acquaints future chairs with both the fundamentals and subtleties of health care and hospital operation. "You [frequently] hear comments from board members [who say] that it takes two to three years to even start to understand what the health care business is all about," Thieme says.

This process also introduces board members to hospital leaders and serves as an on-the-job test. "You don't go to find a board chair who is unknown to everyone. You want someone who's been in training for a while so the board, medical staff, and administration have some idea of who this person is and how he or she responds in meetings and under stress and how this person works with colleagues," says Brian Rines, former chair of Maine General Medical Center–Augusta Campus.

At the Right Time

Board chairs with specific skills may be needed at different times in an organization's life, believes Rines, who became chair as a result of a hospital merger. "If you've just come through a merger, to some degree you need a chair who's able to say, 'We're a new institution; we have to forget the past and move on.' You need a chair who will create a new mission statement that will become the script for what the organization will become and how the board will direct that focus," he says.

When a hospital is stable, the board chair should accurately reflect the needs of the board to the CEO, balance the feelings of the board against the CEO's plans, and preserve its strengths. "Continuing stability in this field really means avoiding being whacked by the next tidal wave," Rines says.

A hospital on the brink of massive change in order to survive needs a board chair who can reassure its community that values will be preserved as the organization downsizes or restructures. It also needs a chair who can prepare the community for the inevitable— "the idea that the hospital isn't going to be doing things much more elaborate than tonsillectomies or appendectomies and setting bones and that people will have to drive six miles for more sophisticated work," Rines observes. The message is a difficult one to deliver, but, says Rines, "it's far better for the board chair and board to prepare the community than for people to wake up some morning and read in the local newspaper that the hospital is out of money and nobody is going to be there a month from Thursday."

With the Right Qualifications

In ideal circumstances, a board will have a nominating committee or a committee on governance to recommend the next chair. Many nominating committees are composed only of board members, but some include the hospital chief of staff as a voting member and the CEO in an ex-officio capacity. Committees also apply a series of criteria to their selection of a chair. Regular board meeting attendance is a basic one. After all, says Joanne Meehan, former chair of Memorial Hospital in South Bend, Indiana, "someone who doesn't attend board meetings regularly is not able to get a feeling for the hospital."

Then there's the person's savvy in running meetings. "One of the challenges of a board leader is to make sure meetings are packed with substance, not simply with reports," says Mount Sinai's Stickler. "You also want lively board meetings, where people can freely express their opinions, ask questions, and explore ideas. When you bring together businesspeople, physicians, and members of the community, not everyone's perspective will be the same. And that's good;

you want diversity. But it takes a lot of energy and focus to keep the meeting active, aggressively seek the counsel of various board members, and still finish on time," he adds.

The nominating committee also considers experience and background. Meehan had chaired several not-for-profit groups in the community and served on a local bank's board before joining Memorial Hospital. As a lawyer, Stickler brought expertise on legal, audit and financing issues.

Finally, there's the ability to meet the time commitment. "If the world is running calmly and sensibly, the board chair will have spurts of activity around the planning and budgeting cycle and community celebrations—dinners or rituals—as well as routine monthly board activities, board meetings, and subcommittee meetings. My guess is this takes up 15 to 20 percent of the board chair's time. When things are noisy, difficult or unpleasant, it's obviously more," says Annison.

For the Right Length of Time

Although some boards allow chairs to serve as long as 25 years, others impose term limits, which vary anywhere from two years to a maximum of three three-year terms. It's probably a good idea to have board leadership change on some reasonably regular basis to provide a fresh perspective and avoid the dangers of long-term board leadership: "The board tends to become narrowly focused rather than more broadly oriented, so ideas that are different are more easily rejected, and there tends to be a habit of thought that makes it harder to hold people accountable," Annison says.

Because many boards have such short terms of office for their chairs, they tend to forgo their formal performance evaluation and opt instead for self-evaluation through interviews or focus groups that assess how well they are achieving agreed-on goals and outcomes. On the other hand, long-term board chairs can become too chummy with the CEO or start acting like the CEO, Thieme says.

The ultimate test of a board chair is how well he or she maintains balance between the board, the administration and the medical staff. Rines likens it to having a sturdy three-legged milking stool. "If one leg is too short or too long or wobbly, the other two have a hard time holding the weight. Board chairs have as much strength and ability to support the concerns of the community as the physicians who are responsible for delivery of care and the CEO who must ensure that the medical staff can practice its craft effectively. But if the board chair exerts an overly strong influence or allows himself or herself to be bullied by the medical staff or the CEO's plan and doesn't reflect the community's needs or desires, then the stool will be unstable and the institution will suffer," Rines says.

Characteristics of
Effective Boards

By Lawrence D. Prybil

Throughout the nation, increasing attention is being devoted to the performance of governing boards in the health care field and other sectors. This is due not only to the inherent importance of governing boards' fiduciary and moral responsibilities, but also to the visible consequences of inadequate governance in both investor-owned and nonprofit organizations; closer scrutiny by Congress, the Internal Revenue Service, and a growing number of state legislatures and attorneys general; and growing evidence that effective governance contributes positively to good organizational performance.

There are, of course, many factors beyond quality of governance that affect the performance of hospitals and other health care organizations; for example, the caliber of clinical staff and executive leadership, the resources to acquire the best technology, the effectiveness of information systems, and so on. However, governmental agencies, bond rating agencies, donors and other stakeholders are recognizing that the quality of governance is important, and they are pressing for higher standards and better board performance.[1]

Lawrence D. Prybil, Ph.D., is professor and senior advisor to the dean at the College of Public Health, University of Iowa, Iowa City, and vice chair of the board of directors at Sisters of Charity of Leavenworth Health System, Kansas City, Kansas. This paper is based on a presentation given at the National Symposium on Governing and Leading Healthcare Organizations sponsored by the AHA Center for Healthcare Governance, Chicago.

Key Characteristics

So what are the key characteristics of effective health care boards? Based on the work of numerous authorities, existing empirical evidence, and my own experience in working with and serving on boards over the past 35 years, key features and practices include

1. A corporate philosophy and policies that support the governance structure and functions within the organization. Whether we are talking about a free-standing hospital or a large, multiunit health care system with facilities in several states, governing boards are unlikely to be effective without strong support by the corporate sponsor or parent body. This support is demonstrated by clear expectations, appropriate resources and thoughtful oversight.

2. A clear, consistent understanding by the board and CEO of the board's role, responsibilities, authority and organizational relationships. Lack of clarity and/or misunderstanding of the board's role and duties are major causes of governance problems and breakdowns. To have a productive board, it's essential for the board members, management team, and medical staff to share a clear, common understanding of their respective responsibilities and authority.

3. The support and leadership of a CEO who is committed to building a strong governance structure and practices. The impact of CEO support and leadership in determining the board's effectiveness is too often overlooked and too seldom discussed. The threshold questions are whether or not the CEO believes in the importance of governance and how strongly he or she is committed to board development. These factors will heavily influence the energy and institutional resources that are devoted to governance structure and functions. Trying to build a strong board without the CEO's interest and commitment is akin to driving a car with the brakes on. Forward movement is possible, but it's slower and more difficult than it should be. On the other hand, the pace of positive change can be accelerated greatly through the active engagement and support of the CEO.

4. Sustained organizational commitment to a solid board development program. The concept of "board development" is not defined consistently in the health care field or in other sectors. In general, however, a comprehensive board development program certainly should include the following:

- An ongoing process for assessing the board's changing needs for expertise
- An active recruitment effort to attract trustees who can meet those needs
- A well-planned orientation process (not a one-time, one-day event) for new board members
- A comprehensive, needs-based board education program
- An ongoing board evaluation process with the twin goals of objective appraisal and continuous improvement
- Clearly assigned responsibility to oversee the board development program. This responsibility can be given to the board's executive committee or to a designated "governance committee" for which planning and guiding the board development program is its principal, if not exclusive, function.

Additionally, every board development program must have a succession plan for board officers and committee leadership positions. To be effective, boards must have highly capable and committed persons in these leadership roles. An ongoing process that focuses on identifying and preparing trustees for board and committee leadership responsibilities is absolutely critical.

There is agreement throughout the field that competent hospital and system governance has become increasingly complex due to economic, environmental, legal and technological changes. In this context, the argument for a solid board development program is clear and compelling. Boards that have development programs in place are much more likely to be effective than those that do not.

5. A sound structure and staff resources to assist the board and its committees. It is not possible for a governing board or its committees to function efficiently without staff and logistical support. Boards need and deserve good secretarial, technical and consultative assistance. However, this support varies widely within hospitals and other health care organizations. In some instances, support still is largely limited to scheduling meetings, packaging and mailing meeting materials, and taking minutes. Minimalist models such as these are inadequate today. The quality of board performance and board member satisfaction are enhanced by top-notch staff support. For some board committees—such as those with oversight responsibility for audit and compensation functions—independent advice and counsel by persons or firms with direct responsibility to the committee is increasingly important. Board leaders and CEOs who want effective boards should review their existing infrastructure and be prepared to invest more resources to support the board and its committees; it is likely that relatively modest investments will produce valuable dividends in terms of board engagement and performance.

6. *Ongoing access to important information coupled with well-constructed board and committee agendas that focus the members' time and energy on key governance priorities.* The evidence clearly shows that effective boards insist on receiving accurate and pertinent information (not excessive and/or unanalyzed data) in a timely manner. They also insist on board and committee agendas that are linked directly to key strategic issues and governance priorities. Unfortunately, a recently completed national study indicates that the proportion of board meeting time devoted to discussing strategy and setting policy has actually declined in recent years—from 38 percent in 2002 to 31 percent in 2005.[2]

Effective board meetings concentrate on matters that involve interactive discussions and deliberations, rather than passive listening to reports and presentations; they also employ "consent agendas" for routine items that require formal board action but no deliberation, and for which the necessary information can be read in advance of the meeting. Effective board meetings do not begin with a series of routine reports, a practice that tends to be mind-numbing and a waste of the board's energy. They also minimize repetition of matters that can and should be handled at the committee level. Board committees can be empowered to perform certain functions on behalf of the board as long as delegation of responsibility and accountability are clearly defined.

7. *Core governance processes that are well-designed and reviewed regularly to identify opportunities for improvement.* Corporate experience and academic research have demonstrated that carefully designing and continually improving core processes and systems is essential to achieving excellence in complex organizations. It is

increasingly clear that designing, monitoring, assessing and refining core processes cyclically is a fundamental key to effectiveness in every enterprise.

This principle applies directly to governing boards whose duties largely involve carrying out a defined set of processes—for example, board evaluation, board development, CEO evaluation and quality-of-care review. The simple truth is that boards that design their core processes carefully, implement them rigorously, and seek ways to improve them on a continuous basis are likely to be more effective than other boards.[3]

8. Substantial engagement of clinicians—chosen by virtue of their commitment and expertise—as members of governing boards and board committees. A host of recent reports by The Commonwealth Fund, the Institute of Medicine, and others have underscored the necessity of improving the quality of care in our nation's hospitals, and health care governing boards have the ultimate responsibility for that improvement. As one strategy for strengthening their collective knowledge base and capability to carry out their quality-of-care duties, the National Quality Forum and other authorities have urged boards to improve their communication with clinical leaders—physicians and nurses—and expand their involvement on boards and board committees.[4] To prove the point, a recent study found that boards of high-performing hospitals had a greater proportion of physician members than a matched group of hospitals whose performance was midrange.[5]

When clinicians serve on the governing boards of health care institutions where they are employed or affiliated, the potential for conflicts of interest must be recognized and addressed. However, in an era where improving the quality and safety of patient care is a national priority, clinician input into governance deliberations is vital. Board leaders and CEOs should review their board's composition to ensure that clinician voices are heard.

9. A board culture that is characterized by proactive engagement of its members, a consistent pattern of constructive dialogue and debate, and enlivened decision-making processes. The Coalition for Nonprofit Health Care, the Conference Board Commission on Public Trust and Private Enterprise, the Panel on the Nonprofit Sector in its Final Report to Congress, and other authorities have urged boards to be more inquisitive and vigorous in carrying out their fiduciary responsibilities. The American Bar Association Task Force on Corporate Responsibility found that "many corporate boards have developed a culture of passivity" and that boards "must engage in active, independent, and informed oversight of the corporation's business and affairs, including its senior management."[6]

These organizations are addressing governance culture—the pattern of beliefs, traditions and practices that prevail when a board of directors convenes to carry out its fiduciary duties—and are advocating for a proactive culture. All boards have a culture that has developed over time and each culture has many elements, including those depicted in "Some Dimensions of Governance Culture" below. Governance cultures vary greatly from organization to organization and honing and strengthening that culture is very important to improving board effectiveness. Studies in the health care field and other sectors have indicated that organizations whose boards are involved, interactive and proactive are more likely to perform better than similar organizations with less engaged boards.

Some Dimensions of Governance Culture*

Low-Functioning Board	High-Functioning Board
Passive and Reactive	Highly Interested and Engaged
Unclear Priorities	Sharp Focus on Well-Defined Governance Priorities
Spotty Attendance with Low Energy Level	High Attendance and Enthusiasm
A Lot of Listening and Little Discourse	Extensive Questions, Dialogue and Deliberation
Challenges and Disagreements Are Squelched	Constructive Dissent and Debate Are Welcomed
Decision-Making Is Pro Forma	Decision-Making Is Enlivened

*The author wishes to extend appreciation to Dennis D. Pointer, Ph.D., for the presentation and discussions that provided the foundation for this model.

Suggestions for Board Leaders and CEOs

Governing boards of the nation's health care organizations vary widely in size, composition, structure, cultural features and effectiveness. From many quarters, there is a growing cry for more accountability and better performance by these boards as well as those in other sectors. Board leaders and CEOs who share a commitment to improving the quality of governance in their organizations may wish to consider the following steps.

First, they are encouraged to initiate and complete a serious re-examination of their board, including how it is organized, what it does and how it does it. To be useful, such a review should be close and thorough. This requires strong board chair and CEO leadership, the board's willingness to look at itself objectively, and readiness to make changes. Without these ingredients, a review process is likely to be pro forma and minimally beneficial.

Second, trustees need to reflect on their review findings and decide what kind of board they want to have and what it will take to achieve that vision. If the re-examination has been thoughtful, it is unlikely that the status quo will seem satisfactory. Even the finest governing boards in the health care field have plenty of room for improvement.

Third, boards and CEOs should set clear priorities and timetables for strengthening their governance, including fuller engagement of physician and nurse clinical leaders as voting board members, and a sequenced assessment of core governance processes. The priorities and timetable for these changes should be pragmatic; revamping governance processes takes time and effort, and everything cannot be done at once. Responsibilities and expectations should be clearly defined, with specific target dates for progress reports and formal recommendations.

Fourth, the board chair should assign long-term responsibility for building (or refining) a board development program to a standing committee. The overall re-examination outlined above will yield valuable insights and produce some important building blocks that can be acted upon promptly. However, board development should be viewed as an ongoing process and become the permanent responsibility of a board committee.

For all of these steps, strong leadership by board officers and firm support from the CEO and his or her management team are essential. Effective governance is rewarding in many ways, but it is hard work and requires sustained leadership and organizational support. Boards that embrace a real commitment to continuous improvement and that invest the necessary effort will increase their ability to provide effective governance for their organization. Their communities will receive the benefits.

Notes

1. See, for example, J. Green and D. Griesinger, "Board Performance and Organizational Effectiveness in Nonprofit Social Service Agencies," *Nonprofit Management and Leadership,* Summer 1996; I. Millstein and P. MacAvoy, "Active Board of Directors and Performance of the Large, Publicly Traded Corporation," *Columbia Law Review,* Vol. 98, 1998; A. Adams, "Quality of Board Governance in Nonprofit Healthcare Organizations," *Journal of Healthcare Administration,* Vol. 2, 2003; and *Governance of Not-for-Profit Healthcare Organizations* (Moody's Investors Service, June 2005).

2. *Raising the Bar: Increased Accountability, Transparency, and Board Performance* (San Diego, Calif.: The Governance Institute, 2005), p. 8.

3. See, for example, L. Prybil, R. Peterson, J. Price, S. Levey, D. Kruempel, and P. Brezinski, *Governance in High-Performing Organizations: A Comparative Study of Governing Boards in Not-for-Profit Hospitals* (Chicago: Health Research and Educational Trust, 2005).

4. See, for example, J. Meyer, et al., *Hospital Quality: Ingredients for Success—Overview and Lessons Learned* (The Commonwealth Fund, July 2004); *Taking a Strong Stance on Quality Oversight* (Boardroom Press, October 2005); and D. Nash and N. Goldfarb, eds., *The Quality Solution: The Stakeholder's Guide to Improving Health Care* (Sudbury, MA: Jones and Bartlett Publishers, 2006).

5. The study found that medical staff members are a more prominent component of high-performing hospital boards (30.3 percent) as compared with hospital boards whose performance is midrange (20.8 percent). In five of seven high-performing hospitals, medical staff members comprised 25 percent or more of the board's voting members; this was true in only one midrange performing hospital. Prybil et al., op. cit., p. 4 and pp. 16–19.

6. "Report of the ABA Task Force on Corporate Responsibility," *The Business Lawyer,* November 2003, pp. 159–160.

Criteria for Selecting Physician Trustees

By Errol L. Biggs

Having worked with health care boards for a number of years, I have learned that boards would be well-served to use several important criteria when selecting physician members.

As a general guideline, a hospital board needs to consider a membership comprising 15 percent to 25 percent physicians—going beyond the traditional president or chief of the medical staff, who usually serves in an ex-officio capacity and represents the medical staff's position. This percentage seems to provide a good balance between physician trustees and other board members as well as adequate medical input for the board.

Physicians understand the hospital's product line. They understand high-quality versus low-quality health care. They bring a clinical perspective to the board's mission, which assists the board in making better quality-related, patient-centered decisions. Selection criteria for physician board members (other than the chief of the medical staff) should be basically the same as for other board members. However, when reviewing physician candidates, the nominating committee must always remember not to ask the medical staff for trustee recommendations. The chief of staff already

Errol L. Biggs, Ph.D., is the director of graduate programs in health care administration at the University of Colorado, Denver.

represents the medical staff, so the board does not need additional physicians to represent that perspective.

Nor does it want to run the risk of a conflict of interest between the hospital and its physicians, such as a competing surgery center. As a first step, the nominating committee should not consider any physician candidates who have contracts with the hospital. This generally includes most pathologists, radiologists, anesthesiologists, hospitalists, intensivists, medical directors, directors of education programs, and emergency department physicians.

A hospital administrator told me recently that about 50 percent of his medical staff had some sort of contract with the hospital. I told him that made the nominating committee's decision 50 percent easier because it only needed to consider the other 50 percent for potential board membership. It also goes without saying that physicians who compete with the hospital in any significant way are not eligible.

Other worthwhile criteria for selecting physician board members include:

- *Experience.* The nominating committee should consider only physicians who have some type of previous governance experience, whether with physician organizations, banks, homeowners' associations or churches. The modern hospital is too important a community asset for people to learn governance there.
- *Education.* Many physicians are getting MBAs or taking business courses through professional organizations. The American College of Physician Executives (ACPE) now has more than 14,000 members and offers management and business courses to physicians. The American College of Healthcare Executives (ACHE) offers business and management courses to physicians regardless of their membership status in the organization. The right physician with this kind of education could be a real asset to a board.
- *Collaboration skills.* Team players can and do think collaboratively about issues, and are able to formulate opinions that integrate the perspectives of the team or board. There are always exceptions, but it has been my experience that primary care physicians seem to be better team players, probably because they have to coordinate patient care among numerous specialists and continually work to be a vital part of a team.

- *Objectivity.* As with the selection of all board members, the nominating committee must look for physicians who in no way represent any particular constituency, such as other physicians, a geographic area or any one group of stakeholders. As with any board member, the physician's primary concern must be the good of the hospital and its patients.
- *Commitment to the hospital.* As it does with all potential board members, the nominating committee should be certain the physician under consideration believes in the hospital's mission and will take the time necessary to serve on the board. If any nominee to the board, including a physician, cannot commit to the necessary time required, he or she will be of no value.

In some instances, boards may feel it is better to go outside the community for physician members. Care should be taken, however, to ensure that the individual is not competing with physicians on the medical staff, and is not affiliated with a hospital in competition with the board's institution.

At the end of the day, having physicians on your board can help the board arrive at better decisions regarding quality of care, competitive strategies, and community health needs.

Who's the perfect physician trustee? One who is a good listener; has an MBA, MHA, MPH or other business or management education; is in primary care; has no conflict of interest with the hospital; has some board experience; and values collaboration. Who knows, he or she may even help the bankers, lawyers and business people on the board better understand hospital financial statements!

PART TWO

The Governance Process
and Trustee Education

Best Practices in Action: Orientation

By Mary K. Totten and James E. Orlikoff

In the April *Trustee* Workbook, we discussed the concept of governance best practices and the essentials of great governance. We also talked about three key dimensions of governance—personality, process and culture—that provide a framework for ongoing assessment and improvement to help boards move from good to great performance.

Personality refers to the characteristics, skills and style of board members and leaders. *Process* encompasses the structures, policies and practices that guide and direct board functions. And *culture* emerges from the interaction of the personality and process of governance.

A board culture can be defined as "the way we do things around here." It includes such diverse elements as how boards handle conflict, as well as how they recognize how past behavior and practice influence the present and even future board functions.

This workbook looks at one key process—orientation. It discusses how boards can assess and improve their current practices in order to move toward greater effectiveness. It also illustrates how boards are integrating the personality, process and cultural dimensions of governance to develop innovative orientation practices.

Mary K. Totten is president of Totten & Associates, Oak Park, Illinois. James E. Orlikoff is president of Orlikoff & Associates, Inc., Chicago.

Orientation: What's Involved?

A thorough and meaningful orientation lays the foundation for effective governance. Rather than viewing orientation as a one-time educational event or sharing of written information and resources, many boards today consider orientation to encompass resources and a variety of activities that take place over several months to a year. While several approaches and techniques can be used to conduct board orientation, effective processes typically have several common characteristics, including:

- A clear understanding of the purpose and desired outcomes of the orientation for both the organization and the new board member
- Well-defined roles and responsibilities for those conducting and participating in the orientation
- A written outline of the orientation process, curriculum and specific activities, including a time line
- Ongoing evaluation of the orientation process and outcomes, in order to regularly refine and revise the process as necessary

Whether your board is planning its first orientation process or routinely evaluating its ongoing practices, consideration of the following questions under each of the key dimensions of governance can point out strengths and areas for improvement.

Personality

1. Who plans and oversees the board orientation process? How is the board involved?
2. Who participates in conducting the orientation (i.e., executive management, clinical leaders, board members, board leaders, outside speakers/facilitators, others)?
3. Who attends orientation (i.e., new board members, seasoned board members seeking a refresher, new senior executives or clinical leaders, others)?
4. Who evaluates the effectiveness of board orientation?

Process

1. What are the purposes of our orientation—for example, to orient trustees to the health care field and the hospital? To ensure that trustees understand the organization's strategic direction and financial status? To review key leadership relationships among the organization's boards and among the board, executives and physician leadership? To convey board roles, responsibilities and trustee performance expectations?
2. How do we conduct our orientation (e.g., educational sessions, written materials, mentoring of new board members by more seasoned trustees)?
3. What specific topics/activities will our orientation cover?
4. What is our expected time line for completing orientation?
5. What outcomes do we expect from the orientation—for individual trustees, the board as a whole and the hospital?
6. Do we have an explicit policy or requirement that all board members participate in our orientation process?
7. What mechanisms do we have in place to periodically evaluate our orientation processes and outcomes?
8. How do we use feedback from our evaluations to improve board orientation?

Culture

1. What elements of our board's culture do we address in orientation (e.g., how the board makes decisions, how it handles conflicts of interest, how it deals with confidentiality issues, whether the board encourages debate and dissenting opinions, how it seeks and develops its leaders, etc.)?
2. Do our orientation processes take into account the different learning styles and preferences of trustee participants?
3. Is our orientation to board culture consistent with the culture in action? In other words, is our definition of board culture consistent with how the board actually works?
4. How does our board's culture inhibit or support governance effectiveness?

Culture Check

Of the three dimensions of governance discussed above, culture is perhaps the most amorphous, and therefore the most easily neglected. Yet it is the culture of the board that often has the greatest impact on its effectiveness. A board may be strong in the personality and process dimensions of governance, with a highly qualified, diverse membership and sound policies and practices. However, if it fails to follow its policies and practices, or if board leaders discourage dissent or input from members, board performance is likely to be, at best, mediocre and, at worst, a liability to the organization and its members.

To test your board's culture, ask members to participate in the following exercise:

1. Write a brief description that characterizes your board and how you think the board goes about its business.

2. Listed below are several characteristics that describe how a board could function. Check all that you think apply to your board.

    a. ☐ decisive leadership
       ☐ encourages debate and dissent

    b. ☐ behaves according to its policies
       ☐ handles conflict well
       ☐ effectively uses member expertise

    c. ☐ dedicated to ongoing learning
       ☐ continuously improves performance
       ☐ lacks focus at times

    d. ☐ rubber stamps committee decisions
       ☐ has little member participation
       ☐ rarely evaluates its performance
       ☐ meeting preparation is uneven

    e. ☐ is collegial
       ☐ collaborates with executives and physicians
       ☐ adds value to the organization's leadership

3. Compare your description of the board's culture to what you learned about the culture in your orientation program. Is it the same or different?

4. Do you think the board's culture supports or inhibits board effectiveness? Why?

Best Practices in Action

Spring Harbor Hospital

Spring Harbor Hospital is a 100-bed, not-for-profit psychiatric facility in South Portland, Maine, that was acquired by MaineHealth (a not-for-profit integrated delivery system comprising five hospitals in southern and western Maine) in 1998. Its 24-member board took on several challenges when it began governing the replacement facility in 1998. One of the challenges was to bring its consumer-majority board quickly up to speed. More than half of the board's 21 outside members have used the hospital's services, or are family members of patients.

"Our board had a mix of experienced trustees who sit on other boards and some who were less familiar with governance, so we decided to develop a detailed orientation process that focused on mental health issues and finance and reimbursement," says CEO Dennis P. King. "Board members also have to become educated about teaching [hospitals] and research because we have two residency [programs] and a growing research function. We also are in the process of building a new hospital."

Prior to attending the orientation at the hospital, new board members are given an orientation manual (see page 40) that provides background on the hospital and its services, current and future directions, and trustee roles and responsibilities. The CEO's assistant devotes a portion of her time to board support.

"Our new trustees spend time with senior clinical and administrative staff during their orientation session and tour both our current hospital and the new facility site," King says. "During lunch, they meet with current members of the board to discuss how the board functions and the expectations we have for our board members."

Trustees also spend time on hospital units and keep current on issues facing mental health facilities through board meeting educational sessions. An extensive annual board self-assessment provides feedback about members' educational needs. Feedback is then incorporated into planning for future board educational sessions and resources.

"We have a different governance dynamic here," King says. "Our board is very involved . . . and very mission-focused. They have a

Spring Harbor Hospital Board Orientation Manual

Table of Contents

sense of purpose like I've never seen, a sense of urgency to accomplish our goals. Our board members are very concerned with the needs, rights and safety of our patients; are active in fund-raising and [donating] to the hospital; participate in political advocacy at the state level; and take seriously their commitment to attend board meetings and participate on board committees."

"There's no question that our orientation and education processes get trustees up to speed quickly," says board member Frank Parker. "Our challenge is to continue to balance the information we send to trustees, so they don't get overwhelmed. The results of our board self-evaluation show us that trustees understand their roles and responsibilities. They also are very complimentary about the information the hospital provides."

He adds, "I think all trustees have an obligation to educate themselves beyond the information they receive at board meetings, and the majority of our hospital's board members do that. Given the budgetary and regulatory constraints facing hospitals today, being passionate about the organization's mission is a requirement for effective governance."

Spring Harbor's successful approach to governance is gaining attention—other hospitals have contacted the organization to learn more about how the board functions. "We have a very committed and energized board," King says. "I'm very fired up about what we have been able to accomplish."

Bronson Healthcare Group

At the Bronson Healthcare Group, a community-owned not-for-profit health care system in southwest Michigan, orientation and continuing education are considered critical board success factors.

"Orientation and ongoing education are cornerstones of board development and effective governance," says President and CEO Frank Sardone. "Through orientation, our board members become well-prepared for their role on the board. They gain an understanding of our organization as well as their role in policy-making. Our detailed orientation process uses a variety of interactive, video and written learning formats conducted over a period of months to immerse the new board member in Bronson's governance structure, processes, roles, responsibilities and leadership culture. Board members also can customize their orientation process to best meet their individual needs and preferred methods for learning," Sardone adds. (See the system's New Board Member Orientation Plan below.)

Bronson Healthcare Group
New Board Member Orientation Plan

The Orientation Process
The CEO and senior management team, along with the board executive committee, will oversee and be responsible for orienting new board members and creating an annual education plan for all Bronson board members.

Orientation Purpose
- Provide a general overview of the health care field to give new board members a context in which the Bronson Healthcare Group functions.
- Provide specific information about the Bronson organization, its vision, structure, relationships, programs and services.
- Outline the culture and values of Bronson to show how the board recognizes and acts to perpetuate these key organizational characteristics.
- Provide a sense of the organization's history to help new board members contribute to continuity in governance.
- Inform new board members about Bronson's strategy and how the market has led to the development of its current strategic plan.
- Review the structure, function, bylaws, roles and responsibilities of the board so new trustees clearly understand.

Mechanisms for a Successful Orientation Plan
A meaningful orientation is not a one-time event. Instead, it will be constructed as an ongoing process over a period of several months, using various mechanisms and formats including: lectures, meetings, videotapes, written materials, one-to-one discussions, tours, "auditing" board committee meetings, attendance at outside educational sessions, and board member mentoring. New

Continued →

---

board members actively participate in designing the orientation process so that it best meets their personal needs, schedule and desired learning format. The orientation process will be evaluated regularly to make sure it is effective in preparing board members for their demanding roles and modified as various changes in the health care field, the Bronson organization, and the process of governance occur.

Vision
Bronson will be a national leader in health care quality.

Strategic Objectives

Clinical Excellence
The Bronson Healthcare Group will deliver excellent clinical care through continuous improvement and coordination of services, technology and human resources.
• Quality & Patient Safety
• Technology & Innovation
• Bronson Programs & Services

Customer Service Excellence
Bronson Healthcare Group will provide excellent service through recognizing and meeting internal and external physician and customer needs.
• Customer Service & Satisfaction
• Human Resources & Workforce Development
• Marketing, Public Relations & Communications

Community Accountability & Long-term Viability
Bronson Healthcare Group will maintain long-term viability and community accountability through achievement of efficiency, growth and financial targets.
• Health Care Governance
• Compliance/Legislative Issues
• Community Benefits
• Finance
• Physician Relations, Integration & Regional Relationships
• Insurance Services
• Risk Management, Security & Safety

Bronson developed its orientation process by reviewing the governance literature and working with several governance experts and organizations to help determine the right approach for its organization and board.

"From the tools and information we gathered, we created our own approach to orientation and education that we consider to be 'best practice' and that is very effective for our organization," says Assistant to the President Michele Serbenski, who is the point person for governing board communication and support. To maintain its best-practices approach to board orientation and education, Bronson conducts a formal review of its programs and processes each year, engages in ongoing assessment and evaluation, and involves the board in all aspects of these processes.

"We have shared some of our board development tools with other health care organizations with which we work closely in our region and through publications as well," she says. "We also use information from our membership in the American Governance & Leadership Group to seek new ideas and look for better ways of doing things in the future."

Conclusion

Boards that are serious about pursuing excellence regularly examine their policies and practices and establish a solid governance foundation through orientation. Any board can improve its value to the organization by systematically examining its personality, processes and culture and determining strengths and areas for improvement. Boards that are developing best practices in governance understand how these key dimensions interrelate and continually look for new ideas and approaches that will best meet the needs of their organization and its trustees.

The Governance Audit: Assessing and Improving the Board

By James E. Orlikoff
and Mary K. Totten

The post-Enron/AHERF backlash against ineffective, negligent or fraudulent governance has led to new legislation and regulations designed to hold corporate boards to much greater standards of accountability, performance and functional transparency. The Public Company Accounting Reform and Investor Protection Act of 2002 (also called the Sarbanes-Oxley Act) and the new Corporate Governance Standards of the New York Stock Exchange both impose standards and requirements on public boards to protect investors.

Although these laws and regulations will have almost no direct impact on boards of not-for-profit health care organizations, they will likely form the foundation of expectations and standards for them and establish the framework for future legislation and case law. Clearly, board scrutiny and the drive to enhance governance performance and accountability are gaining momentum.

Thus, boards of health care organizations would be wise to "get ahead of the curve" and to rigorously examine and improve all their activities. An effective way to do this is to conduct a comprehensive governance audit.

James E. Orlikoff is president of Orlikoff & Associates, Inc., Chicago. Mary K. Totten is president of Totten & Associates, Oak Park, Illinois.

This audit should be a detailed and integrated review of the board's structure, processes and function, with particular attention paid to those areas of highest liability exposure or risk of performance failure (see "Effective Governance after Enron and AHERF," *Trustee* Workbook 3, July/August 2002). A governance audit is much more focused and demanding than a traditional board self-evaluation, as it requires an unflinching willingness to ask difficult questions, to examine challenging and highly charged strategic situations, and to "look under the rocks" to uncover and address problems. Further, a governance audit involves a detailed legal review of the board to determine if there are any areas of function, structure or process that are inconsistent with legal or regulatory standards.

How a Governance Audit Can Help Your Board

Many boards may resist conducting a governance audit under the theory that it is better to "let sleeping dogs lie" or to not look for problems if everything seems to be working well. Yet the benefits of conducting such an audit far outweigh the excuses not to do one. According to Monte Dube, head of the health law practice for the law firm McDermott, Will & Emery in Chicago, the many valuable benefits for a board to conduct a governance audit include:

- Minimizing the risk of exposure to litigation and legal liability
- Minimizing the risk of financial or strategic damage to the organization
- Reducing the risk of regulatory sanctions
- Minimizing the risk of adverse publicity for the organization, thus avoiding embarrassment for trustees
- Proactively enhancing effective mission and corporate stewardship
- Helping the board to adopt best practices (as opposed to simply complying with minimum legal and regulatory requirements), thereby preventing the imposition of onerous regulatory requirements

When to Do a Governance Audit: Case Studies

A governance audit is beneficial for any board at any time. However, there are particular situations or circumstances when it may be immediately useful. According to Jeannie Frey, also of McDermott,

Will & Emery, and Dube, there are several such situations, high-lighted in bold type below.

Evaluating a Prospective Merger/Affiliation Partner. An audit of the governance structure, processes and practices of one or both of the prospective affiliating parties can provide insight into potential clashes of governance culture, processes and assumptions, as well as any problem areas that might affect the synergies desired by both parties.

Case Example: Hospital A and Hospital B have decided to create a two-hospital system to provide more cost-effective service to their community. The board of Hospital A has 30 members, many of whom have served for 15 or more years. The board has had the same chair for the past 10 years, and although he presides over every board meeting, the chief executive determines the meeting agendas and supporting materials, which are often delivered to board members a day or two before the meeting. The board meets monthly and has seven committees, each meeting at least monthly. Board meetings begin with dinner and often last late into the evening, with committee reports taking up most of the time. Little discussion occurs around agenda items, and deliberation and dissenting views are discouraged. Frequently, the board simply rubber-stamps management's recommendations in order to get through an agenda packed with reports and required votes.

Hospital B has an 11-member board. The chair, a well-known local business leader who has chaired many corporate and community boards, believes in strategic leadership. He works closely with the hospital CEO to develop each meeting agenda and to provide focused agenda materials that help brief the trustees about key issues and provide multiple courses of action for board discussion. The board meets monthly for two hours. Board decisions are made early in the meeting using a consent agenda; the majority of meeting time is spent deliberating one or two key strategic issues facing the hospital. Every trustee is expected to attend each meeting, prepared and ready to participate in discussion. Healthy debate and expression of diverse opinions and perspectives are encouraged.

The hospitals are considering the formation of one parent board, with half of the membership coming from each of the current hospital boards.

Questions for Discussion

1. How would you characterize the leadership style and governance culture of each hospital board? Which governance style and culture do you think would be most likely to generate liability or embarrassment? Why?
2. Which style and culture are likely to guide the new organization most effectively into the future? Why?
3. How could an understanding of how each organization is governed help the leaders of both organizations determine how best to move forward?

Distressed Health Care Provider. When a facility or system has fallen on hard times and faces possible insolvency, it should take a good look at the adequacy of its governance structure and processes for dealing with the difficult times ahead. Even strong boards will be challenged to balance the organization's responsibility for its mission and the need to ensure continued provision of care for the community with financial and business realities. A thorough review of board structure and function can help answer the following important questions.

Questions for Discussion

1. Does the board have a firm understanding of its fiduciary duties to its creditors—and what that means to the organization's mission?
2. Are the board's audit committee, internal and external audit functions, and financial operations up to the scrutiny of potentially hostile outsiders?
3. Has the board evaluated what kinds of decisions may need to be made by the outside directors, and is there a process in place for those directors to obtain appropriate support from corporation staff and external advisors?
4. Should the board communicate the hospital's story to key stakeholders?

Public Hospitals. As government-sponsored institutions, public hospitals are subject to several additional levels of oversight compared with their private counterparts. Elected officials, the general public, and the press have greater access to information about public hospital operations and may hold such hospitals to higher standards than they do private facilities.

That's why a public hospital board must be acutely aware of its governance-related requirements, including conflict-of-interest standards and open meeting laws—whether mandated by statute, governing ordinance or public expectation. In addition, a public hospital board should ensure that solid reporting mechanisms exist to alert it to potential operating problems, especially in finance and compliance.

Questions for Discussion

1. Has our board ever audited its structure and function to ensure that it complies with statutory and other governance requirements?
2. What reporting processes and mechanisms does our board have in place to ensure effective operational oversight?
3. To what extent have our board members been made aware during recruitment, orientation, ongoing board education or other methods of the specific duties and responsibilities of serving on a public hospital board?

New Board Member Recruitment. It is no secret that good directors/ trustees are hard to find. Yet health care organizations have a critical need for a savvy, hard-working and diverse board. A governance audit can be an invaluable recruiting tool, allowing prospective directors to get an accurate sense of board operations and culture. To the extent a governance audit reveals or results in the use of "best practices" in such important areas as audit committees, D&O insurance, indemnification and use of independent directors, the governance audit report can be an effective marketing tool for wooing qualified, desirable board candidates. Further, it makes board membership more attractive to the potential trustee by suggesting that potential liability exposure or embarrassment has been minimized.

Questions for Discussion

1. To what extent do prospective board members understand our board structure and how it conducts its activities?

2. What questions do prospective board candidates ask about serving on our board? How do we address them?
3. To what extent is our board aware of governance best practices and how, if at all, do we incorporate them into our structure and function?
4. How might the results of a governance audit help improve our recruiting process?

Executive Searches. For organizations needing to fill key executive positions, such as the chief executive, chief financial officer, or chief operating officer, a governance audit can help recruiters better understand the organization's governance culture and practices, and thus identify candidates who either complement them or who bring needed skills to shore up weaknesses. A governance audit can also help prospective executives understand the organization they may join.

Case Example: A hospital has had three CEOs in five years, and the board is in the process of recruiting a new one. The most qualified candidates have requested independently that the board explain the reasons for the high CEO turnover rate, and several wish to examine the board's policies and practices. They have made it clear that they will not consider accepting the position unless these questions are answered.

Questions for Discussion

1. Are these requests for information appropriate?
2. How should the board respond to them?
3. Has our board experienced conflicts with previous executives that stemmed from differences in leadership styles or approach? Could these have been minimized or avoided by providing them with a better understanding of how the board governs?

Donors and Grant Makers. In light of the recent governance and financial scandals and investigations in both the public and nonprofit sectors, such as Enron, WorldCom, AHERF, United Way, Baptist Foundation, Allina Health and Bishop Estate, donors and grant makers may be very interested in obtaining assurance that the organization they are funding is well managed and governed. Especially for any institution that has recently suffered "public relations nightmares," such as conflicts of interest, federal compliance investigations or highly publicized incidents of poor care, a governance audit and implementation of practice standards can be used to win back key donors and grant makers and provide assurance that past problems will not recur.

Questions for Discussion

1. Have we lost grants or donations because of donor concern over the integrity of our organization's leadership and governance? What have we done to address this?
2. If our organization were to approach a potential donor or foundation, how would we assure them of our board's integrity?
3. Do we have mechanisms in place to ensure continuous board improvement?
4. It was recently reported that, except for health care organizations, philanthropy rose in 2001. Why do we think this happened? How might our board address this situation?

Patient Care Quality and Safety. Quality of care and patient safety top the list of concerns about our nation's health care. Therefore, board oversight of these areas has never been more important.

In the corporate world, investors and legislators are demanding greater financial transparency and accountability in the boardroom. The equivalent of financial transparency in the health care sector is quality. Health care boards are responsible for ensuring that all aspects of their organization's quality and patient safety are exemplary and, further, that all actions of the board and other leaders are in the best interests of patients and stakeholders.

Case Example: A hospital has the highest-level trauma unit designation possible in its state, one that requires certain specialist surgeons to be on-site 24 hours a day. Several months ago, two surgeons notified the hospital that they would no longer take trauma calls or be on-site during the early morning hours. This leaves the hospital's trauma unit with no on-site surgical coverage for several 12-hour periods each week. Yet the board wants to keep its current trauma unit designation, even though this coverage gap clearly disqualifies it.

Case Example: According to several medical staff leaders who have spoken to the hospital's board chair and CEO privately, one of the physicians on staff has serious quality problems. The medical staff refuses to take any formal action against this physician. An external review concludes that the physician is indeed consistently providing substandard care. Still, the medical staff will not recommend that any action be taken against the physician; on the other hand, they will not refer their patients to him or allow their family members to be treated by him. Several medical staff leaders have privately advised their friends on the board not to use this physician's services. Unfortunately, this problem physician is the only specialist at the hospital in his field and is a major contributor to the hospital's bottom line.

Questions for Discussion

1. What do these two cases have in common?
2. Who bears the ultimate responsibility to act in both situations?
3. To be true to the hospital's mission as well as to the best interests of patients and public safety, what should the board do in each situation?
4. If each board does not "do the right thing," what are the potential consequences for patient outcomes? For the board's liability exposure? For regulatory sanctions and community embarrassment?

Effective Boards Have Effective Social Systems

A recent review of governance and leadership practices in both thriving and failing organizations suggests that boards at both types of organizations do not always follow the conventional wisdom of good governance—that is, a lean structure, age and term limits for board members, few insiders on the board, the right mix of skills and talent, regular meeting attendance, and the like. (See "What Makes Great Boards Great," *Harvard Business Review,* September 2002.) What does seem to distinguish high-performing boards is that they are effective social systems. In short, effective boards do the following:

• Operate with a high degree of trust and open, honest communication among members

- Encourage healthy debate and dissent
- Allow members to play a variety of roles and encourage them to develop and debate various courses of action before making decisions
- Ensure individual accountability
- Regularly evaluate both individual member and full-board performance

Thus, boards would do well to ensure that attention to governance structure supports and strengthens effective and robust governance communication.

Questions for Discussion

1. How many of these social characteristics of effective boards does your board consistently demonstrate?
2. Which ones does your board fail to demonstrate consistently? Why?
3. Does your board encourage respectful dissent?
4. Does your board have a culture that leads to the vast majority of votes being unanimous? If yes, why? Is this a problem? If not, why not?

Getting Started

If one or more of the scenarios or case studies described here sound familiar to you or depict a situation you could see developing for your board in the future, performing a governance audit should be one of your board's near-term goals. Conducting an audit and acting on its results can enhance trustees' confidence in the board's integrity and guide governance improvement.

Listed below are sample diagnostic questions developed by health care governance and leadership consultant Dennis D. Pointer for beginning a thorough governance audit:

1. Has our board formulated a set of specific trustee expectations?
2. At least every other year, does our board engage in a formal assessment of its performance and contributions and use the results to improve governance?

3. Has our board specified the competencies and capacities that all members must possess?

4. Does our board annually formulate a set of specific, quantifiable financial objectives for our organization?

5. At least quarterly, employing specific, quantitative indicators and standards, does our board assess how well the organization is meeting its quality objectives?

6. Are management "insiders" and medical staff members less than 40 percent of board membership?

7. Does our board have an audit committee and does it meet at least quarterly?

8. Does board policy prohibit our organization's audit firm from performing consulting work for our organization?

9. On average, is less than 40 percent of board meeting time spent listening passively to briefings and reports from management, the medical staff or the board's own committees?

10. Does our board employ a formal system, with explicit criteria, for assessing the qualifications of potential members?

11. Does our board have a written work plan that details annual priorities?

12. Does our board review its fiduciary duties of loyalty and care before it discusses, deliberates and votes on major issues, such as mergers, acquisitions and disposition/transfer of significant assets?

13. If we are part of a system, does our parent board review the annual audits of its subsidiary organizations?

14. Does our board have a formal conflict-of-interest policy that requires directors to disclose any and all potential material conflicts of interest annually and refrain from discussing, deliberating and voting on any issue in which they have a material conflict of interest?

15. Does our board have a formal and explicit plan for developing the capacity/competence of the board as a whole and the knowledge/skills of individual directors?

In addition to Pointer's recommended list of governance audit questions, consider applying the following New York Stock Exchange Corporate Governance Standards:

1. Does our board have an audit committee composed entirely of outside directors?
2. Does the sole responsibility for hiring and firing the independent external auditor rest with the audit committee or another committee (such as the finance committee) composed entirely of outside, objective board members?
3. Do our board and certain board committees meet in occasional executive session to discuss issues other than executive compensation?
4. Does our board have a policy that prohibits any outside board member from doing business with the organization?

Although these lists of questions are not meant to be exhaustive, they provide insight into the breadth and level of specificity a comprehensive audit should undertake.

Conclusion

Insurers, employers, regulators and the courts have begun holding boards accountable to higher standards of behavior and performance and punishing those organizations with ineffective governance. A governance audit can help a board prepare for this new reality. When conducting an audit, the most important questions to ask are the ones that will generate the most discomfort. However, not asking such questions can be far more damaging to the board, the organization, patients and the community.

How to Run
Effective Board Meetings

By James E. Orlikoff
and Mary K. Totten

And while the Great Ones repair to their dinner,
The Secretary stays, growing thinner and thinner.
Racking his brains to record and report
What he thinks they will think that they ought to have thought.
—London Institute of Directors' 1971 *Standard Manual*

A truly unique aspect of governance is that a board exists only when it is actually meeting. So the most valuable commodity a board has is the time its members spend together between raps of the gavel. The art of governance largely involves maximizing the use of this precious time, and the effectiveness of a board is predominately determined by how effective and efficient its meetings are. Conducting board meetings that are as focused and productive as possible and continuously evaluating and improving them is a hallmark of effective governance.

Long, rambling, inconclusive and inefficient meetings are a chronic complaint of many board leaders and members. Meetings dominated by one or two people, those focused on incidental issues or those that get sidetracked from important agenda items

---

James E. Orlikoff is president of Orlikoff & Associates, Inc., Chicago. Mary K. Totten is president of Totten & Associates, Oak Park, Illinois.

are also common barriers to meaningful gatherings. Effective board meetings are the result of a clear purpose, a focused agenda, summarized governance information and an explicit decision-making process.

The Board as a Decision-Making Body

Many boards concentrate on the content of their meetings, but very few focus on the process. A key characteristic of an effective board is that it has a clear process for making decisions. Further, the board chair clearly communicates this process to each member and makes sure that all trustees understand it. Board meetings are often rendered ineffective when different members have different ideas about the decision-making process, or different decision-making processes are inconsistently applied to different situations.

Some boards use a consensus model of decision-making, where a decision is "made" without a vote as long as no member strongly disagrees. Some boards have a unanimous model of decision-making, where dissenting votes are implicitly discouraged and the vast majority of votes is unanimous. Some boards have a culture where a simple majority vote will carry any issue, whereas other boards require a "supermajority" (i.e., a percentage of board votes greater than 51 percent to carry the decision) on important issues. Some boards have a culture where the issues presented for vote have been "predecided" by the executive committee, the board chair, or the CEO, and the board votes are simply pro forma approvals. Different situations may call for different methods, and effective boards prospectively determine when specific decision-making methods will be most appropriate.

Effective boards have a clear, agreed-on process that they routinely use to both frame and make decisions. Their meetings are facilitated by the consistent use of a defined process that addresses such issues as these:

- How much discussion is encouraged prior to a vote? Are all members encouraged to speak, or are established positions articulated by designated individuals?
- Which issues, if any, require a supermajority vote of the board?

- Does the board have a policy that, except in emergencies or rare situations, it will not vote on issues at the same meeting where they are first presented or discussed? This policy permits trustees to consider an issue between board meetings, request more information, and then make a more informed decision.

Questions for Discussion

Boards can make a decision by consensus, a unanimous vote, a supermajority vote and a simple majority vote.

1. Which decision-making process does your board use? Why?
2. If your board uses some other process for making decisions, how would you describe it?
3. If your board uses different decision-making processes at different times, is it clearly understood which process is used in which situations and why? (For example, a board may use simple majority votes on routine issues but require supermajority votes on specified issues of importance.)
4. Is the decision-making process used by your board the result of conscious discussion and deliberation, or is it used because "it has always been done that way"?
5. Does your board routinely make decisions on issues at the same meeting where the issue is first presented?

Agenda Control

A key component of effective board meetings is an effective agenda. Efficient boards control their agendas, yet many boards are prisoners of static agendas. Many still place the most mundane, trivial issues first on their agendas and take the majority of their time discussing them. The issues of greatest significance are then placed at the end of the agenda, when there is time pressure to end the meeting or trustees are tired and eager for it to end.

This can give rise to the "Law of Triviality," that is, "The amount of time a board spends on an issue tends to be in inverse proportion to the importance of, and dollar amount involved in, that issue."

To avoid falling prey to this law, an effective meeting agenda focuses first on issues that have been prospectively identified as

Tips for Effective Meetings

Try one or more of the following tips to help make your board meetings more productive and dynamic.

1. Make sure your board understands the decision-making processes it uses and how and when to apply them. Consider reviewing this information as part of a board meeting educational session and building it into your trustee orientation program.

2. Help board members prepare in advance. Set and circulate an annual schedule of meetings and board education sessions and send out board meeting agenda materials at least a week in advance.

3. Require trustees to come prepared for meetings and evaluate their performance as part of your trustee evaluation and development process.

4. Use a consent agenda to address items such as approval of board committee minutes or reports, which require board action but do not require significant discussion by the full board.

5. Organize your agenda to allow participants significant time for discussion of strategic issues.

6. Use e-mail to distribute agenda materials in advance of board or committee meetings. Some organizations use their Web site or a designated board-only subsite to post information as well.

7. Follow an action-oriented agenda for your board meetings. Set a time limit for the meeting itself and time limits for each agenda item. Circulate the schedule in advance of the meeting.

8. Ensure strong leadership. Include information about how to run efficient, effective meetings into your board and committee chair leadership development process. A knowledgeable and skilled chair who keeps the meeting on track, ensures productive participation from all members and handles conflict appropriately (see "Resolving Conflict," page 64) is critical to meeting effectiveness.

9. Build meeting etiquette and participation skills into trustee orientation.

10. Take time out to evaluate the effectiveness of each board meeting. Continual feedback is essential to continuous improvement.

most urgently needing the board's attention. The board identifies these critical agenda issues through the strategic plan and the organization's annual goals and objectives, as well as its own annual goals and objectives. Focusing on these issues enables a board to develop a collective sense of what is important and a shared understanding of purpose and priorities. These purposes and priorities are then reflected and emphasized in board meeting agendas throughout the year.

A very useful agenda control technique is a *consent agenda*. Agenda planners (usually the executive or governance committee, but occasionally the board chair with the CEO) divide the board agenda issues into two parts. The first part contains those items that must be acted on by the board because of legal, regulatory or other requirements but are not significant enough to warrant discussion by the full board. Issues such as receipt and approval of reports and minutes, along with related materials, are combined into a single section, or consent agenda. Trustees review this section prior to the meeting, and if no one has any questions or concerns, the entire block of issues is accepted or approved with one board vote and no discussion. This frees up a tremendous amount of time that would otherwise be squandered on minor issues.

Important issues that require thoughtful discussion, deliberation and action by the board constitute the second part of the agenda. Items are addressed one by one, with the board spending the time that has been freed up by the consent agenda to address these more critical issues.

In addition to the use of consent agendas, other techniques to leverage better board meetings through the agenda include:

- Placing the most important agenda items first to provide the most time for board discussion
- Clear agenda distinctions between action items, discussion items in preparation for future board decisions, and information and board education items
- Distributing a timed agenda for each board meeting to all board members in advance
- Setting a realistic agenda not packed with too many items
- Adhering to the established agenda, with the board chair keeping a tight rein on digressions, members' side discussions, and issues

that have already been addressed or that will be addressed later in the agenda
- Sticking to beginning and ending times; in this way, meetings become more efficient, and trustees are not likely to feel their valuable time is being wasted

Exercise: Assess Your Board's Agenda

1. At your next board meeting cross out the date of the agenda so that it is unreadable. Have the board secretary bring an agenda from a board meeting from two years ago and cross out that date. Now, mix up the two agendas and have the board compare them. Can the board identify the agenda for today's meeting? If the answer is no, that implies the board is addressing the same issues today that it did two years ago—it is a prisoner of its own agenda.
2. Effective board agendas change as the strategy of the organization changes and as the issues change. A "living agenda" also means that the board meetings change as well. Does your board have a living agenda or a fixed one?
3. Has your board ever fallen prey to the Law of Triviality? If so, how often and why? If not, why not?

Board Meeting Evaluation

A very useful technique to continually improve meetings is to conduct a brief evaluation at every meeting's conclusion. After each meeting adjourns, trustees take no more than five minutes to complete an evaluation that assesses that meeting's effectiveness and efficiency. The board chair, with the help of the CEO or governance committee, analyzes the results and uses them to monitor and improve all processes relating to the conduct of effective meetings. Further, the aggregate results of each meeting evaluation should be presented to the full board at its next meeting, along with any plans for improvement.

Asking each trustee to list anonymously what worked well as well as what did not and why can help a board constantly fine-tune and improve its meetings. In doing so, the effectiveness and efficiency of the board meetings will continuously evolve, and the cohesiveness of the board and the quality of governance will grow.

Personal Advice on Improving Board Meetings

"We had very traditional board meetings until our new board chair engaged members in a collaborative effort to make our meetings more interesting and dynamic. Every month we build into our meetings a half hour or so of board education. Because we felt the full board needed a better understanding of financial and quality issues, we have disbanded our board finance and quality committees for the time being and use meetings of the full board to discuss these issues. We also use a consent agenda, and everyone understands they have to do their homework and come to meetings prepared. Our board meetings are more exciting, and I look forward to them. The quality of questions that board members now ask also shows that they are more knowledgeable and involved."

—Sr. Catherine Manning, president and CEO,
Saint Vincent Health System, Erie, Pennsylvania

"The single most important ingredient for a great board meeting is having a chair who's a really good meeting manager and facilitator. Running an effective, efficient meeting is an acquired skill. To do the 'acquiring,' here are some of the best books around that board chairs can read":
- *Meetings That Work,* by Richard Chang
- *First-Aid for Meetings,* by Charles Hawkins
- *The Strategy of Meetings,* by George Kieffer
- *How to Run Successful Meetings in Half the Time,* by Milo Frank
- *How to Make Meetings Work,* by Michael Doyle

—Dennis D. Pointer, Ph.D., principal,
Dennis D. Pointer & Associates, and John J. Hanlon,
professor of Health Services Research and Policy,
San Diego State University, La Jolla, California

"The most important thing we have done to improve our board meetings is to switch the agenda around to lead with education and discussion on a topic that our board members want to know more about. We now put the committee reports and consent agenda items in the second half of our two-hour meetings. This new order of agenda topics sends a message of priority to our board members— that we want to invest time and energy in helping them keep abreast of industry issues and trends."

—Michele Serbenski, assistant to the president,
Board Relations and Communications,
Bronson Healthcare Group, Kalamazoo, Michigan

Sample Board Meeting Evaluation Questions

Consider the following:

- Did the meeting agenda relate to, or support, the mission and vision of the organization?
- Did the agenda focus on the organization's strategic priorities?
- Did the meeting have specific objectives and were these objectives accomplished?
- Did the agenda book contain information that facilitated informed decision-making?
- Did every board member have an opportunity to express his or her views?
- Did every member participate?
- Was more time spent on future issues than on past issues and organizational monitoring?
- Did the board micromanage?
- Did every board member come to the meeting prepared—having read and considered the agenda information?
- Did the meeting start and end on time?
- Did you think that the meeting was challenging and productive?
- Did the chair run the meeting efficiently and objectively?
- Did the board use its meeting time well?
- Did everyone learn something from this meeting?
- Did everyone leave the meeting energized and excited?
- How could the meeting have been better?

Questions for Discussion

1. Of the preceding sample questions, which do you think would be most valuable for assessing and improving your board meetings? Why?
2. Which questions do you believe would be least valuable for your board? Why?
3. What other board meeting evaluation questions would you suggest for your board?

Who Should Attend Board Meetings?

People who are not board members often attend health care organization board meetings. These individuals may include senior executives, perhaps medical staff members, and invited guests.

Frequently, nonboard members participate freely in the meetings and can even dominate them. To an outside observer or a new trustee, it may not be at all clear who is a board member and who is not.

As a general rule, if a board is meeting, those attending should be primarily, if not exclusively, board members. Other than the CEO, management staff should be present only during their reports

---

Resolving Conflict at Board Meetings

One of the most difficult aspects of board meetings to manage is the eruption and resolution of conflict between trustees or others present at the meeting. Conflict is a frequent presence in health care boardrooms today and can be expected to increase as a result of the significant changes in health care that make governing a hospital or system very stressful. A consistent and rational approach to conflict resolution will help any board conduct more effective meetings.

Conflict resolution techniques that can be applied by board chairs, CEOs or trustees to minimize board and committee meeting disruption include the following:

- Define the problem as objectively as possible and get participants to agree to the definition of the problem before suggesting or even allowing the suggestion of solutions.
- Use active listening to restate each person's perspective and concerns regarding the problem or conflict in order to both understand the problem and to demonstrate that the perspectives of all those involved are understood accurately.
- Confine the debate and discussion of the problem to principles and issues, not personalities.
- Facilitate a brainstorming session among those who are involved to generate a comprehensive list of possible solutions.
- Once a list of possible solutions has been generated, take a break from the issue or conflict (perhaps even tabling it until the next board meeting) to allow all board members and meeting participants to consider the problem, generate additional solutions and identify the most effective solution.

It is very important to remember that how a board or chair addresses a conflict or problem will be remembered long after the actual conflict is resolved.

---

to the board and a follow-up question period, and should then excuse themselves. The more nonboard members present during a meeting, the less effective that meeting is likely to be. Having non-members routinely attend board meetings inhibits free discussion and deliberation, and prevents the board from developing into a cohesive unit.

Questions for Discussion

1. How many nonboard members routinely attend your meetings? Why?
2. Do you think that meetings would be more productive without the presence of nonboard members throughout the meeting? If so, why? If not, why not?

Conclusion

Every board meeting is an opportunity to build trustees' knowledge and understanding and to advance the board's effectiveness. Establishing ground rules about trustee preparation, participation and decision-making; developing agendas that allocate the majority of meeting time to discussion of strategic issues; ensuring that meeting chairs are skilled in how to run an effective meeting; and taking time out to evaluate the content and process of each meeting are some of the ways that boards can make the best use of the precious time they spend together.

Governance 101

By Shari Mycek

*What are the fundamentals that every trustee
should know, and how do they learn them?*

When I was in the seventh grade, Charles Dickens' *Oliver Twist* was
mandatory reading. I wish I could say I devoured the gloomy London tale, but the truth is, I didn't. I procrastinated reading it, and
when it finally came time to deliver my analysis to the class, I did
what any self-respecting, enterprising student would do—I spoke
articulately from *Cliffs Notes*. I also wish I could say the report was
a disaster and that I learned this oh-so-valuable life lesson I can now
pass to my own eighth-grade daughter. But the truth is, I didn't. I
aced that presentation.

As a journalist reporting on everything from health care to the
world's most exotic spa (it's in Malaysia, by the way), I'm required
to gather information quickly, pare down the essentials, and report
intelligently and objectively. I am not (nor do I need to be) an expert
on any one subject; but rather, I seek out the experts for the subject
at hand.

Health care trustees should have it so easy.

In the September 2003 issue of *Trustee*, Edward Kazemek and
Michael Peregrine (in their article, "Health Care Boards: Who Will
Serve?" page 33) wrote a hypothetical "want ad" for trustees. They

---

Shari Mycek is a writer based in Belle Mead, New Jersey.

contended that prospective hospital trustees should be "willing to assume a position of tremendous responsibility overseeing an organization in one of the most complex industries in America . . . be subject to intense scrutiny . . . and receive little or no pay."

They might have added that the ideal candidate should also be an expert on everything related to hospital care. And that this expertise should come magically overnight.

While there are no published statistics on trustees' educational and occupational backgrounds, anecdotal indications are that most (if not all) trustees come from outside the health care industry.

So how and where do new trustees obtain instant knowledge of the complex health care industry? There are no hospital trustee *Cliffs Notes*. But that's not to say there isn't hope.

From her home in Massachusetts, Lois Green offers insight. For years, Green served as a trustee at the University of Massachusetts Medical Center in Worcester, and, recently, as chair of the AHA's Committee on Governance's education committee. These days, she's a faculty member at the university, but hospital stewardship remains close to her heart. Educating trustees, she believes, starts with the fundamental task of outlining their responsibilities.

"My hair stands on end when I read about boards and some of the trouble they're in because I really think a lot of it goes back to [board members] not knowing their responsibilities," Green says. "So much time, especially orientation time, is spent showcasing the organization, highlighting its services—and not on the responsibilities of trustees and what's expected of them."

In his recently released book, *The Governance Factor: 33 Keys to Success in Healthcare* (Health Administration Press, 2003), Errol Biggs, Ph.D., a former hospital CEO and current director of graduate programs in health administration at the University of Colorado, Denver, addresses this topic.

Biggs became "intrigued" with the gap in trustee education and its impact years ago while serving as vice president of then Hospital Affiliates, now Texas-based Quorum Health. He traveled through the mountains of Colorado, attending 10 to 12 management-contract hospital board meetings a month in hospitals ranging from 200 to 400 beds in like-sized communities (approximately 15,000 to 18,000 people). He says he was struck by how one board could function so well while another didn't. And then the light switched on: "I realized one board was educated, another was not. There was this very incompetent group, made up of extremely competent individuals. It was as if these highly competent people walked into the hospital board room and checked their brains at the door," says Biggs.

"First off, they didn't speak the language," he continues. "Doctors use big medical words, administrators copy [them], so board members, especially new ones, are intimidated—a person who runs the largest corporation in the city suddenly feels ignorant."

In addition to the language problem, trustees on the ineffective boards simply didn't seem to know what their job was.

"The single, most important way to educate board members is to provide them with written job descriptions," says Biggs. "The board chair—not the hospital CEO (remember: the CEO works for the board)—must sit down with each new board member and say, 'Here is your job description. Here's what you're expected to do.'" (See "Trustee Job Description," page 69.)

When Biggs speaks around the country about board job descriptions, he tells audiences offhandedly to leave a business card if they'd like to receive a copy of his presentation. Every time, a line snakes around the room—hospital CEOs, board chairs, presidents of medical staffs, all clamoring for information.

Once trustees know what's expected of them, a formal board orientation may then follow. But according to governance expert Dennis Pointer, Ph.D., professor of health care management, School of Public Health, University of Washington, Seattle, and vice president of the American Governance & Leadership Group, Bozeman, Montana, orientation for the new trustee "must be a process, not an event." With a new book just out, *The Health Care Industry: A Primer for Board Members* (co-authored with Steve Williams, Jossey-Bass, 2003), Pointer adds, "Orientation needs to be spanned over the course of trustees' first year and not crammed into one or two days . . . board orientation must be multichanneled and consciously thought out, as opposed to us taking new board members by the hand, marching them down the dock, kicking them in [the water] and telling them to have a nice swim. It should include many facets and be ongoing."

Pointer concludes, "One of the greatest disservices we can do is to take intelligent people who want to make a contribution and not support their development."

Trustee Job Description

The idea of written job descriptions for hospital chairs and board members seems so simple. But every time Errol Biggs, Ph.D., speaks on the topic, he is inundated with requests for more information. What do the job descriptions look like? What are the functions, relationships and responsibilities of hospital trustees? No need to wait in line: Biggs, director of the graduate programs in health administration and director for the Center for Health Administration, University of Colorado, Denver, shares his model here.

Function:
A board member serves to elect, monitor, appraise, advise, stimulate, support, reward, and, when necessary or desirable, change top management.

Relationship:
A board member exists to meet the needs of the people the organization serves.

Responsibilities:
- Attends board meetings
- Reads agenda materials carefully prior to board meetings
- Participates in board orientation and continuing education
- Keeps all board deliberations confidential
- Avoids potential personal and/or professional conflicts of interest
- Approves annual budgets
- Understands the organization's mission and vision
- Avoids interference in hospital operations
- Establishes corporate policy
- Oversees physician recruitment and selection processes
- Develops and recommends strategic direction and financial plans for the organization
- Establishes evaluation criteria for key board officers and the CEO
- Elects officers (chair, vice chair, treasurer, and secretary at annual board meeting)
- Represents the hospital to the community
- With the board officers, monitors the performance of the CEO
- Reviews management's achievement of the organization's mission and goals

Source: Used with permission from *The Governance Factor: 33 Keys to Success in Healthcare* by Errol L. Biggs (Chicago: Health Administration Press, 2003), p. 159.

"Boards have really good people [serving on them]," says Biggs. "The problem is that no one has ever told them what their job is." Only when trustees know what's expected of them, say Biggs and Green, can ongoing education begin.

Given that trustees have busy professional and personal lives, and thus time constraints on their hospital work, what does the ideal "curriculum" look like? Perhaps something like this:

1. Trustee Education Appears as a Line Item in the Budget

Ideally, 1 percent of the total hospital budget is dedicated to trustee education (retreats, outside speakers, magazine subscriptions, etc.).

2. Once a Year, the Entire Board Goes on a Retreat

"Most hospitals routinely send their board chair, president of the medical staff and CEO to leadership conferences. And the three play very well together," says Biggs. "But when they come back, the rest of the board doesn't grasp the concept [of what they have learned]. It's important to get the entire board out of town for one or two days, even if it's only 20 miles away. Half of the time should be spent on speakers, presentations and formally educating board members. The other half should be spent on play. Board members really need to play together—to golf, talk, learn to get along. No matter how small a town they come from, these people don't travel in the same social circles. The rich farmer is different from the banker [who] is different from the teacher. They don't really know each other. Trustees need to learn to play together in the sandbox, understand each other's backgrounds and get along together. And they just might be able to govern together."

In northern Virginia, "Knox" Singleton, CEO of Inova Health System, which comprises five hospitals, is no stranger to boards or the need for board education. Twice a year, Inova devotes one to three days to off-site trustee education. In the spring, the Inova parent board (19 members) goes on a retreat; in the fall, everyone involved in Inova governance—from subsidiary to foundation boards—convenes.

"There's great value in board members getting to know one another and spending time together," says Singleton, who notes that one-third of "formal" education time is spent listening to outside speakers, while the other two-thirds is spent looking at how industry issues affect Inova specifically. "We explore what a particular issue means for Inova, and it may change our strategy, our priority," he says. The Inova group has convened close to home, a few hours away, and has even flown to far-off locales.

"There are pluses and minuses to both," says Singleton. "But in this cost-conscious environment, I'm finding it best to stay local. There's the expense of travel, but even more so, there's the expense of time. The amount of time trustees can give today is less than it was even three years ago. So if you want good attendance, you have to make it convenient."

3. Every Board Meeting Starts with an Educational Update

According to Green, one of the most productive educational practices boards can follow is to devote the first 20 minutes or so of every board meeting to updating trustees on breaking federal, state, local and hospital issues. "It's not just the new trustee who needs to be educated, but also those who've been there forever," she says.

Back in northern Virginia, Singleton says his boards religiously devote 20 minutes to "JIT" (just in time) education.

"We typically address an internal area—something the hospital is working hard on, such as patient safety, but with which the average trustee may not be conversant. If you wait until you have a full hour, or until the time is right, you'll never do it," Singleton says.

4. All Board Members Read from the Same Page

Most trustees don't have much time to read health care literature. "Again, these folks aren't from the health care industry," says Biggs. "They may not know *Trustee* magazine or [other publications]. So it's up to the CEO or board chair to figure out which media outlet best serves the board and give every trustee a subscription."

5. All Board Members Speak the Same Language

In *The Governance Factor,* Biggs includes a 21-page appendix of common health care terms (adapted from the Iowa Hospital Association's

Common Health Care Abbreviations & Terminology (www.ihaonline
.org/publications/termsweb.pdf).

"As with many other industries, the health care arena has spawned
its own lexicon, inhabited by a seemingly unending stream of abbreviations and jargon that can be confusing," says Biggs. He tells of
entering a doctoral program at a major university (after having been
a hospital CEO and merging two hospitals) and hearing about the
horrendous "OB" problem. It made no sense to him why the class
discussion centered on obstetrics. Then, someone enlightened him.
"OB" stood for "organizational behavior."

6. Everyone Gets a Mentor

"People often [hang back] in new situations. It's just human nature,"
says Green. "So nine times out of 10, new board members stay
silent, don't ask questions. Of course, when they do ask questions,
they ask the best ones: 'Why aren't you doing this?' or 'How did
you come to this decision?' because they see the issue from a fresh
perspective. For this reason, I like [assigning] new board members
a mentor—someone who sits next to them at board meetings, takes
an interest in them, meets them for coffee, and answers the questions they feel may be 'dumb' and therefore are too timid to bring
up before the full board."

Pointer, also a major advocate of mentors, adds that every board
meeting should be preceded by a short telephone conversation
between mentor and new board member as to what's on the agenda
and why; and that each meeting should be followed with a 10- to
15-minute personal "recap" of what just happened. "So much of
what happens in governance is subtle," says Pointer.

7. Trustees Only Receive Information Helpful in Governing

Most hospital boards receive way too much information: statistics
and reports—all of which ends up as mounds of paper for each
trustee. But what to cut? What to expand? Biggs offers the following advice: "Think of governance versus management. If you give
trustees management information, they will manage. Give them
governance information, and they will govern."

8. Trustees Use the Web as a Resource

Cyberspace is vast and not necessarily efficient if users don't know where to go. For those trustees who have time to peruse the Web, even if just occasionally, a number of sites may prove especially helpful. Among those worth visiting: www.americangovernance.com (the Center for Healthcare Governance); www.governanceinstitute.com (the Governance Institute); www.greatboards.org (governance consultant Barry Bader's site); and Lois Green's favorite, www.trusteeresources.com (from the AHA).

And finally, in the quest for a highly educated and competent board:

9. There Must Be a Constant Vigil for New and Qualified Recruits

In the last few years, term limits on board members and board chairs have become a hot issue. According to Biggs, a number of boards around the country have tried, then rejected, term limits because of the time it takes to bring new board members up to speed and educate them about health care, about the organization and about their governance responsibilities.

When recruiting new talent for the board, Biggs suggests "figuring out what criteria/skills you need, and if you don't find them in your own community, go outside"—maybe even to a neighboring state—perhaps inviting a noncompeting hospital CEO to serve. While not the norm, such individuals can "bring a lot of knowledge and objectivity to the board and help the board put its own situation in perspective by sharing how similar problems are handled in another location," says Biggs. "Most boards and CEOs who've taken this approach seem very satisfied with it and support the idea."

As for physician recruitment? Using physicians who double as members of both the medical staff and the board seems, perhaps, to be the most obvious way to increase the number of trustees with health care expertise. Their expertise, in turn, can "bring along" those board members without a health care background.

But according to many governance consultants, not all boards have enough physicians. And those hospitals that do have physicians on board do not necessarily have the right ones.

"The harsh reality is that any physician who has any contract whatsoever with the hospital—for whatever reason—cannot be considered to serve on the board," says Biggs. "Don't even talk to them. Don't ask. They're not eligible."

What Do Boards Need to Know?

By Laurie Larson

Most hospital boards understand that they need to become more sophisticated, more transparent and more facile at bringing their new members up to speed more quickly. In other words, health care governance needs to be a savvier, leaner machine than ever before.

"We'll see more and more of governance functions under a microscope, because of the scandals in health care and private companies," says Edward A. Kazemek, CEO and chair of Accord, Ltd., Chicago. "So much more attention is being paid to how governance is carried out, how [board members] are selected, oriented and educated . . . ratcheting up the concrete criteria [for board membership] is a good idea."

His list of preferred skills for today's trustees includes expertise in:

- Information and clinical technology
- Strategic planning
- Finance and banking experience, including audit expertise (i.e., a financial expert for the audit committee)
- Legal matters, preferably health care law, contract law and/or mergers and acquisitions
- Human resources, to assist with workforce issues
- Quality improvement, including knowledge of private sector approaches to quality
- Marketing

Laurie Larson is the senior editor for *Trustee.*

- Faith-based sensitivities, to be attuned both to faith-based health care systems and strongly spiritual communities
- Community advocacy

"This is a new dimension of what we're looking for in board members . . . those who can advocate to state, federal and local governmental representatives, making sure the community is represented," Kazemek says. "Board members have a bigger influence on elected officials than CEOs; they are more credible because they are viewed as being from the community."

Broadening these criteria to a wider set of overarching skills, Errol Biggs, director of graduate programs in health administration at the University of Colorado, Denver, encourages boards to look at the following criteria when recruiting new members:

- *Board experience.* Biggs recommends that the hospital's governance committee go to its local Chamber of Commerce "looking for corporate people within a 20-mile radius, those who have some board experience of some kind . . . you don't [want to have] people 'practicing' being a board member [for the first time] in the community's most complex organization." He adds, "Even small town boards should look for outside directors for certain skills. Outsiders are less emotional." Health care foundation boards and committees within the hospital are also great places to look for new members, he says.
- *Achievements.* Look for those individuals who have achieved something in their careers, whatever the field, as well as those who have specific skill sets, such as a background in construction, finance, marketing, etc.
- *Willingness and time to serve on the board.* "You don't want people who are on too many other boards," Biggs says. For example, there should not be CEOs on the board who have too many commitments. "Time is very important," he adds.
- *Objectivity.* "You can't have anyone on the board who represents some kind of constituency," he warns.
- *Strategic focus.* Trustees should be skilled in looking at "dashboard" indicators to analyze such areas as quality of care and financial ratios to keep a "governing not managing" perspective, Biggs says, maximizing big-picture over day-to-day thinking.
- *Commitment to the hospital.* Trustees need to truly understand and act from a firm knowledge of the hospital's mission.

To ensure these qualities, Kazemek says many boards have a written "expectations agreement" that candidates are required to review before accepting the board's nomination, spelling out such minimal requirements as: attending at least 75 percent of meetings, reviewing all materials for meeting preparation and fulfilling all board education requirements. "The agreement should ask, 'If we nominate you, will you abide by this agreement?' It's about being clear," Kazemek says.

Physicians definitely belong on the board, but as with other board members, Biggs recommends seeking them from outside the community when possible. Even when they are local, however, physician trustees should be chosen by the board, not based on their colleagues' recommendations, Biggs says. Ideally, on the average 12-person board, one physician trustee should represent staff and two more should be on the board who do not.

Indeed, as an overall trend, Kazemek says, "The days of hiring friends . . . picking people willing to write a check . . . and general 'good people' are over."

To determine who they need most on the board, Kazemek says more board nominating committees are developing a greater number of competencies for potential candidates, including competence "matrixes" or scorecards listing out all skills the board deems important for its members. Once those competencies already covered by current members are noted on the scorecard, it becomes clear which missing competencies to seek when recruiting new members. From this, the board can generate a "wish list" for new trustees, ranging from candidates with job titles the board is seeking, such as an accountant, to specific skills, such as IT or clinical quality expertise.

However, Kazemek says, "Boards are moving away from job titles and toward skill sets that [reveal] what the person really knows— their formal education, their work experience." Examples might include seeking trustees with turnaround experience for a system in financial trouble, or professionals who understand conflict resolution to improve physician relations.

Regardless of the overall level of business experience new members may bring to the board, they must still be able to "hit the ground running" as health care trustees. Here, Biggs says a highly focused, crystal clear orientation is key.

"If there is only one thing a board does to make itself more effective, it would be to get a job description for each new trustee from the chair," Biggs recommends. The CEO's and the chair's job should also be explained, along with the structure of the organization, its bylaws, strategic plan and mission. The job description should also include a review of the health care industry overall, along with a market overview and an analysis of the hospital's competitors. He adds, "You can't do orientation in one session, you need several."

However, Kazemek thinks a solid full day of orientation can be enough, provided all of the areas listed above are covered, including a hospital tour and the participation of experienced board members. He also advises an orientation follow-up after six months to see how new members are doing and what questions they may have. He further recommends that experienced board members become "coaches" to new board members, talking informally with them and providing an outlet for them to ask questions they may feel are too basic to bring up during meetings.

But, of course, learning is never over—and education is the best way to keep the board sharp.

By Kazemek's estimate, the average board spends about 20 hours a year on education, which he asserts is "not good enough." He recommends 30 to 40 hours a year, which he says is not as difficult as it sounds. "If boards didn't waste time in meetings getting into operational details, there would be tons of time for education."

He advises breaking education down into three types: "just in time" topics injected into each board or committee meeting; one annual retreat, including formal education, board self-assessment and strategic planning; and at least one off-site meeting or educational session each year.

Most importantly, all board education curriculum should be developed in conjunction with the strategic plan.

"What you are currently educating your board on, after the basics, is tied directly to those areas where the board will make strategic decisions or enact policies," Kazemek says. "Be focused before you choose your topics for education, don't be general."

Biggs sums it up: "The most important thing for the future for any trustee is to be able to think strategically . . . and [for the board] to function as one voice."

Knowledge Building:
How to Raise Your Board's IQ

By Shari Mycek

Label on a child's Superman costume:
"Wearing of this garment does not enable you to fly."
—Unknown

"I've been a trustee 33 years. My, how that dates me," says Joan Soriano, a trustee at Harrison Medical Center in Washington's scenic Olympic Peninsula. "In that time, I've seen many changes take shape in health care. And, of course, some of the same problems resurface."

Among the most common problems for health care trustees? How to stay on top of the consistently changing, complex health care industry while maintaining high-profile careers, coaching their kids' sports teams, raising families, and serving as stewards for their community.

Larry Walker, president of The Walker Company, a leading health care consulting firm based in Lake Oswego, Oregon, says he works 60-plus hours a week researching and trying to understand health care issues and challenges and feels he's "still just scratching the surface of what's important to know. Every day, my inbox is overflowing with new studies, new insights, new information and new

---

Shari Mycek is a freelance writer based in Belle Mead, New Jersey.

perspectives." He adds, "The field is so complex, so profound it's difficult to stay on top of it all."

If seasoned governance experts are admitting to information overload, what's a volunteer trustee to do? Before throwing in the gavel, Soriano and Walker—and a handful of others—offer survivors' insight, beginning with the distinction between orientation and continuing education.

"The two are not [the same]," says Walker. "Board orientation is board orientation: a two-hour tour of the hospital, meet-and-greet with administration, and handing out of job descriptions and bylaws."

"Board orientation is facility familiarization," adds Soriano. "During orientation, one learns the organization structure, the responsibilities and obligations of the board commitment, the facility plan and the particulars of the institution. But learning about your hospital is very different from learning about overall health care and the topics of the moment that we need to know about to stay in business and serve our communities. Continuing board education is ongoing and, aside from seminars, should be just what it says. This means reading provided educational materials, being a political advocate and making the effort to seek out knowledge at every opportunity."

Walker takes the concept one step further, encouraging boards to replace the term "ongoing education" with the idea of "board knowledge and intelligence building—the end result being greater knowledge and heightened leadership intelligence that ensures trustees are fully prepared to engage around critical issues and make evidence-based versus 'gut-based' decisions," he explains.

Simple questions such as, "What does this board know and what does it need to know?" and "Who is going off the board in the next three to four years and what will the impact be in terms of knowledge and experience loss?" can get the ball rolling. But while the strategy may appear broad-brushed and collective, it's not, according to Walker, who advocates "personalization down to each individual trustee. If someone made me God, as scary as that sounds," he laughs, "I'd say that the CEO or board chair should have a one-on-one discussion with every trustee to assess where 'Dave' is in the health care learning curve and what 'Doris' needs next. Every trustee is in a different place in terms of his or her level of awareness and knowledge of the issues being discussed and the decisions being made. But every trustee has the same fiduciary obligation, the same responsibility to be well-informed and the same vote," Walker says. "The best way to assess where 'Dave' is in the curve is to talk to him."

According to Walker, such an assessment might go something like this:

- What do you think are the trends or other factors that will most affect or influence our success in the next few years?
- What major assumptions should we make about the environment that will have an impact on our ability to achieve our strategies (e.g., the economy, competition, reimbursement)?
- What does "health care reform" mean to you?
- What issues do you think should occupy our governance time and attention in the next year? In the next three years?
- What areas do you think you need to understand better in order to contribute most effectively as a trustee?
- How do you learn best? By reading? Presentations? Interactive dialogue?

"The individualized knowledge assessment is not a 'test,' and should not be intimidating," says Walker. "It's a conversation to help determine the areas where pinpointed education can be focused most quickly to get the trustee up to speed on the issues and decisions for which he or she is fully responsible."

Larry Walker, meet Bob Kiely, CEO of Middlesex Hospital, Middletown, Connecticut. Kiely allocates $100,000 per year specifically to trustee "knowledge building." And he personally conducts the type of one-on-one conversations that Walker envisions.

"Some years we don't spend that much; other years we spend more," says Kiely. "[Spending is] contingent on where we are. Hospitals, I think, have an obligation to bring new board members up to speed, while simultaneously keeping their most experienced trustees moving forward. They are our jewels, and so we must buff them— make sure we can tailor educative opportunities to their needs."

When Kiely arrived at Middlesex Hospital 17 years ago, he found a board of trustees who met once a month and a score of subcommittees that did the same. About six months later, Kiely said to the board: "Ladies and gentlemen, we are no longer going to meet once a month. Everyone in this room is busy, we're very geographically dispersed. (Middlesex Hospital serves residents and culls trustees from 22 towns in the region.) Instead, we're going to allocate our time differently."

Today the 12-member Middlesex board meets only five times a year. But in between every meeting (roughly six times per year), Kiely, along with an executive or clinical team member, meets one-on-one for 30 to 60 minutes with each trustee in the trustee's own office.

"I try to make it as convenient as possible by going to them," Kiely says. "By far, these one-on-ones are among our greatest board successes. For me, they provide an opportunity to get to know each board member, assess where they are on the health care learning curve, and to update them on any hot-button issues that may be pressing, so that when we do come together, we're all singing on the same page of the hymnal, everyone is up to speed."

He adds, "Bringing members of the executive team also enables board members to get to know them and to feel comfortable with someone other than myself, so that if they have a question or hear something [about the hospital], they are comfortable picking up the phone and contacting the team member closest to that specific issue."

Kiely says that "every two weeks, like clockwork," he dispatches a "Board Update" via e-mail or hard copy—a simple, double-sided page—briefly highlighting a pressing national or state health care issue and how it applies specifically to Middlesex (see "The CEO Brief," page 83). He also encourages (and pays for) trustees to attend one major educational conference at least every other year.

"We tried holding an annual retreat and bringing in top speaker(s)," says Kiely. "But for various reasons, it just didn't get the priority that a 'clear-your-calendar, you're-flying-to-Florida-this-week' gets in terms of attendance. The last time we tried an annual retreat, we had an absolutely magnificent speaker, but only half of our board attended. So now we focus more on clearing a few days and sending a handful of trustees at a time to major educational conferences."

Kiely adds that there is also "tremendous benefit" in an educational venue socially. "Due to our wide geographic spread, our trustees don't have a common playing field outside the hospital," he says. "They don't sit on the same bank boards or belong to the same country club, so these external, get-away-from-the-hospital meetings enable board members to interact with one another away from the board table."

While not every hospital can follow Middlesex's lead and devote six figures annually to trustee knowledge building, the concept should be anchored by some sort of "budget with purpose," Walker says. This means it should define, for several months out, the issues and topics for exploration, he explains, including their expense.

The CEO Brief

"Every two weeks like clockwork," as he describes it, Bob Kiely, CEO of Middlesex Hospital in Middletown, Connecticut, sends a double-sided "brief" to hospital trustees, updating them on pressing national or state health care issues and how they directly correlate to Middlesex. Following are two excerpts from recent briefs:

- "The article that ran in *The New York Times* this weekend (copy attached) is an example of the reporting on hospital performance that we are likely to see more and more of in the months ahead. While it focuses on acute myocardial infarction and pneumonia care, it highlights both the benefits and pitfalls that will inevitably be part of the increased scrutiny of hospital performance. Middlesex Hospital was in the highest rated group (top quartile of all hospitals) for acute myocardial infarction and chronic heart failure. The hospital's performance in pneumonia was cited as being in the third quartile. The data were for the time period from Jan. 1, 2004, through June 30, 2004."
  —Aug. 22, 2005

- "Attached is a copy of The Governance Institute's 'Fast Track Board Self-Assessment' instrument. As you know, we have routinely performed board self-assessments alternating between our 'homegrown' version and instruments designed by The Governance Institute. The Governance Institute recently revised its self-evaluation instruments and I felt it would be beneficial to use their instrument so that we can gain comparative 'benchmarking' information against their client database. . . . Below are some thoughts on board self-evaluation."
  —Dec. 14, 2005

For starters: what is the cost (lodging, meals, registration and mileage) for every board member to go to two in-state educational programs per year? What is the cost for every trustee to receive subscriptions to the industry's "must-reads" (*Trustee, Hospitals & Health Networks, AHA News, Modern Healthcare, The Wall Street Journal*) and online reports such as *HealthLeaders* and the Kaiser Family Foundation? What is the cost of one two-day board retreat per year to focus on knowledge and new insights? Or to send every trustee to one out-of-state educational conference per year?

"Trustee knowledge building needs to take place continuously and through a variety of venues, including state hospital association conferences, reading and absorbing information and ideas in trade journals and online versions of national newspapers, and through targeted education at every board meeting," says Walker. "The key to success is to develop trustee knowledge that enables governance leaders to put the bigger issues and challenges into a local market framework, identify local market implications . . . and lead with confidence."

Back in Washington state, Soriano's hospital adheres to such a philosophy. While there is no set governance education budget, Harrison Medical Center requires each of its 15 board members to complete 45 hours of education per term.

Any in-state educational meeting (i.e., state hospital association) trustees want to attend is covered in full, as is one out-of-state conference per year (and once a term, trustees may take a spouse). In between conferences, every monthly board meeting begins with an education session.

A new format, introduced about a year ago, has trustees arriving at 4:30 p.m. for an educational update. Dinner is served promptly at 5:30 p.m., and the board meeting is under way by 6.

"The new format has been very well received," says Soriano, noting that about 80 percent of trustees consistently arrive early for the educational component. "We used to start our board meetings at 5:30 and try to build education into the agenda, which didn't always work. We'd eat dinner after, and it was a really late night, especially for those who'd been working all day."

Time, no matter how you look at it, factors into board knowledge and intelligence building.

"This sounds so basic, but the success of any continuing board education effort very much depends on the job you do first on board selection," Kiely says. "If a board member simply can't or won't allocate time to learn, all the educative efforts in the world won't work. We try to be very careful about who we bring onto the board and to seek people with intellectual curiosity and excitement to learn."

Designing the Education Process

In building a board's knowledge and intelligence capital, Larry Walker, president of The Walker Group, a health care consulting firm based in Lake Oswego, Oregon, recommends the following six steps:

1. Define the broad issues that every board member needs to understand in order to be a high-performance trustee. These can range from reimbursement, regulation and workforce to quality and safety, community benefit and medical staff issues. The hospital's current strategic plan should serve as a basis for determining the issues that have an impact on success.
2. Assess each individual trustee's awareness and understanding of the issues and situations likely to come before the board in the coming months. This can be done through the board self-assessment, a simple survey, casual one-on-one conversations—typically between the trustee and the board chair and/or the CEO—or a combination of all.
3. Assign an experienced board colleague to work closely with newer trustees to help them understand issues, questions, nuances, etc.
4. Develop a 12-month or longer "curriculum" of topics that are essential to effective governance and determine the most appropriate resources to access or deliver that information. Ensure that every trustee is committed to and involved in the process.
5. Leverage enriched trustee knowledge through coordinated community outreach, including political advocacy, community discussions and presentations.
6. Continuously refine and improve the process.

During his 17-year tenure at Middlesex, Kiely admits having to "counsel off" three board members. "Not happy occasions," he says. "But they simply couldn't commit the time and 'do' the education. And without doing the education, trustees cannot be effective in their jobs."

Thomasine Kennedy, a former elementary school principal and long-time trustee at Duplin General Hospital in Kenansville, North Carolina, couldn't agree more.

"Trustees are typically very busy people, who come into the boardroom with an intense desire to serve their community, but often with very little health care background," she says.

Explaining the road she took to learning the field, Kennedy says, "I had very limited health care background when I came on my hospital board, but my educator background kicked in, and I took advantage of the many regional, state and national offerings available to me via the North Carolina Hospital Association and the American Hospital Association. As a trustee, you have to. Trustees are, above all, advocates and must be able to [be] articulate in the boardroom, in the grocery store, at the Rotary Club and at the local, state and [national] political levels."

She adds, "It's impossible to be an effective advocate if you don't have a good talking knowledge of your subject. It's impossible to go into a senator's office and try to articulate the impact of a health care issue if you don't understand it yourself. And so you must put yourself out there, take advantage of the wonderful offerings."

But that doesn't mean you have to do all of them.

"Some people learn better by reading," says Kennedy. "Others by listening. And others by interacting. To say that every trustee has to build his or her knowledge in the same way is a burden on the trustee. And a fallacy to what we know to be true about learning styles. An educative variety must be offered."

PART THREE

In the Boardroom

Judging Fiduciary Duty

By Karen Sandrick

*Do you understand the full extent
of your fiduciary duty and how to fulfill it?*

The directors of Granada Hills (CA) Community Hospital thought they had done everything they could to discharge their fiduciary duty. After the hospital was plunged into Chapter 11 bankruptcy because of the unexpected failure of a national accounts receivable management firm in 2002, trustees heeded the advice of the hospital's bankruptcy counsel, its bondholders and a committee of unsecured creditors and hired a turnaround/crisis management firm to handle day-to-day operations while it attempted to reorganize.

Over the next seven months, board members were told the hospital was making real progress, verified by reports showing apparent gains in admissions, physician support and nurse staffing.

But the picture was not nearly as rosy as the turnaround company's CEO and CFO painted. Within hours of learning that payroll taxes had not been paid, board members met in emergency session and immediately terminated the contract with the turnaround company for cause. A week later, faced with stark financial numbers showing that the hospital could not survive, the board agreed to file for Chapter 7 insolvency and the hospital closed.

Karen Sandrick is a writer based in Chicago.

But the story for these trustees did not end with the closing of Granada Hills Community Hospital. Three years later, board members were hauled before a U.S. District Court in California, charged with breaching their duty to the hospital and threatened with personal liability for damages in excess of $10 million. Finally, this January (2006), Judge George Schiavelli ruled that the former directors of Granada Hills Community Hospital were protected from personal liability by the state's business judgment rule because they had acted in good faith and took steps they believed were in the best interest of the hospital (see "The Granada Hills Case," pages 92–93). To some observers, the ruling in this case reaffirmed that state laws provide strong protections to hospital trustees.

"The way this particular federal court judge looked at the issues and the manner in which the judge sided with the directors, based on his application of the business judgment rule, should be encouraging for other nonprofit directors who may get in a situation like this," says Cary W. Miller, the principal attorney who defended the trustees and a partner in the law firm of Hooper, Lundy & Bookman, Los Angeles.

But to others, it's a warning shot. "The fact that this case was thrown out against the directors in terms of personal liability under the California business judgment rule on the one hand is comforting to board members. But on the other, it should raise some alarms," says James E. Orlikoff, president of Orlikoff & Associates in Chicago and senior consultant to the AHA Center for Healthcare Governance.

"Up until now, the issues that got boards into trouble were those of gross negligence and malfeasance," Orlikoff says. "But this case was about making bad decisions. The fact that this lawsuit was filed is indicative that the areas of safety for boards are getting smaller, and that boards should rely more on good governance and the effective discharge of their fiduciary duties than on legal protections." He warns, "It's only a matter of time before things start to crack and there is a successful penetration of a state's business judgment rule."

The Changing Face of Fiduciary Duty

The definition of *fiduciary* seems clear enough. A fiduciary is a person who has the legal duty to act in the interest of other individuals connected with an enterprise. "A fiduciary has to act for the benefit of other people and [his or her] actions have to be consistent with what the mission of enterprise is," says John Combes, president and COO of the Center for Healthcare Governance. "So, for a hospital, a fiduciary has to act for the benefit of patients, the community, the workforce, the physicians—all those different groups of stakeholders."

Virtually every state applies the same three legal criteria to describe the fiduciary's responsibilities: the duties of care, loyalty and obedience. But the concept of fiduciary duty is broad, vague and confusing. It should come as no surprise, therefore, that many hospital and health system board members are not aware of all its ramifications and simply presume *fiduciary* is a synonym for *financial*.

"When they hear the term 'fiduciary duty,' too many people assume the board's duty is to make sure the organization is doing well financially," Orlikoff says. "Certainly that's a part of their duty, but a small part of it." In fact, adds Combes, since hospitals are not primarily financial institutions, it's more important for trustees to represent the organization's commitment to its mission rather than to concentrate predominantly on its finances. The ebb and flow of marketplace demands, as well as those of employers and employees over the last few years, have altered the role and responsibilities as well as the accountability of hospital boards.

John Leech, an attorney and principal with Dynamis Healthcare Advisors Inc., Chagrin Falls, Ohio, has served on hospital boards since the 1970s and witnessed these changes. In the 1970s, he recalls, hospital boards "were given the total presumption that they were doing everything right." He explains, "the difference now is that people are applying today's facts against broad standards, and although the standards [of fiduciary duty] haven't changed, the attitude has. People are saying, 'Prove to me that you did everything right. Were you prudent if you just showed up to two meetings a year and a huge institution went under, left a lot of debt, didn't serve the medical interests of the population, and got a tax exemption?' It means hospital boards have to work harder at their good faith due diligence."

The shift in attitude from "we know you're doing a good job" to "show me you're doing a good job" for hospital boards has happened at least in part because the stakes have gotten so high. It's well-recognized that today's hospital trustees govern extremely complex organizations that are navigating through periods of immense pressure and transition.

The Granada Hills Case

Along with five other members of the community and the president-elect of the medical staff, Steven Hicks joined the newly constituted board of 139-bed Granada Hills Community Hospital, Los Angeles County, as chair in November 2002. Hicks was recruited to help guide the hospital as it put together a financing and restructuring plan for affiliating with one or two other hospitals in the area in order to improve its financial status, meet statutory requirements for seismic retrofitting, and better negotiate managed care contracts with local providers. Except for John Weitcamp, who remained on the hospital board, all 20 members of the hospital's previous board had stepped down to streamline its structure and bring on individuals who had more experience with health care.

Less than 10 days after the new board convened, the company that was managing its accounts receivable, National Century Financial Enterprises (NCFE), filed for Chapter 11 bankruptcy protection. As a result, more than 2,000 health care providers, including major clinics, physicians' office practices, and hospitals across the country also immediately filed for bankruptcy. With $18 million in debt and its accounts receivables frozen, Granada Hills Community Hospital had no choice but to file for Chapter 11 bankruptcy itself. To shepherd them through the process of reorganization under Chapter 11, board members retained the services of Coudert Brothers, LLP, a national law firm based in Los Angeles with a well-established bankruptcy and creditors' rights practice.

After Coudert Brothers, as well as the hospital's bondholders and an official committee of unsecured creditors strongly urged the board to hire a turnaround company to operate the hospital during its reorganization, board members spent weeks interviewing individuals from as many as a dozen firms that performed turnaround work.

Because all other candidates refused to take on the job or represented one of the other health care providers involved in the NCFE bankruptcy, the board eventually hired Healthcare Resource Specialists Inc., a subsidiary of Bay Management Group, LLC. Healthcare Resource Specialists had been in existence for only a few months and had no prior experience as a turnaround manager for a hospital or any other financially distressed company. From Jan. 17, 2003, when the company was hired, to July 9 of that year, the board and the representatives from Healthcare Resource Specialists had a positive working relationship.

"We were getting good feedback through our bankruptcy counsel that things were really turning around," says Hicks. "The management

Continued →

company was working well with a number of our unsecured creditors. One of the officers of the firm had been appealing to physicians in the community to bring their patients back to the hospital, and we saw a significant increase in admissions." Hicks adds, "Based on nurse staffing levels in the hospital at the end of February (2003), we were at capacity. For the first time in a couple of years, the hospital was in a diversion mode. We had to divert patients coming to the hospital because we had approximately 100 patients and couldn't accept any more."

But on July 9, 2003, the chief operating officer of the turnaround company, who had just taken over as CEO of the hospital, learned through reports from department heads that payroll taxes had not been paid. Within minutes, he relayed the information to Hicks, who met with bankruptcy counsel and convened an emergency meeting of the board the next day. Two days later, after receiving approval from the bankruptcy court, the board fired the turnaround firm.

"As a result of an assessment and report of the financial viability of the hospital under these new circumstances, it was obvious the hospital could not survive, even in Chapter 11," Hicks says. "It was the board's recommendation that the hospital close, that the bankruptcy be converted to Chapter 7, and that the court appoint a bankruptcy trustee."

On June 30, 2004, the bankruptcy trustee filed three lawsuits in the Superior Court of the State of California—one for breach of fiduciary duty of due care and good faith against the board, and two against the representatives of Healthcare Resource Specialists. The lawsuits alleged that the actions of the board and the turnaround company had a significant impact on the hospital, its estate, creditors, and others and incurred damages of more than $10 million.

"The effect of the . . . Board's failure to supervise and make reasonable inquiries about the Hospital's operations and finances was to drive the Hospital deeper into insolvency," the complaint stated. "If the Board had addressed the worsening financial condition of the Hospital and the Hospital's nonpayment of critical post-petition obligations, it could have taken steps to close the Hospital sooner with a resulting benefit to the Hospital and its creditors. . . ."

On Jan. 31, 2006, the District Court of the Central District of California ruled that the lawsuit against the board members was "circumspect and unmeritorious," and there was no basis for imposing liability on the trustees.

While the case against the board members has been decided, the decision may be appealed. The lawsuits against the officers of the turnaround company are continuing.

—Karen Sandrick

This change also is occurring because of the migration of provisions from the Sarbanes-Oxley Act into the not-for-profit sector. Although the Sarbanes-Oxley Act on its face applies only to for-profit corporate boards, it is setting standards for not-for-profit organizations that may be tested in a court of law or an administrative law procedure. "The number of cases on the books involving hospital not-for-profit directors has been relatively small," Miller says, "but Sarbanes-Oxley being what it is, the concern now is that [as] there is greater scrutiny, greater regulation over boards and directors of corporations on the for-profit side, that same scrutiny is going to seep over into the not-for-profit side, so cases like this will become more regular."

Indeed, state legislatures and state attorneys general are beginning to hold boards of not-for-profit corporations accountable to principles of governance similar to those of Sarbanes-Oxley. A "Charity Integrity Bill" and "Nonprofit Integrity Act" have been introduced in California. Massachusetts has proposed the "Act to Promote the Financial Integrity of Public Charities," and New York is considering the "Nonprofit Accountability Act." The attorney general in the state of Hawaii is seeking the authority to remove directors of not-for-profit organizations when necessary.

Health care attorneys are not noticing a significant upsurge in litigation involving hospital boards of directors. They are, however, seeing novel causes of action that project liability onto hospital trustees in pushing for a settlement. Plaintiffs in the Granada Hills case applied the "deepening insolvency theory," which has been increasingly advanced over the last decade. The question in the lawsuit was not whether the hospital could have or should have been saved, it was whether its trustees should have allowed the hospital to go into Chapter 7 bankruptcy much earlier and thereby preserved more of the bankruptcy estate for creditors, Miller explains.

Recognizing the relationship between creditworthiness and good governance, bond issuers and bond insurers are critically examining the quality of governance structures and processes and focusing, in particular, on such issues as conflicts of interest among board members. Additionally, companies that issue directors and officers' (D&O) liability insurance are using assessment scales and evaluation instruments to determine the risk a particular board may present to them before they decide to write a D&O policy or set premium or coverage levels.

Perhaps the best example of the heightened interest in the performance of fiduciary duties exercised by not-for-profit boards is the vigilance of the U.S. Senate Finance Committee, which has been conducting inquiries of some of the major not-for-profit organizations in this country, such as the American Red Cross, American University, and the Nature Conservancy, says Michael Peregrine, partner in the law firm McDermott, Will & Emery, Chicago.

In light of recommendations to improve the oversight and governance of charitable organizations from the federal Panel on the Nonprofit Sector, which includes provisions on financial audits and reviews, and conflict-of-interest disclosure, "the onus of due care on nonprofit directors has never been stronger," Peregrine says. "There has never been more focus on the burden of good governance placed on nonprofit directors."

In addition to a greater willingness to hold hospital trustees accountable for existing standards of fiduciary duty, over time the definitions of those duties will most likely expand. "You might say the duty of loyalty already has been expanded or might be applied more rigorously as boards are held to task in terms of conflicts of interest and director independence," Orlikoff says. "The duty of obedience is being applied more rigorously as boards are held accountable to IRS requirements, Medicare regulations, as well as their own governing documents."

Beyond this, an argument could be made that trustees of an organization that is facing or is in the midst of bankruptcy may be subject to higher standards of fiduciary care. "There's a real debate in the law, from my perspective, whether the duties do change in the circumstances of a bankruptcy," Peregrine says. As soon as a corporation enters a period of insolvency, he explains, the directors owe duty partially, if not primarily, to corporate creditors, the thought being that when an organization is insolvent, the creditors become the business's owners. But while some court cases have concluded that this concept applies to directors of organizations in the not-for-profit world, others have not. "If I were advising a client in that situation," Peregrine says, "I would say there's no clear guidance, so assume the worst, assume that you have a much higher standard in terms of your actions in overseeing a failing business organization because the creditors and their counsel will seek to hold you to higher standards."

D&O Insurance

The realization that they were being sued was devastating enough for the trustees of Granada Hills Community Hospital. But the prospect of being held personally liable for actions they believed they had taken in good faith to try to save a struggling hospital was positively chilling. "When you serve on a board, your personal assets are at stake, but the organization provides indemnification, and it pays for any legal expenses you or the organization may incur as a result of a lawsuit," explains Beth A. H. Strapp, vice president, Chubb and Son, health care industry practice leader and portfolio product manager for Chubb Specialty Insurance. "When an organization is bankrupt and there is no other financial resolution, the only thing that protects you from creditors coming after your personal assets is your D&O insurance."

D&O liability insurance indemnifies directors and officers of not-for-profit organizations for damages and defense costs arising from lawsuits that allege any number of "wrongful acts," including discrimination, harassment, wrongful termination of employees, waste of assets, libel and slander. D&O insurance fills in the gaps left by state business judgment laws and covers the boards and staff of not-for-profit organizations that may face a case brought in federal court or an employment practices lawsuit.

Although there have always been liabilities associated with serving on a not-for-profit board, exposures to liability have changed in the last few years. The severity of D&O insurance claims has been on the uptick, as shown by the number of hospitals that have not been able to meet their financial obligations and have reorganized or filed for bankruptcy. The frequency of D&O claims involving employment practices has also particularly risen, Strapp says.

Trustees may actually use their D&O insurance policy as a tool to minimize their exposure to liability and improve their governance. "Every D&O policy has a section called 'limitations and exclusions,' which identifies the areas of greatest risk," Orlikoff explains. "If I'm on a board and my D&O policy flags three areas, that tells me where my governance needs to be based on best practices and where we as a board need to be most aggressive." So while there are a number of protections from liability for hospital trustees—statutory immunity, D&O insurance, indemnification by the organization—the best defense nevertheless is good governance, Orlikoff says.

On top of the general obligation to act in good faith in the best interest of the organization, trustees also need to act with care to make reasonable inquiries. That's why it's important for board members to keep the minutes of meetings up to date, ask the right questions, get the right kind of information, and have access to outside experts if they need clarification. Says Leech, "It's just being a little more prudent."

Orlikoff's advice: "The best way of protecting your good name, avoiding embarrassment or media or regulatory scrutiny, and even potentially protecting personal loss, is doing your job right."

Accountability Stops Here: Educating the Board to Meet Its Responsibilities

By Shari Mycek

We've all been there—stuck bumper to bumper in a sea of fuming cars and SUVs—deadlocked on the highway, unable to turn back or accelerate forward. Inevitably, we resign ourselves to our place in line—make a phone call, turn up the radio volume, creep forward ever so slowly. When we finally reach the site of the accident, our necks crane. We can't help it. We look.

If it's only a minor fender bender, we may resume our previous pace. But if the accident is serious, if people are hurt, or, worse yet, if there appears to be a fatality, we slow down and heed the reminder.

It's that same type of moment to which Seattle-based governance expert Dennis D. Pointer says health care trustees must increasingly pay attention. In the past five years, the governance highway has witnessed two fatal crashes: first, the collapse of AHERF (Allegheny Health Education and Research Foundation in Pennsylvania) in 1998; and, most recently, the demise of Houston-based Enron, which declared bankruptcy in December 2001.

Pointer raises the question, "Where were the boards?" in his presentation to trustees around the country. He works with more than 500 trustees, 70 percent of whom are on health care boards. And

Shari Mycek is a contributing writer to *Trustee*.

although he doesn't claim to have all of the answers in this new age of accountability, he does offer this insight: "Boards are as high up in organizations as one can go and still remain inside them. They bear ultimate fiduciary responsibility, authority and accountability for their organization's affairs. As the plaque on Harry Truman's desk said: 'The buck stops here.'"

But increasingly, the governance "job" is tougher than it used to be.

"Ten years ago, health care trustees served on boards because it was a feather in their cap and a nice thing to do for the community," says Pam Knecht, vice president of Accord Limited in Chicago, a national consulting firm specializing in governance and organizational strategy. "What's expected of trustees today is very different. The world of health care—with its mergers, acquisitions, takeovers, dispositions of assets—has become very complex, and trustees are being held accountable in ways never seen before." She also points to Enron, AHERF, and Intercoastal in West Palm Beach, Florida, where a community didn't want its hospital turned into an ambulatory care center.

"Communities are speaking out; attorneys general are stepping in, but trustees cannot and should not count on the state attorney general or the community to hold them accountable," says Knecht. "Accountability has to be self-imposed. Boards have to create and maintain a culture of holding themselves accountable."

But how?

Both Pointer and Knecht first suggest board education. The old adage that knowledge is power is perhaps nowhere more true than in the health care governance arena. But educating well-meaning, time-stretched trustees may be easier said than done.

Mary Walker, president and CEO of Texas Healthcare Trustees in Austin, speaks fondly of a trustee in her home state. Like many, this individual serves on multiple boards, is committed, and is a hard worker. But like many, he feels unsettled about his new responsibility as a not-for-profit hospital trustee. "Health care looks a little complicated," he told her. "But I'm sure I'll figure it all out. I didn't need any special training to be a bank trustee."

But "special training" is exactly what Walker and other governance experts are prescribing.

"Being on a board today is not about sitting down and having a cup of coffee," says Walker. "There are consequences to making bad decisions—of not having the right information, not asking the right questions."

"Health care governance is definitely not a competency-free zone," says Pointer. "Knowledge, skills and experience (of the right type) are a board's most important and precious assets. Trustees need to understand the industry, the market and their organization. What we're asking of them is really a lot."

And the job doesn't come without a hefty time commitment. The typical not-for-profit hospital or system trustee already clocks more hours in a given year than a director of a Fortune 500 corporation, so it's difficult to ask trustees to give more. The issue, therefore, is not how to get more time out of trustees but how to make the time they already spend more effective. Following are some thoughts on how to do that.

Focus, Focus, Focus

"Many of the boards I work with simply don't have a clear sense of what their obligations are and [what] type of work they need to do to fulfill those obligations," says Pointer. "They spend a great deal of time on issues that are irrelevant, inconsequential, and don't add a lot

---

Board Skills

What are the core competencies that all health care trustees must possess to keep themselves and their organization accountable? Governance expert Dennis Pointer, of Pointer and Associates, Seattle, says that all trustees must understand:

- Governance obligations, functions, processes and best practices
- The health care industry as well as their individual market and organization
- Key success factors, including strategic, financial, operational and clinical variables
- How to read, analyze and interpret basic financial statements

Pointer further notes that at least some board members must possess specific competencies in law; accounting and financial expertise; and clinical care.

of value. If you have a 15-member board and five members think the board should be concentrating on A, B and C; another five think the focus should be on D, E and F; and the remaining five haven't much thought about either, that board is going to be ineffective by definition. To be effective, a board must have a collective notion of what it needs to do and how to go about doing it," Pointer says.

"One of my favorite quotes comes from the greatest philosopher around, country-western singer Willy Nelson, who says that 'if the next pot of chili tastes better than the last, it's probably due to something you left out versus something you put in,'" Pointer says. "I think that's true for governance. If the board has a laserlike focus on the things that will add value and make a difference—if it can clear everything else from its plate—it will be effective."

Defining Expectations

Knecht adds that trustees should be aware—up front—of what is expected of them. "When the nominating committee is out there trolling for potential board candidates, it is critical [that they] ask, 'Are you aware of what it is we're requesting of you?' Otherwise, we do our trustees a great disservice." She tells of one health care system that has instituted a covenant that board members must sign when they agree to serve on the board, stating how many hours they will spend in meetings, the number of educational sessions they're expected to attend, and so on.

"It takes guts to do this," she says. "In wooing potential board members, you don't want to make them feel like [governance] is a big bad job, but the truth is that it is a very serious responsibility."

In Kalamazoo, Michigan, former Borgess Health Alliance CEO Tim Stack demonstrated exactly that type of "guts." While at Borgess, Stack and his board chair sat down with the board and created a very realistic job description detailing the commitment required to serve on the board, the amount of time it would take, and the number and types of mandatory meetings. Now, as the new president and CEO of Piedmont Medical Center and Piedmont Hospital in Atlanta, Stack has asked the board there to follow suit.

"Right now, we're getting to know each other [at Piedmont]," says Stack. "But in a few months, we're going to start laying some serious expectation groundwork. Trustees have an awesome responsibility. The better prepared they are, the better off the organization is. Trustees of nonprofits do a great job, but it's a tremendous amount of time, and I think we have to be sensitive to their time—make it a little easier for them by letting them know what the expectations are ahead of time."

Stack describes the time spent with the Borgess board as "a wonderful process. It really set in place—in front of the board—the requirements. Then there's no surprise down the road when we say, 'Okay, we're going to meet 10 times a year, once a month on Tuesday mornings for three hours,' everyone knows the expectations. When the dialogue took place, some folks—for a variety of reasons—chose not to proceed because they couldn't meet the demands."

Board Development

Formal, didactic education is yet another critical way to help trustees. But rather than budget for a once-or-twice-a-year educational session, Knecht suggests that boards themselves create a complete development curriculum.

"Most often, boards hold a retreat, figure out the 'hot topic,' bring in a speaker to talk to the board, and that's it. We should approach board education and development the same way we would management education and development. Board members [usually] say that it takes two years to really learn—to be a good, functioning board member. That's a crime. We have to figure out how to orient our board members so that within two months they are feeling relatively comfortable, and by six months they're functioning."

And that begins with a comprehensive orientation.

Pointer says he has personally served on all different types of boards: nonprofit, hospital, health care system and corporate. And despite his knowledge of governance and health care, there is a learning curve on every board.

"So many times, the idea of orientation is to grab new board members by the hand, walk them along the dock, throw them in the water and tell them to have a nice swim," he says. "I can't tell you how many times that's happened to me. Orientation should instead be a series of well-designed activities that last the better part of the first year of a board member's tenure. I'm a huge advocate of orientation through mentoring—of pairing a new board member with a really excellent, experienced board member so that after a meeting, the new member can ask, 'Hey, what just happened in there?'"

Teaching Moments

As important as formal education are "teaching moments"—opportunities (Knecht advocates 30) built into every board meeting, where education is framed around a specific issue or challenge that trustees are facing.

If the hospital is contemplating a merger, a "teaching moment" might be to offer trustees insight into the board's roles and responsibilities for its fiduciary obligation and mission. Monthly reporting mechanisms (such as the well-known "dashboard" approach—see "The Data Game" in the April 1997 issue of *Trustee,* available from the archives on www.trusteemag.com) are also recommended. But more important than the actual dashboard format is the assurance that every trustee knows how to interpret it.

"How can you serve as a member of the board and really govern if you can't read the basic financial statements of the institution?" asks Pointer. "How can you sit on a hospital board and not truly understand the factors that affect the quality of medical practice? The answer: you can't. So when trustees come on board, when we get the people [we want] to serve, we have to help them read, analyze and interpret the data."

And, finally, trustees must continually engage in self-assessment.

"Feedback," says Pointer, "is the breakfast of champions." As with orientation, Pointer asserts that self-assessment needs to be a serious board activity. Boards must constantly ask themselves whether they are focusing on those issues that make a difference to the organization. Are they executing their proper roles? Meeting their obligations and responsibilities, their fiduciary duties? And they must courageously broach that "third rail" of governance—individual trustee assessment.

"Everyone knows [individual assessment] is important," says Pointer. "But no one wants to touch it. Yet it is critical in making reappointment decisions and for individual board member development."

In his presentation to trustees, Pointer repeatedly draws striking comparisons between what went wrong at Enron and what failed at AHERF (both of which he calls the "poster children of bad governance").

"Both boards formulated flawed business models, stumbled badly in executing their strategies, were blindsided by unanticipated industry and/or market forces, employed hyperaggressive accounting [practices], and engaged in highly questionable management and financial practices," he says.

The two boards also shared specific and similar behavioral characteristics. On both were highly intelligent, competent, experienced and successful individuals, yet, according to Pointer, "most knew very little about their organization's industry, markets, business, and key strategic, financial, or operational success factors. Board meetings were highly scripted events, produced, choreographed and performed by executives (board members spent meeting time listening passively); proposals were floated as faits accomplis; and board members who questioned or objected and expressed reservations were pushed aside or removed.

"Essentially, executives employed a 'mushroom management' strategy—keep the board in the dark and feed 'em manure," Pointer adds.

One of the most effective strategies against such "mushroom management" is to raise flags and ask questions. The issue of decreased reimbursement provides a perfect example.

"Decreased reimbursement continues to be a problem," says Knecht. "As it becomes more and more difficult, hospitals have to figure out where to get revenues. Creative strategies are devised—some of which are great and fit directly with the mission of the organization and employ good ways of utilizing resources. Other strategies may be on the edge. Boards need to be educated about health care in general, and about various strategies in particular, to recognize a bad idea when they see it. And they need to call a 'stop action' if they find themselves in a position where management is suggesting something they think may be a little harebrained. Trustees need to be able to say, 'Hang on a sec,' and ask intelligent questions," Knecht says.

The same concept holds true in maintaining individual trustee accountability, and for this the board chair is key.

"The board chair has to be a person knowledgeable in governance and in health care, and also an individual who has the strength to make sure the board is, indeed, doing what it is supposed to be doing," she continues (see "Board Skills," page 100). "It's the board chair who really sets the tone for whether the board is going to serve as a social entity or whether it's going to do real work. If, for some reason, a person ends up on the board who simply shouldn't be there, the chair must be able to privately take that person aside and say, 'Hey, you haven't attended the educational meetings; you haven't even been to the last three board meetings. Shape up or ship out.'"

Avoiding Conflict of Interest: How Boards Can Withstand Close Scrutiny

By Karen Sandrick

Since Enron, Worldcom, HealthSouth and the Sarbanes-Oxley Act—Congress' legislative response—the public perception, as described in news reports and discussed by business pundits, is that the corporate world is infested with conflicts of interest. And no one, the thinking goes—not the outside auditors or the lawyers or the inside directors or CEOs—is doing anything about them. The perceived "tainted" corporate environment is making the public wonder whether they can trust any boards of directors to conduct business at arm's length and help—or at least not harm—their companies and stakeholders.

"Everyone has 'Enronitis.' The public doesn't differentiate between for-profit and not-for-profit structures. They just see multimillion-dollar budgets and a hospital industry that says it's not being reimbursed enough. They think the marketplace is charging too much and providing too little service," says John Leech, principal with Dynamis Healthcare Advisors Inc., Chagrin Falls, Ohio. And the public is growing more cynical about the trustworthiness of the governance process in making appropriate decisions about how those dollars are spent.

Karen Sandrick is a health care writer based in Chicago.

Conflicts of interest have become such fodder for the popular press and television talk shows that even when a board acts responsibly and legally, it may not pass the "smell test." It's a tinderbox atmosphere, says Leech, and any perceived or real conflict of interest can spark a blaze of public outcry.

To keep hospital boards from reaching a flash point, *Trustee* asked board members, governance consultants and lawyers to identify the most common pitfalls that might lead to real or perceived conflicts of interest, and suggest ways to avoid them.

Inadequate Management of Existing Conflicts of Interest

Some boards may believe they've adequately complied with their conflict-of-interest policy simply by developing forms that ask trustees about their conflicts, then collecting and filing that information. But that's just the first step, says Samuel A. Friede, manager of the Governance Initiative, Health Policy Institute at the University of Pittsburgh. The real challenge is to have a process for managing that information.

Especially in small communities where there may be a limited pool of board talent, some trustees will inevitably have conflicts of interest. Hospitals in these areas need to be sure they are managing actual and potential conflicts at several stages of the board decision-making process. On the most basic level, hospitals should not allow conflicted board members to cast a vote on any decision that may lead to their personal gain. In addition, boards should not permit a conflicted trustee to participate in a meeting or even remain in the room during a discussion if the chair or other trustees believe that the trustee's body language could influence the eventual vote, Friede adds.

Conflicts should be managed not only when an issue is up for a final vote, but also during planning phases when the board is considering whether it has sufficient resources to proceed with a project. If Mr. Jones' firm stands a good chance of getting the contract for a new construction project, for example, voting in favor of the project may very well constitute a conflict of interest for him, Friede says.

Reluctance to Change Corporate Culture

"Some [board members] think, 'We're not Enron or HealthSouth. So why do we need to go through any kind of internal, gut-wrenching self-analysis about conflicts? We have more important priorities than examining our conflict-of-interest policy or our compliance with general corporate responsibility laws, like Sarbanes-Oxley, that are now in vogue but don't legally apply to us,'" says Monte Dube, partner and head of the health law department at McDermott, Will & Emery, Chicago.

But, says Pam Knecht, vice president of Accord, Ltd., Chicago, many hospital boards operate in a culture that ignores uncomfortable issues. When board members think "Joe" has a conflict related to an upcoming discussion item, they often lack the nerve to ask him about it straightforwardly. And they don't have a process for tactfully bringing up the question.

Boards can develop tools to make addressing conflicts of interest less personal. They can prepare a booklet or add a specific section to their board manuals that defines their overall policy on dealing with conflicts of interest and lists specific steps that should be taken when someone may be conflicted on an issue. For example, a board member could invoke "Procedure 103" and say, "I'd like to stop the conversation now and vote as a board on whether or not we think Joe has a conflict of interest and should be allowed to participate in further discussion."

Creating a new policy on conflicts of interest—or revising an old one—gets boards thinking about how they can change their culture to recuse a member from voting, discussing, or even being present during debate on a controversial issue. "When the full policy is put before the board for approval, it notifies the members that, 'We are going to change our way of doing things and we are doing it for good reason,'" says Friede.

Inadequate Leadership

Policies governing conflicts of interest don't actually specify what constitutes a conflict; that determination must be made when an issue arises. And it ultimately falls to the board chair to ask an individual, openly or privately, if a conflict exists. It's the chair who asks a conflicted trustee to abstain from voting or to leave the room during a discussion. It's the chair who decides to reopen an issue if a conflict may have unduly influenced a board decision.

"One of the most important things that any chair does is to be certain that board members use due diligence in the performance of their duties and that they have loyalty to the hospital," says John Horty, managing partner of Horty, Springer and Mattern, Pittsburgh.

The board chair consequently has to be knowledgeable about conflicts of interest and savvy about group process. The chair also should be willing to obtain a legal opinion when it's unclear whether a conflict exists. He or she should seek outside help from a consultant if the hospital is unable to resolve a conflict of interest on its own, and the board needs education, facilitated discussion and action planning, Knecht suggests.

Inadequate Vetting

Hospital boards often don't think about conflicts of interest when they're evaluating prospective members. They fail to be sufficiently wary of individuals who have considerable investments in competitive ventures or who represent the only game in town when it comes to bank loans, legal advice, architectural design or construction.

But astute governance or nominating committees are looking deeply into each candidate's potential conflicts of interest and limiting their choices to individuals who have the fewest outside, competitive interests. These committees are also weighing the candidate's personality and willingness to discuss conflicts openly, while explaining carefully the board's policy for handling them. "The governance committees that are doing this job well set clear expectations about what actually will happen if someone with a potential conflict of interest comes on the board. They are realizing that dealing with conflicts of interest can't be kept on the back burner any longer and that they have to get ahead of it in terms of selecting and educating board members," Knecht explains.

Difficulty Dealing with Physician Trustees

Over the last 20 years, physician participation on hospital boards has grown significantly. At one time, only the president of the medical staff was an ex-officio, non-voting board member of Jewish Hospital and Healthcare Services, Louisville, Kentucky. Now physicians comprise 15 percent or more of the voting membership.

Physician involvement on hospital boards was at least manageable when physicians and management tended to work more as partners, says Henry "Sonny" Altman Jr., chair and lifetime trustee of Jewish Hospital and Healthcare Services and chair of the American Hospital Association's Committee on Governance. But as circumstances in the health care environment have shifted, turning physicians and hospitals into adversarial competitors in the outpatient services market, trustees increasingly have had to wonder whether the physician sitting across the conference table is considering a competitive venture and listening for his or her own purposes to the board conduct hospital strategic planning, Altman notes.

Governance experts acknowledge that it's beneficial to have physicians serve on hospital boards; some advocate that physicians occupy 25 percent of board seats. But hospitals in small communities often have a difficult time finding physician board members who aren't currently competing with them, or who may be planning to do so.

"Whether or not physicians have a culture of trying to cooperate with the hospital, or a history of being very independent and doing whatever the heck they want to do, [the sentiment] 'forget about the hospital' varies from community to community," says Ed Kazemek, chairman and CEO of Accord, Ltd. Overall, however, "there's a real need for physicians to protect their incomes, which are being threatened by low-pay payers. And they're doing it in a variety of ways, many of which are in direct competition with the economic well-being of the hospital, such as putting an MRI in an orthopedic office, starting a for-profit ambulatory surgery center or specialty hospital," he adds.

Physicians who get a seat on the board when they become chiefs of staff may be understandably confused about their role on the board, says Dube. "Many times, the chief of the medical staff will say, 'I'm here because I represent the medical staff, so my votes will be in the best interests of the medical staff.'" But the obligation of not-for-profit boards is to act in the best interests of the entire organization, which does not always coincide with those of the medical staff. For example, an anesthesiologist who wishes to vote on every decision to grant privileges to other anesthesiologists may be doing the hospital a disservice by protecting his specialty from additional competition.

There's no easy answer to managing conflicts of interest that arise with physician board members. "Trying to get physicians, boards and management to work together for the well-being of the community and the hospital is, in fact, the Mount Everest issue in health care," says Kazemek.

Some hospital boards, frustrated with conflicts involving physician ventures, have thought of asking the physicians on their boards to give up their votes and attend meetings simply as advisors. Kazemek's immediate reaction is to refrain from that route because it may create distrust among the physicians. Instead, he advises working harder to have frank discussions with physician board members, explaining conflict-of-interest issues and loyalty to the organization in detail, as well as the need to exclude them from discussions about sensitive issues, such as plans for an outpatient surgery center that might tread on the physicians' turf.

After all, if physicians are going to enter into a business venture that is contrary to the well-being of the organization they have sworn to protect and oversee as trustees, they at least should comply with a rigorous conflict-of-interest disclosure policy. "Instead of going behind the back of the board and setting up or investing in an ambulatory surgery center or specialty hospital, physician board members should inform the board of their intention to do so," Kazemek says.

Hospital boards can do a better job of vetting physicians before they even join the board. Kazemek advises boards to screen physicians much more closely, not only in terms of their character and knowledge, but also for the likelihood that they may end up competing with the hospital.

So that physicians understand and buy in to their legal responsibilities, board chairs should have a dialogue with them before they join the board, Dube suggests. Physicians need to learn, just as other prospective board members do, the full extent of their fiduciary duties and responsibilities.

A Higher Standard

Some hospital boards are conducting comprehensive audits that assess how well they comply with the state and federal laws governing conflicts of interest for private companies. These boards also are look-ing at Sarbanes-Oxley and other laws that affect publicly traded cor-porations to find germs of ideas that could be translated into best practices or higher standards than they are legally required to meet.

The net result is a policy that gives trustees a choice: They can serve on the board and not conduct business with the hospital, or they can decline to serve on the board at all.

Dube has worked with increasing numbers of hospitals, par-ticularly in urban settings where there are plenty of vendors to choose from, that prohibit outright any business dealings with cur-rent directors. "They believe that trustees ought not to leverage or potentially leverage their status in the organization into a business-making opportunity with the corporation, even if a transaction may be at arm's length, at fair market value and of very high quality. They don't want their organization to be second-guessed by the public, so they'll find someone else to do business with rather than a board member," he explains.

These hospitals, and others that are addressing conflict of interest proactively, realize that revealing potential conflicts of interest and abstaining from voting on problematic issues isn't good enough. "The recent regulations promulgated by the Securities and Exchange Commission and the New York Stock Exchange are sending the message that if something has the appearance of a conflict, if it can't 'pass the smell test,' don't do it," Kazemek says. "In conferences with health care board members, we're seeing this same kind of heightened awareness that they're all operating under a microscope, and we're moving into the era where hospital and health system boards are going to be much more sensitized and restrictive in their dealings with board members."

"The appearance of conflicts can be just as harmful from the stakeholders' perspective as actual conflicts," says Dube. Therefore, hospital boards are trying to be totally transparent. Kazemek adds, "Hospitals are trying to raise the awareness of conflicts of interest so everyone knows what they are supposed to do, and in the process they're shining a bright light on the issue."

Director Fitness

By Michael W. Peregrine

A sensitive issue requires a serious response.

Governing boards' current attention to sensitive matters concerning "director fitness" may prove beneficial in the future if they are called upon to address a director's continued ability to serve in a fiduciary capacity with a nonprofit corporation. Although term limits may solve some of these issues by removing directors who may have grown stale in the job or ceased to function effectively, mandatory board turnover may also force the resignation of very effective and experienced directors who bring great value to the organization.

Fitness relates to the qualifications of an individual to serve (or to be retained) as a director of a nonprofit corporation. As such, it encompasses several factors ranging from fundamental competence and unique qualifications, to a director's potential for a conflict of interest, and to attentiveness and personal ethics. In the corporate environment that has emerged since Sarbanes-Oxley, the board's focus on fitness has become more important, for many reasons.

First, the clear theme of the corporate responsibility environment is that both corporations and their governing boards must pay more attention to maintaining the highest level of ethical behavior at both the operational and strategic levels.

Michael W. Peregrine is a partner with the law firm McDermott, Will & Emery, Chicago.

Secondly, federal regulators and Congress are demanding assurance that directors of nonprofit organizations possess qualifications commensurate with the needs of the corporations that they serve. For example, several state attorneys general have challenged whether nonprofit organization boards comprise individuals with the business, financial or other types of acumen necessary to oversee a large, sophisticated charity. This scrutiny is occurring without any law or legal principle mandating specific or general qualifications for nonprofit organization board members. Rather, state charity officials are, in certain instances, exercising more vigilance on director qualifications as part of a broader effort to preserve and protect charitable assets.

There is also an increasing breach-of-duty risk to the board as a whole from the actions (or inaction) of the director who is inattentive, uninformed or otherwise fails to properly prepare for or attend meetings, or exercise judgment with due care. Where such inattention is limited to one or two board members, the liability exposure is most often also limited to those directors. But in an environment of enhanced regulatory and judicial scrutiny of a board's overall decision-making process, a board is materially disadvantaged and placed at an increased level of risk to the extent that it tolerates board membership by such "non-participating" directors.

Boards also need to pay attention to changes in the personal or professional status of a particular director who may have originally been asked to serve because of his or her professional position, or because of a relationship he or she may hold with another organization deemed supportive of the health care organization's charitable mission. Many times, such a board member is akin to an ex-officio trustee. For example, a hospital director may be selected because he or she is an executive with a local grant-making organization. When that person no longer holds that position, his or her value to the hospital may diminish greatly. When does the separation of the director from such a position or relationship affect his or her continued value as a board member?

For these and other reasons, the attentive board will want to be aware of its options for dealing with fitness-related issues that will inevitably arise. There is no single approach. It depends on the institution, its board members and its history of and/or potential for fitness-related issues. Any or all of the following options may be perceived as appropriate solutions for determining director fitness, ranging from the "blunt instrument" approach for an unfit board member (i.e., removal), to more discreet tactics, such as conducting extensive board education on fitness matters.

1. Code of ethics. Incorporating fitness-related provisions into the corporate code of ethics may be one means of addressing the issue. Many organizations have adopted the broad statement of corporate ethical standards promulgated in the Office of Inspector General's Draft Supplemental Compliance Guidance for Hospitals. While "ethical business conduct" is a concept somewhat distinct from "director fitness/qualifications to serve," it may still be useful to incorporate guidelines that address the potential for director conduct that could embarrass the corporation/health system.

2. Director questionnaire form. Another effective method for identifying potential director fitness problems might be to adopt more sophisticated information questionnaires for directors and director candidates that incorporate fitness-related questions into the nomination, conflict-of-interest disclosure and/or director renomination process.

Adding fitness-related questions to a director questionnaire is intended to help trigger disclosures about a director's background, education and independence. Sample questions might relate to: the level of business experience and/or financial literacy that candidates or current directors possess; how directors may have participated in litigation that related to issues of personal integrity; how directors may have participated in litigation that was adverse to the interests of the corporation; and the number and type of other boards on which candidates or directors may serve. There has been considerable concern in the post-Sarbanes environment about directors who may be stretched too thin by serving on multiple boards and are therefore unable to devote the time and attention needed to govern responsibly.

By adding such topics to director and candidate questionnaires, the board establishes an "advance warning system" for potential fitness-related issues. To be effective, however, board members should be encouraged to fill out such questionnaires again whenever circumstances occur that materially change their initial responses. Furthermore, the corporate general counsel should review and evaluate questionnaire answers.

3. Governance policy. Director fitness standards should be included in the charter or policies of the board's governance and nominating committees. Standards should emphasize the importance of identifying board candidates who possess needed business, financial and/or corporate expertise. Candidates should possess: an overall understanding of the organization's business; a general understanding of provider regulatory, financial and quality-of-care issues; understanding and support of the organization's charitable mission; appropriate educational and professional qualifications; and the highest ethical standards, integrity and business judgment.

4. Removal. Clearly, unequivocal removal authority as stated in the bylaws of the corporation is the most obvious means for addressing fitness issues, even if it is often the most politically difficult option to pursue. While removal powers are not uncommon, care should be taken to assure that the most efficient language allowable under state law for the removal of appointed/elected directors is used in the bylaws.

On a related matter, nonprofit organizations may wish to consider a separate removal provision dealing with non-employee directors who change the position they held when they were first nominated to the board. For example, if a CEO of a major local business leaves his job, he might no longer be considered as valuable to the board without the knowledge of current local commerce trends he previously brought to the table.

Such a removal provision typically requires that directors offer their resignation to the board when their job responsibilities change or when they retire. Such a provision does not mandate director removal, but should prompt the nominating/governance committee (or committee with similar duties) to review the circumstances of each situation to determine the director's continued fitness. The affected director should then follow the committee's recommendation.

The question of removal is ultimately a matter for the governance, nominating or similarly charged board committee, working in consultation with the general or outside counsel. When fitness-related problems occur, they often cannot be resolved by mediation. That's why some types of mandatory resignation clauses, as discussed above, can be useful. The bottom line is that the board must always look out for the best interests and charitable mission of the organization—that's what comes first.

Board members' reputations are a very important consideration, and no one wants to do anything that will create unnecessary problems or concerns for well-intentioned directors. However, when push comes to shove, mission comes first.

Governance in the Spotlight: What the Sarbanes-Oxley Act Means for You

By James E. Orlikoff and Mary K. Totten

Following a wave of high-profile corporate business and governance scandals, Congress passed the Public Company Accounting Reform & Investor Protection Act of 2002 (Public Law 107-240), better known as the Sarbanes-Oxley Act. This legislation contains the most sweeping and comprehensive set of public-company governance, financial and accounting reforms enacted in more than 30 years. The Sarbanes-Oxley Act, intended to protect investors and renew public trust in corporations and their boards, set the stage for even broader reforms promulgated by the stock exchanges and other business and investor protection groups.

These emerging requirements and standards are widely perceived as governance "best practices" for both for-profit and not-for-profit organizations alike. Attorneys, consultants and governance experts agree that it is only a matter of time before the Sarbanes legislation, and the rules and regulations designed to implement it, will be broadly applied to not-for-profit governance and used as the

---

James E. Orlikoff is president, Orlikoff & Associates, Chicago. Mary K. Totten is president, Totten & Associates, Oak Park, Illinois.

yardstick against which board performance and accountability are measured.

Sarbanes at a Glance

While the Sarbanes-Oxley Act leaves many questions unanswered and allows federal agencies broad discretion in enforcing its requirements with publicly held companies, the following provisions are applicable to nonprofit organizations:

- The role of independent directors and their representation on audit and other key board committees
- Executive compensation and loan arrangements
- New disclosure requirements for changes affecting the company's financial status and the adequacy of company financial statements and controls
- Detailed codes of ethics, business conduct and comprehensive conflict-of-interest policies

Each of these areas is discussed in more detail below.

Independent Directors

Independent directors are the linchpin of many of the public-company reforms. To be considered "independent," directors must be free of relationships with the company/organization or its management that might influence their decisions. Relationships affecting director independence include employment, vendor or consulting arrangements, as well as indirect links through family, business or charitable organizations in which the board member may hold an officer or director position.

Sarbanes-Oxley and the related rules of stock-listing organizations (such as the New York Stock Exchange) sharpen the focus on the role of independent directors by specifying governance oversight activities in which only independent directors should be involved. For example, independent directors must meet together at regular intervals without either inside directors or management present. Several important governance-related committees, such as the audit committee, the nominating committee, the corporate governance committee and the compensation committee must be staffed solely by independent directors.

Audit Committee

The new reforms make it clear that the audit committee bears direct responsibility for hiring and firing the CEO, determining CEO compensation, and overseeing the company's external auditors. Because of the importance of maintaining the audit's integrity, committee members are prohibited from receiving any compensation from the company other than directors' fees and expense reimbursement.

The act also requires that:

- The external auditor reports directly to the audit committee, not to company management.
- Audit committees must be given the authority and resources to hire outside attorneys, consultants and other advisors as they think necessary.
- The audit committee must oversee the external auditor directly and resolve any disagreements between management and auditors about financial reporting.
- Audit committees must establish procedures to receive anonymous employee concerns about accounting or auditing practices.
- External auditors are prohibited from providing certain non-audit services to the companies they audit, such as consulting, bookkeeping, appraisal or valuation services; design and implementation of financial information systems; actuarial services; legal services unrelated to the audit; and management or human resources functions.
- The audit committee must rotate the lead external audit partner at least every five years.
- All audit committee members must be financially literate.
- Audit committees must have at least one member who is a financial expert; if no committee members are financial experts, the company must disclose that fact in its financial filings.

The Securities and Exchange Commission (SEC) is proposing to define a *financial expert* as someone who has an understanding of generally accepted accounting principles (GAAP); experience in applying GAAP to how estimates, accruals and reserves are accounted for; experience in preparing or auditing financial statements; experience with internal controls and procedures for financial reporting; and a detailed understanding of audit committee functions.

Most likely, a health care financial expert would be defined somewhat differently—with a more specific emphasis on health care that reflects the field's unique and complex financial, reimbursement and regulatory demands.

Nominating Committee

This committee is responsible for setting board membership criteria and identifying qualified candidates. By requiring that the nominating committee comprise only independent directors, the reforms place key decisions about board candidates in the hands of independent directors, rather than management.

Corporate Governance Committee

The role of this committee is to prepare and recommend corporate governance guidelines to the full board that would address such issues as director qualifications, duties, and educational needs and programs. The governance committee would also be responsible for recommending appropriate ethics and business-conduct codes for directors, officers and company employees. These duties could also be carried out by the nominating committee.

Executive Compensation

The duties of this committee include all issues related to the CEO's and other senior executives' compensation, including identifying future performance goals, evaluating whether past goals have been met and overall assessment of appropriate standards for the CEO's and other senior officers' compensation.

The public-company reform rules reflect the strong and growing congressional and regulatory concern about excessive executive compensation and "perks." Some of these concerns are reflected in the requirement that only independent directors sit on a company's compensation committee. However, in case this committee is not rigorous enough in its procedures for relating CEO performance to compensation, Sarbanes-Oxley also requires CEOs or CFOs to pay back any bonus or similar "reward" for good financial results, if the company's financial statements are later restated, as a result of misconduct or significant failure to comply with financial reporting standards. Another notable reform emerging from Sarbanes-Oxley is the flat prohibition against loans or other kinds of "extensions of credit" to directors and senior officers (e.g., the CEO of a for-profit corporation) including guaranteeing or securing personal loans for officers or directors. The act also raises questions about a number of other practices, such as reverse split-dollar life insurance, a fairly common executive benefit provided to not-for-profit hospital CEOs; salary advances; or advancement of expenses for legal defense incurred by an officer or director.

In addition to their roles in the above key committees, independent directors must also make sure there are ways for concerned shareholders and employees to communicate directly with them in order to avoid situations in which legitimate whistle-blower and stakeholder concerns are "brushed under the rug" and never communicated to non-management directors.

Disclosure Requirements and Executive Certifications

To enhance the quality and timeliness of important financial and operational information available to public-company investors, Sarbanes-Oxley specifies numerous events and transactions that must be disclosed promptly to investors, such as information about off-balance-sheet transactions; cancellations of significant contracts; and incurrence of significant debt and defaults, or potential defaults under current debt instruments. As has been widely reported, Sarbanes-Oxley has also imposed rules that the CEO and CFO certify the accuracy of financial statements and other information filed by the company with the SEC. Certification of all quarterly and annual reports must stipulate that:

- Financial statements fairly represent the organization's financial condition and operational results.

- The report does not contain any untrue statement or omit material facts.
- The CEO and CFO have designed internal controls to ensure that: they possess all relevant information; they have personally evaluated the effectiveness of internal controls within the last three months; and that they have presented their conclusion about the effectiveness of the internal controls in the report.
- The CEO and CFO have disclosed to the auditors and audit committee all significant deficiencies in the organization's internal controls and any fraud, whether material or not, that involves management or other employees who have a significant role in the company's internal controls.

Codes of Ethics and Business Conduct

In a clear nod to the Enron debacle, Sarbanes-Oxley requires public companies to adopt a code of ethics for the company's CFO and other senior financial officers. Furthermore, any waivers of the company's conflict-of-interest policy must be reported promptly in an SEC filing. The New York Stock Exchange has proposed requiring all companies listed on the exchange to adopt a code of business conduct. Other exchanges and listing organizations, as well as shareholder activists, can be expected to demand that companies both have and comply with such codes of ethics and conduct.

Sarbanes-Oxley Creep

As anticipated, several developments indicate that the bar on governance of not-for-profit organizations is already being raised in the wake of Sarbanes-Oxley. In other words, the governance-related requirements of Sarbanes-Oxley are beginning to "creep" into the not-for-profit health care world.

The Internal Revenue Service (IRS) recently stated that it was likely to implement modifications to the Form 990 reporting requirements for tax-exempt organizations. The IRS Announcement 2002-87 stated:

> It may be argued that there are similarities between the need for veracity in the public information used by shareholders in making investment decisions and the need for veracity in the public information

used by contributors and others in making decisions regarding exempt organizations.

The modifications are intended to increase the public's confidence in the integrity of information disclosed by tax-exempt organizations and in their leaders' integrity. Some of the measures include requiring that tax-exempt organizations:

- Disclose whether they have adopted conflict-of-interest policies
- Disclose whether their board audit committee members are all independent
- Disclose other information concerning transactions or financial relationships with substantial donors, officers, directors and key employees

The IRS has also recently announced that it is aggressively increasing its scrutiny of CEO compensation in tax-exempt organizations.

Clark Consulting–Healthcare Group, an executive compensation and benefits firm based in Minneapolis, recommended in its September 2002 issue of *CEO Hotline* that not-for-profit organizations discontinue eight compensation practices common in the health care field. (See "Risky Compensation Practices," below.)

Risky Compensation Practices

1. Employing stock option look-alikes as compensation mechanisms.
2. Offering reverse split-dollar life insurance.
3. Providing loans to executives.
4. Using the organization's financial performance as the primary basis for providing incentive awards.
5. Hiring the same firm to provide both audit and consulting services.
6. Conducting piecemeal reviews of executive compensation and benefits.
7. Reporting less than total compensation on IRS Form 990.
8. Asking management to prepare data on executive compensation and benefits for board review.

Source: Clark Consulting–Healthcare Group, Minneapolis, Minn., 2002.

In November 2002, the Coalition for Nonprofit Healthcare published the *Corporate Responsibility Guidebook* urging not-for-profit health care organizations to "implement selected Sarbanes-Oxley provisions now."

Further, the Office of Inspector General last year released a questionnaire-style guide targeted at health care boards. The guide is designed to help governing boards ensure that their organizations have effective compliance programs and meet Medicare requirements.

Several states are also considering applying Sarbanes requirements to state statutes. For example, a bill introduced in California in May 2004 (Senate Bill 1262) would hold nonprofit, tax-exempt organizations in that state to many Sarbanes-like standards, including the composition and function of their boards and board committees. In addition, the New York State Attorney General introduced legislation modifying the state's Not-for-Profit Corporation Act to incorporate a number of provisions similar to those included in the Sarbanes-Oxley Act.

But, perhaps, most importantly for health care organizations, many financial, legal and governance experts believe Sarbanes-Oxley requirements will eventually be extended to not-for-profits by the courts, legislators, regulators, bond underwriters or liability insurers as the rules come to be viewed as best practices in governance. For example, Moody's Credit Rating has said its ratings may take governance practices into account. The Coalition for Nonprofit Health Care, the American Governance & Leadership Group, the Governance Institute and the American Health Lawyers Association have all urged health care organization boards to take the new rules seriously. The Health Care Compliance Association, Minneapolis, is even starting to consider good governance a compliance issue.

Two hundred and thirty health care organizations responding to a 2003 survey conducted by Clark Consulting suggest that hospital boards are already reviewing how their corporate and governance policies, procedures and practices compare with Sarbanes-Oxley and other governance reform mandates and are taking steps to adopt reforms. (See "Ahead of the Pack," page 126.)

Writing in the January 2004 issue of *American Governance Leader,* Clark Consulting's Managing Director David Bjork said that boards may be focusing too narrowly on Sarbanes-Oxley, which concentrates primarily on the audit function, not on governance generally.

According to Bjork, the proposed listing requirements of the New York and American Stock Exchanges and NASDAQ are broader, clearer and more useful for real governance reform than those

---

Ahead of the Pack

Some 230 health care organizations responding to a 2003 survey conducted by Clark Consulting–Healthcare Group, Minneapolis, indicated that they have already implemented several reforms recommended by Sarbanes-Oxley and the stock exchanges.

Specifically, consultants found:

- More than half have separate audit, compensation and governance committees. Most have had these committees for more than two years.
- More than two-thirds already have a governance committee charged with periodically reviewing the governance process and evaluating the effectiveness of the board, its committees and individual members. Most of these have had one in place for more than two years.
- More than half (66 percent) are bringing information on CEO compensation to the board as a whole, and a similar number have been doing so for more than two years.
- A majority (86 percent) have had a policy addressing directors' conflicts of interest for more than two years.
- Almost as many (70 percent) have had a policy on business ethics and practices for more than two years.
- Three-quarters of surveyed health care organizations periodically review total compensation for all executives, not just the CEO, and 64 percent have been doing so for more than two years.
- Most (83 percent) have formally reviewed their governance process to evaluate its effectiveness.
- Roughly the same number (84 percent) have formally reviewed their corporate bylaws and policies to ensure that they match actual practice.
- A majority (72 percent) have changed their bylaws and policies to better match actual governance practices and processes.
- More than half (64 percent) have reviewed the new rules set by Sarbanes-Oxley and the SEC.

required by Sarbanes-Oxley, and they represent a consensus based on many governance reform proposals, such as those by the Conference Board, the Business Roundtable, the National Association of Corporate Directors, and the Council of Institutional Investors. Yet, few Clark Consulting survey respondents indicated they had looked at the broader set of recommendations coming from these organizations. The survey found that:

- Only 14 percent had formally reviewed the new rules proposed by the stock exchanges.
- Only 46 percent had formally reviewed other proposals for governance reform.
- Only 21 percent have a policy calling for regular meetings in executive session.
- Very few of the boards that do not already have separate audit, compensation and governance committees are considering establishing them.
- Very few of the responding organizations that do not already bring CEO compensation information to the board as a whole are considering doing so.

Next Steps for Health Care Governing Boards

Governance reforms, such as Sarbanes-Oxley, are likely to be applied to not-for-profit health care organizations in a variety of ways. Forward-looking boards will voluntarily adopt relevant public-company financial and governance requirements because they consider them to be best practices. State attorneys general will likely apply them to help protect the public interest in nonprofit organizations. Bond underwriters, insurers and investors in debt instruments will likely require that such standards be met before they issue, insure or invest in debt securities. Over time, the courts and the IRS are likely to hold not-for-profit organizations to standards of performance and accountability similar to those required for their public company counterparts. Underwriters of directors and officers' liability insurance also will take such standards into account when writing and pricing D&O coverage.

Given that Sarbanes-Oxley and other similar reforms are moving their way, not-for-profit health care organizations should consider taking a number of steps now. (See "First Steps," page 128.)

Clearly, health care boards are rapidly entering a new era of accountability, scrutiny, and perhaps even increased exposure to regulatory sanctions and liability. Whether or not boards are held directly accountable to the provisions of Sarbanes-Oxley, effective boards will read the handwriting on the wall and begin to seriously evaluate their structures and practices to ensure that they would, at a minimum, pass regulatory, legal and media muster. More importantly, boards should aggressively adopt governance best practices to assure that they actively contribute to the ongoing success of their organizations.

First Steps

- Hospital and health system governing boards should decide which of the new recommended standards should be adopted by their organizations.
- Boards should review their composition to ensure a majority of board members are independent or outside directors.
- If the board has not already done so, it should establish a board audit committee composed solely of outside directors and seek individuals for that committee who would be considered financial experts in health care.
- To foster transparency and full disclosure, health care organizations should decide how to best communicate with their communities. For example, should a health care organization's annual report disclose such material facts as Joint Commission violations or malpractice litigation, which may have a bearing on the organization's future, much like the information that publicly traded companies are expected to disclose?
- Boards also should determine what types of responsibilities they will take on that may have been previously delegated to the CEO, such as oversight of executive compensation and succession planning.
- Boards should ensure that they have a strict conflict-of-interest policy in place that they actively enforce.
- Boards should regularly conduct and document rigorous self-assessments. Such assessments should lead to an action plan for improvement that guarantees that their policies and practices will result in a high level of board performance and accountability.

Show Them the Data

By Michele Bitoun

*What do trustees need to know,
and how do they need to know it?*

As dubious business and accounting practices at U.S. corporations continue to dominate the news, hospital trustees aren't above the fray. The hospital industry, too, has its share of boards that have not lived up to their oversight responsibilities. (See the article "Accountability Stops Here" on page 98 of this book.) These cases are a sobering reminder of the professional and personal liabilities that hospital trustees face if they're not regularly reviewing the data and activities at their institution. In fact, many experts say these cases have underscored the need for board members to track more information than they have in the past.

"Boards need to know more than they used to—about business, the organization, competition, all those sorts of things," says L. Edward Bryant Jr., a partner in the Chicago law offices of Gardner, Carton & Douglas, specializing in health care and governance. Bryant has served as counsel to many hospital boards and is currently board chair of the Sisters of Charity of Leavenworth (KS) Health System.

Unlike the past, when "there wasn't a great deal of oversight" and board members who weren't involved in committees or leadership

Michele Bitoun is an assistant professor at the Medill School of Journalism, Northwestern University, Evanston, Illinois, and a freelance writer.

roles "just came [to meetings] and participated in social events," the stakes are now higher, Bryant says. "Boards have fiduciary obligations to [the hospital's] employees and medical staff to [govern] an enterprise that doesn't go bankrupt."

The same goes for unethical practices.

"I think [trustees] have concluded, based on AHERF, Allina, and other cases, that they [have] personal liability for a number of things," he says. Federal intermediate sanctions adopted in 2001, for example, assess serious penalties for deriving excess benefits from a tax-exempt entity. "This pertains to every transaction, including compensation, between the tax-exempt entity and an insider," Bryant adds.

But in order to stand firm at the helm, trustees need to be knowledgeable. Bryant refers to "the Sergeant Schultz Defense," a term coined by one of his partners and inspired by the *Hogan's Heroes* television sitcom character who feigned innocence with the frequent refrain, "I know nothing." Says Bryant, "Many hospital trustees or directors take the position, 'Nobody ever told me.' That's no longer a viable excuse . . . they're supposed to ask about these things."

What information do trustees need? James Lifton, a director with Arista Associates, a health care consulting firm in Northbrook, Illinois, emphasizes the difference between reviewing mere data—which is, no doubt, available to any hospital trustee in truckloads for the asking—and reviewing meaningful information that's presented by the administration in a clear, concise format.

"What we're really talking about is information. . . . Voluntary trustees can get a lot of data and not understand what they mean or not have time to review all of them," Lifton says. "I've seen boards get a three-ring binder or a large packet, and sometimes they don't know what to make of it, or they're unwilling or unable to take the time to go through it."

That's where a tool commonly referred to as a "scorecard" or "dashboard" comes in. The tool's indicators reflect the organization's goals and help trustees quickly gauge how well they are meeting their targets. "It's a very powerful approach that allows the board to look at information as you would on the dashboard of your car," Lifton says. More detailed information can be scrutinized in committees.

Experts have different opinions on the exact indicators to use, in part because they depend on a hospital's or health system's goals and strategies, which can change over time. Richard Umbdenstock, president and CEO of Providence Services, a nine-hospital system based in Spokane, Washington, and former head of the American Hospital Association's division of governance, says boards should be regularly reviewing indicators in several areas: finance, quality, patient and employee satisfaction, operations, and community benefit.

"I think within each [area], you have to decide what the important indicators are, and then within those [determine whether] the bells and whistles are going off on one or two of them. If they are, how are you attending to them?" says Umbdenstock. "It would be good if the board and management agreed on the critical 10, 15 or 20 indicators that span the enterprise and [treat] them as a balanced set of indicators so that they're not just looking at finance, which is the general tendency, because it's the universal language [that most people understand]."

Lifton agrees. The dashboard or scorecard concept isn't new, particularly in the business world, but what is changing, he says, is the breadth and complexity of chosen hospital indicators evolving from basic financial measurements to criteria reflecting a variety of strategic goals, including quality, staffing, and even charity care.

"I think that most boards, in fact the majority, probably started with financial indicators because that's what they're most comfortable with. They understand operating margins. They understand [patient] days and accounts receivable. They understand equity as a percentage of total capitalization," Lifton says.

Umbdenstock says it's the CEO's job to recommend a set of indicators to the board, "but it's up to the board to then say, 'Yeah, that makes sense,' or 'I'd be interested in these, and, oh, by the way, maybe quarterly I want to know what our liability experience and lawsuit experience has been,' or 'In my business, X, Y and Z are really important. How come they're not here?'" Some of the current significant issues to track include medication errors and overall patient safety issues, such as wrong-site surgery, he says, as well as pain management for those with chronic or terminal conditions.

For instance, Providence uses four indicators to monitor quality: medication errors; risk-adjusted mortality rates; severity-adjusted length of stay versus expected length of stay; and severity-adjusted complication rates. In the area of charity care, the system looks at dollars as a percent of non-government patient revenue. Umbdenstock says the format was challenging for the individual hospitals of the system to implement because:

> People have been defining these [indicators] their own ways for years. They're not used to having to change those definitions to conform to a group process. Secondly, sometimes they're not set up to collect this particular set of data, so it's either costly or culturally challenging to get people to organize their systems to produce the data. But generally, I think, what most people would have on this type of balanced scorecard is stuff that the field has started to focus on as key potential hot spots that a board ought to be aware of.

The Sisters of Charity of Leavenworth Health System, a nine-hospital system spanning four states, instituted a 30-indicator report (see pages 134–135) for its 15 board members about a year ago. The approach has streamlined meetings and reduced confusion at board meetings. In fact, the approach has cut the number of board meetings from six to four per year.

"It really allows the board to get a good sense for whether the administration is moving forward and whether, in fact, the organization is moving toward its vision for the future," says Bill Murray, president of the Sisters of Charity system. "In the past . . . as [trustees] would look at reports, they had a difficult time determining whether we were actually making progress. And . . . this report has helped them . . . to look at the total operation and understand whether or not we're doing the things we need to do."

The indicators reflect the system's four strategies: mission and culture; physician relations; health care transformation (such as new service lines); and consumer value. Within each of those four areas, the board tracks specific quarterly indicators delineated by red dots (which means the target has not been met), white dots (which means the target has been met), or green dots (which indicates that the target has been exceeded). The indicators include traditional financial markers, such as profit margin, but also cover employee vacancy rates and turnover, free care, community service, medication errors that cause patients harm, and physician and patient satisfaction.

Murray and all the system's hospital CEOs created the indicators together. "Some came out of our strategic plan, some of them are actually the measures we use for performance-based [manager] compensation, and some of them are indicators we would be tracking anyway," Murray explains. The targets, plus or minus 3 percent, reflect either internal standards (systemwide goals) or external standards (such as industry norms).

Bryant says dashboard indicators have been key to improving his trustees' efficiency, setting incentive compensation, making strategic moves in local markets, setting agendas, and bringing in speakers to discuss trouble spots. Especially for a diverse board that may have difficulty reaching consensus on specific issues to study, "this helps you do it," he says.

"It's amazing how much time you save and how much it helps you focus your interest," says Bryant. "You don't have to spend 40 minutes going over 60 pages of financials. Literally, within two minutes, you can figure out where your problems are, then go to that part of the financial statement or the feasibility report, or whatever it is."

Homing in on what criteria to put on a dashboard does take some trial and error. "It's a couple of years before you fully feel these systems work," Bryant says. For example, his board initially used AOIM (area of interest management) to measure operating margin until trustees finally switched to EBIDA (earnings before interest, depreciation and amortization) to factor out depreciation, over which the hospital board had no control.

"Sometimes it's those accounting nuances that you [need to] keep adjusting your dashboards to pick up," he says.

But for Bryant, the 30-indicator dashboard now used by the Sisters of Charity of Leavenworth provides just the right amount of depth because it encompasses every area in which board members need to be informed, including incentive compensation, strategic planning and operations. "We started out with 16 and worked our way up to 30," he says.

"[The indicator report] is really a red flag report, if you will," adds Murray. "It's a rollup of a lot of other reports that [the board] might have been seeing." But it works better. Previously, he says, board members "were frustrated that as they would look at reports periodically, they had a difficult time determining whether we were actually making progress. And that's what this report has helped them to do—to be able to look at the total operation and understand whether or not we're doing the things we need to do. And we're not looking just at finance. We're really looking at volume growth and quality indicators to get a sense of whether there are any areas of concern."

SISTERS OF CHARITY OF LEAVENWORTH HEALTH SYSTEM

Performance Indicators

Outcomes as Compared to Internal Targets for the Fiscal Year Ended May 31, 2002

| | | | Providence Health | | | Montana Region | | | | |
		SCLHS	Providence Medical Center	Saint John Hospital	St. Francis Health Center	Holy Rosary Healthcare	St. James Healthcare	St. Vincent Healthcare	Saint John's Health Center	St. Mary's Hospital & Medical Center
Mission and Culture										
Quality of Worklife										
Nurse Turnover	E	X	♦	♦	X	X	♦	■	X	♦
RN Vacancy Rates	I	X	♦	♦	X	X	X	X	X	X
Employee Turnover	E	X	♦	♦	X	■	X	X	X	♦
Employee Satisfaction	E	X	X	X	■	X	X	X	X	X
Social Accountability										
Social Accountability/Community Benefit Expense	I	X	X	X	X	X	X	X	X	X
Care of the Poor Expense**	I	X	X	X	X	X	X	X	X	X
Physician Relations										
Physician Satisfaction										
Physician Admissions Growth	I	X	X	X	■	■	X	■	X	■
Physician Satisfaction	I	■	♦	♦	■	X	♦	X	X	■
Health Services Transformation										
Growth										
Adjusted Admissions**	I	■	X	■	X	X	■	X	■	■
Inpatient Surgeries	I	■	X	♦	X	♦	♦	■	X	■
Outpatient Surgeries	I	X	X	♦	■	♦	X	X	■	♦
Emergency Room Visits (Admitted)	I	♦	♦	X	■	■	♦	X	♦	♦
Births	I	■	X	♦	♦	X	♦	♦	X	■
Open Heart Surgeries	I	♦		na	♦	na	na	♦	♦	♦

Consumer Value

Quality

	Benchmark
Unscheduled Readmissions	E
Pain Management	E
Patient Falls	I
Medication Errors	I
Surgical Site Infection Rate—	
Hip Arthroplasty	E
Post CABG Mortality	E

Financial*

	Benchmark
EBIDA Margin**	I
Days in Net Accounts Receivable	I
Days Cash on Hand	I
Debt Service Coverage Ratio	I

Operational*

	Benchmark
Paid Hours per Adjusted Admission	I
Total Expense per Adjusted Admission, CMI Adjusted**	I
Compensation Ratio	I
Medicare Average Length of Stay, CMI Adjusted	I

Customer Satisfaction

	Benchmark
Adult Inpatient Satisfaction**	E
Emergency Room Patient Satisfaction	E

Legend

- X — Greater than 3% Favorable Variance
- ■ — Within 3% of Internal Targets
- ◆ — Greater than 3% Unfavorable Variance
- O — Not Available
- E- External Benchmark or Target
- I- Internal Benchmark or Target

*Inclusive of System Office (net of Eliminations) and Exempla/Saint Joseph Hospital

**Key Performance Indicators

Source: Sisters of Charity of Leavenworth Health System, Leavenworth, Kansas.

The approach has also helped board members spot trends that could affect their future significantly. "There's a change taking place in cardiovascular surgery—with the introduction of beta-blockers and the use of stents, the number of open heart [surgeries] is going down . . . and . . . we saw it right across the whole system, and we're able to take that [finding] into consideration as we're projecting our long-range plans," Murray says.

Murray adds that the approach has also allowed the system to zero in on nurse vacancies and turnover rates to such an extent that it's now looking at them on a systemwide basis. "We're able to really get a sense for [which hospitals in the system] have problems," he says. No more than 30 indicators are used at one time, but they may change with shifts in the system's priorities and long-range plans.

Committing to the targets associated with these indicators, especially financial ones, such as operating margin—and holding management accountable by tying them to compensation—is critical to a hospital system's success, says Nathan Kaufman, senior vice president for health care strategy with Superior Consultant Holdings Corp., San Diego. For-profit hospitals operate this way as a matter of course, but the same should hold true for not-for-profits, he says.

"Even when tax-exempt hospitals quantify things and hold people accountable, they achieve [their target], so that's what the game's all about," he says. What often happens, however, is that management will look at a margin that isn't 5 percent and cite a nursing shortage or some other problem to justify why the goal was not achieved, he says. "What the board of trustees should be asking is, 'Okay, what are we going to do to get it to 5 percent?'" The board may not achieve the target immediately, but it should adopt a sense of urgency about working toward it, he says.

The critical performance indicators Kaufman recommends tracking, with some targets subject to modification to reflect local market conditions, include: operating margin (at least 5 percent); earnings before depreciation, interest, taxes and amortization (at least 15 percent); personnel expense (less than 45 percent of net revenue); supply expense (less than 16 percent of net revenue); growth in net revenue per adjusted patient (at least 6 percent); growth in net revenue (at least 8 percent); inpatient surgery per 100 admissions (at least 28); bad debts as a percent of net revenue (less than 8 percent); accounts receivable (less than 65 days); growth in ER visits (at least 3 percent), as well as other key services; RN turnover; employee turnover; patient satisfaction; and quality indicators (see "Strategic Vision" in the July/August 2002 issue of *Trustee*).

Kaufman says these indicators should be reviewed by the board every month, and if the system isn't within its targets, "there has to be an action plan to get them back in place. . . . When there's a variance from the target, there needs to be some sense of urgency and some activity and action plan in place that brings it back over time into compliance." For instance, if staffing costs went up because the hospital raised nurses' salaries, one option might be to raise prices in the next round of pricing, even if it's not for another six months.

Methodist Hospital in Arcadia, California, starting tracking about a dozen performance indicators a few years ago, including inpatient and outpatient activity, patient satisfaction and quality information, cash position, and a case mix index. Holding itself to these targets has encouraged the board to improve its operating margin significantly, which started out at 1.3 percent, says CEO Dennis Lee.

"Nate's message to us [during a retreat] was that even though we're tax exempt, most hospitals need a 5 percent operating margin in order to generate sufficient cash surpluses to be able to replace our equipment, buy new equipment, invest in new technologies and invest in our facilities," says Lee.

The 5 percent goal prompted the 18-member board to assemble a task force comprising board members, medical leaders and administrators to identify three or four "attack points" to boost their profit margin. One of those strategies was to negotiate higher rates with managed care companies. It worked.

"Virtually all the HMOs have [agreed to] our rates," says Lee. "Sometimes they jockey for position, and they do it at the 11th hour. Sometimes [they miss] the expiration date and then come back a week later and agree to [the new rate]. There's that kind of game-playing going on. But in just about every case, we've been successful in getting higher rates." The board expects to hit a 3.3 percent operating margin this year, followed by 4 to 4.5 percent the next year, and 5 percent after that.

Methodist's scorecard is designed as a bar graph using individual months, as well as a 12-month rolling average. To the left are targets (set internally) and prior years' performance so that board members can see trends. "The variances that occur from month to month—that's really what a board needs to see," Lee says.

He says the dashboard format has been well-received by the board. "My impression and the direct feedback [I receive] is that [trustees] really do understand it; they like seeing the graphs; it's meaningful information to them; and they really do have a sense for how well the hospital is doing—for example, is our volume growing? Are our inpatient admissions going up or down or remaining stable? Is our outpatient activity going up, down, or remaining stable? Are revenues above our costs?"

In the past, Lee says, he'd get all that information to trustees, then ask them for their general impression of the hospital's status. "They'd say, 'Gee, I don't know,' because it was too much detail for them. Now it's a digestible amount of information."

The targets used have been established in the budget, Lee says. "We don't routinely give industry standards on the key performance indicators, because we don't have access to that information on a real-time basis, but generally once every year or two we will engage a consultant to get us the benchmark information to show the board how we compare."

Bryant says that boards must track services that make their hospitals and systems unique, as well as typical financial indicators. And they need to be just as vigilant about tracking losing operations as they are about winners. "In hospital language, cross-subsidization was what always solved everything," says Bryant. "It didn't matter that you lost money in arthritis center operations because you made money in cardiac. Or it didn't matter that you lost money in the emergency room because you made money in oncology. But you never quite knew how much money you were making or losing on a per-service basis, so you could never make actual tactical or strategic decisions about what to do and what not to do. It's that discipline that [boards] can bring to hospitals—knowing whether an enterprise is viable or not doesn't mean looking at just the bottom line."

Diagnosing the Health of Your Organization: Early Warning Signs

By Mary K. Totten
and James E. Orlikoff

Trustees who believe it is their role to help create their organization's future understand that good stewardship first requires a solid understanding of their performance today. Tools and processes that allow boards to routinely assess and compare their hospital or health system's performance over time can identify potential problems early on that might erode the organization's overall health—sometimes more rapidly than board members could have thought possible (see "*Trustee* Workbook 1: Stewardship of the Future," January 2000 issue of *Trustee*).

Rather than being forced to confront a turnaround or other drastic crisis measures, governing boards should engage in ongoing performance monitoring, getting the information they need to keep their organizations on track. In order to be a good steward, anticipation is the name of the game. So to help boards identify the early warning signs of a business failure, we talked with John Tiscornia, principal, Wellspring Partners, Ltd., Chicago, a financial consultant with more than 30 years' experience advising health care organizations.

Mary K. Totten is president, Totten & Associates, Oak Park, Illinois. James E. Orlikoff is president, Orlikoff & Associates, Chicago.

"Prudent health care organizations routinely engage in risk management activities to help evaluate and improve the quality of the services they deliver," says Tiscornia. "Boards need to conduct risk management from a business perspective to help their organizations regularly assess and improve their overall performance. Once problems hit the bottom line, it may be too late."

He adds: "Research tells us that about 70 percent of health care organization failures are due to flawed strategies. All of us are familiar with some of the more high-profile failures, such as hospitals or health systems engaging in large-scale purchasing of physician practices or getting into the insurance business by buying a health maintenance organization. Yet the problem of flawed strategy runs deeper.

"Some hospital boards will authorize the purchase of expensive imaging equipment, such as an MRI, without asking for a specific business plan, what risks [the purchase of such equipment] might pose for the organization, and what plans management has to minimize those risks," Tiscornia says. "After the purchase, the board may never look back to assess results."

Trustees often fail to ask whether the programs or services they approved actually fulfilled their volume or financial projections and, if so, over what period of time, Tiscornia says. And unlike many of their corporate counterparts, health care boards, for whatever reason, often fail to act when performance is not on target.

"I know organizations that purchased physician practices and planned to lose money in the first year and break even after four years," Tiscornia says. "Four years later, the practices were still losing money, and no action had been taken. In an uncertain environment, boards need to be tolerant of risk-taking, yet they also must act appropriately when a project doesn't deliver."

What's on Your Board's Radar Screen?

Although most boards and their finance committees regularly review selected indicators of the organization's overall financial performance, many need to perform a more comprehensive evaluation. And though boards will frequently step back and study the big picture once their own organization is in trouble, Tiscornia says a better approach is to look for cracks in the dike—early warning signs that, if addressed, can prevent financial disaster.

Governing boards should routinely complete a diagnostic checklist that broadly assesses overall organizational performance. Tiscornia recommends that boards and executives complete and review such a checklist two to four times a year to help diagnose potential problems in market, money, people, management, medical staff and governance.

Market

Tiscornia believes "it all starts with the market." Health care organizations, however, often focus too much on their internal indicators. They look at how many inpatients are on today's census or how many outpatients came through the door during a given period. Many don't spend enough time looking at market share trends; and when times get tough, marketing is often one of the first areas to see staff or budget cuts.

Boards need to receive monthly or, at least, quarterly revenue and expense summaries for their hospital's top five product lines in order to track profitability, Tiscornia advises.

Having ongoing processes in place to monitor how strategies are carried out can help prevent failures down the road. For example, "if an organization has a strategy to improve employee satisfaction through recruitment and retention, yet no additional dollars have been budgeted for recruiting or retention activities, the likelihood of success is slim," he says.

"It's also important to know where board members and their families receive their own health care. The answer to that question is a 'gut check' about what trustees really think of the organization's quality," he adds.

Money

Even though boards should routinely review financial indicators, some health care boards don't pay enough attention to their cash position until they have difficulty paying their bills. Tiscornia recommends developing and using daily cash flow projections and trends to help both executives and the board stay current on their performance and prevent denial.

Assessing Your Organization's Market Orientation

To assess its market orientation, the board should answer the following questions:

	Yes	No
1. Are key strategies and investments aligned?	☐	☐
2. Do you monitor your corporate strategy?	☐	☐
3. Do you and your families use this hospital when you need care?	☐	☐
4. Are your top five product lines profitable?	☐	☐
5. Is market share increasing for your top five product lines?	☐	☐
6. Are customer perception and organizational image key strengths?	☐	☐
7. Is satisfaction improving for these groups:		
• Patients	☐	☐
• Physicians	☐	☐
• Employees	☐	☐

Board Checklist for Monitoring the Organization's Financial Position

	Yes	No
1. Are your financial, quality, and other key indicators identifying the right information?	☐	☐
2. Are your operating, financial, and quality reports providing timely information in a format you can understand and use?	☐	☐
3. Are your operating and financial projections on target?	☐	☐
4. Do you have a consistent program to evaluate revenue improvements?	☐	☐
5. Do your net revenue/admissions compare favorably with those of your competitors?	☐	☐
6. Do you review monthly and daily cash flow projections?	☐	☐
7. Is your operating cash flow sufficient to meet future investments?	☐	☐
8. Has your revenue cycle—from admission, treatment, and discharge—been evaluated and updated recently?	☐	☐
9. Are nonsalary contracts competitive with others in your market?	☐	☐

Continued →

Board Checklist on Workforce Issues

	Yes	No
1. Do you have appropriate performance indicators for the organization and each business function?	☐	☐
2. Have you developed benchmarks for each performance indicator?	☐	☐
3. Does the organization support management's educational and skill needs with appropriate resources?	☐	☐
4. Are accurate performance data available to key users?	☐	☐
5. Are protocol-driven processes in place to support the appropriate use of resources?	☐	☐
6. Are managers accountable for the deployment of resources to enhance their staff's performance?	☐	☐

Board Checklist for Monitoring Management

	Yes	No
1. Have you reviewed your organizational structure recently?	☐	☐
2. Is management accountable for organizational performance?	☐	☐
3. Does your organizational culture support your vision and mission?	☐	☐
4. Are managers trained to use performance management tools, such as mentoring and evaluations?	☐	☐
5. Does the incentive compensation formula encourage "stretching" accounting rules?	☐	☐
6. Is financial management focused on the future rather than on past performance?	☐	☐
7. Are finance executives and managers rather than members of your finance department accountable for operating variances?	☐	☐
8. As labor costs are reduced, are adequate internal and business controls maintained?	☐	☐
9. Is the hospital's infrastructure adequate to handle additional patients?	☐	☐

Continued →

Board Checklist for Monitoring Medical Staff Issues

	Yes	No
1. Does physician compensation align with your strategy and mission?	☐	☐
2. Do you have a system for monitoring the value the organization receives relative to physician compensation?	☐	☐
3. Do physicians have communication channels outside of the formal medical staff organization?	☐	☐
4. Does the hospital have an active and effective medical staff human resources plan?	☐	☐
5. Does the hospital or system offer a leadership training program for physicians?	☐	☐
6. Are periodic physician satisfaction surveys completed and reported?	☐	☐

Governance Checklist

	Yes	No
1. Are the roles of board committees and the full board clear?	☐	☐
2. Are the roles of the board and management clear?	☐	☐
3. Are decisions made appropropriately and effectively?	☐	☐
4. Are decisions made in a timely manner?	☐	☐
5. Does the board have no more than 15 members?	☐	☐
6. Does the board use specific criteria for selecting new members, including personal characteristics and functional skills?	☐	☐
7. Does the board conduct a self-evaluation each year?	☐	☐
8. Does the board spend 60 percent of its time on strategic issues?	☐	☐
9. Do the board and individual trustees have good relationships with key physicians?	☐	☐

Source: John F. Tiscornia, principal, Wellspring Partners, Ltd., Chicago.

"A 'bad month' can easily become a 'bad six months' unless the board recognizes the trend, asks how soon management plans to get 'the train back on track,' and then holds everyone accountable," Tiscornia says. "Focusing on the organization's performance in this area can help avoid the need for big year-end adjustments."

People

If people are an organization's key asset, then it's important to know how the organization invests in them. The board and management need a real-time picture of employee satisfaction to help assess staff needs. The problem with satisfaction surveys is often in the lag time—frequently as long as a year—between when a survey is fielded, the results analyzed and problems addressed. Tiscornia recommends that health care organizations conduct satisfaction studies on a rolling basis, surveying a portion of employees or physicians each quarter to provide more timely data and faster problem identification and resolution.

Management

So much of an organization's performance relates to its culture and to the tools and resources available to managers. In many hospitals, managers of clinical services have had little or no management training, Tiscornia says, and performance accountability is lacking. Boards and executives need to monitor regularly the extent to which they provide clear expectations for management's performance, as well as whether they provide appropriate training and incentives to help managers achieve desired results.

Medical Staff

Many organizations have development and succession plans for their key employees and executives, but few have such plans for their medical staff, Tiscornia says. The lack of such a plan should be a warning sign to boards of a potential problem. Board members should ask for a breakdown of medical staff by highest admitters, age and specialty. If data show that all of the medical staff's heart surgeons are 55 years old or older, for example, it's time to begin recruiting

Tips for Using a Performance Diagnostic Checklist

Listed below are several suggestions boards can use to help them note early warning signs of performance problems in their own organization.

1. Customize the checklists shown here (pages 142–144) to enable the board and executive management to broadly evaluate the hospital's or system's overall performance.

2. Consider completing and reviewing the results of the checklists on a quarterly or biannual basis as part of a scheduled board meeting or retreat.

3. Have both trustees and executives independently complete the checklists and discuss results.

4. Clarify and discuss every negative response and follow up with corrective action where needed.

5. Make sure the board has processes in place for timely follow-up and resolution of identified performance problems.

6. Move toward implementing organizationwide, ongoing processes for gathering and tracking performance-related information.

7. Board committees should incorporate specific performance indicators or sections of the performance checklist into their work plans to promote more frequent board performance monitoring.

8. Make participation in performance monitoring part of the board's job description.

9. Include an evaluation of how well the performance monitoring process works as part of the board's self-assessment.

10. At least annually, summarize and share performance problems with the full board that were resolved through performance monitoring.

new, younger surgeons. Other medical staff issues to consider are shown in the Board Checklist for Monitoring Medical Staff Issues (page 144).

Governance

Dysfunctional governance is a clear indication of organizational performance problems. For example, boards that don't understand the distinction between the role of the board as a whole and the role of committees or that increasingly cross the line between governance and management often see their organization's financial performance deteriorate eventually, Tiscornia says. Other board performance questions include those listed in the Governance Checklist (page 144).

Discussion Exercise

In "The Success Syndrome" (in *Leader to Leader*, Jossey-Bass: San Francisco, 1999, pp. 201–212), David A. Nadler and Mark Nadler write that sustained success can foster organizational complacency, which can lead to reduced innovation, increased costs and bureaucracy, and an organizational inability to act, adapt or learn. Nadler and Nadler suggest that leaders take the following eight steps to prevent the success syndrome from infecting their organizations:

1. Create and sustain an external focus. Leaders need to communicate constantly and reinforce by personal example that the organization must continuously focus on customers, competitors, new technology and market forces.
2. Maintain a contrarian mindset. Even if things are going well, performance can always be improved.
3. Never underestimate your competition. Don't assume your competitor's recent win is just a flash in the pan. Understand that even a small competitor might have a better strategy, market assessment or product than you.
4. Anticipate change through systematic, periodic environmental scans. Anticipating disruptive change can give your organization time to experiment with ways to minimize potentially negative effects.

5. Think of yourself as your own biggest competitor. Don't be afraid to innovate and be out front with a new product or service, even if it means getting out of existing business lines or taking business away from a profitable product or service.

6. Don't wait until a crisis to bring in new, experienced leaders from outside your organization or industry. Be willing to question why your organization does things the way that it does.

7. Pay close attention to the observations of frontline employees. These people are often the first ones to sense when something is going wrong.

8. Create formal processes to analyze your successes and failures so that lessons learned can be applied throughout the organization.

Conclusion

To secure their hospital's future, boards must first find firm footing in their present performance. Tools and resources that help governing boards routinely and systematically monitor their organization's performance and provide early warning signs of performance problems can give boards the information they need to make corrections today that can avert disasters tomorrow. Although hindsight can help us see the past more clearly, foresight is the foundation of true vision.

PART FOUR

Finance

Hospital Finance: What Every Board Needs to Know

By Jan Greene

The next time you're tempted to complain about sipping cold coffee at a late-night hospital board meeting or missing a golf tournament for a weekend board retreat, just be glad you weren't on the Fletcher Allen Health Care board over the past couple of years. In a very public bloodletting, all 16 trustees for the Burlington, Vermont, system left their positions, many under pressure to resign. They were held responsible for failing to properly oversee a giant, scandal-tainted $356 million building project. Aggressive administrators, hoping to outwit the state's certificate-of-need process, skipped getting proper state approval for a parking garage, ultimately costing the system $1 million in fines and exposing its former management to possible criminal prosecution.

It's not often that hospital board members get caught up in a mess that big and ugly. But the Fletcher Allen story is a cautionary tale to all trustees about the real meaning of fiduciary duty and the board's weighty responsibility to oversee hospital or system finances. With so many health care organizations engaged in major capital projects—from building a new wing to outfitting the hospital with a new computer system—the board needs to be more savvy than ever about allocating and monitoring large capital expenses.

Jan Greene is a freelance writer based in Alameda, California.

151

Boards must approve large-scale investments for operations, employee pensions and capital projects—a task complicated by a roller-coaster stock market and rock-bottom interest rates. At the same time, hospital boards are coming under more scrutiny by bond-rating agencies such as Moody's Investors Service and Standard and Poor's, which want to ensure that hospitals hoping to make a significant bond sale are governed well enough that they'll be able to pay off their debts. And in the future, trustees of not-for-profit organizations are likely to face new governance rules similar to those enacted under the Sarbanes-Oxley Act for public corporations and their boards.

"There's a sea change going on in what's expected from boards in overseeing the financial dimensions of the organization," says governance consultant Edward Kazemek, chairman and CEO of Accord, Ltd. in Chicago. "Even though many boards spend the bulk of their time on finances, there's pressure to upgrade the quality of that oversight."

All these new pressures on boards of trustees may be intimidating, but there's no need to panic. The best way to navigate the new challenges is to follow the rules of good governance and to assign specific tasks, such as overseeing audits and monitoring investment advisers, to those trustees who have the best understanding of finance. Most boards have a finance committee, and many will end up with a separate group just to handle audits as pressure mounts on not-for-profits to adopt the same governance best practices as public corporations.

While these responsibilities don't require everyone to be an accountant or have an MBA, they do call on each trustee to pay attention to any and all financial education that management provides. And, most importantly, anyone who doesn't understand must ask questions.

That's where the former trustees of Fletcher Allen went wrong, says Henry "Sam" Chauncey, a new Fletcher Allen trustee and finance chairman. They were afraid to challenge administrators who may have been using poor judgment. "It was a unique set of circumstances," says Chauncey, a former administrator of a rehabilitation hospital. "You had a secretive administration and an acquiescent board. I've been on a lot of nonprofit boards, and that's the first time I've seen both at the same time."

Forget about an accounting degree or an MBA. Any trustee can cultivate the following financial skills, most of which involve reading your favorite health care publications and asking questions of the CFO and other managers.

Trustees need to have:

- Ability to analyze and interpret trends
- Understanding of whatever ratios the organization uses to track financial health
- Awareness of Medicare and Medicaid policy and payment changes
- Ability to forecast implications of trends for the future (e.g., How will the new Medicare drug bill affect the hospital?)
- Willingness to ask penetrating questions
- A focus on the strategic implications of each financial decision
- Access to a glossary of financial terms used by hospital leaders

Source: Larry Walker, president of The Walker Company, a health care consulting firm based in Lake Oswego, Oregon.

To change that, William Schubart, a businessman who chairs the brand-new board, has established a spirit of openness that encourages questioning. "It's really the job of the chair to ensure that everyone on the board understands that any question, whether clarifying or challenging, is OK," he says.

Board/CEO Relations

The new Fletcher Allen trustees feel a particular responsibility to get good, detailed information from management—and they're starting from scratch with newly named top executives.

Because of his experience in health care administration, Chauncey sees both sides of the trustee-management relationship, and believes a good partnership based on trust will ensure that he gets the information he needs to fulfill his fiduciary duties. He's been working with interim chief financial officer Ken Fisher, with whom he's built a good, trusting relationship.

"There is no hard and fast rule about how much information a board member should have," Chauncey says. "We see ourselves as a team, and that makes Ken call me up and volunteer information. If we see ourselves as a team, we tell each other things, good and bad, so the other person can be well-informed."

Still, Chauncey leaves open the possibility that he might not always see eye-to-eye with the administration about priorities or information gathering. For instance, he got impatient with how slowly system managers were moving to bring an investment review to the board finance committee. "They kept putting it off because they thought other things had a higher priority," Chauncey says. But as chairman of that panel, he felt it was his responsibility to ensure the project got done sooner. "I said, 'We are going to do it at the next meeting and spend "X" amount of time on it,'" Chauncey relates.

And if he doesn't get the information he needs on a particular financial topic, Chauncey says he feels free to walk into the hospital's finance department and look it up himself.

Across the country at Marin General Hospital, just north of San Francisco, Finance Chairman Tim Wilson has learned the same lesson. But not until after he'd dealt with a previous administration that wasn't as open to board input as the current one.

"When I joined the finance committee [four years ago] the CFO wanted to run the finance committee," recalls Wilson, who recently retired from the board. "At that point it was really a dog and pony show. We'd listen to highly tailored presentations. If you asked a question [the CFO] would kind of look at you in a way that made you feel, 'Gee, I asked a dumb one.'"

But with a new management team came a new attitude that allowed the trustees and management to have a more free-flowing exchange of ideas. "There was a lot more give and take," Wilson says. "Of course, that meant our meetings went on longer than they had. But I felt it was a trade-off I was delighted to make. People who are volunteering their time like to feel their time is valued and their input is valued."

Skills and Committees

A finance committee needs to have people with some business or financial savvy, Kazemek advises. That may be difficult in small rural areas that lack financial professionals. Still, it's helpful to have members who have been exposed to managing or overseeing a company's or organization's finances. "It's not necessary to have a 100 percent bunch of green-eyeshade [wearing] board members, but it sure does help to have people who are reasonably conversant on the basics of financial management," says Kazemek. "They might be retired accountants, CFOs, treasurers or just a person who owned his or her business."

As for the financial acumen of the remaining board members, there should be a balance, says Richard Clarke, president and CEO of the Healthcare Financial Management Association (HFMA). "I wouldn't [want to] see a whole board made up of finance people," he says. "You want to have a balance of patient care, community, mission and finance [expertise]. A board that isn't relatively diverse is not going to be as effective as one that is very diverse. You just need enough members of the board who have the financial acumen that allows them to understand in an easy and fast way."

The board as a whole should expect regular education on the specifics of health care economics, particularly for new members. "It's almost borderline irresponsible when a new person comes on, and the orientation program is either silent or superficial on the basics of health care finance," Kazemek maintains. "It's one of the most complex industries there is. You bring in a couple of board members, and by osmosis they're expected to pick up what's going on and fumble through reams of data on finances, full of acronyms and jargon, and expect to be intelligent about making decisions."

Reviewing Ongoing Finances

One of the board's essential duties is ensuring the organization's ongoing financial health. While everyone should examine the financial statements in preparing for board meetings, they shouldn't spend too much meeting time picking over small details. "Boards can waste a lot of time going down a detailed monthly or quarterly financial statement asking relatively picayune questions about numbers without having deep knowledge or understanding of how the entire function should be overseen," warns Kazemek. He tells of a board that spent so much time on a monthly statement that trustees were literally asking, "What is that $250 for?"

"That's really wasting everybody's time. They [trustees] need to get their heads up above the treetops," Kazemek says. Of course, the level of discussion in the boardroom depends on the size of the forest. At a small, rural hospital, it might be appropriate for trustees to discuss tweaking billing code procedures to maximize income. "If you sit in those board meetings it's almost like a family-run business," Kazemek says. "They roll up their sleeves and get in there, pounding the nails and turning the screws. They're almost like adjunct staff to the CEO and CFO on financial issues." But in a big system, coding is too small an issue for the board, says Kazemek. "When you get to a big, multistate system, a board member should absolutely not be diving into that. Coding is a little, tiny cog in a vast, complex machinery."

No matter what size the hospital or system, though, the board should try to keep its focus on the bigger strategic questions. One way to do that is to define a list of a dozen or so critical indicators for monitoring the financial health of the organization and review them regularly, asking plenty of questions. Those indicators can be straight numbers, such as revenues and margins, or ratios that split up the data in useful ways.

The list of indicators is likely to look a little different in each hospital, depending on its strategy, market position and mission. Consultant Larry Walker helped an 80-bed rural hospital choose its top metrics, paring down a list of 37 potential factors to a handful that could easily be surveyed during a monthly board meeting. These indicators comprised aspects of profitability, pricing, volume, length of stay and efficiency. Using a relatively inexpensive national database of hospital benchmarks, his client could compare itself with similar hospitals. "We called them vital signs and put them in graph form," says Walker, president of The Walker Company, Lake Oswego, Oregon. "If this is done in a structured way it doesn't have to take a lot of time."

However, when given a list of ratios, boards need to be sure they're not hiding bad news, says HFMA's Clarke. "Days outstanding in receivables is a good, broad measure, but it can hide a lot of things," Clarke says. For instance, the number can be reduced by simply writing off hard-to-collect bills. To guard against this, Clarke advises governing boards to build in a countervailing measure such as bad debt and have a benchmark for both.

Consultant James Grobmyer of St. Petersburg, Florida, recommends that the board set specific goals for each important indicator.

That kind of direction gives management clear messages and reminds trustees to ask whether the goals are being met, and if not, why not. "Too often, hospitals find that the financial direction is not specific enough to give management a clear understanding of what their goals and objectives are," Grobmyer says.

Investment Oversight

The hospital board—primarily the finance committee—is also responsible for overseeing how the organization's money is being invested. The funds are usually split into different pools for such purposes as employee retirement, short-term operations, self-insurance, foundation/endowment, and replacement of buildings and equipment (known as funded depreciation). Each of these pots of money will call for a slightly different level of risk or investment philosophy. For instance, pension funds tend to be invested largely in stocks and bonds because of their long-term nature, while operating funds are kept in cash-type holdings for liquidity.

The board's responsibility is to help decide what level of risk the organization is comfortable with to get better returns. While razor-thin margins prompted by Medicare cuts in the late 1990s tempted organizations to put more money in stocks, they were frightened away from the stock market after its big drop in 2000. "None of them [trustees] wants to see [his or her] name in the newspaper," says Timothy Solberg, an investment consultant to hospitals with CCM Advisors in Chicago. "They believe they are doing something that benefits the entire community, and they want to make sure [the hospital's money] is invested and monitored appropriately," he says.

To help boards make these decisions, most hospitals use investment managers, and the board monitors their performance. "Most hospitals are very conservative and risk-averse," Solberg says. "They don't want somebody who's going to be a high-risk manager." More hospitals look to national or regional managers to get the most sophisticated financial advice they can, he says. Board members are also getting more involved in the process for rating their creditworthiness by bond rating agencies such as Moody's Investors Service and Standard and Poor's. It's now standard practice for hospitals to send representatives from the board—usually the chair and chair of the finance committee—to New York City along with hospital executives to visit the bond rating agencies and make the case for a top rating.

Capital Planning

The new Fletcher Allen board is left with the task of monitoring a $350 million rebuilding project with state regulators and legislators, while the news media watches over its shoulder. The best way to keep tabs on a capital project such as that, governance consultants say, is to plan from the start: Establish goals to assess the project's progress along the way and when it's done.

It's also smart to assess retrospectively whether the project was a good use of precious capital funds. For instance, if the hospital is going to spring for a computerized physician order entry system, a baseline measurement should be taken before the project gets under way, and then measured again after implementation to find out whether the investment was worthwhile.

The board's role in strategic planning also applies to creating a capital spending plan that sorts out the many competing big-ticket requests for money, the most common of which are high-tech imaging equipment, new outpatient buildings and information technology. This kind of planning first requires a big-picture, long-term analysis of the hospital's future, one that boards sometimes miss when they're trying to take advantage of an immediate market opportunity, Walker says. "The reason for the capital project has to tie into the strategic plan," he advises. "You have to understand the implications on the total debt structure, and the impact on other programs and services. Boards need to have a conversation about those issues."

Audits and Sarbanes-Oxley

The Sarbanes-Oxley Act was passed in the wake of illegal corporate behavior that neither the board or outside auditors took the responsibility to stop. To prevent such lack of oversight in the future, the law requires that for-profit corporate boards institute various conflict-of-interest and auditing practices. And there's a strong push coming from various sources for not-for-profit boards to follow many of these best practices, both because they represent basic good governance and because there's a strong chance that similar rules will become law for not-for-profits as well.

The biggest immediate impact on boards is the growing need for a separate audit committee to review the hospital's audit process. This committee needs to have at least one member who has extensive knowledge about the arcane world of accounting standards and processes. Boards that don't yet have such a member should be scouting their communities for candidates, according to Kazemek. "[A hospital board] is no longer a place for amateurs. You need at least one person to be the go-to person when there's a question around, 'Is our auditor performing properly?'" he says.

Marin General's board has felt increasing pressure to be responsible stewards of the organization's finances, and now has a more rigorous recruitment process for all new members. "In the past, people would end up on the board because they had helped fund raise or had donated, and the idea was to get them on the board as thanks," says outgoing finance chairman Wilson. "That kind of thinking has gone out the window."

In fact, one of the latest board recruits, a CPA, was sought out especially for her accounting background. And, in a twist that reflects the increasing complexity and responsibility of being a hospital trustee, the recruit vetted the hospital and its board at the same time. "She did a thorough job of being sure we knew what we were doing," says Wilson. "We're getting more sophisticated people who are asking more sophisticated questions about being a trustee."

Board Oversight of the Revenue Cycle: Tools for New Levels of Performance

By Jeffrey D. Jones

Stewardship of hospital finances and assets, always a key governing board responsibility, has come into sharper focus as failures of high-profile organizations have raised demand for improved board performance and accountability. Effective stewardship in an environment of elevated standards and expectations, whether from stakeholders or stockholders, requires more than closer scrutiny of past and current performance.

Governing boards are being increasingly called upon to expand their leadership horizons and become stewards of the future, spending the majority of their time strategically guiding their organizations toward a tomorrow built on strong financial, clinical and service performance that continues to improve over time.

Although much has been written about the need for boards to govern more in the future tense, many boards continue to monitor the past, lacking the resources and approaches necessary to shift their governance focus forward, thereby capitalizing on opportunities

Jeffrey D. Jones is western regional director, Stockamp & Associates, Inc., Portland, Oregon.

for significant financial gains that will improve overall organizational performance. Clearly, new leadership tools and processes are needed that enable trustees and other organizational leaders to collaborate for improved performance, both today and into the future.

The revenue cycle—the process of providing and receiving payment for patient care and services—is the engine that drives a hospital's or system's business and operational performance (see "Understanding the Revenue Cycle" in the June 2003 issue of *Trustee*). Governing boards that understand and can monitor the revenue cycle hold an important key to organizational success. However, even boards that regularly review revenue cycle function often lack the information they need to get an accurate overview of long-term performance. Without such information, boards do not have the tools they need to raise key questions and adequately discuss performance assessment and improvement. And without appropriate governance information and tools, boards will never be able to make the valuable contributions of which they are capable.

Monitoring Revenue Cycle Performance

Most hospital and system governing boards review a number of traditional financial performance indicators that provide an overview of how well the revenue cycle is performing. These typically include such measures as: days in accounts receivable (A/R days); how long it takes to resolve receivables; cost of collections; and bad debt and charity care write-offs, expressed as a percentage of revenue. These measures are frequently used to compare the organization's performance over time, or against the performance of other hospitals or health systems. As long as these indicators are trending downward, the board can assume performance is improving.

However, the way these indicators are calculated, as well as the many differences between hospital service areas and operating environments, make them, at best, meaningless indicators of performance. Even worse, reliance on them may cause the board and the organization to overlook real opportunities for financial performance improvement.

Let's look at days in accounts receivable. Perhaps the most frequently used measure of how well the revenue cycle is functioning, the number of A/R days shows how long it takes for the hospital to be paid for care and services delivered. Health care organizations with fewer than 80 A/R days are usually thought to have efficient revenue cycle performance, and organizations with fewer than 50 to 60 A/R days are believed to be best of class.

Unfortunately, hospitals often fail to account for several variables—such as contractual allowances (i.e., discounts that hospitals have agreed to in their payer contracts), billing credits and difficult-to-collect accounts receivables—that can increase the A/R day calculation. Meaningful A/R data would include such factors to give a more accurate revenue cycle performance picture, but typically, such calculations fail to account for some or all of these variables.

Net A/R day calculations, which are supposed to adjust for the variables mentioned above, also are based on differing assumptions, making them subject to equally inconsistent methods of calculation. While such A/R day calculations may help the board accurately understand the cash value of its receivables, they do not give enough detail to truly get a clear picture of revenue cycle performance. In fact, they typically make revenue cycle performance look better than it is. This satisfies the board, and no further attempt is made to look deeper to uncover the millions of dollars of potential performance-improvement opportunities that lie below the surface.

Hospitals lose millions of dollars annually from contractual allowances in which payer-approved charges are less than the hospital's standard rate for any given procedure. Some of these allowances could have been avoided by improved account processing.

Also, boards often look at write-offs for bad debt or charity care as another way to evaluate revenue cycle performance, yet there is great variability in the ways hospitals classify their write-off categories. The overall result of relying on these indicators is that they may give the impression that revenue cycle performance is better than it really is. The same is true of "aging" statistics—the length of time that accounts remain unresolved. The older the unresolved account, the less efficient the revenue cycle. Problems with this indicator occur when accounts receivable that have been deemed hard to collect are not included in the A/R aging statistics. When this happens, the revenue cycle may appear to be performing more efficiently than it really is.

Inconsistencies in calculation methods for these indicators and differences among hospitals' payer and service mix, patient populations, access to labor pools (some hospitals rely on higher-cost agency labor because they can't recruit enough employees, or they outsource functions that could be done more economically in-house; therefore, comparing hospitals with these differences does not result in apples-to-apples comparisons), economic conditions and other operational elements make analysis using these performance measures flawed, often resulting in missed opportunities for financial and overall performance improvement. Gaining a true and comprehensive picture of revenue cycle performance requires different performance measures that boards can use in new ways.

Gaining a Clear Picture of Revenue Cycle Financial Performance

Governing boards that want a clear, accurate picture of the ongoing financial performance of their hospital's revenue cycle should work with their executive team to obtain information from two sources: a dashboard of revenue cycle performance indicators for ongoing board review and a periodic, comprehensive assessment of overall revenue cycle performance. A dashboard set of revenue cycle financial performance indicators designed for both full board and finance committee review should first be developed. Such a list of full-board indicators, including how each should be calculated, as well as additional finance committee indicators, appears below.

Full Board Indicators

1. Income improvement: Actual income earned each period compared with the target established for that period and year-to-date
2. Cash factor: Gross cash receipts divided by gross patient revenue
3. Expense factor: Gross expenses divided by gross patient revenue
4. Net cash flow: Operating income adjusted for investment gains/losses, depreciation and amortization

---

At each of its meetings, the full board should review actual performance, displayed on a quarterly basis, for each of its designated indicators. For each indicator, performance should be compared with the organization's quarterly goals. Performance trends over the past three years also should be provided for each indicator to help the board view performance patterns and variations longitudinally.

To help ensure that board members have had the opportunity to review revenue cycle financial performance in greater detail, the board finance committee should review an additional set of financial indicators (see below) that shows how these aspects of the cycle affect broader revenue cycle performance.

Actual monthly performance should be displayed for each of these indicators as well as compared with monthly performance goals set by management. The board should also see 12-month performance trends for each indicator to help identify performance patterns over an annual business cycle.

To ensure overall revenue cycle performance reliability, the board also needs information about revenue cycle performance from a second source. At least annually, the board should ask management for a detailed assessment of the hospital's entire revenue cycle. This comprehensive assessment involves the steps outlined below and is only done periodically to ensure that the overall revenue cycle is running at top performance.

Board Finance Committee Indicators

1. **Secure Rate:**
   The percentage of patient accounts that are financially secure or complete at the time of service

2. **Revenue Capture Rate:**
   Total revenue recorded as a percentage of total revenue expected (i.e., average revenue per service times patient volume)

3. **Revenue Cycle Efficiency Rate:**
   The percentage of overall revenue tied up in the organization's revenue cycle processes compared with the percentage of overall revenue billed and owed by payers

4. **Monthly Cash Factor:**
   Gross monthly cash receipts divided by gross monthly revenue

The indicators simply monitor ongoing performance but could indicate the need for a periodic in-depth assessment if performance declines. Such an assessment should be based on a sample of accounts, including those that are active, as well as those that have been written off, or for which payment has been denied by an insurer. Every patient account should be reviewed to establish whether proactive, timely and efficient processing occurred at each step in the revenue cycle. Results of this evaluation should be reported to the finance committee and to the full board, accompanied by management's plan to either address performance shortfalls or to continue to sustain and improve upon good performance.

Using Information to Improve Performance

Accurate, timely and meaningful revenue cycle performance information should become the foundation for a board/management dialogue about both existing and expected performance. For each indicator, the full board and finance committee should ask management to discuss the two or three factors that most affected performance—whether that indicator exceeded, met or trailed performance goals.

Management should also share anticipated performance for the next two upcoming review periods with the board and finance committee. With both actual and predicted performance in hand, the board and management can then discuss how management intends to address expected performance.

The case examples below look at two important dashboard indicators of revenue cycle performance: cash factor and secure rate. The cash factor indicates how effectively the organization collects each dollar of revenue, a key performance measure since cash is critical to an organization's overall financial health and ongoing viability. Secure rate is important because it is the best predictor of the amount of future revenue being currently generated, which strengthens and helps the organization better manage future cash flow.

Case Example: Analyzing Cash Factor Performance

Table 1 (page 166) shows cash factor performance for the second quarter of 2003 and the previous 12 quarters, beginning in the second quarter of 2000, as well as quarterly and annual performance goals. This report was presented for review to the full board at its July 2003 meeting.

Report information indicates that second quarter performance met the performance goal and that management expected to maintain the performance gains over the rest of the year. Past performance trends indicated opportunities for significant improvement, so in September 2002 management completely redesigned the hospital's revenue cycle, the only proven way to achieve sustainable improvement.

Table 1. Cash Factor Performance

Current Performance

Second quarter 2003 performance	46.8%
Second quarter 2003 goal	46.5%
Third quarter 2003 performance forecast	46.5%
Fourth quarter 2003 performance forecast	46.5%
Annual goal: Cash factor at or above	46.0%

Three-Year Performance Trends

Cash factor for second quarter 2000	43.3%
Cash factor for third quarter 2000	43.5%
Cash factor for fourth quarter 2000*	42.5%
Cash factor for first quarter 2001	42.6%
Cash factor for second quarter 2001	42.8%
Cash factor for third quarter 2001	43.2%
Cash factor for fourth quarter 2001	43.4%
Cash factor for first quarter 2002	43.1%
Cash factor for second quarter 2002	43.1%
Cash factor for third quarter 2002**	43.2%
Cash factor for fourth quarter 2002	44.8%
Cash factor for first quarter 2003	46.3%

*Hospital initiated a 15 percent price increase in October 2000 to achieve parity in the market and to drive increased revenue.

**Comprehensive revenue cycle improvement project began in July 2002.

The redesign process examined each step in the revenue cycle to ensure proactive, efficient and timely account processing, and performance has continued to trend upward since the project began.

In reviewing this performance information, board members might ask the following questions:

- What key factors caused cash factor performance to improve so dramatically over the past several months?
- How might cash factor performance vary with ebbs and flows in the hospital's business cycle?
- What is a realistic best-performance goal for this indicator? Do we need to adjust our current goal to reflect this level of expected performance?
- How does management plan to continue to sustain and improve cash factor performance?
- If our organization achieves peak cash factor performance, how will that affect our organization's overall financial performance?

Case Example: Analyzing Secure Rate Performance

Table 2 (page 168) shows secure rate performance for the current month, as well as performance trends for the past year. The report was presented for review to the board's finance committee at its July 2003 meeting.

The report information indicates that the current month's performance reached its performance goal and that secure rate performance has been trending upward since the organization undertook a revenue cycle redesign and performance improvement project in September of the previous year. Given these trends and additional opportunities that have been identified for further gains, management expects performance to continue to improve for July and August 2003.

In reviewing this performance information, the finance committee members might ask the following questions:

- What key factors dramatically improved secure rate performance from June 2002 through June 2003?
- How might secure rate performance vary with ebbs and flows in the hospital's business cycle?

Table 2. Secure Rate Performance

Current Performance

Secure rate for June 2003	93%
Monthly goal	92%
Performance forecast for July	96%
Performance forecast for August	98%
Annual goal: Secure rate at or above	98%

12-Month Performance Trends

June 2002	25%
July 2002	28%
August 2002	26%
September 2002*	35%
October 2002	44%
November 2002	56%
December 2002	67%
January 2003	74%
February 2003	78%
March 2003	84%
April 2003	87%
May 2003	90%
June 2003	93%

*Beginning of comprehensive revenue cycle improvement project.

- What is a realistic best-performance goal for this indicator? Do we need to adjust our current goal to reflect this level of expected performance?
- How does management plan to sustain and improve secure rate performance? If we continue to achieve peak secure rate performance, how will that performance affect our cash flow?

Sharing and discussing both actual and expected performance on a regular basis, using accurate, timely and meaningful revenue cycle performance information, allows the board and management to work together to maximize performance outcomes and establish a collaborative process for performance accountability. Ongoing dialogue using the information and process described above provides clarity, not only about current performance, but also on what the organization anticipates future performance to be.

Conclusion

As performance trends become more predictable over time, forecasting can extend further into the future. This longer-term view should allow the hospital board and management to work together in order to influence performance outcomes positively. By focusing in this way, rather than on the past, the governing board and management can work together to help create a better, more successful future for the hospital.

Strategic Financial Planning: What Every Trustee Needs to Know about Facility Replacement

By Mark E. Grube

Driven by a confluence of factors—capacity constraints, increased demand for services, changes in care delivery and facility inadequacies—hospitals and health care systems nationwide are wrestling with whether to replace their aging facilities, and if so, how. These decisions have enormous strategic and financial implications. A thoughtfully planned and financed replacement facility can enable an organization to meet community needs well into the future. Conversely, a facility replacement initiative that lacks a balanced strategic and financial plan can easily sink the organization by overextending its ability to sustain the required high level of capital investment.

Given their fiduciary duties and core responsibilities, trustees need to be well-informed about the essential characteristics of an integrated facility planning and decision-making process. Integrated planning involves thorough consideration of five components: mission, vision and strategy; market and competition; operations and technology; site issues; and financial requirements and projected financial impact.

Mark E. Grube is a partner of Kaufman, Hall & Associates Inc., Northfield, Illinois.

Mission, Vision and Strategy

An organization's mission and vision statements provide the foundation for its strategy, which focuses both on external market needs and how to meet such needs given the organization's strategic and financial resources. In the earliest stages of evaluating whether to replace a facility, executives and the board should be able to answer the following five questions:

1. What is the organization's vision (i.e., where do we want to be five and 10 years from now)?
2. Who do we intend to serve, and what needs do we wish to meet?
3. What mix of programs and services will meet defined needs?
4. How might a replacement facility improve care quality and our ability to provide the desired programs and services?
5. How will our constituents (the community, physicians and other staff, and the capital markets) respond to our choice and how should we communicate our plans?

The board and senior management are responsible for strategic planning. Building a replacement facility is a major strategic decision. A hospital or health system's management and board must be confident about the organization's ability to meet real market needs through a facility replacement. Trustees should be concerned about a strategy that lacks clarity or a strategy that is well beyond an organization's means.

KishHealth System comprises two hospitals in Illinois—100-bed Kishwaukee Community Health in Dekalb and 25-bed Valley West Community Hospital in Sandwich. The two hospitals are approximately 60 miles west of Chicago, serving a region that is rapidly growing and evolving from a primarily rural to a suburban area.

KishHealth's mission, vision and strategy is to provide its growing community of approximately 120,000 with a broad range of health care services, from primary care to highly specialized services, including surgery, ophthalmology and cancer care, as well as orthopedic and rehabilitation outpatient facilities and a diagnostic imaging center.

"In 2002, the board and management team articulated a vision of moving from a community acute care provider to a health system

with a broader and deeper mix of services and a more regional fla-
vor," notes Kevin Poorten, KishHealth's president and CEO. This
vision responds to favorable market trends in DeKalb and surrounding counties, including rapid population growth (forecasted at 19
percent) and an increasingly affluent population with higher income
and education levels.

While its two distinct community hospitals are well-known
throughout DeKalb County, its patient draw and market share are
heavily dependent on the communities of DeKalb, Sycamore and
Cortland, with a more limited presence in other portions of the
county. By developing into an independent regional health system,
KishHealth expects to be able to increase market penetration within
both its core market and other portions of DeKalb County. Dewey
Yaeger, who chaired both the hospital and new system board,
describes the board as very representative of the community, committed to the organization's mission and vision.

Market and Competition

The approach to integrated strategic financial planning starts with
an assessment of the market or community served and the current
and potential emerging competition. Key questions are:

- What is our prospective market and what are its demographics by
  market cluster (e.g., primary market, etc.)?
- Who refers patients to the hospital/health system and what are
  their expectations?
- Who competes with us now and who is likely to do so in the
  future?

Collection and analysis of demographic and socioeconomic data
on current and potential service areas, and on market share data
by geographic location and service line, provides a profile of an
organization's performance in core and non-core service areas and
its competitive strengths and weaknesses. Trustees should be aware
that such data are not just "nice to know" information, but rather
"need to know" information. Market strength and/or a differenti-
ated competitive position are central to maintaining strategic and
financial viability.

KishHealth defined its service area by patient origin, analyzed demographics by market cluster, identified current competitors and potential market entrants, and assessed market share by cluster and program/service line. Growth in the east market was strongest (14 percent), but population growth in all markets exceeded national rates, indicating strong organizational growth potential for the health care system.

A detailed analysis of the competition indicated which services and geographic areas offered the greatest future potential. "There was no one dominant provider in numerous market clusters, which reinforced our strategy to become a regional provider, drawing patients from a broader geographic area," says Poorten. An analysis of overall inpatient market size and KishHealth's share by program indicated an opportunity to move from a 36 percent of total market share to higher systemwide market share, conservatively projected to be between 40 percent and 45 percent. The closest competitor had a market share of approximately 16 percent, and more than 10 other competitors captured only 2 percent to 7 percent of the remaining market share.

The analysis also indicated which service lines should be further developed based on market demand and financial considerations (see figure 1 on page 174). As the figure indicates, KishHealth provides a broad range of services. Its development as a regional health system is focused on expanding the depth of existing service lines. For example, its basic orthopedic service program is expanding to include subspecialties such as spinal problems and the full range of joint replacement services, such as knee, hip and shoulder. The gastroenterology department is recruiting new physicians, and imaging-based diagnostic services such as cardiac MRI and angiography are growing significantly. Physician recruitment is a high priority; to achieve its targeted program/service expansion, KishHealth successfully recruited nearly 40 physicians over a recent two-year period.

Operations and Technology

The integrated approach continues with an operations analysis. Key questions include:

- Does the current facility provide the opportunity to add or expand services?

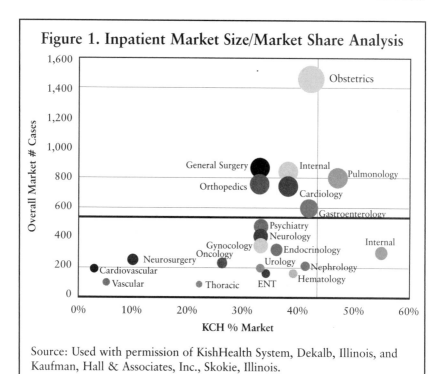

Figure 1. Inpatient Market Size/Market Share Analysis

Source: Used with permission of KishHealth System, Dekalb, Illinois, and Kaufman, Hall & Associates, Inc., Skokie, Illinois.

- What operating model, such as decentralized nursing pods, might be used in a new facility for service and patient care? Has this model been tested and proven effective in other facilities?
- What are the opportunities for change in health services and how might technology enable these changes?
- What service, quality and efficiency improvements are expected? For example, might new technology decrease the number of staff required?
- Will a new facility reduce unit service costs?

Recent research conducted by Kaufman Hall indicates that better-performing hospitals are able to achieve operating savings of 6 percent to 8 percent in replacement facilities by the fifth year after replacement. Such savings derive from new labor-reducing technologies, more efficient designs of patient floors, improved logistics, more efficient work processes and building systems, and volume growth. If an organization's executive team and board decide to meet expanding market/service needs by building a replacement facility, but do not believe that operational efficiencies will be achieved, the organization's revenue growth projections need to be even more impressive to meet financial goals.

KishHealth's executive team and board considered how operations and health care technology might change in the next decades. "The bottom line question for us was this—'Might our current facilities or a replacement facility be able to meet the need for expanded services for a growing patient population with increasingly sophisticated technological needs and facility expectations while increasing our efficiency?'" Poorten explains. Yaeger adds, "Although the current hospital was aging, we were very sensitive to its 30-year heritage and the emotional commitment of the many stakeholders who worked hard to build it."

Site Issues

Costs and risks associated with facility replacement are substantial and must be evaluated carefully in the context of meeting community needs while maintaining a sound financial position. Key questions for the board include:

- Can the existing campus expand, and if so, how accessible is it to target growth markets?
- Is land available, and can it be acquired for a fair price?
- How much land will be needed, and where should that land be located?

Common pitfalls in replacement facility planning include undersizing the facility, underinvesting in infrastructure, and overinvesting in non-revenue-generating space. Hospitals or systems that make the decision to replace their facilities at a new site should take full advantage of the opportunity to redesign care, but they should avoid untested concepts, such as a patient care model with decentralized diagnostic testing in which imaging and other technology-based services occur in multiple locations throughout the facility. Other planning challenges include disposition of the existing campus; scope, budget and schedule controls; organizational culture; gaining and/or maintaining community support; and effective communication.

KishHealth's five options for addressing its aging facilities and expanding utilization were to:

1. Make minimal investments to keep current system facilities operational
2. Invest incrementally in existing facilities over the next 10 to 12 years
3. Focus facility development on the addition of a patient tower that would provide needed space for expanding clinical services
4. Replace the entire facility adjacent to the existing building on its current site
5. Replace the current facility at a new site

"We wanted to identify the option that would enable the organization to achieve the vision and strategic goals previously articulated by the board," explains Poorten. "To evaluate each of these options, we carefully assessed where the community was expected to grow in the next 10 to 20 years, the cost and availability of land, our ability to expand current facilities, and the facility design alternatives for options 3, 4 and 5."

Projected Financial Impact

Replacing an aging facility has enormous financial implications. Costs of $1 million to $1.5 million per bed are not unusual. Organizations planning to replace a facility must have deep financial resources, or the ability to access significant capital in the debt markets. Key financial questions include:

- What is the organization's credit profile?
- How much additional debt can the organization support?
- What other capital sources are available to fund the project? Do we need to consider partnering with others to create the necessary financial means?
- What is the organization's projected financial performance if we build a replacement facility? What level of cash flow must the organization generate?
- If we go ahead with a new facility, when do we start construction? Do we do it in phases?

Few health care organizations have the operating cash flow and available cash reserves to fund strategic investments of the magnitude of a replacement facility. A replacement facility project almost always requires incurring significant debt, and increased debt will most likely have a negative impact on the key financial ratios used by rating agencies to evaluate an organization's financial performance and current credit rating. A lowered credit rating will increase the cost of capital. In addition, once a rating is lowered, it may be difficult to bring back up.

Trustees are responsible for ensuring the continued financial integrity and creditworthiness of the organizations they direct, so detailed analyses of the future financial impact of additional debt and projected revenues are critical. Partnerships or consolidations could provide funding support if the organization is unable to create or access capital on its own. If this is necessary, boards must consider how such a loss of independence would affect the organization.

Notwithstanding the fact that KishHealth was in the unusual position of having no publicly traded outstanding debt, the first step of their board's financial analysis involved studying the organization's credit position and identifying the amount of debt it could support within the desired "A" credit rating category. "The management team and board needed to know what performance benchmarks (such as profitability, debt and liquidity ratios) the credit markets, specifically the rating agencies, would use to assess the organization's financial condition and how we performed against these benchmarks," Poorten says.

On most measures, KishHealth compared favorably with other A-rated organizations, but its revenue base was considerably smaller—a factor the board and management would address through growth over time. A capital position analysis, comparing projected sources with fund use over a five-year period, indicated the estimated five-year and annual cash flow requirements.

"Actual annual cash flow in 2002 and 2003 exceeded estimated requirements, which increased management and board confidence that we could incur additional debt without harming our credit position, while also maintaining future financial flexibility to address changing market, strategic and technological issues," Poorten says.

Next, the organization assessed the financial implications of each of the five facility options by projecting their volumes, revenues, costs, profitability, debt, liquidity and capital capacity impact. "The board challenged us to add an 'Option 4B,' which involved replacing the facility adjacent to the current site and growing market share to the levels forecasted to be achieved with Option 5 at a new site, located closer to target market areas," Poorten says. "We started by projecting the volume we could expect, given market share changes forecasted under each option." Feedback from separate physician and community focus groups provided critical information for volume projections and option preferences by constituency. "Public perception and preferences were vital to us, so listening to focus group input was extremely helpful," says Yaeger. As it turned out, physicians and community members preferred Option 4B and Option 5. "The board and management team met in November 2003 to evaluate the options," Yaeger explains. "We went into the meeting with no preconceptions about building a new hospital. That was just one among the options we were considering."

"The financial projections for both Options 4B and 5 were so close that we decided to replace at a site adjacent to our existing facility (Option 4B) rather than take the risk of moving to a 'green-field site' (Option 5)," Poorten says. "Facility replacement was and is viewed as a key enabler for achieving our goals." Groundbreaking took place last August (2004), and construction is expected to be completed within the next 25 to 27 months.

A comprehensive strategic and financial assessment of all the alternatives gave the board, management, physicians and the community confidence in the selected option. Physicians and community members on the board and physicians on the management team helped build buy-in. An extensive communication effort using mailings, Web site announcements and newsletters continues to inform these important constituents. Additionally, organizational commitment to generating the level of financial performance required for capital access was critical to the execution of strategy.

Expected results for the new facility include an enhanced ability to meet both primary care and specialty physician needs; the ability to offer an expanded scope of services to the community and to assume a more regional approach to health care; and improved market share and financial performance. (See figure 2, page 179, for the complete process and its time line.)

Figure 2. Strategic Facility Plan Project Time Line

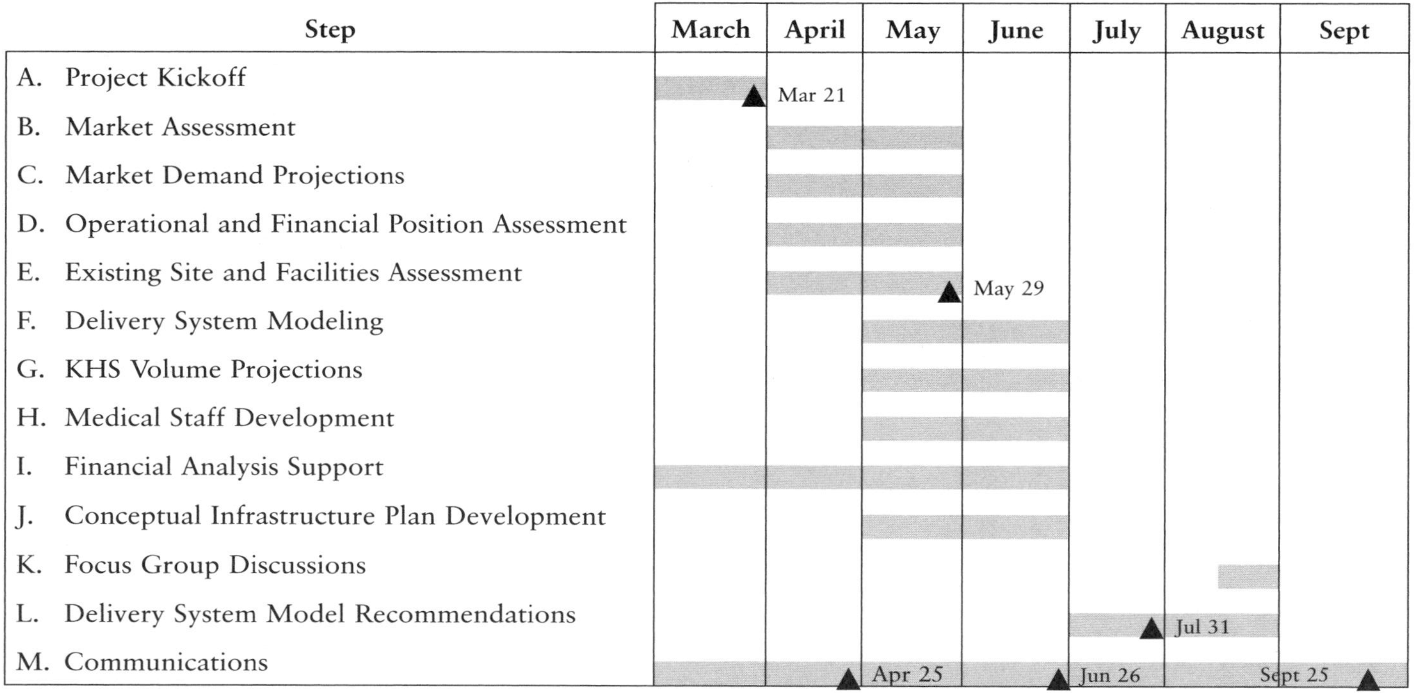

Step	March	April	May	June	July	August	Sept
A. Project Kickoff	◀ Mar 21						
B. Market Assessment		▓	▓				
C. Market Demand Projections		▓	▓				
D. Operational and Financial Position Assessment		▓	▓				
E. Existing Site and Facilities Assessment		▓	◀ May 29				
F. Delivery System Modeling				▓			
G. KHS Volume Projections				▓			
H. Medical Staff Development				▓			
I. Financial Analysis Support	▓			▓			
J. Conceptual Infrastructure Plan Development				▓			
K. Focus Group Discussions						▓	
L. Delivery System Model Recommendations					◀ Jun 26	▓ Jul 31	
M. Communications	▓ Apr 25			◀			◀ Sept 25

Source: Used with permission of KishHealth System, Dekalb, Illinois, and Kaufman, Hall & Associates, Inc., Skokie, Illinois.

Developing a replacement facility represents a high-risk, but potentially high-reward endeavor. In a competitive marketplace, health care organizations must be able to give increasingly sophisticated patients and providers an effective, efficient and pleasing environment that meets their health care needs.

"Our guiding principles included supporting patient-centered care concepts, assuring future flexibility, optimizing operational efficiency, and incorporating concepts of evidence-based design to promote a healing environment," Yaeger says. "But integral to all the principles was this: All decisions must be made within the context of fiscal responsibility."

Looking Harder:
The Audit Committee
under Sarbanes-Oxley

By Jan Greene

Governing a hospital is difficult enough without trying to comply with rules and regulations that aren't even required. But directors of not-for-profit hospitals across the country are hearing the echoes of corporate financial scandals and investing time and effort to ensure that their organizations don't end up in court or making newspaper headlines.

That's why they're taking a good hard look at the 2002 Sarbanes-Oxley Act, which tightens up accountability requirements for financial reporting by public corporations. The act doesn't cover not-for-profits, so theoretically, the vast majority of hospitals could ignore it. But fears of a homegrown financial mess and the prospect of future accountability rules targeting not-for-profits are prompting many boards to reconfigure committee assignments and take a stronger hand in overseeing the books.

"While nobody likes more rules and regulations, most trustees are welcoming this as a way to avoid a potential problem down the road," says Steven Albertalli, a long-time board member of a 99-bed hospital in Corning, New York. A financial glitch that gets by the board, Albertalli says, "could hurt the reputation of the hospital and hurt [a trustee's] own personal reputation."

Jan Greene is a writer based in Alameda, California.

Governance consultant Larry Walker sees boards of larger hospitals responding to the issue early, while most boards of smaller hospitals, which usually have fewer resources, are waiting to act until rules are written specifically for nonprofits, possibly by the federal government or by attorneys general of individual states.

"We're seeing a lot of activity among boards of larger hospitals because they see Sarbanes-Oxley and the implications—particularly with regard to audit functions—being something they'll be expected to respond to," says Walker, who is based out of Lake Oswego, Oregon. "Smaller hospitals tend to be less aware of the implications and increased government accountability and feel they are complying with the spirit of the law through existing committee structures."

That may not be good enough, Walker warns, contending that hospital size should not be a factor in documenting financial accountability or assuming that the board has the right expertise for the job. "There's no reason why even small hospital boards can't recruit someone in the community who has good financial skills and enhance those skills with some targeted knowledge and skill building," he says. "It takes time and commitment, but even if it's a very small community hospital in a rural market with a small board, I think there is still an opportunity and an expectation that they should not just use their size or lack of resources as an excuse for not doing it [preparing for Sarbanes-Oxley]."

In New York State, where all the hospitals are not-for-profit and Attorney General Elliot Spitzer has proposed legislation that would apply many provisions of Sarbanes-Oxley to nonprofits, many hospital boards are taking action. "Trustees [are] not only aware of the issue, but itching to be proactive," says Joanne Cunningham, executive director of the Healthcare Trustees of New York State. "They [are] very motivated by the fact that they are fiduciaries of very important community-owned assets. There's a heightened awareness that the climate has changed."

Some of the specific changes hospital boards are making include creating a separate audit committee comprising only independent board members, avoiding conflicts of interest and overseeing their external auditor. Some hospitals are committed to following Sarbanes-Oxley to the letter, while others are using its principles as a general outline and making the specifics fit their own situations. "They're figuring out how to do it so it makes sense for their culture," says Cunningham.

Corporate Accountability Guidelines Inspired by Sarbanes-Oxley

- [The board should] maintain a code of ethics

- The full board should adopt a conflict-of-interest policy

- [The board should] establish an audit committee or assign its functions to an existing board committee

- [The board] should maintain an internal control program

- The CEO and CFO should provide the board with certified financial documents such as the Medicare cost report, the IRS Form 990 and the management representation letter provided to external auditors

- The board should set policy on what constitutes an "interest" in a hospital-related business transaction or compensation arrangement that would preclude a board member from participation in a vote

Source: *Non-Profit Corporate Accountability, A Guidebook,* from the Healthcare Association of New York State and Healthcare Trustees of New York State. See "Audit Resources," page 190, for ordering information.

Creating an Audit Committee

Some hospitals, mostly larger ones, are establishing a separate committee to handle audit functions. Other boards are giving those duties to a finance or compliance committee and altering the panel's name to reflect its double duty.

The board at Corning Hospital, for instance, is creating a new audit subcommittee of the board's finance committee. The subcommittee's role is to closely examine the assumptions behind management's financial statements. "Where you can get into the most trouble is making financial assumptions about things such as funding the [employee] pension," says board member Albertalli, who is retired from a 44-year career with Corning Inc., where he was most recently a vice president and director of investor relations. "We felt we had to have a special subcommittee that would be able to spend more time looking into just the financial assumptions."

In Massachusetts, another state where there's been talk of an accountability law for nonprofits, the Cambridge Health Alliance board has made several organizational changes over the past six months. One such change resulted in the board "peeling off" an audit panel from the financial committee. The groups will share some members, including their chair, who is a certified public accountant. "We've always been reasonably prudent and tight in our oversight activities on finance," says Richard de Filippi, board chair. "This hasn't represented a major change in what we're doing."

Once a board has established a separate audit committee or explicitly given those duties to a financial or compliance panel, it should put the audit group's responsibilities in writing, in the form of a charter, Walker recommends. "Be sure the audit committee has a good, solid, well-articulated charter," he says. "They need a charter that describes what [the committee's] function is and its responsibilities with regard to the audit." The charter should address what questions the committee should ask, what documents it should review, what issues it should address, the timeframe in which it does its work and how it reports results. "The audit committee is used not only to strengthen the hospital's financial accountability but also its trust with employees and external audiences so people know what kind of governance oversight is taking place," Walker says.

Audit Committee Independence

To comply with Sarbanes-Oxley, all audit committee members must be independent—that is, not tied financially to the hospital. This means changing the committee's composition if the CEO or CFO has been a member. In Cambridge, the health alliance chose to keep its CEO on the audit committee as an ex-officio member in order to retain his expertise without compromising the committee's objectivity.

But audit committee panelists' independence goes beyond hospital employment. Any financial tie can be a problem. Some boards, in fact, are struggling with their desire to maintain hard-won physician input on their fiscal committees when those doctors may receive some remuneration from the hospital as medical directors or even as heavy admitters.

This is an issue Sparrow Health System in Lansing, Michigan, faces as it seeks to comply with Sarbanes-Oxley, explains Jonathan Raven, chair of the system's audit and finance committee. "We have a core value that we believe physicians have to be involved in everything we do," Raven says. "We have to ask ourselves what role they can continue to play if they are large-volume referrers. Though Sarbanes-Oxley would probably preclude a lot of physicians from being involved [on the board], we don't feel comfortable disenfranchising them."

The Sparrow board is finding that the federal law, written for the corporate world, is not always a good fit for not-for-profit hospitals. But using Sarbanes-Oxley to confirm that the organization has all the proper financial controls in place is still a good exercise, Raven maintains. "If you are running a nonprofit hospital already with due care to appropriate compliance and reporting standards, I don't think Sarbanes-Oxley is going to improve anything. But maybe other institutions that haven't been as proactive as Sparrow may be well-served by looking at things in Sarbanes-Oxley. They may not be as cleanly governed as they could be."

Sarbanes-Oxley also requires that a corporate audit committee maintain at least one member who is an "expert" in accounting. Meeting that standard can be especially challenging in a small community. Corning Hospital serves about 40,000 people in rural New York, where locating hospital trustees with specific expertise in nonprofit or hospital finance is tough. "In a small community like this, we haven't yet found an outside person with hospital experience," says Albertalli. "We'll have to back off and pick someone who's a non-board member who can add more of an auditing background. We probably can't find somebody with a medical accounting background."

The new accountability standards also require extra care in avoiding conflicts of interest on the board. Again, that can be difficult in a small town. "We have a limited number of contractors in our community, and we have one person on our board who is the head of a contracting group we have used," Albertalli explains. "With this one we're a little more rigorous. We've dealt with it over the years by having a very careful bidding process. This person has won some contracts and lost some contracts, and always recuses himself from any board decision on a contract where his firm could be a candidate."

External Auditor Relationship

The audit committee is also responsible for maintaining the relationship with the external auditor who reviews the organization's financial statements. Under Sarbanes-Oxley, the audit panel takes responsibility for choosing the auditor and monitoring the firm's relationship with management.

Sarbanes-Oxley provisions recommend that organizations regularly change audit partners—those individuals (if not audit firms) who actually conduct the external audit. Of course, frequent change is simply disruptive. But fresh eyes looking at the financial statements every five years can keep the process robust.

The Cambridge Health Alliance board recently opened up its external audit contract for bid for the first time in many years. The organization had maintained the same external auditor for 15 years, and while it was doing a fine job, the board felt it was time to allow other organizations a chance to vie for the position. A new audit firm won the bid. "We'll probably do that now on a routine basis," de Filippi says.

It's also important to know what external auditors can't do for your organization—they may only examine the financial statements. They aren't responsible for uncovering fraud or for examining the risk profile of the hospital's big decisions on new construction or business partnerships. That's up to the audit committee and, in hospitals with enough resources, an internal auditor should analyze that profile. (See "The Internal Auditor's Role," page 187.) "We've been working with our external auditors to learn what it is they do and what they don't do," says Corning's Albertalli. "We found they might not check into some things that could get [us] into trouble."

On the other hand, external auditors are good resources for information about the best accountability practices. Some hospitals have asked their audit firms to give their boards a presentation on Sarbanes-Oxley.

"External auditors have a heightened awareness of the changes in the climate," says Cunningham. "They're being sticklers on making sure they're working with folks that have created the right process and structure that abides by the spirit of Sarbanes-Oxley."

The Internal Auditor's Role

Internal auditors examine high-risk hospital processes of all types under a microscope and suggest ways to make them safer. "We're looking at the things that are the most crucial to the organization, what keeps [managers] up at night," explains Bryon Neaman, director of internal audit for the giant Bon Secours Health System, based in Maryland and ranging over nine states.

Internal auditors are most often employed at medium to larger size hospitals and systems. They often report directly to the board's audit committee or a financial or compliance committee that also handles audits.

Interestingly, internal auditors are quite different from the external auditors that practically every organization, no matter its size, uses to examine its financial reports. Internal auditors can study the financials, but they're not restricted to that. Some, in fact, get asked to look at the risks posed by clinical processes or by materials management. Some may analyze regulatory decisions that could affect the organization.

"A good internal audit program can look within any part of an organization; it's really irrespective of financial reporting," Neaman says. "We look at anything we believe poses a significant risk to the organization."

For example, a new piece of legislation may have an impact on Bon Secours hospitals. "One of our roles is to evaluate those areas within our organization that legislation may directly affect," he explains. "We provide some objective advice and counsel on how well we meet that legislative requirement."

At Bon Secours, the system board's audit committee helps direct the internal audit's annual plan, a strategy that changes from year to year, depending on the health care environment. The current year's audit plan includes review of Bon Secours' pharmacy vendors along with drug administration practices and pricing and how well a new information system in finance, materials management and human resources is being implemented. Bon Secours' internal audit department is also revamping more than 200 financial policies to ensure systemwide consistency.

Continued →

Internal auditors may have financial training. Or, in Bon Secours' case, the 21-person department includes lawyers, laboratory and physician practice managers, information technology experts, and accountants. Some internal audit departments may also choose to include nurse managers.

Chris Boutin, now audit director at three-hospital Baystate Health System in Springfield, Massachusetts, started out as an accountant for a small hospital—small enough that he was able to learn all about his hospital's operations. He moved into public accounting, performing external hospital audits, then went to an individual hospital as a controller, and then returned to Baystate as an internal auditor, where he's been for 15 years. "Because health care is so dynamic and challenging for me, it's just become a pleasure to come to work every day," he says.

And while everyone doesn't enjoy having an auditor look over his or her shoulder, most hospital employees accept auditors, he says. "The philosophy here is that the internal audit function is part of continuous improvement," Boutin says of his seven-member department. "It becomes a partnership with management. We help them assess their controls. We provide a service to them to allow them to sleep better at night."

At the same time, it's crucial that internal auditors maintain a certain distance from operations and management, reporting directly to both the board audit committee and to one of the hospitals' top executives. They are also careful not to get too involved in hospitalwide initiatives or day-to-day operations so they may independently review the progress and results of those projects later.

To be most effective, a hospital's internal auditors need to have the board's support. "The [message] from the board to the CEO to the CFO needs to say that [the] internal audit function is good for the organization, good for governance," says Boutin. "Having the support from the audit committee and the board is very important to any audit executive in any health care organization."

Neaman agrees. "The key attribute to ensure the independence of the internal audit function is to have a direct-line reporting relationship to the audit committee of the board," he says.

—Jan Greene

Audit Committee Best Practices

- A board-level committee, whether the "audit," "audit and compliance," "finance," or some other denominated committee, should assume all duties and responsibilities for auditing oversight.

- The purpose, membership and function of the committee should be [written] in a charter or other document adopted by the board.

- Committee members should meet articulated and strict independence criteria.

- Committee members should possess [at least] a minimal level of financial expertise.

- The duties and responsibilities of the committee should encompass specific matters relating to external auditors, internal financial controls and internal audits, corporate conflict-of-interest policies and the corporate compliance program.

- When a single committee takes on multiple roles, such as an "audit and compliance" or "audit and finance" committee, the various roles of the committee should be clearly articulated, and reporting relationships well-defined.

- The committee must be provided with adequate resources to allow it to effectively carry out its functions.

- The committee may appropriately rely on information and advice from management and independently retained advisors and counselors and make decisions on the basis of such information and advice.

Source: *Non-Profit Corporate Accountability, A Guidebook,* by the Healthcare Association of New York State and Healthcare Trustees of New York State. See "Audit Resources," page 190, for ordering information.

Audit Resources

1. *Non-Profit Corporate Accountability, a Guidebook,* by the Healthcare Association of New York State and Healthcare Trustees of New York State. These organizations studied the implications of Sarbanes-Oxley on not-for-profit hospitals and devised useful recommendations. Available for $100. Order forms are online at www.hanys.org. Click on "Library" and then on the green box "Order HANYS Publications."

2. "Trends in Board Accountability: Conducting the Audit," by Mary Totten and James E. Orlikoff in *Trustee,* January 2003. Detailed advice on the audit process.

3. "Responding to Governance Challenges: The Audit Committee," by Christopher Boutin in *Trustee,* April 2003. General discussion of audits.

4. "Charity Oversight and Reform," a staff white paper from the U.S. Senate Finance Committee on specific proposals that could affect governance of not-for-profit organizations. Available online at http://finance.senate.gov/hearings/testimony/2004test/062204stfdis.pdf.

5. "Sarbanes-Oxley: Relevance and Implications of Certain Provisions for Non-Public Healthcare Organizations," by PricewaterhouseCoopers, January 2004. Available online at www.healthcare.pwc.com/cgi-local/hcregister.cgi?link=pdf/sarbanes.pdf. Useful overview of advice for nonprofit hospital boards.

Implications for Trustees

While organizations that have already made voluntary compliance with Sarbanes-Oxley a high priority are finding that doing so is not a big stretch, it does add to an ever-increasing burden on trustees. "Boards and individuals are putting a lot more time into structure and process and making sure they are getting it right," says Cunningham, who works with trustees throughout New York state. "There are a lot more meetings, a lot more time spent. I kind of worry . . . that the job will become less attractive."

Albertalli's board in Corning has found that learning a newly rigorous oversight role is time-consuming. "I think it will end up taking more time," he says. But his board hasn't lost anyone yet to the fear of added fiscal responsibility. "You probably pick people who you know are ready to take on that responsibility. In a small community, you know them pretty well and know if they're willing to put in that time."

The Sparrow board is also putting in more time, but the position of trustee continues to be a popular one. "The time it takes for board members to educate [themselves] has increased tremendously in the last 10 years," says Raven. "But we are fortunate to have a list of 80 to 90 people waiting in line. At this point . . . [they believe] it's an honor to participate."

Most board members view compliance with Sarbanes-Oxley as an opportunity to prove to the community that they are committed to good governance. "It really provides hospitals and health systems with an opportunity to . . . tell people what they're doing and why," says Walker. "Even though it's not required to have this level of scrutiny, it's the responsible thing to do."

Establishing Principles for Hospital-Physician Joint Ventures

By James Lifton and L. Edward Bryant Jr.

When properly structured, joint ventures can increase access to capital as well as clinical and management resources, while offering financial incentives for investors. Improperly structured, however, they can lead to poor financial results, hard feelings between participants, and disrepute in the community. Regulatory and legal problems can even arise, since Medicare has declared certain hospital-physician relationships unlawful.

Typical Joint Ventures

Hospital joint ventures with physicians typically involve procedures that generate a technical, or facility use, fee from Medicare and other payers. Ambulatory surgery centers, endoscopy suites, and imaging centers are common examples.

In the face of reduced professional fees, physicians may seek to maintain their income through facility ownership, which generates a facility fee. Hospitals may decide to participate in such joint ventures, even though they reduce hospital revenue, on the rationale

James Lifton is principal consultant, Policy Studies Inc., Chicago. L. Edward Bryant Jr. is partner, Gardner, Carton & Douglas, Chicago.

that "half is better than none"—assuming that the physicians would find another partner or move ahead alone if the hospital was unwilling to participate.

The hospital may also be able to set conditions on its partnership with physicians—for example, resolving concerns about "cherry-picking," a business practice where physicians refer paying patients to the joint venture and send low-pay or uninsured patients to the hospital or wholly owned hospital facility.

A typical joint venture is structured as a limited liability company (LLC). Under this non-taxable structure, income passes directly through to the owners, which benefits both physicians and hospitals. For taxable owners, such as physicians, the income is not subject to "double taxation" (where earnings are taxable both to the corporation and to the individual investor). And for a nonprofit entity, such as a hospital, being a partner in an LLC strengthens its financial status because its share of the income is tax exempt.

The Board's Role in Joint Ventures

Board involvement and support for a joint venture is important because of the high stakes involved. Moreover, because a joint venture typically involves the creation of a new legal entity, board approval is required. With hospitals and physicians as co-investors in a joint venture, the hospital will have more at risk than its capital investment; if the venture does not work out, it may also be jeopardizing the hard-won goodwill of key physicians.

A board-adopted policy, along with a set of principles to guide hospital participation, can help maximize the benefits of joint ventures while minimizing the associated risks.

A Mindset for Joint Ventures

To create the right mindset for determining joint venture principles, think about the implications in practical terms. Assume that the transaction and resulting joint venture will:

- *Be entered into for profit.* Certainly the expectations of physician investors will be to realize a profit. However, not all enterprises in health care can be profitable. Keep in mind that no investment vehicle will make a bad business venture into a good one. Is the business fundamentally sound? Are the forecasted financial results realistic?

- *Be subject to public scrutiny.* Would it embarrass the organization if the press, government or non-investing physicians were to learn details of the joint venture? Worse yet, would it put the organization in legal jeopardy?
- *Have to be unwound.* Investors may need to exit the deal, and defining the exit terms in advance makes this easier for everyone concerned. Keep in mind that, in most instances, the hospital will not be able to bail out the physician investors.
- *Set a precedent for other deals.* Ask yourself: "Would we do the next joint venture the same way we did this one?" If the answer is no, then it's probably best not to do it that way the first time.

Some Issues to Consider

The following issues and questions point out principles that typically need to be investigated regarding joint venture structures and participation:

1. *Business activity.* Is the proposed business one that, by law, can be owned by a hospital and physicians who refer their patients to it? For instance, will it "practice medicine" or is it a "designated health service" under the Stark Law?
2. *Scope of businesses.* Can the parties define the businesses in which they are willing to invest, and those they are not? Will the hospital put existing, wholly owned services into a joint venture? If so, under what circumstances?
3. *Ownership.* Will the hospital accept less than 51 percent ownership? If so, under what circumstances? Will the hospital's ownership stakes render income from the joint venture taxable to the hospital?
4. *Control.* Will control reflect the ownership percentages? Will the venture have a board or will the owners control it directly?
5. *Investors.* Will there be any restrictions on investors? For instance, if a group of orthopedic surgeons proposes to enter

into a joint venture with the hospital, will the hospital require that the opportunity be open to all orthopedists on the medical staff at the time? What about orthopedists who subsequently join the staff? Will for-profit firms, such as a management company, be allowed as investors?

6. *Reserved powers/guarantees.* Over what must the hospital reserve powers? (A Catholic hospital, for instance, would have to ensure compliance with the Ethical and Religious Directives for Catholic Health Care Services.) Will the hospital require, and be willing to enter into non-competition agreements prohibiting the parties from investing in other, competing ventures? Will physicians need to be given control over clinical standards?

7. *Payment and free care.* What will the joint venture's policy be regarding patients who cannot afford to pay for services? Will the joint venture be required to accept Medicare and Medicaid patients? Concerns about cherry-picking can be addressed by establishing a charity care policy for all hospital joint ventures.

8. *Valuations.* Are participants willing to deal with each other on an "arm's length" basis, that is, using objective third-party valuations of assets going into the deal and unwinding it? Although this arrangement adds expense, it also protects all parties under both the Medicare laws and Internal Revenue Code.

9. *Unwind provisions.* All businesses with two or more owners need unwind provisions written into the organizational documents. Have the parties considered what might require the deal to be unwound and how each scenario would be addressed? Are these various situations fully addressed in the organizational documents?

10. *Structuring the joint venture.* Are there alternatives to a joint venture? A joint venture should be viewed as a "means"—the best means—not an "end." There are many ways to share rewards, but true joint ventures require sharing risks as well.

Getting Started

As with many challenges facing health care leadership, commitment and common sense are good places to start:

- Commit to developing (or reviewing) the organization's policy on joint venture participation.
- Identify a working group that can consider the issues listed above.
- Consider the hospital's circumstances and, perhaps, its past experience.
- Develop a standard policy format for the organization.

Legal counsel and the hospital's business advisors can provide feedback on the policy draft, offer input on additional issues to consider and ensure that the policy works from legal and business perspectives. The resulting joint venture policy and principles will support timely, informed, consistent and fair joint ventures, as well as legal and regulatory compliance.

Where's the Money?

By Karen Sandrick

*Small rural hospitals have more access to capital
than they might think.*

When it comes to gaining access to affordable capital, many small
rural hospitals give up before they even try. The board and administrators believe they will never be able to get a favorable bond
rating because the big three rating agencies—Standard and Poor's,
Moody's, and Fitch—equate small size with high risk. They may
also believe they will never get investment bankers interested in
shepherding a bond issue through the financial markets because the
paper will just be too hard to sell to institutional investors.

Many small, rural hospitals therefore continue to scrimp and
save, dip into their endowments, or get an occasional loan from a
local bank that doesn't really understand health care dynamics or
isn't set up to make long-term, fixed-rate loans. Hospital management and boards are left hoping that a larger financial institution
with deeper pockets buys the bank.

In the process, these hospitals may end up relegating themselves
to the absolute minimum number and scope of capital projects they
need to survive. Rather than plan renovations or expansions that
will help them flourish, small and rural hospitals focus on little
projects that will keep the linoleum on the floors and the tiles on

---

Karen Sandrick is a Chicago-based health care writer.

the ceiling. No doubt about it: Access to affordable capital is limited for small, rural institutions. But financially viable hospitals with fewer than 100 beds can and do get outside financing for large-scale projects.

"Over the better part of 30 years, I've seen tiny hospitals make an investment of $1 million, $3 million, $5 million and have a dramatic effect on their ability to expand their services and recapture patients," says Steve Weyl, director of the law firm Sheehan, Phinney, Bass & Green, Manchester, New Hampshire, and chair of its Healthcare Practice Group. And it's possible for them to get this financing at reasonable costs.

For example, in the last few years:

- Community Memorial Hospital, a facility with fewer than 25 beds in Oconto Falls, Wisconsin, raised $9 million for its first capital renovation by selling non-rated bonds to institutional investors at an average interest rate slightly over 7 percent.
- Because of its strong financial performance—more than 120 days cash on hand—and an affiliation with the Gundersen Clinic outside Lacrosse, 53-bed Vernon (WI) Memorial Hospital got an investment-grade rating on a $13 million bond issue at an interest rate in the neighborhood of 6.5 percent.
- Twenty-five-bed Shoshone Medical Center, Kellogg, Idaho, secured $18 million in outside financing, locking in a low-cost, privately placed Ginnie Mae collateralized direct loan that eliminated the negative arbitrage associated with a bond financing, reducing its closing costs by $100,000, and captured an interest rate of less than 6 percent.

The ability of small, rural hospitals to access capital has been hampered by the perception that these facilities are teetering on the edge of solvency. But there are a number of alternative funding structures for fiscally sound institutions, such as bank-qualified bond issues, letters of credit and obligated group financings. Even some struggling small, rural hospitals can improve their overall financial performance and creditworthiness through U.S. Department of Housing and Urban Development (HUD) mortgage insurance programs. But hospitals often don't know about these options.

"Small and rural hospital [managers and boards] don't have a sense of what the possibilities are. That's nobody's fault. It's just because they haven't been around investment bankers and capital markets and haven't understood that there are strategies they can implement at one time, or over the course of time, to borrow money at favorable tax-exempt rates of interest," says Weyl.

In fact, he adds, "If a hospital's future configuration involves capital expenditures for projects that are reasonable and will generate revenue, it most likely will find someone to fund the projects in some form. The question is, what is the best way to do it?"

Financing Strategies

Small, rural hospitals don't have as many financing options as their larger counterparts, and those options they do have differ from state to state.

In Maine, small, rural hospitals can improve their creditworthiness by joining pools of other borrowers. This strategy is not common, and it can be chancy in states where financial status can't sustain a high credit rating. But if a state has an "AA" rating, bonds issued with some limited reserves to fund expenses will carry an "A" rating for a hospital that otherwise couldn't come near that category.

Likewise, bank-qualified bonds are not widely available because they depend on the existence of a statewide authority for issuing tax-exempt debt. Nevertheless, they provide a gateway to capital for hospitals that have a reasonable record of financial performance—for example, enough revenue to generate 1.25 times their annual debt service coverage over the course of a loan and about 50 days cash on the balance sheet—and provided they are seeking less than $10 million in debt financing, says Don A. Carlson Jr., senior managing director, Ziegler Capital Markets Group, Chicago. He explains that, because of a provision in the 1986 tax reform act, commercial banks can purchase up to $10 million of tax-exempt bonds from a tax-exempt borrower, such as a city or county, on behalf of a hospital in any one calendar year.

A successful strategy for small hospitals in states without a central conduit for issuing debt, such as New Hampshire, is a partnership with a local bank that doesn't lend money for tax purposes but provides support for the loan in the form of a letter of credit, says Weyl. His firm recently closed an $8 million transaction between a non-rated hospital and a non-rated commercial bank that linked with a nationally rated bank to issue "A"-rated debt. Instead of making an $8 million taxable commercial loan to the hospital, the bank issued a letter of credit for which it charged a fee. The bank therefore generated income from letter of credit fees, and the hospital not only received a rating it would not otherwise merit, it also obtained financing at a lower-than-anticipated interest rate by issuing debt on a variable rate basis, which currently carries incredibly low interest rates—around 2 percent or 2.5 percent. "Variable rates can go up in the future, but historically, they have never averaged more than 3.5 percent over a 10-year period, so this is a fairly inexpensive way to borrow," Weyl says.

Although rarely used, the Rural Development Program run by the U.S. Department of Agriculture offers limited amounts of capital through grants ($40,000 to $50,000 per institution); loans (up to $7 million divided among all hospitals); and guaranteed, equity-linked loans (beginning at $25 million) to small hospitals that compete against other hospitals for funding on a state-by-state basis.

Allying with a health care partner is another way for small, rural hospitals to access capital. An alliance with a larger health care institution may serve as a direct source of capital financing. Large academic medical centers may provide funding to small, rural hospital affiliates they see as feeders to their secondary and tertiary care practices. Obligated group financings, which couple small rural hospitals with large institutions for economic purposes, strengthen the small hospitals' financial picture in the investment community by focusing investors on the blended credit of the entire group.

"If you have a hospital with a $5 million bottom line and two little hospitals that just break even, you look at the debt capacity of the larger hospital, which almost cross guarantees the debt for small hospitals," Weyl explains.

The HUD Stealth Program

One of the most effective routes to low-cost capital for small, rural hospitals is the least well-known—HUD's 242 Federal Housing

Administration (FHA) mortgage insurance and Critical Access Hospital (CAH) programs. Many hospital CEOs and CFOs have never heard of CAH, and they tend to shrug off FHA mortgage insurance, thinking it's too time-consuming, difficult to navigate and restricted to hospitals in New York state.

Although 80 percent of the 242 program's insurance portfolio includes hospitals in the state of New York, the FHA has operated in 40 states and Puerto Rico since it was created in 1968. And the FHA is actively working to diversify its portfolio geographically, says Christopher D. Boesen, director of the HUD Office of Insured Health Care Facilities, Washington, D.C.

"Our program isn't limited," he says. "We don't have a cap on how many hospitals we can help. We don't have a cap on how large the mortgages can be. There's no ceiling on that. Any hospital we believe is a needed facility and can pay its mortgage for 25 years [that] applies, we're going to approve," Boesen stresses.

And just as FHA's single family program helps homebuyers borrow money to purchase a house, the 242 program allows acute care facilities to build, refinance, modernize, remodel, purchase capital equipment or expand, by guaranteeing that lenders will be repaid. With an FHA-insured mortgage note, a hospital can get an "AA" rating on a bond issued from one of the rating agencies. To enhance the marketability of the bonds even further, the hospital may then obtain private bond insurance and raise the rating to "AAA," explains Carlson.

"Even 'BBB'-rated hospitals are pursuing FHA insurance because of the economics," says Stephen R. Pack, managing director of the Health Care Public Finance Group, Bank of America, New York City. "When you factor in the spread between a 'BBB' health care uninsured and an FHA-insured deal with commercial bond insurance as a wrap on top, a hospital can get a full 'AAA' rating. When you factor in the 50 basis points and the fees paid to FHA, the hospital is still way ahead economically," Pack says.

The CAH program, which is part of the Medicare Rural Hospital Flexibility Plan approved by Congress in the Balanced Budget Act of 1997, increases the Medicare revenue stream and fast-tracks FHA mortgage insurance for small and rural facilities that are willing to limit their inpatient capacity by carrying only 15 acute care beds and limiting inpatient stays to an average of 98 hours. "In return for reducing the inpatient load, converting to an outpatient mode of care, and providing services necessary to support physicians in the community, Congress allows hospitals to go back on cost-based reimbursement," explains Charles Davis, who manages the program.

As a result of CAH, one hospital was able to borrow $20 million for new construction at an interest rate of 5.5 percent, which saved $8.2 million over the life of the loan, says Boesen. CAH status allowed 46-year-old Shoshone Medical Center to build a new 48,000-square-foot, 25-bed facility, overcoming the hospital's negatives in the eyes of potential investors, such as its limited balance sheet and restricted physician base, as well as the project's location on a SuperFund site, recalls Alan Richman, president and CEO of InnoVative Capital, LLC, a Springfield, Pennsylvania–based mortgage banking and financial advisory service for rural, community and critical access hospitals.

Downsizing to meet CAH criteria also made it easier for two small, rural hospitals to raise money in the debt markets even though they had been losing money. Some $9 million worth of bonds were well-received by investors at least partly because Community Hospital of Oconto Falls was viewed as a critical access institution, Carlson says. In addition to an affiliation with Howard Young Medical Center, which has a "BBB" rating, critical access status allowed 25-bed Eagle River (WI) Hospital to obtain private bond insurance guaranteeing the principal and interest on an $11.6 million bond issue, he adds.

HUD deals can be somewhat expensive, Carlson points out. FHA charges one-half of 1 percent annually for its insurance premium and three-tenths of a percent for its application fee. On top of that are the financing costs associated with underwriting bonds, etc. "But you're getting pretty low interest rate financing because of the FHA guarantee and in some cases the third-party insurance wrap over that," Carlson says.

HUD transactions also have been known to take as long as 12 to 18 months to wend their way through an analysis of audited financials, underwriting, a preapplication assessment of architectural plans, legal and engineering reports, and the application itself. But HUD is streamlining its operations, cutting the mortgage insurance process for critical access hospitals in half.

"Especially in rural areas, people have been afraid of a program like CAH," says Davis. "They think it's very complicated, and they don't see themselves as having the expertise to apply and successfully navigate through the process. But there's a lot of help out there from this office and banking institutions that are active in this program." (See "CAH Information" below.)

Trustees at the Threshold

From a board perspective, being able to ascertain whether or not a hospital can access capital in the future is the threshold question because the long-term financial viability of the institution in large part will be driven by its ability to obtain financing, says Carlson. "Maybe a hospital won't need capital this year or next year, but at some point, to keep up with technological changes, the aging of the population, and the sophistication of services and equipment, it will need to borrow. And if it can't, it will need to affiliate or merge with an organization that can," he says.

Fortunately, although small and rural hospitals may not have many financing choices, they shouldn't assume they won't be able to borrow when they need to. "It may take some creativity and work, but bankers who specialize in this area have a good record of raising money for these hospitals," says Weyl.

Boards typically aren't involved in day-to-day management of a financing plan but approve an overall concept, letting the hospital CFO and finance committee sort through the details of debt structuring. But "to preserve stewardship of a hospital on a local basis, it's incumbent on the board to understand and fully evaluate what the hospital is getting into, not only from a financial commitment but also from an operational standpoint and a legal perspective. It comes down to an issue of vigilance," says Richman.

CAH Information

Hospitals interested in the Department of Housing and Urban Development's Critical Access status may call (877) 263-0763; contact the program's manager, Charles Davis, at (202) 708-0599; or visit the HUD Web site at www.hud.gov.

In order to determine whether the hospital will be able to pay back debt, trustees need to receive realistic projections about the likelihood that capital projects will generate revenue and help the hospital thrive in the marketplace. "Trustees need to know what the financial effects are, what the current debt service requirement is, what ratios bond underwriters look for, how new monies will be used for expansion, and how specific projects are being justified," says Ben Wheeler, board treasurer for 62-bed Monadnock Community Hospital, Peterborough, New Hampshire.

With that information under their belts, trustees can turn to capital outlets with some degree of confidence. For many small, rural hospitals that need to borrow, says Weyl, "There's going to be a buyer out there somewhere, and because rates are low, this is a good time to do it."

Mission Possible:
A Financial Assistance Policy

By Dina Maas

As the number of uninsured and underinsured patients continues to increase in the United States, financial assistance policies in health care organizations are playing an increasingly important role in making sure patients receive the care they need with little or no financial burden. If these policies are going to work, however, all staff must be well-educated about them and patients must have easy access to both policy information and the application process.

Alegent Health, a not-for-profit health care system based in Omaha, Nebraska, operates nine acute care hospitals in Nebraska and southwestern Iowa. The system has created a financial assistance policy that ties in closely to its mission.

"The mission of Alegent Health is to further the healing ministry of Jesus Christ," explains Scott Wooten, senior vice president and chief financial officer for the system. "We see all people as children of God and deserving of dignity and respect at all times, including when accessing health care. Our financial assistance policy is one way we live this belief, allowing individuals and families without the necessary resources to pay for their health care by receiving care at a lesser cost or no cost, depending on their circumstances."

Dina Maas is coordinator of corporate communications for Alegent Health, Omaha, Nebraska.

When first developing its financial assistance policy, Alegent Health wanted a design that worked directly with patients to find solutions. Tim Meier, chief financial officer at Alegent Health Bergan Mercy Medical Center in Omaha, was part of the team that designed the policy. He says, "We used a combination of what we felt were best practices across the nation and what we felt worked best for our patient population."

For instance, when the policy was first revised in 2001, Alegent was using the federal poverty guidelines. However, Catholic Health Initiatives, which is a sponsor of Alegent Health, was using U.S. Department of Housing and Urban Development (HUD) geographic low-income guidelines, so Alegent decided to adopt that practice into its policy.

"We felt it was a better fit with our mission," Meier says. "HUD guidelines are not based on a 'one-size-fits-all' solution and [they] allow Alegent Health to get specific income levels for our service area. We also added a catastrophic clause, which is a unique aspect of our financial assistance policy."

The catastrophic clause limits the amount of a patient's bill to no more than 20 percent of his or her income. For example, a former patient at Alegent Health had an annual income of $150,000 and had good health care coverage. However, he needed some medically necessary services that were not covered by his particular health plan, and ended up with a bill of $100,000.

Therefore, the catastrophic clause went into effect and the patient was only responsible for $30,000 of the bill. The clause also allows Alegent Health to work with patients to set up a bank loan with an interest rate that fluctuates with the prime rate. While the catastrophic clause is not used often, it provides an important safety net for patients.

Beyond the catastrophic clause, patients qualify for the policy's assistance for medically necessary procedures based on their income levels and HUD guidelines. The policy works on a graduated scale covering a 30 percent to 100 percent write-off. This scale is also based on family size, which means the more people there are in a family, the more income that family can make and still qualify for assistance.

An interactive application process can be found online, which is one of the more unusual aspects of the plan. Patients can complete the online form and immediately find out whether they qualify for financial assistance and, if so, at what percentage. The process is very similar to that of online mortgage calculators.

And, since Alegent Health must have proof of income before approving financial aid, the online process allows patients to upload scanned documents that provide proof of their income and savings.

Meier also stresses the importance of staff education about the policy at every level of the organization, in both hospitals and clinics. He says the policy will not accomplish its purpose unless everyone in the organization can talk knowledgeably about it.

Alegent Health has also spent a considerable amount of time ensuring that patients are well-informed about the policy, what it might mean for them and how to use it. Brochures and application forms are available at every point of registration, and the policy is built into the preregistration process.

Financial assistance information is also printed on billing statements and anyone calling Alegent Health for information will be able to speak immediately to a knowledgeable employee.

Setting up or revising a financial assistance policy can be a complex process and the board needs to understand it. "It is very important for the board of directors to get involved and stay involved," Meier advises. "They need to continue to monitor the policy even after it is established to make sure it is meeting the changing needs of the patient population."

Lawrence J. Beckman, Alegent Health's board chair, says, "Our board is fully cognizant of the ever-growing population of uninsured and underinsured [people] in our communities. We feel it is essential that this population receive a discount similar to what we give contracted payers. Our financial assistance policy is an extension of our mission and a reflection of our commitment to promote community health."

Through continued monitoring of its patient population, Alegent Health also realized that some patients who didn't qualify for financial assistance did not have insurance coverage, so last May, the system added a self-pay discount clause to its existing policy.

Funding a financial assistance policy is yet another challenge. Alegent Health does not fund its financial assistance policy per se; rather, it is budgeted for in aggregate. Some states maintain funds to help hospitals fund their financial assistance policies, but neither Nebraska nor Iowa have such funds.

The biggest challenge the nation's health care system faces is its cost. Alegent Health's CEO, Wayne A. Sensor, says, "As we focus on the future of health care, we must not lose sight of the underserved in our communities, who need our help now. The proactive approach we take with our financial assistance policy is just one example of our commitment to assisting patients with high medical bills. No one who comes through our doors is denied access to the high-quality health care that they need—no matter their ability to pay."

PART FIVE

Quality

Hospital Governing Boards and Quality of Care: A Call to Responsibility

By the National Quality Forum

It is well-established that hospital governing boards have responsibility for the quality of care provided in the institutions they govern.[1] However, hospital boards generally have been rather passive in their approach to quality improvement, leaving this responsibility to the medical staff or delegating it to the quality committee of the board.

The board's role in ensuring quality of care is of increasing importance as public reporting of quality data and rewarding performance activities become more prevalent; however, board members often express confusion and uncertainty about what exactly they need to do to fulfill their responsibilities in this regard. Indeed, the specific responsibilities of hospital governing boards for improving quality and the most effective methods by which boards can assure that management is fulfilling its obligation regarding quality of care are not well-defined. More clearly defining these responsibilities would likely benefit hospital quality of care.

At present, the Joint Commission sets forth a set of expectations and responsibilities for hospital boards, and various hospital governance experts promote algorithms detailing board responsibilities. However, there is no comprehensive, consensually produced guidance

---

This article was contributed to *Trustee* by the National Quality Forum, Washington, D.C.

available for trustees who wish to measure the quality of their governance against objective standards. This is especially so in the area of clinical quality improvement.

National Quality Forum Workshop on the Role of Hospital Trustees in Quality Improvement

During the past two years, the National Quality Forum (NQF), Washington, D.C., has been approached by multiple entities about whether it would be willing to articulate specific expectations of boards of trustees regarding their roles and responsibilities and the degree of their oversight for quality improvement.

On March 30, 2004, the NQF convened a meeting to help determine how it might best help hospital trustees monitor their governance of and accomplish their obligations for quality improvement. In light of recent reports raising concerns about patient safety and health care quality, the meeting especially focused on three questions:

1. What strategies and tactics should boards employ to best fulfill their responsibility for improving the quality and safety of care in their facilities?
2. How can hospital governing boards assure that facility management is fulfilling its obligations regarding quality improvement?
3. How can the NQF help motivate and support hospital trustees in the accomplishment of their obligations regarding health care quality improvement? More specifically, what role might the NQF play in articulating expectations, strategies or standards regarding the role and responsibility of boards of trustees in improving quality and safety?

One of the recommendations of the participants at the NQF Workshop on Hospital Governance and Quality Improvement was that the NQF should issue a "Call to Responsibility" for hospital governing boards.

Following the workshop, the NQF prepared a draft statement, which then underwent review by the workshop participants. The statement then was reviewed and amended per widespread public and NQF member comment before its ultimate endorsement by the NQF Board of Directors.

Call to Responsibility

The National Quality Forum, representing nearly 300 consumer, health care provider, health care payer and other organizations, endorsed the following "Call to Responsibility" for hospital governing boards on Dec. 2, 2004:

Principles for Boards of Trustees

The NQF strongly encourages hospital governing boards to become actively engaged in quality improvement. The NQF calls upon hospital governing boards to review their policies and practices to make sure that they are consistent with the following principles. The NQF recognizes that hospital boards vary widely in composition and governance authority but believes that these principles are intended to apply to all boards:

1. *Hospital governing boards play a vital role in monitoring and improving hospital care to ensure that it is safe, beneficial, patient-centered, timely, efficient and equitable.[2] Indeed, hospital governing boards are responsible for ensuring the quality of health care provided in their institutions.[3] To fulfill their role in ensuring quality, hospital governing boards should:*
   a. Ensure that health care quality is a paramount priority and a primary focus of board activities. Pragmatically, boards may wish to take a more active role in ensuring quality by beginning with a focus on patient safety, recognizing that safety is a subset of quality and that the infrastructure needed to ensure safety is materially the same as that needed to ensure high quality.
   b. Prominently place patient safety and quality issues (e.g., reviewing errors and their impact on hospital resources) on board meeting agendas to ensure that the treatment by board chairs accorded to these issues equals—or exceeds—that accorded to finances.
   c. Proactively oversee and evaluate patient safety and health care outcomes and the creation of a culture of safety by engaging in patient safety and quality improvement projects, establishing governance practices that support a system of performance measurement and quality improvement, and holding

management accountable for poor performance, adverse outcomes and their remedies.

d. Ensure that a system of performance measurement and quality improvement is in place and that credible results enable the evaluation of the organization's effectiveness.

e. Recognize physicians' roles, the role of the medical staff within the hospital, and the roles of nursing executives and other clinical leaders (e.g., pharmacists, infection control professionals) in achieving quality by engaging them in quality improvement efforts.

f. Assure that hospital leadership adopts human resource policies and physician staff bylaws that articulate specific expectations of staff's involvement in quality improvement, adheres to hospital policies designed to ensure the safety of patients and staff, and receives adequate training (e.g., educational preparation, technical competency and continuing education) in quality-related content areas (e.g., performance measurement, quality improvement).

g. Ensure that hospital management is capable of and focused on the analysis and improvement of organizational design that supports the ongoing, systematic assessment and optimization of patient safety and quality of care, including the facilitation of internal reporting mechanisms between management and line staff, and that resources are made available for this purpose.

h. Align budget development and financial resources with the organization's quality and patient safety goals to ensure dynamic and ongoing review and consideration of such priorities—and plans for continuous improvement—when developing and executing capital budgets and other financial strategies and decisions.

i. Actively support management's negotiation of payment contracts that do not penalize the organization for its investment in quality and safety, recognizing that such investments are equal to, if not more important than, those designated for service capacity and/or facility improvements.

2. *To enable effective evaluation of their own role in enhancing quality, hospital governing boards should:*

a. Advocate for diverse board composition with specific expertise in quality, patient safety and clinical areas including, but not limited to, physicians, nurses, industrial engineers, pharmacists, consumers and others with qualifications in modern business management, organizational design, and health care administration.

b. Review their own performance—individually and collectively through established measures developed for this purpose—in improving hospital care by assessing the extent to which the board's oversight and leadership influences quality and safety in the facility.

3. *Hospital governing boards should develop "quality literacy" regarding patient safety, clinical care and health care outcomes. This literacy should:*

a. At a minimum, include education in the infrastructure of patient safety, health care quality and performance measurement, incorporating clinical education, as appropriate, as well as the business case for quality.

b. Recognize the role of the board of trustees in representing consumers and the community it serves.

c. Be comparable and akin to their knowledge and understanding of the institution's financial health and well-being vis-á-vis the Sarbanes-Oxley Act.[4]

d. Where appropriate, utilize existing organizations (e.g., the Governance Institute, the Health Care Trustee Institute, the Center for Healthcare Governance, the Joint Commission) and their resources to provide courses, training and information to assist in fulfilling these expectations for quality literacy. In instances where existing tools and resources are not available, boards should collaborate with organizations to develop and commission such tools.

4. *Hospital governing boards should oversee and be accountable for their institutions' participation and performance in national quality measurement efforts and subsequent quality improvement activities.*

a. Hospital boards should ensure that their participation in national quality improvement activities focus on nationally agreed-upon priorities[5] and those that are critical to their own institution.

b. Participation in one or more existing efforts, including, but not limited to, the Hospital Quality Alliance,[6] NQF-endorsed national voluntary consensus standards,[7] Joint Commission National Patient Safety Goals,[8] the Leapfrog Group and other national performance reporting/benchmarking systems[9] should be realized.

c. Performance data derived from participation in national quality improvement efforts and presented by appropriate hospital personnel (e.g., chief medical officer, nurse executives, pharmacists) need to be consistently reviewed by the board, no less frequently than the board reviews the institution's financial metrics, to determine performance and drive improvements in patient safety and health care quality.

d. Based on such data, a determination of the cost implications of adverse events and poor performance that have an impact on profitability and compromise organizational performance—and an understanding that quality improvements can result in cost savings—should be calculated, including, but not limited to, legal, personnel, regulatory and marketing costs.

e. Performance should be evaluated in the context of the six NQF aims (i.e., safe, beneficial, patient-centered, timely, efficient and equitable) for quality improvement.

f. Hospital boards should hold accountable and require full and complete explanations from management when safety and quality performance levels differ significantly from national benchmarks or fall below expectations, with specific attention devoted to the organization's plan for improvement (e.g., its development, performance expectations, and the basis on which expectations are established). Boards should then monitor management's progress with these plans at least quarterly and consider action if shortfalls are not eliminated in a timely manner.

g. In the context of these performance levels, hospital boards should facilitate the adoption of incentive programs for hospital executives and management based on explicit rewards for results and related quality improvements.

Principles for Other Hospital Stakeholders

Although hospital governing boards play a pivotal role in improving patient safety and health care outcomes, it should be recognized that other hospital stakeholders influence successful hospital governance. To this end, the NQF calls upon other hospital stakeholders to support boards of trustees and hospitals in this enterprise.

1. *Policy-making organizations responsible for establishing standards and/or developing regulations in this area should ensure currency with scientific evidence and federal and/or state regulations.*
   a. Policymakers should ensure that any regulations in this area address the highest standards for the role of hospital governing boards in quality improvement.
   b. Specifically, the Joint Commission and the Centers for Medicare & Medicaid Services (CMS) should continue to review and update their hospital accreditation standards to ensure currency, consistency and alignment.

2. *Consumers—both individually and in organized forums—should expect hospitals' boards of trustees to represent their interests in overseeing quality of care.*
   a. Consumers should expect to be represented on boards and/or be vocal to the board about their experiences and expectations with hospital care.
   b. Consumers should urge and encourage hospitals in their community to participate in local, regional and national public reporting initiatives.

3. *Payers (i.e., public and private entities) should align payment systems with hospital quality and safety improvements.*
   a. Purchasers and health insurance plans should consider the role of hospital governing boards in quality improvement, including public accountability, in their contracting and purchasing arrangements (e.g., "shared savings" arrangements).
   b. They should also consider the impact of improvements in safety and quality on payment mechanisms (e.g., analyzing and evaluating the quality and safety ramifications of all major financial negotiations, rewarding for performance).

Future Action

In approving this document, the NQF Board of Directors agreed that it should be distributed widely with the expectation that hospital trustees exert their appropriate role in quality improvement. This document will be reviewed periodically for the need to update it.

Conclusion

The business of hospitals is to provide high-quality, safe health care. It is critical that trustees endeavor to collect and analyze performance measurement results as often as they do financial results and with as much rigor. It is not sufficient for boards to declare "zero tolerance" for medical errors. To be good stewards of their hospitals, boards cannot simply leave the business of health care to the professionals; instead, they should judge quality using standardized measures of performance and judge management accordingly.

Workshop Participants

- Kenneth W. Kizer, M.D., M.P.H. (Co-Convener)
  President and CEO, National Quality Forum, Washington, DC

- Eric D. Lister, M.D. (Co-Convener)
  Healthcare Trustee Institute and Ki Associates, Portsmouth, NH

- Daniel T. Roble, J.D. (Co-Convener)
  Ropes & Gray LLP, Boston

- Harris Berman, M.D.
  Tufts University School of Medicine, Boston

- Carmella Bocchino, R.N., M.B.A.
  America's Health Insurance Plans, Washington, DC

- Frank E. Carlton, M.D.
  Memorial Health University Medical Center, Savannah, GA

- Gordon R. Clark, M.B.A.
  The Governance Institute, San Diego

- Carmela Coyle
  American Hospital Association, Washington, DC

Continued →

- Robert M. Dickler
  Association of American Medical Colleges, Washington, DC
- Richard de Filippi, Ph.D.
  Cambridge Health Alliance, Cambridge, MA
- Irene Fraser, Ph.D.
  Agency for Healthcare Research and Quality, Rockville, MD
- John R. Griffith
  University of Michigan, School of Public Health, Ann Arbor, MI
- Neil Jesuele
  American Hospital Association, Washington, DC
- Charles N. Kahn lll
  Federation of American Hospitals, Washington, DC
- James R. Knickman, Ph.D.
  The Robert Wood Johnson Foundation, Princeton, NJ
- David J. Lansky, Ph.D.
  FACCT-Foundation for Accountability, Portland, OR
- Russell Massaro, M.D.
  Joint Commission, Oakbrook Terrace, IL
- Catherine E. McDermott
  National Committee for Quality Health Care, Washington, DC
- Linda Miller
  Volunteer Trustees of Not-for-Profit Hospitals, Washington, DC
- Woodrow A. Myers Jr., M.D., M.B.A.
  WellPoint Health Networks, Thousand Oaks, CA
- Debra L. Ness
  National Partnership for Women & Families, Washington, DC
- James E. Orlikoff, M.A.
  Orlikoff & Associates Inc., Chicago
- Karen Titlow, M.A., P.T.
  Leapfrog Group, Washington, DC
- Susan Van Gelder
  Federation of American Hospitals, Washington, DC
- National Quality Forum Staff:

  Ellen T. Kurtzman, R.N., M.P.H.
  Senior Program Director

  Christine M. Page-Lopez
  Research Assistant

References

1. Lister E, Cameron DL: The role of the board in assuring quality and driving major change initiatives—part 1: maintaining organizational integrity. *Group Practice Journal,* 50:13–20, 2001.

2. In *Crossing the Quality Chasm: A New Health System for the 21st Century* (National Academies Press 2001), the Institute of Medicine identifies six aims of the health care quality system: that it should be safe, effective, efficient, timely, patient centered and equitable. In 2002, the NQF endorsed the consensus document, "A National Framework for Healthcare Quality Measurement and Reporting," which lays out similar aims for the health care system but states that one aim should be beneficial, which encompasses but also goes beyond effectiveness.

3. This responsibility can be delegated to a hospital-level committee that reports directly to the board in those cases where an institution is part of a larger multihospital system.

4. On July 30, 2002, President George W. Bush signed into law the Sarbanes-Oxley Act of 2002, which added many new—and revised many existing—provisions of the federal securities laws. To protect the interests of investors and, more generally, the public, this federal law establishes the status, duties, composition, powers, rules and reporting of boards for all public companies that are subject to securities law. See www.sec.gov/divisions/corpfin/forms/exchange.shtml. Last accessed Jan. 30, 2005.

5. National Priorities for Healthcare Quality Measurement and Reporting. Washington, D.C.: NQF, 2004.

6. The Hospital Quality Alliance was initiated in December 2002 by the American Hospital Association, the Federation of American Hospitals and the Association of American Medical Colleges. Since that time, a number of additional organizations have joined this effort to make critical information about hospital performance accessible to the public: the Joint Commission, NQF, CMS, the Agency for Healthcare Research and Quality, the American Medical Association, the Consumer-Purchaser Disclosure Group, the AFL-CIO, AARP, the National Association of Children's Hospitals and Related Institutions, the American Nurses Association and others.

Continued →

7. To date, NQF has endorsed national voluntary consensus standards for acute care hospitals, nursing homes, cardiac surgery, nursing and diabetes, and has endorsed national consensus standards on safe practices for better health care and serious reportable events in health care. Additionally, NQF has endorsed frameworks for a national health care quality and measurement and hospital performance evaluation.

8. As of Jan. 1, 2004, all Joint Commission–accredited health care organizations began to be surveyed for the implementation of the 2004 National Patient Safety Goals.

9. National performance reporting/benchmarking systems include those operated by the Joint Commission, CMS, the American College of Cardiology, the Society for Thoracic Surgeons, the Vermont Oxford Network, the American College of Surgeons, the Leapfrog Group and others.

Understanding and Improving Clinical Quality: The Role of Trustees

By James L. Reinertsen, M.D.

Hospital trustees often express uncertainty about their role in overseeing and improving the quality of their hospitals' services, particularly when it comes to clinical measures. At a recent American Governance & Leadership Group conference for trustees, administrators and medical staff leaders from hospitals across the country, when the subject turned to improving intensive care services, evidence-based medical care, risk of hospital-acquired infections and other clinical matters, typical trustee reactions were:

"These clinical quality problems are the job of the doctors, nurses and administrators. I wouldn't know the first thing about those issues. I'm a banker. The board's job is just to make sure that our physicians are excellent and credentialed properly, and then the clinical quality should take care of itself. Isn't that right?"

And, "At our last board meeting, the [information] packet included 322 separate so-called 'quality indicators,' ranging from the time to answer a call button on 5 West to the percentage of heart attack patients who received aspirin, to the hospital's overall mortality rate. I have no idea what all these things mean and what's

---

James L. Reinertsen, M.D., is president, The Reinertsen Group, Alta, Wyoming, and senior fellow, the Institute for Healthcare Improvement, Boston.

important and what's not. I assume the administrators and doctors must know. Don't they?"

The purpose of this article is to address these and other questions about the board's key responsibilities in overseeing the primary work of their institutions—caring for the sick.

The board's roles can be summarized as:

1. To understand the community's expectations
2. To ensure that a few organizationwide measures of those expectations (these are the "big dots") are established, understood and monitored
3. To hold management accountable for improving the big dots and linking that improvement to the organization's strategic goals
4. To build the hospital's will to achieve these aims
5. To maintain constancy of purpose for the long-term quality transformation of the hospital
6. To promote collaboration across the community for redesigning care

What Do Patients Want?

If you were to ask your patients and community why they need the hospital and what they want it to do for them, you would get a variety of answers. But the core themes, particularly with regard to clinical care, would sound something like the following:

- "Cure me. If I get sick or injured, I want you to cure me if a cure is possible."
- "Heal me. I want you to help me to heal, even when a cure is not possible."
- "Don't hurt me. I don't want you to make my condition worse in the course of diagnosis and treatment."

These needs form the three pillars of the hospital's clinical mission: cure when cure is possible; heal even when cure is impossible; and throughout the process, do no harm. The first is about clinical effectiveness—about organizing and delivering care in such a way that all the known science of medicine is applied to each patient and produces the best possible results. The second need is about building healing relationships between patients, doctors and nurses and centering the care design around each individual patient and family. The third need primarily concerns safety and confidence, but it can also be broadened to include unnecessary costs as another form of harm. Hospital boards must understand and accept all three of these drivers of the hospital's clinical mission.

Know Your Big Dots

If curing, healing and avoiding harm form the hospital's core clinical mission, trustees must ensure that the hospital has organizationwide measures of their components—in other words, measures of how the hospital performs as a whole, rather than how each individual part performs. Trustees don't need to know how 5 West compares with 5 East in safety. Rather, they need to know how the entire hospital is performing on these measures. Trustees should not be reviewing information packets that contain scores of detailed performance measures for individual floors, units, physicians and conditions.

On the other hand, administrators and clinicians do need to understand these detailed measurements—often called "dots" because they appear as data points on charts and other graphic displays—as they work on improvement.

Examples of system-level performance measures of curing, healing and harm prevention include:

- Hospital mortality rate (curing, harm)
- Functional outcomes for a few major procedures and conditions—for example, mortality rates for coronary artery bypass grafting, outcomes for total knee and hip arthroplasty (curing, harm)
- Patient satisfaction (a good proxy for healing)
- Nursing staff voluntary turnover (another good proxy for healing)
- Rate of adverse drug events (ADEs) per 1,000 doses (harm)
- Cost per admission (harm)

Trustees often say, "That's all well and good, but I'm not a doctor. I might understand measures of service quality, but I don't understand clinical numbers, such as mortality rate. So what good does it do to measure these things and report those measures to the board?"

Perhaps the best response to this question is simply to ask another question, using mortality rate as a specific example: If saving the lives of badly injured or critically ill patients is one of the hospital's most important roles, shouldn't trustees know how well the hospital is doing that? Shouldn't they understand the hospital's performance on something as important as "alive or dead" at least as well as they understand debt service coverage ratio and days cash on hand?

If you answer this question affirmatively, read "Understanding the Biggest of the Big Dots" below. It provides a primer on hospital mortality rates as an example of a system-level performance measure that every trustee should understand.

Understanding the Biggest of the Big Dots: Hospital Mortality Rates

Among the various system-level measures of clinical quality, hospital standardized mortality rate (HSMR) is a powerful indicator of performance and should definitely be on every board's list of "big dots." Mortality rate has a lot of advantages over other measures. Death is a unique, unambiguous event unlike many other measures such as morbidity and functional status. By law, hospital deaths must be recorded, so the data are more complete and accurate than most other clinical indicators. Furthermore, death rates are clearly understood by the public.

In addition, adjusted death rates can be used to compare hospitals, and it is highly likely that your hospital's death rate will be published in the newspaper alongside regional and national comparisons. (See the British version of these hospital quality reports at www.drfoster.co.uk.)

One of the world's finest health services researchers, Sir Brian Jarman, senior fellow with the Institute for Healthcare Improvement (IHI), Boston, recently spent a year working with publicly available data from the Medicare database and has produced an exceptionally well-adjusted set of HSMRs for U.S. hospitals. The important points to note:

- There is no obvious correlation between standardized charges and HSMR.
- The risk of dying in the worst hospitals is four times higher than in the best hospitals.

Continued →

So what does this really mean? How are these rates determined? If one hospital gets all the tough cases, is it fair to compare it with hospitals that get easy cases? Trustees should understand the answers to these questions as well as they understand the issues around such performance measures as operating margin. The following outline might help trustees understand the process by which the HSMR is calculated:

1. Each patient admitted to a U.S. hospital is placed into one of hundreds of "cells" according to that patient's diagnosis, age, sex, race, payer type, admission source (e.g., referral, no primary physician, etc.), and admission type (e.g., emergent, elective).

2. All patients in a particular cell (e.g., all African-American women, age 70 to 75, admitted on an emergency basis with septic shock, with no primary physician) are then analyzed to determine an "expected" death rate—the average for that cell—for the time period in question (e.g., January–June 2002).

3. The experience of each of these patients admitted to a hospital in 2002 is then compared to the predicted experience, cell by cell.

4. The hospital's data are adjusted for regional characteristics, such as the availability of hospice resources or the prevalence of the presenting condition(s). For example, if the community has no hospice facilities, it's likely that a higher percentage of all deaths will take place in the hospital, rather than elsewhere, so the data are adjusted for this regional characteristic.

5. The results are then "normalized" so that the average performance for a hospital is an HSMR score of 100. If an HSMR is 125, that means that patients being admitted to the hospital have a 35 percent higher chance of dying in that hospital than in a hospital with an HSMR of 90.

Some important points for trustees to know about HSMRs:

• The HSMR for any given hospital tends to be fairly stable from year to year. It is a predictable result of the system of care in that institution.

Continued →

- The "our patients are sicker" argument really doesn't hold much water, given the method by which the HSMR is calculated. Comparison at the level of individual patients, cell by cell, makes this issue much less important. For example, when leaders of a hospital with a high HSMR say, "Oh yes, that's because of our Stroke Center. We get all the tough stroke patients in the community," they are often puzzled to find out that eliminating the stroke patients from the analysis doesn't change their HSMR at all.

- A bad HSMR is not the result of a bad doctor or two or bad processes of care for a couple of diseases or conditions. Hospital standardized mortality rate is a system attribute of the hospital—related to broad operational and cultural issues such as nurse staffing levels, the degree of teamwork between doctors and nurses, and how the ICUs are organized.

- Being an academic health center or a "Top 100" hospital is no guarantee of having a good HSMR. In aggregate, the HSMRs of these prestigious clusters of hospitals look pretty much like the rest of U.S. hospitals.

How would you go about learning your hospital's mortality rate? A number of options exist. You could send an e-mail to moveyourdot@ihi.org and learn where your mortality "dot" is. You could also join IHI's IMPACT network and participate in a collaborative of dozens of hospitals aiming to improve their mortality rates. The Institute for Healthcare Improvement (www.ihi.org) is a quality improvement organization in Boston led by Donald Berwick, M.D. Other means of learning your mortality rate include membership in organizations such as Premier, which often have excellent data systems. A number of other vendors (e.g., CareScience, www.carescience.com, and The Delta Group, www.thedeltagroup .com) also provide good data on hospital mortality.

Although the methods by which each vendor calculates mortality rates vary somewhat, it's probably less important which report the board chooses than that it chooses one, understands what it means, and establishes a goal for improving hospital performance wherever it falls on the mortality spectrum. The last place the board wants to learn about its hospital's mortality rate is on the front page of the local newspaper!

Establish Aims for Your Big Dots

Once it knows how the hospital is doing as a whole, the board should establish system-level aims for improvement. Supposing the hospital's mortality rate is 125 (25 percent higher than the national norm), what would constitute an appropriate aim for improvement? The same type of question might be asked of nurse voluntary turnover rates, patient satisfaction ratings, ADEs per 1,000 doses and other big dots.

There are probably as many methods for setting board goals as there are boards, but some general rules for quality goals are:

Aim high. If patients are dying unnecessarily in your hospital every year, incremental improvement is hardly an appropriate goal. Similarly, if patients are being harmed by adverse drug events all over the country, and your hospital is currently worse than the average, is it enough to say, "Let's get our rate down to the point where we only hurt as many patients with medications as the average American hospital"?

The highest you can aim for is perfection, that is, the "theoretical ideal of performance." This is a daunting idea, and since perfection is never really achievable, setting goals at this level generates a lot of cynicism. But you can use perfection as a point of reference for your goals. For example, most hospitals have ADE rates of 5 per 1,000 doses or higher. Perfection would be zero per 1,000. Could you set the aim to close the gap between current performance and zero by half, to 2.5 per 1,000, in the next year?

Another approach is to set your goals based on the best performance you can find. Would it help if you knew that at least three hospitals have achieved ADE rates of 0.5 per 1,000? They have. If you can't aim directly for perfection, isn't it reasonable to set a goal that targets the best known performance rather than the average?

Connect your quality goals to your strategy. When I ask hospital CEOs, "What are the one or two things that you simply must accomplish in the next three years or your job will be on the line?" the answers are usually framed in terms of key strategic directions for which they are held accountable by their boards. They say, "We must grow by 15 percent," or "We must improve margins from break even to 5 percent," and "We must become less dependent on government payers and more attractive to a diverse group of patients."

But when I ask the next question, "And how does your work on quality improvement—say, on mortality rates or nurse satisfaction—relate to those key strategic directions?" their answers often sound a lot more vague.

The important point about quality and strategic goals is that the board and the CEO must develop a logical and quantifiable relationship between the two. This isn't always easy, but it's critical to success. Far too often, strategically important work and quality work are unconnected and therefore occur in two separate parts of the organization. Line managers and key executives work on the strategic goals, and the quality staff and a few doctors and nurses work on the quality goals, along with other activities, such as getting ready for a Joint Commission survey. When the going gets tough, is it any mystery why the quality work suffers? Treating quality as a staff function, of no real strategic importance, is a recipe for mediocrity.

The board can forestall this by demanding that the CEO work with it to make logical, quantifiable connections between quality and strategic goals. In essence, boards need to ensure that a coherent strategy is developed and that it includes the right quality goals. This will also help it prioritize among various quality aims. For example, if growth is the most critical strategic imperative, which system-level measures of quality will be the most powerful drivers of growth? The answers might vary by market and institution, but the board must ensure that its institution has addressed the question.

Build Organizational Will

Although boards can make sure that system-level measures of quality are in place, can learn how to interpret them, and can set aims for improvement, do they have any role in actually moving the big dots?

Leading major change is sometimes described as a mix of will, ideas and execution. With regard to clinical quality, it isn't likely, or even appropriate, that board leaders should be responsible for generating ideas on how to reduce mortality rates or implementing changes in clinical processes to improve their reliability and safety. But boards do, and must, have a powerful role in establishing an institutional will to improve.

If a hospital hopes to improve its mortality rate, for example, the board must support its CEO and medical staff executive committee as they work through some highly controversial issues—such as how ICUs are organized and staffed, how nurse staffing levels are determined, and how the medical staff organization can ensure the consistent practice of evidence-based medicine across a diverse staff. This will require the board to demonstrate backbone and send a clear set of signals to the organization that it intends to achieve its quality aims, even if the changes are painful. There are at least five ways in which trustees can send these signals:

- *Attention.* The currency of leadership is attention. If the board reviews the hospital's financial performance monthly, but only reviews mortality, ADEs and other quality data annually, the organization's attention is not being channeled toward quality. The board can build will by giving at least as much attention to the "big quality dots" as to capital projects and the bottom line.
- *Accountability.* Other than overall stewardship of the institution's mission, the board's four main responsibilities are overseeing quality, finances, strategy and management. The board can build will by establishing clear accountability for the CEO's achievement of quality aims.
- *Resources.* Staff tend to watch resource allocation to determine whether the board is really serious about its goals. Boards can build the will for quality by making sure they don't flinch at budget time.
- *Policy.* Boards don't usually decide which managers get promoted or which physicians are appointed to key positions. But boards can and should establish policies that help drive the quality transformation of their hospital, that is, requiring a demonstrated ability to improve quality as a non-negotiable prerequisite for any candidate's promotion or new appointment.
- *Courage.* As stated before, when boards start to move the big dots, they're going to face resistance. For instance, what should the board do if the medical staff president reports that one of the hospital's highest volume admitters refuses to adopt the medical

staff's recommended best practices and threatens to leave the hospital? An institution that is undergoing a quality transformation will face many such issues. The board can demonstrate its will by acting steadfastly and courageously in the face of these predictable challenges.

Maintain Constancy of Purpose

Improving system-level performance measures from their current level to something closer to the ideal will involve deep, fundamental change in the institution's culture, structure, processes and strategies. It's not unreasonable to think of such a transformation as occurring over 10 to 20 years, at minimum. It's the board's role to maintain constancy of purpose for this transformation over the long haul.

The tenure of hospital CEOs is typically less than five years. Medical staff presidents, chief nursing officers, vice presidents of medical affairs and other key leaders have similarly short periods of influence and responsibility. It is clear that long-term quality transformation will not occur if it is seen merely as the pet project of the CEO or some other powerful individual because these roles are too transient. The only leadership constant throughout the years of transformation is the board (not the individual trustees), and, therefore, the board must take this responsibility.

In addition to these methods for building organizational will, the most important way the board can maintain its constancy of purpose is through CEO succession planning. Therefore, boards must design structures and systems that will ensure that each new CEO will continue the quality transformation.

Collaborate across the Community

If you are to achieve truly patient-centered clinical quality, it is highly likely that your hospital cannot work in isolation from physician office practices, home health agencies, nursing homes, and even competitors. For example, suppose you learned that by joining with a competing hospital to develop a common physician order entry system, you could reduce serious medication "reconciliation" errors between hospital and office practices by 90 percent. To achieve this, your hospital would have to invest $2 million, and the competitor only $500,000. The benefit to all the patients in your community, however, would be enormous. This decision has elements of competitive strategy, quality improvement, financial oversight and physician relations. Who could make such a decision?

When cooperation across otherwise "sovereign" organizations is required, only the board has the authority to decide to share resources, invest in radical redesigns of care and other actions that transcend the boundaries of the institution. As a trustee, you play an important role in encouraging and permitting such cross-institutional clinical improvements.

The most important point for trustees to understand about quality transformation is that it can be accomplished. There are hospitals that have achieved ADE rates of 0.5 per 1,000 and mortality rates in the 40s. You can and should expect your doctors and administrators to be able to make dramatic improvements in these and other big dots.

Conclusion

Trustees are often confused about their role in clinical quality. Most boards know they must establish a process for credentialing physicians—a process that is usually delegated to the medical staff, with only cursory review by the board. But after credentialing, then what?

In hospitals at the forefront of quality, boards are not merely passive recipients of reports on what the administration and medical staff are doing to improve quality. Rather, they are the principal drivers of the quality transformation.

One Giant Leap for Quality

By Karen Sandrick

When boards get behind quality initiatives,
patient care benefits.

Soon after the Institute of Medicine released its disturbing report about safety in U.S. hospitals in 1999, the board of 400-bed Meritor Hospital in Madison, Wisconsin, realized it needed to understand quality and safety issues more fully and how they might affect some upcoming decisions about major expenditures and strategic planning. So in 2001, vice chair Regina Millner formed an ad hoc board committee to learn about safety and quality and how to make improvements, what costs might be involved, and how corporate culture needed to change. Based on their analysis, in 2002, Meritor trustees took a fairly revolutionary step for a hospital board: it approved spending $8 million to $9 million over five years to install a computerized physician order entry system (CPOE).

Computerized physician order entry is one of the key tenets of the Leapfrog Group, formed in 2000 by the Business Roundtable, Washington, D.C., an association of CEOs from major U.S. corporations that advocates public policies to ensure a well-trained and productive workforce as well as vigorous economic growth. The Business Roundtable launched Leapfrog to spur giant leaps forward in health care affordability, quality and safety by promoting high-value health care. (Leapfrog is now a separate 501(c)(3) organization.)

Karen Sandrick is a Chicago-based health care writer.

According to Leapfrog's 2004 survey of 1,019 hospitals that agreed to participate, only 4 percent have fully implemented CPOE, while 16 percent plan to implement it by 2006.

Although the American Hospital Association has partnered with many of the same employer members of Leapfrog in the Consumer Purchaser Disclosure Group (which includes leading employers, consumer groups and labor groups that are working to ensure that all Americans have access to publicly reported information about health care performance), it has not been on the same page with Leapfrog regarding its initial "leaps," particularly CPOE.

"We fully support the notion that CPOE, electronic health records, bar coding and other information technologies can be important tools for hospitals and other health care providers as they strive to provide more effective and efficient care to their patients. But we know hospitals need to be able to exercise judgment in choosing which technologies, which strategies are going to be most effective for their own patient populations. So the thought of requiring that particular strategies, such as CPOE, be implemented is not one we can support," says Nancy Foster, the AHA's vice president for quality and patient safety policy.

Survey results were similar for two other Leapfrog measures. Nineteen percent of 914 hospitals with intensive care units (ICUs) met Leapfrog's criterion for staffing intensive care units with trained ICU specialist physicians or "intensivists," and 13 percent plan to have intensivists on board by 2006.

Fewer than 20 percent of hospitals met the group's standards for high-risk procedures, which are based on volume and a proven track record. Basing the decision to perform high-risk procedures on volume is a good first step, says Edward Walker, M.D., chief medical officer of the University of Washington Medical Center, Seattle. Data do show a crude correlation between volume of procedures performed and mortality. However, other measures of quality around volumes need to be considered. After all, says Walker, "If you are doing something wrong and you do a lot of it, you just do it wrong multiple times."

And, despite the merits of CPOE, it is fraught with problems, Walker believes. He explains that CPOE is actually a series of processes beginning with the physician's initial decision to administer a drug, followed by entering the order into a computer. That command then triggers a software interface that checks for drug interactions and treatment substitutions and compares the current prescription with the patient's present and past history. From there, the system has to link both with the pharmacy to control inventory and the drug management process and with the nursing stations on hospital floors to govern drug delivery through a bar coding mechanism.

Some hospitals may have an electronic prescription system that computerizes drug ordering, but all it really does is send an e-mail to the pharmacy. Everything else is manual. "The only safety issue that's being improved is that the physician's handwriting isn't getting in the way anymore," Walker says. "But every other error that can come with medication administration, with interactions of drugs, [or a drug] going to the wrong patient, is still there."

This is not to say that Walker eschews Leapfrog's efforts. Quite the contrary. He is an enthusiast. But he acknowledges that both hospitals and Leapfrog are still finding their way.

When Walker first became medical director of the University of Washington Medical Center in 2002, he and his colleagues on the medical staff, both rank and file and department leaders, weren't fully informed about Leapfrog, nor did they understand it in context. The overall feeling was that the group focused too narrowly on a subset of safety standards.

In the last year, however, the Leapfrog Group has expanded its scope to include all 30 safety practices endorsed by the National Quality Forum (NQF), Washington, D.C. It has operationalized its assessment of hospitals' compliance with its own safety criteria as well as those of the NQF, by asking hospitals about four key aspects of meeting quality and safety standards: awareness, accountability, ability and action.

As a result, Leapfrog's Hospital Quality and Safety Survey is now able to provide a comprehensive assessment of hospitals' progress in meeting Leapfrog criteria as well as the NQF safety practices. The latest Leapfrog survey found that 80 percent of the 1,019 surveyed hospitals had procedures to prevent surgeries on the wrong body part, and 70 percent required a pharmacist to review all medication orders before a drug was dispensed to a patient.

The survey also points to trouble spots: 70 percent of surveyed hospitals lacked an explicit protocol for ensuring adequate nurse

staffing; 60 percent had no procedures for preventing patient mal-
nutrition; 50 percent had not established procedures for preventing
bed sores; and 40 percent lacked policies governing handwashing
by all members of the staff.

Leapfrog's efforts have helped align hospitals with employers'
concerns. "In our dialogue with employers, they are interested in
how we are doing on Leapfrog criteria and what we are doing to
improve quality and safety," says Gary R. Yates, M.D., chief medical
officer of Sentara Healthcare, a six-hospital system in southeastern
Virginia.

Although Leapfrog has not provided a platform on which hospitals and employers can engage in cross-cultural collaboration, it
has raised hospitals' awareness of the employer community, which
is leading to some interesting initiatives. For example, Sentara is
working with members of the nuclear power industry to learn about
and adapt some of the safety techniques used in other high-risk
industries. The hospital system is working to create a culture of
safety among employees and physicians in its acute care facilities,
nursing homes and medical group office settings by developing a
series of behavioral-based expectations. "The idea is to change our
culture by practicing safe behaviors throughout the organization.
By having these behaviors become habits, we will help to make sure
that an adverse event will be less likely to happen to a patient,"
Yates says.

Leapfrog's work has also spurred innovations. Sentara was the
site of the first electronic ICU (e-ICU), which uses technology,
intensive care specialist physicians and critical care nurses to monitor patients in multiple ICUs across several facilities. This provides
a heightened level of care to patients whose conditions can change
quickly and dramatically. The e-ICU includes cameras to observe
patients, as well as data and imaging monitors to collect and display
vital signs, laboratory values and radiology scans.

Since it instituted the e-ICU system five years ago, Sentara has
seen a 20 percent reduction in mortality among ICU patients.
"Using the e-ICU, we're able to provide this intensive specialist
[type of] care to more patients, use scarce resources wisely and meet
the Leapfrog criteria," Yates says.

Now that Leapfrog has removed the first barrier to data quality
by standardizing responses to its survey questions, the accuracy of

reporting about compliance to Leapfrog criteria should improve. Walker believes the group needs to institute an auditing mechanism to substantiate that responses to survey questions are based on reality. "You want to be sure people take the quality analysis seriously and they are representing quality as it exists in their hospitals, not some dream vision of where they want it to be," he says.

Adherence to Leapfrog criteria also needs to be linked more directly with employer contracting. Although more than 160 Fortune 500 companies and other large private and public sector purchasers have joined the Leapfrog Group, hospitals interviewed by *Trustee* have not seen that employers are basing their health care purchasing decisions on quality and safety.

In some markets, it may be just too early to realize a benefit in contracting. "We are doing safer, higher quality care. I don't know that you need much more of a reward than that. Whether or not that translates into dollars is to be seen," Walker says.

However, in many markets, employers are basing their contract decisions on price. Over the last few years, Exempla Healthcare, Denver, has negotiated a pay-for-performance contract with one of the city's major employers that provides financial incentives to the hospital system for meeting specific quality measures in several service lines, including cardiac and respiratory care. The system was able to earn additional revenue by meeting the goals, says William Jessee, M.D., chair of the board's quality committee.

However, when Exempla opened a new hospital, the same payer that had been paying for quality improvement decided not to contract with the facility because it got a better rate from a competing institution. "It was a sobering lesson for us that payers are interested in quality so long as it doesn't interfere with their ability to get cheaper prices," Jessee says.

This showed Exempla that, while Leapfrog has captured the attention of large employers, smaller companies, such as those in their community, are still not on board. So Exempla is now shifting its marketing efforts away from seeking rewards for the quality it is able to achieve and concentrating instead on educating employers. "We'll not be successful with quality as a market strategy unless the employer community starts demanding it. Right now, although a lot of lip service is paid to quality, price is still a more dominant factor," Jessee observes.

Still, Leapfrog, like the Joint Commission and other quality and safety initiatives, helps focus health care professionals' attention on issues they might not think of as important to the quality and safety of the care they provide, Jessee says.

For instance, Leapfrog criteria set Meritor Hospital on a path it might not otherwise have taken. Vice chair Millner recalls that the members of the ad hoc committee spent considerable time educating themselves about quality within their institution as well as about issues related to quality and safety throughout the hospital community. The committee learned about the difficulty of translating CPOE systems developed in other hospitals to their own setting and the "horror stories" about instituting bar coding too soon. The hospital consequently is introducing a CPOE program in phases throughout the hospital and eventually into physicians' offices. It will not complete the installation until trustees are confident that the switch to computerized order entry will not eliminate some existing human safeguards, Millner says.

Exempla is also following a measured approach to CPOE. A computerized system is being rolled out in Exempla's new hospital, Good Samaritan Medical Center, Lafayette, Colorado, in a culture where the nursing and medical staffs are committed to electronic order entry and results reporting. By getting the bugs out of the system in that single setting, Exempla believes it will be easier to install in its other two facilities over the next year.

"It's not a matter of being able to take these kinds of tools and plunk them into an existing setting and turn them on, and everyone will be happy. You have to take into consideration the culture of the organization and do it in such a way that you make sure the tool will be used," Jessee explains. Leapfrog has also reminded trustees that they do not only oversee the hospital's fiscal health.

"Trustees need to balance their time on finance and business development with quality and safety and tie the organization's values back to strategic planning," says Charles Denham, M.D., chair of the Texas Medical Institute of Technology, Dallas, which administers Leapfrog's quality and safety survey.

Denham points out that most trustees spend 90 percent of their time on finance, and 10 percent on quality because they don't feel qualified to look into it. But trustees don't need to know all the answers or much about content; they need to know the right questions to ask, Denham believes. In particular, trustees need to ask whether their hospital is pursuing initiatives such as Leapfrog and if not, why not?

Trustees also can gain insight about their hospital's quality and safety efforts through the Leapfrog survey, which reveals gaps in performance—gaps that may go unrecognized by administrators and trustees during routine oversight. But awareness still only goes so far, Denham believes. Management and governance must be accountable for closing those gaps.

"We've been investing in procedures that generate revenue and volume, such as new molecules that turn into new drugs, new devices that take pictures," Denham adds. "We haven't been investing in information systems, communication systems, in how teams work together. But hospitals must be willing to invest the resources and capacity into becoming able to change."

As business and community leaders, trustees have a natural understanding of the sources of system failure. The goal now is to translate that comprehension into action. As Denham notes, "Trustees need to attack inertia and synchronize action with smart targets by picking the area the organization is going to work on, like Leapfrog, and demand disciplined activity."

In addition to Leapfrog's "leaps," there are other strategies that have been shown to improve medication safety and the care of patients in the ICU.

"Hospitals need to look at the evidence and the strategies that are available to them, look at financial and other resources, and make wise decisions in collaboration with their community boards, medical staffs and others,"says the AHA's Foster. "Wise decision-making means looking at all of the options that are available and choosing the one that would be best."

The Rural Case for Quality (and Why It Matters)

By Laurie Larson

As concerns multiply about the state of America's health care system, so do the analyses and measurements of ways to improve quality and patient safety. And, although no federal edicts have been issued about the best ways to make care better and safer, one pronouncement has become sweeping: Every hospital, large or small, must step up to the quality challenge and provide data on its performance. With a host of challenges already unique to their situation, rural hospitals must address the quality imperative as well.

"These days, every provider has to prove [its] quality," says Richard Umbdenstock, president-elect of the American Hospital Association and executive vice president of Providence Health & Services, Spokane, Washington. "There are no more exceptions, no levels of omission that are acceptable anymore." And, although rural hospitals have typically sought even standing with their urban counterparts, it's a case where being considered their equals may not be an advantage.

"Historically, because of small volumes and not enough data, small, rural hospitals have not been allowed to participate in federal and other initiatives for reporting quality," says Ira Moscovice, professor and director of the Rural Health Research Center at the University of Minnesota, Minneapolis. "But now, policy-makers are

---

Laurie Larson is *Trustee*'s senior editor.

asking what they're getting for the money they are spending, asking for public reporting and quality improvement initiatives—and rurals need to participate."

As a prime example, the Centers for Medicare & Medicaid Services (CMS) recently began offering all prospective payment system (PPS) hospitals an increase in their Medicare reimbursement of four-tenths of a percent in exchange for voluntarily submitting data to CMS' "Hospital Compare" Web site on specified sets of quality measures. This year, that incentive increased to 2 percent. And, even though the country's nearly 1,000 critical access hospitals (CAHs) receive cost-based reimbursement, they must still pay attention to what CMS is asking of PPS hospitals and report quality data, because the same quality expectations will eventually affect them as well, Moscovice and others believe.

"The federal government will not allow more than a quarter of all the nation's hospitals to not participate in public reporting initiatives," Moscovice says. "Rural hospitals have to believe it's important."

Apparently, a good portion of them do. Last year, 41 percent of CAH hospitals participated in some level of Hospital Compare, Moscovice says, submitting data that allow consumers to compare how well hospitals in their area perform against each other relative to acute myocardial infarction (AMI), pneumonia, heart failure and prevention of surgical infection.

They're doing so to show their commitment to quality and transparency, explains Mary Wakefield, chair of the Center for Rural Health at the University of North Dakota in Grand Forks.

"Rural hospitals can't afford to not be part of public reporting on quality," she explains. "Pay for performance is driving quality improvement [and] rurals can't be left out of tying payment to performance. Meaningful reporting measures will allow them to be held up to scrutiny, but measurement and payment strategies must really work."

Measurements that Matter

The key term is *meaningful*. To help determine what measurements make sense and will allow rural hospitals to be equal players on the quality playing field, the Institute of Medicine (IOM) produced a report in 2004 called *Quality Through Collaboration: The Future of Rural Health Care.* Wakefield chaired the committee that produced the report, and Moscovice was also a committee member.

The report examined both the general level of quality among rural hospitals as well as what quality improvement approaches could be tailored specifically for them. It was written at the request of the Federal Office for Rural Health Policy, the Agency for Healthcare Research and Quality, the Kellogg Foundation and others, who wanted to "drill down separately" on rural health care quality, Wakefield says, since most quality research to date has focused on urban health systems or been more generalized.

"Rural providers have said that the focus of quality measures is irrelevant to them . . . that quality approaches and expectations don't fit . . . that the rural context is not taken into consideration," Wakefield says. For example, the Leapfrog Group recommends that intensive care units be staffed by an intensivist. Rural hospitals typically don't have either.

Wakefield says that, while payers and the federal government want to see data from hospitals that report on quality of care, "they need [multiple] cases, sets of numbers, to statistically report with validity, and rurals don't see enough numbers to report on a big enough set" of quality indicators. Collectively, however, with one-fifth of the U.S. population living in rural communities, there is a significant "number set" among rural hospitals overall that needs to be taken under its own consideration—and that bears quality measurement merit.

"There are unique circumstances in rural health that influence delivery and quality, and unique strategies are needed to improve quality," Wakefield says. In addition to large distances between services and facilities, rural hospitals have a unique clinician mix comprising mostly primary care physicians, as well as many nurse practitioners and physician assistants, who provide some primary care. Specialty and more complex general acute care is typically provided in larger towns. Within the patient mix, chronic health conditions and substance abuse are prevalent, as well as large numbers of low-income, uninsured patients and a significant elderly population.

Why is the IOM looking at rural quality reporting now? In addition to seeking process improvements that are more appropriate for rurals, Wakefield explains, "this is part of a broader push over the past five to seven years . . . to make U.S. health quality better. We should never talk about a second-tier health system . . . there should be no geographic quality divide." She adds, "If we don't look at rurals specifically, they will be left out of the debate."

Moscovice explains, "Having [rural] quality information available is important to the local community, and it is [also] externally important, so the world sees that [rurals] are there. When an institution doesn't report [on quality], it looks like they're not good enough to report."

Moscovice's Rural Health Research Center at the University of Minnesota, in partnership with the state's quality improvement organization (QIO) (federally supported in every state to improve care for Medicare beneficiaries, although some QIOs cover more than one state), have done field testing with hospitals in Nevada, Utah and Washington, in addition to Minnesota, to devise quality measurement sets that are aligned with CMS' Hospital Compare data, but that also cover core rural hospital functions not considered in existing measurement sets. In addition to AMI, pneumonia and congestive heart failure, these added rural functions include timeliness of emergency department (ED) care, patient transfer communication and medication safety checklists. Participation is voluntary, and by the end of the trials, 40 rural hospitals will have participated, Moscovice estimates.

Looking at hospitals with fewer than 50 beds, his team has found that CAH hospitals do better with pneumonia outcomes than non-CAH hospitals, but not as well with AMIs when they do not transfer patients out of their facility.

However, transferred AMI patients have done well in study results, which points up an area where rurals particularly excel. Patient transfers, and equally importantly, the decision of whether or not to transfer patients, "that's the rural hospital differentiater," Moscovice says. "To send a patient 40 miles away is a crucial decision, and little research has been done on the timeliness and appropriateness of those decisions, as well as what happens after the transfer and what happens after those patients go home and in their future health care . . . the transfer decision is the quality key . . . rurals can really take the lead here."

Moscovice says rural hospitals should take the same quality lead in ED care, particularly concentrating on timeliness of trauma care. "Rurals need to be good at these things and they can develop measures before other hospitals. These are core aspects of what those institutions provide," he says.

Ideal Laboratories

In truth, there are many factors that make rural health care providers models of particular excellence. "Rurals have historically had to make do with less; there are no extra resources in their infrastructure—it's invention by necessity," Wakefield says. "There are great places that have invented and created because they don't expect resources. That mindset in rural areas is an advantage." In addition, rural providers know each other and their patients, and their facilities "can make changes on a dime for the whole hospital," Wakefield says. "The stakeholders are there, and all the players are easily brought to the table."

The University of Minnesota study has been testing this flexibility, looking at whether designated hospital staff can gather necessary quality data, and then, if the hospital is able to change its procedures based on what it learns—and the answer is yes. As an example, participating hospitals have tracked how well they've transferred necessary patient information, as well as the patients themselves, to receiving hospitals. Moscovice says that "within a week" of tracking their accuracy, those hospitals have been able to fix glitches in patient information transfer, improving care and further avoiding duplication of services.

Because of their size and flexibility, Wakefield says rural hospitals "are perfect learning laboratories. If you want to look at the impact of change, the rural community is small [so] you can look at research immediately . . . you can evaluate clearly what impact changes make. When we think of places to demonstrate new approaches, rurals are ideal."

For example, because rurals excel at transfers, both between facilities and within their own walls, their procedures could potentially determine standardized protocols—an example of rurals acting as these "learning laboratories." Taken one step further, health care quality for entire populations can be evaluated in rural communities, Wakefield believes, since it is easy to engage and track outcomes for all participants in a study, such as improving diabetes management or lowering rates of obesity.

To do all this, Wakefield and others agree that rural hospitals must find ways to put information technology (IT) into their infrastructure that is both cost-effective and functionally tailored for what they do, with high-speed connectivity (see "IT Funding" on page 246). The IOM rural quality report says hospital strategic planning should consider the financial resources that rurals need to participate in quality improvement and encourages federal agencies to ensure rurals have broadband network access. Wakefield believes that CMS and other federal agencies should give financial rewards to rural providers who implement electronic medical records and other IT infrastructures and that the Health Resources and Services Administration should look at ways for rurals to become paperless as well. Bottom line, "Financial resources should be tied to expectations about IT," she asserts.

The Collaborative Imperative

But getting support from the government and other funding sources is only half the equation. Both from the standpoint of cost and standardization, rurals need to collaborate, experts agree. "By natural market and natural service area, that's the way to gather together," Umbdenstock says. "Smaller organizations can get [IT] faster in collaboration with others . . . and the [resulting] scale takes the learning curve up in a hurry." Additionally, he says that "regional collaboration improves and maintains local assets—and people want to keep health care local." His system also works with regional rural hospitals through a Rural Health Care Quality Network to compare quality data with each other.

"You can't work in a vacuum," says Nancy Vorhees, chief operating officer of Inland Health Services in Spokane, an affiliated Providence company. "What are your established relationships with other hospitals? Where is the 'hub' where referrals go? In areas where collaboration can make a difference, who do you want to collaborate with?"

Similarly, in shopping for IT, Vorhees advises against "buying something that only works for you . . . that's where partnerships come in to get it done. The ability to connect with each other is critical." Umbdenstock adds, "When you increase communication and contact [in a health care system] . . . there is better coordination of care. It's financially prohibitive for each hospital to build its own IT system. The more you can build a community utility for health care information, the better you serve people—you have to learn how to collaborate and compete at the same time."

IT Funding

The Institute of Medicine's 2004 rural quality report outlines a multi-faceted strategy for addressing quality challenges in rural communities, including "establishing a stronger health care quality improvement support structure to assist rural systems and providers," and "investing in an information and communications technology infrastructure."

Getting rural hospitals that support and IT infrastructure will require funding and most are already "financially fragile," maintaining low or negative margins relative to their urban counterparts, says Mary Wakefield, chair of the committee that prepared the IOM study *Quality Through Collaboration: The Future of Health Care.*

Fortunately, funding is available, and she recommends the following resources:

- *State offices of rural health.* These exist in every state and receive federal funding. They are a good contact for rural hospitals looking for health care IT funding, Wakefield says, because they should be aware of any targeted programs at the state level to fund IT projects, and may also know about local or regional foundations that might provide funding. Grants from the Health Resources and Services Administration are also available through this office.

- *The U.S. Department of Health & Human Services' Office of Rural Health Policy (ORHP).* The ORHP bestows the Medicare Rural Hospital Flexibility grant (available to critical access hospitals) and the Small Hospital Improvement Program grant, which provide IT funding, among other forms of assistance.

- *The Rural Assistance Center Web site (www.raconline.org).* This site can be used to run rural IT funding searches.

- *The Rural Health Care Program (RHCP) of the Universal Service Fund.* The RHCP supports the participation of rural providers in IT systems by making discounts available to eligible health care providers for telecommunication services and monthly Internet service charges. The program is intended to ensure that rural health care providers pay no more for telecommunications than their urban counterparts. Contact the RHCP Customer Service Support Center at (800) 229-5476 or rhc-admin@universalservice.org.

For more general information about the Universal Service Fund's Rural Health Care Program, go to the Rural Assistance Center's Information Guide on the topic at www.universalservice.org/rhc.

—Laurie Larson

What Rural Connectivity Could Look Like

Providence Health & Services, Spokane, Washington, was a model of rural collaboration even before it came together as a merger between Spokane-based Providence Services and Seattle-based Providence Health System at the beginning of the year (2006). But now the integrated system, which covers most of Washington state, as well as parts of Idaho, Montana, Oregon, California, and Alaska, has forged wide expanses of new collaborative ground.

"Spokane is the largest city between Seattle and Minneapolis," explains Richard Umbdenstock, the merged system's executive vice president. "It's a huge rural area, there are great distances to any other city of our size or larger. We needed to work together to get referrals into Spokane." The region encompasses a half million residents in and around Spokane, plus 50 rural counties, comprising 1.2 million residents total for Providence's service area, he estimates.

The system began by combining its rehabilitation services into one rehabilitation institute, and then combined its air ambulance services. Providence now performs approximately 3,500 helicopter and/or ground transports a year in western Montana, northern Idaho, eastern Oregon and eastern Washington, according to Nancy Vorhees, chief operating officer of Inland Health Services in Spokane, an affiliated company created through a joint collaboration between Providence and Spokane-based Empire Health Services. Inland has three divisions, comprising: the rehabilitation institute; Northwest Health Partners, which oversees the air and ground transport services, 65 telemedicine sites, a community health program, and a wide array of philanthropic and support services for area providers; and Information Resource Management, which manages information technology (IT) for 35 Providence hospitals in Washington and Idaho, as well as a combined group of 20 physicians' offices, imaging centers and labs.

Although this impressive IT system was initially formed as the fortunate result of a class action suit against a regional telephone carrier that had to return money to the community, resulting in a multimillion dollar grant for telemedicine funding for Providence, the system has since received additional federal grants by demonstrating what it has been able to achieve over the past decade.

Continued →

"We built the IT system on our own," Umbdenstock says. "We are still competitors [with the other system], but we have collaborated on [all these services] and have shown community benefit—and there is a definite benefit for quality—all clinical specialties are available across regions through IT capabilities."

That system connects the hospital to an estimated 2.4 million electronic patient records, Vorhees says, providing more than 1,000 physicians and nurses with patient and related services data. "We did it for economies of scale," Vorhees says. "We asked ourselves if we could do more with less and we've proved to ourselves that we can. The level of quality and services escalates and it's a benefit to the region. Linkages, videoconferencing, imaging—all this information can be passed on quickly."

In addition to educational conferences and clinical consults, the health care system has expanded its telemedicine capabilities to include "TeleER" and "TelePharmacy" services. In emergency departments, larger trauma hospitals are electronically connected to EDs in 13 rural hospitals, allowing direct, interactive patient consult videoconferencing. The TelePharmacy processes prescription requests, allowing them to be dispensed from medication "machines" in rural hospitals once orders are approved by a remote pharmacist.

"Overall, there is better access to information, which gives access to patients sooner and, ultimately, will result in better outcomes," Vorhees says. "Electronic patient records allow resources to be better allocated, decisions can be made more quickly, and there are fewer errors."

"The goals should be to have 80 percent of the information on 80 percent of patients on one system," Umbdenstock says. "And if you decide to upgrade, ask yourself what the standard is for your region. Everyone should [eventually] be able to migrate to a common system."

—Laurie Larson

Vorhees says, "Sometimes you have to set aside that competitive edge. I think you have to take a risk and ask what's best for patients. If you don't have patients, you don't have a hospital." And those who need to ask that question first and foremost are hospital leadership and the board.

"Rural hospital board members need to ask for quality and safety data in the same way that urban hospitals do," Wakefield says. "They should get reports on quality at every meeting, ask what can be done to make quality better and allocate resources to improve quality of care." Moscovice adds, "What is clear is that the information can be collected—and it has to be collected identically to CMS—but it depends on [hospital] leadership saying it's important."

"To sustain and strengthen their hospital, trustees need to focus like a laser on quality of care," Wakefield says. "Increasingly, payment policies are being crafted and linked to quality. Boards of directors have to be focused on both payment and quality—they are no longer separate universes—these two tracks are converging rapidly. And you can't lead if you don't have data to measure quality."

"My hypothesis is that rurals can show the rest of the field how we do things," Moscovice says. "We can take the lead on [quality of] patient transfers and timeliness and appropriateness of ED care—and that's better than a model being developed in an urban hospital that rurals are expected to follow." He adds that "rural is not 'small urban.' There is a mythology that bigger is better, that urban is better than rural. I think it's important that rurals show they are interested in providing the highest quality of care and that urbans can learn from rurals, and vice versa."

Pay for Performance

By Jan Greene

Quality and cost control go arm in arm.

Early in 2005, Alan Beason found out that the 10 cardiologists in the Shreveport, Louisiana, specialty practice he managed would be singled out by a major insurer based on the quality of care they provided and how much they spent to provide it. The doctors who met United Healthcare's standards would get a gold star by their names. And for a few big national employers with a presence in Shreveport, employees would pay less for choosing a gold-star provider.

This did not go over well with the doctors in Shreveport. Besides feeling that this new plan came as a surprise with no local physician input, they were upset with the way they were to be assessed and with the possibility that many would be unfairly judged and would lose business because they didn't have stars by their names.

"There is a right way to do this," says Beason. But United Healthcare's evaluation, based on claims data, wasn't it, he says. "The acceptance by the medical community would be much better if this was focused more on touching the bases for quality care and better outcomes."

Beason and others in Shreveport put up a fuss. There was an even bigger dustup in St. Louis, another of the 20 markets where the plan was introduced; BJC Healthcare, one of the nation's largest health

---

Jan Greene is a writer based in Alameda, California.

systems, nearly severed its relationship with United Healthcare over it. Nevertheless, the insurer stood firm and plans to expand its "premium designation" program to 17 more markets.

From the insurer's perspective, it was simply trying to give health care consumers information to choose the best, most efficient doctors in town. "Consumer-directed health plans are placing increasing responsibility on the shoulders of consumers to help make decisions ... and they ought to have credible information in hand to help them," says Roger Rollman, director of public relations for United Healthcare's southeast region. He defended the use of the claims data, saying that United's database is large, varied and statistically sound.

United Healthcare's experiment is just one of dozens around the country designed to put some muscle in all the talk about improving the quality of health care. Some efforts are relatively simple quality reporting systems like United Healthcare's; others are incentive programs that pay a bonus to providers that meet certain quality or efficiency standards. These attempts to orient the health care system in a new way are known as pay-for-performance programs (often called P4P), and they could completely restructure the way health care is paid for in this country.

United Healthcare's gold-star system is not P4P per se, but it's being used by some self-funded employers as one—they're giving employees a lower co-payment for using designated doctors. Some programs offer financial bonuses to providers who meet certain criteria, and others tie future rate increases to quality measures, such as preventive care, chronic disease monitoring and/or investing in information technology. Ultimately quality experts hope to develop standards that measure actual health outcomes.

Hospitals have been dealing with this kind of quality reporting through the voluntary Hospital Compare reporting program and, more recently, through Medicare's move to offer a small increase in the annual reimbursement update to hospitals that report on 10 quality measures. But physicians have just started to see these efforts aimed at them.

"It's much more than a fad," says Michael Millenson, a Chicago-based independent consultant and author of *Demanding Medical Excellence,* noting that the health care system must move away from paying for volume, which is inefficient and expensive. "It's a question of how we are going to reimburse health care. Pay for performance is a recognition of the fact that if you don't link payment to quality, it's not sustainable," he says.

Gimmick or Better Way to Pay?

Some see pay for performance as yet another health care gimmick, the latest in the insurance industry's attempts to control physician behavior and cut costs beneath a thin veil of "quality" to give it respectability.

And yet, many health care policy authorities see the practice of paying for quality as the wave of the future. The most important of those authorities from a practical standpoint is Medicare, which has a series of pay-for-quality demonstration programs under way looking at both physicians and hospitals. Most likely, Medicare will choose to make pay for performance a permanent policy. The impact of that move would be huge for providers of all sizes throughout the United States, including small and rural hospitals.

In November 2005, the Senate approved legislation as part of the budget reconciliation package that would expand Medicare's commitment to pay for performance. The language is not included in the House version of the bill, and by *Trustee*'s press time, it was unclear whether it would survive conference talks between House and Senate members reconciling the two bills. However, Centers for Medicare & Medicaid Services (CMS) officials are optimistic that Congress will ultimately approve new P4P authorization, says Barry Straube, M.D., acting director of the Office of Clinical Standards and Quality for CMS. "Managers and policy-makers don't realize that if Medicare implements pay for performance, [it will] be on the leading edge [of P4P], which is breathtaking," says Hoangmai Pham, M.D., senior health researcher at the Center for Studying Health System Change in Washington, D.C. "This is one of the reasons physicians everywhere accept that [pay for performance] is becoming reality. They see the writing on the wall."

For hospital leaders, the pay-for-quality trend should be a big flashing dot on the radar screen, requiring boards to get reports from both their chief financial officer and the quality folks about how the trend will likely affect their markets. The pressure to measure and report quality—such as giving beta-blockers to heart attack patients and closely monitoring those with chronic diseases—is

Quality/Payment Programs

Three quality-reporting/payment programs working with CMS that will have a major impact on hospitals are:

Hospital Quality Alliance

The Centers for Medicare & Medicaid Services is working in conjunction with the Hospital Quality Alliance, a public-private collaboration on hospital measurement and reporting, comprising the American Hospital Association, the Federation of American Hospitals and the Association of American Medical Colleges. The Alliance has developed a set of reporting measures centered around three clinical conditions: myocardial infarction, heart failure and pneumonia.

About 4,000 hospitals submit quality information to this program, which posts the data on the "Hospital Compare" Web site at www .hospitalcompare.hhs.gov. New measures are being added regularly.

Hospital Quality Initiative, CMS

In this initiative, CMS has focused on an initial set of 10 quality measures that link reporting of those measures to the payments hospitals receive for each discharge. Hospitals that submit the required data receive the full payment update to their Medicare diagnosis-related group (DRG) payments. Nearly all (98.3 percent) of hospitals eligible to participate (Medicare/Medicaid recipients) are doing so.

Premier Hospital Quality Incentive Demonstration, CMS

The Centers for Medicare & Medicaid Services is additionally analyzing pay for performance through a partnership with Premier. Under this demonstration project, CMS is collecting data on 33 quality measures related to: heart attack, heart failure, pneumonia, coronary artery bypass graft, hip replacements and knee replacements. Hospital-specific performance will be publicly reported on CMS' Web site.

In the first year of the program, participating hospitals improved care an average of 6.6 percent. CMS paid about $8.85 million in first-year incentives, the agency reported in November 2005. Hospitals scoring in the top 10 percent for a given set of quality measures received a 2 percent bonus payment on top of the standard DRG payment for the relevant discharges. Those scoring in the next highest 10 percent received a 1 percent bonus. By the third year of the demonstration, those hospitals that do not meet a predetermined threshold score on quality measures will be subject to small reductions in payment. More than 260 hospitals, members of the Premier hospital alliance, are participating.

moving from being a best practice to a standard with a direct impact on the bottom line. And the more providers can influence the decidedly evolving science of defining just what "quality" means, the better off they'll be in the long run.

Quality, Efficiency, IT Problems

Pay for performance is a market response to several trends. One is the growing body of medical journal articles documenting the distressingly high prevalence of medical errors in hospitals, along with inconsistent and inadequate care for a large proportion of the U.S. population. Then there's the American health care industry's slowness to use information technology's potential to standardize care. Voluntary measures haven't done a lot to improve commitment to change, so some believe financial incentives might do the trick.

At the same time, employers are watching their health insurance premiums rise in double digits each year. They're looking for ways to regain control of costs that they lost when managed care's hold on the market loosened in the late 1990s.

This situation raises an essential question behind the pay-for-performance trend: Is it all about quality or is it all about saving money? The answer will vary, depending on who's sponsoring the program and what their motivations are. Many would argue it should only be a quality issue.

"Pay for performance is not about cost control," says Kenneth Kizer, M.D., president and CEO of the National Quality Forum, Washington, D.C. "It's about quality improvement and getting a better outcome. It just so happens that a side effect, or collateral benefit, of improving quality is that we are likely to save money for at least some things and for some period of time."

But if there are employers who believe P4P is the antidote for their rising premiums, they will be disappointed, Kizer says. "We shouldn't delude ourselves into thinking pay for performance is going to solve the health care cost problem. It will not," he says. "It may help in some ways, but fundamentally it's about incentivizing the system to provide better care."

Whether pay-for-performance programs actually produce higher quality care is an open question. Bruce Vladeck, who directed the Medicare program in the mid-1990s, is skeptical. He believes the health care system is too complex to allow simple financial incentives to align everything in a positive direction. "Why doctors do what they do and hospitals do what they do is complicated," he says. "The notion that you can add $4 to a payment, and it's all taken care of doesn't make sense."

Payment systems can be used to change behavior, but only to a point, Vladeck says. "We have a long-standing tendency to try to load too many other kinds of expectations on payment systems. People think they are magic." He also worries that payment systems will become too entrenched to adapt to evolving best practices, and that pay for performance misses what motivates the vast majority of doctors. "Health professionals want to provide the best quality care. That's what gets them up in the morning," he says. "Not that they'll make another $1.19 that day."

On the other hand, Millenson argues, what is the alternative to finding some way to pay for quality? Continuing to pay for volume, which results in higher costs? Or going back to managed care, which was unpalatable to consumers?

What's Happening Out There

Because hospitals and physicians are generally on different payment systems, pay-for-performance programs thus far have focused on either one or the other. A more integrated approach might be developed in the future that would make sense, providing a more comprehensive and sophisticated way to encourage quality across the continuum. The pay-for-performance trend hit hospitals first, in part because it was easier to gather data from a large institution than from a small medical practice. But now, physicians are being targeted by a fast-growing number of payers. Med-Vantage, a San Francisco consultant, surveyed pay-for-performance programs and found 35 of them in 2003. The firm expects that number to grow to 160 this year (2006).

Probably the most advanced example of pay for performance is run by the Integrated Healthcare Association (IHA), a consortium of seven large California HMOs that offers financial incentives to participating physicians who post improvement across multiple measures of clinical quality. (See "Integrated Healthcare Association's P4P Measures," page 256.) More than 35,000 doctors in 225 medical groups participate.

Integrated Healthcare Association's P4P Measures, 2003–2004

The Integrated Healthcare Association (IHA) is a California health care leadership group. Some of its members—seven major health insurers in the state—provide medical groups with incentive payments based on quality benchmarks. The IHA program assesses the performance of more than 35,000 physicians in 225 medical groups.

In the middle of last year, the IHA released results of quality measures affecting more than 6.2 million commercial HMO enrollees whose health plans participate in the program.

Results of 13 measures are below, representing improvements between 2002 and 2003.

Selected Clinical Measures

1. Breast cancer screening: 1.5 percent increase (64.4 mean to 65.4 mean)
2. Cervical cancer screening: 8.2 percent increase
   (62.4 mean to 67.5 mean)
3. Childhood immunizations, DTP:* 84.5 percent increase
   (33.4 mean to 61.5 mean)
4. Asthma, all ages: 3.3 percent increase in appropriate use of medication
   (66.7 mean to 68.8 mean)
5. Diabetes care, HbA1c screening: 5.3 percent increase
   (65.8 mean to 69.3 mean)
6. Cholesterol management, LDL screening:* 15.7 percent increase
   (67.7 mean to 78.3 mean)

IT Measures

7. Medical groups meeting IT criteria: 53.8 percent increase
   (34.4 mean to 52.9 mean)
8. Integration of electronic clinical data sets: 70.6 percent increase
   (27.9 mean to 47.6 mean)
9. Point-of-care decision support technology: 69 percent increase
   (20 mean to 33.8 mean)

Patient Experience Measures

10. How well doctors communicate:* 1.6 percent increase
    (85.6 mean to 87 mean)
11. Rating of doctor: 0.9 percent increase (80 mean to 80.7 mean)
12. Rating of health care: 2 percent increase (70 mean to 71.4 mean)
13. Timely care and service composite: 7.3 percent increase
    (69.5 mean to 74.6 mean)

*Indicates a change in the survey questions or measure specifications, which may be responsible for some of the change.

Rewarding Results: Lessons Learned

Pay for performance (P4P) has had some important successes in the field, but still faces challenges before it can become a standard part of health care reimbursement, according to a long-term study involving seven of the nation's most advanced P4P programs.

The Rewarding Results program was coordinated by the Leapfrog Group, a health care quality and cost containment consortium comprising more than 170 companies and organizations that purchase health insurance for their employees. The program was supported by grants from major national health care philanthropies, with the seven project sites aligned with a variety of sponsors across the country, including health insurers, employers, hospitals and broad-based coalitions.

Among the Lessons Learned So Far

1. *Financial incentives do motivate change.* But they need to be large enough to make a difference. One of the program sites, for example, suggests that, at a minimum, an incentive should be set at $5,000 per physician to affect quality improvement. Others suggest that incentive programs need to be structured to account for at least 10 percent of a physician's annual income. All seven Rewarding Results sites are offering incentives at a variety of levels.

2. *Nonfinancial incentives also can make a difference.* Just providing additional support to make a physician's job easier, or supporting the infrastructure to supplement technology can motivate physicians to hit quality targets.

3. *Engaging physicians is a critical activity.* All seven projects have worked hard to engage physicians, with varying degrees of success. If physicians are not brought into the process early as collaborators to ensure that goals are clinically meaningful, they will not adopt and sustain the change.

4. *There is no clear picture yet of return on investment.* Estimating the return on investment of P4P is essential, but few projects are conducting rigorous research on this topic. There are still questions about who should benefit from cost savings and over what time span the return on investment should be calculated.

Continued →

5. *Public reporting is a strong catalyst for providers to improve care.*
However, providers need adequate tools and data to keep improving. To maximize improvement, providers also need to be rewarded
for installing and using health information technology and building
infrastructure to track and compare performance.

6. *Providers need feedback on their performance.* Frequent, clear
and actionable feedback to providers is essential. Many of the
Rewarding Results projects issue public report cards to help
physicians compare their performance to others and make their
performance more transparent to consumers. Physicians need to
understand: what aspect of their performance will be evaluated;
how performance will be measured; and how performance and
incentives are related. They also need to be given tools and guidance on how they can improve.

7. *Providers need to be better educated about P4P.* Physicians are
deluged with clinical and reimbursement information. For any
payer, even those with a large share of the market, it can be challenging to attract provider attention. Still, payers need to find
effective communication tools to raise awareness about P4P; if
they don't, physicians will ignore quality improvement demands
or, as in one case, inadvertently throw bonus checks in the trash
because they aren't aware of the program.

8. *Data integrity is important.* Most health care providers are
inundated with quality measures from a variety of payers. They
are more likely to participate and embrace P4P if they view
payer measures as valid and scientifically based. Quality targets
also need to be clinically relevant.

9. *Experience with managed care matters.* Markets where managed
care has more of a foothold seem to have an easier time with
P4P because physicians and the general public are more
comfortable with issues related to quality improvement, such as
transparency, accountability and performance comparisons.

10. *P4P is not a magic bullet.* It is one of a number of activities under
way by the public and private sectors to improve quality and
change incentives in the way health care is delivered and financed.
If it's implemented well and aligned with other incentives,
including performance feedback, public reporting and support for
systems improvement, it appears to be an extremely useful tool.

Source: The Leapfrog Group, November 2005.

IHA reported second-year measurement results in July 2005 that indicated that pay for performance can offer results. The measures, focused on preventive and chronic care, showed impressive gains in childhood immunizations—an 84 percent increase in children receiving DTP shots—as well as 8 percent more women getting cervical cancer screenings. There was also a big jump in groups meeting IHA's information technology standards, rising from 34 percent to 53 percent in a year. Financial incentives amount to about 5 percent of total capitation rates.

Because California was a leader in using capitation during the heyday of managed care, it makes sense that such an experiment would start there. In fact, an ongoing study of 12 health care markets around the country by the Center for Studying Health System Change found the most active markets in pay for performance were Orange County, California, and Boston.

One potential problem the study's researchers identified is the growing number of conflicting sets of standards each of these programs requires. Add to that the standards set by Medicare and accrediting agencies, and both hospitals and physician groups could easily be overwhelmed, no matter how good their information technology systems are.

"Across 36 hospitals in 12 markets, we counted 38 different quality reporting programs," Pham says. "It gets very complicated. We don't think most of [these] programs . . . appreciate that there is this dizzying array of sponsors and programs."

A Long List of Challenges

There are a lot of potential problems with paying for quality that these experiments must resolve. They raise such questions as:

- How large a financial incentive does it take for a physician to change behavior—1 percent, 5 percent, 50 percent?
- Where does the bonus money come from for incentive programs? Is it new money invested by payers or taken away from some other part of the benefits package or from other providers?
- Are the programs voluntary or mandatory?
- How do you get enough data for a given health plan with an individual provider to make analysis statistically significant?

- How do you avoid penalizing physicians for their patients' non-compliance, such as failing to get follow-up care or a diagnostic test that's been ordered?
- What data are used to evaluate provider claims, which may not be adjusted for risk, or to conduct chart analysis, which is more rigorous, but expensive?
- How will the multitude of health plans, employers and quality accreditors around the country coordinate the criteria they use to measure quality, so providers don't waste time and money answering the same questions many different ways?

Physicians Object

In the past couple of years, nearly every U.S. health care organization, from the American Medical Association (AMA) to the Joint Commission, has developed its own criteria for how P4P should be carried out.

Not surprisingly, physician groups' criteria include those that protect their members from potential harm. For example, the AMA asks that these programs be voluntary, that practicing physicians be involved in their design, that they don't penalize doctors for treating non-compliant patients, and that they involve rewards rather than penalties.

The AMA isn't against the idea of pay for performance, says John Armstrong, M.D., a spokesman for the AMA and chair of its task force on the issue. But it wants to be sure that the intent behind the plans is actually quality, not cost savings.

"AMA believes there need to be pilots and demonstrations to look at P4P and make sure it has its intended effects of quality improvement," Armstrong says. "Physicians are concerned that this is another tactic by payers to reduce costs."

At the same time, it may be hard to find a pay-for-performance model that physicians approve of, argues Millenson. "There has never been any payment model that organized medicine has not opposed," he says. "They have legitimate concerns, but their whining is so pervasive and so self-righteous that it overwhelms any legitimate concerns."

Physicians will have to be willing to give up something to address the quality problems and waste that exist in American medicine, Millenson maintains. "If you're giving [appropriate] care only

55 percent of the time and wasting 30 percent of the money, could you explain to me a way to deal with this that does not cause some doctor, somewhere, to lose some income?"

What Trustees Need to Know

What does all this mean for hospital trustees? Obviously, hospital pay-for-performance programs such as those now being developed by Medicare will have a direct impact on hospitals. And physician incentive plans are likely to alter the local health care marketplace in a variety of ways—particularly, by putting added pressure on physician groups to invest in IT, for which they may look to the local hospital for help.

For hospital trustees, the P4P trend is another reminder that boards can no longer focus only on finances. They need to get regular updates from the quality side of the hospital as well.

"Trustees need to think about performance data beyond just pay for performance," advises Carmela Coyle, vice president for policy at the American Hospital Association. "They really need to think about this in the broader context of sharing that information with their community and with their patients. We are at the point where sharing this information is critical to building your relationship with your community."

That goes for hospitals of all sizes, in all markets. Even without pay-for-quality moves by payers, smaller hospitals are feeling the pressure from their own communities to share information about the quality of care they provide. "In some cases, hospitals have a lot they are proud of and are grateful someone's finally interested," says Suzanne Delbanco, executive director of the Leapfrog Group, whose hospital quality survey is seeing a rapid rise in the number of rural hospitals participating in it.

For trustees, the idea of paying for quality may be easy to understand because they may come from industries where customers expect to get value for what they buy. Trustees should be educating themselves about how health care purchasers are seeking that same kind of value.

"They're all going to have to deal with it, because pay for performance is coming to your neighborhood," says Kizer. "The board should spend as much or more time talking about quality as it does about finances. As boards move forward, the two will be inextricable."

PART SIX

Patient Safety

Creating the Patient Safety Mindset

By Laurie Larson

*Two health systems explain how they are
making safety improvements—and proving them.*

Is it dangerous to be a hospital patient today? It's often difficult to separate the attention patient safety has received in the medical and popular press from its actual condition. But can it improve? Always.

"It seems that the way you create change in a society is to first create fear," says Patrice Spath, president of Brown-Spath & Associates, Forest Grove, Oregon. "That's the cycle now [in health care]. But [safety concerns] are also a part of the public's anger toward managed care and the health care system."

In her work as a health care quality consultant, Spath often goes on-site to interview administrators and help them assess the safety of their institution (see "What's Your Patient Safety Culture?" pages 266–267). She always counsels that improvement in patient safety begins with an analysis of what a hospital will do *when* rather than *if* an unsafe event occurs. And she listens for three common statements that tip her off to an institution's need to become safer:

- *"It's never going to happen to us."* Hospitals that have never had a major sentinel event may say this, keeping them from identifying

---

Laurie Larson is *Trustee*'s senior editor.

What's Your Patient Safety Culture?

The statements below reflect how staff feel about various human factors that affect patient safety in your organization. Place a check in the appropriate box to indicate how strongly you agree with each of these statements.

People in this organization . . .

	Low	Medium	High
1. Are open to hearing how their actions affect patient safety.	☐	☐	☐
2. Can listen to feedback from others without getting defensive.	☐	☐	☐
3. Don't blame others for their mistakes.	☐	☐	☐
4. Don't retaliate against those who make mistakes.	☐	☐	☐
5. Believe that even competent, well-trained professionals make mistakes.	☐	☐	☐
6. Are willing to admit to patients that caregivers sometimes make mistakes.	☐	☐	☐
7. Cooperate with one another to resolve problems.	☐	☐	☐
8. Regularly report all patient incidents.	☐	☐	☐
9. Feel comfortable reporting unsafe conditions to their supervisor.	☐	☐	☐
10. Believe that there are things that can be done to reduce the likelihood of a medical mishap.	☐	☐	☐
11. Are willing to change some of their old habits in order to improve patient safety.	☐	☐	☐

Continued →

	Low	Medium	High
12. Believe that a medical accident could occur in this facility.	☐	☐	☐
13. Take time to discuss what went wrong when a significant patient incident occurs.	☐	☐	☐
14. Are willing to share information about errors they have made and the contributing factors.	☐	☐	☐
15. Believe that most patient incidents are preventable.	☐	☐	☐
16. Agree that patients play a role in preventing medical mistakes and mishaps.	☐	☐	☐
17. Believe that the organization's leaders are committed to improving patient safety at all costs.	☐	☐	☐

Sample tabulations of responses for each item, using percentages (not just raw numbers), will generally suffice. These can be indicated on a copy of the questionnaire, with percentages filled in where the checkmarks would go. Some results may be ignored later, but it is important to begin by tabulating everything.

The next step is cross-tabulation for items that may have some important relation to one another. For example, to determine whether the culture in particular patient units or among particular disciplines is more error-prone, one would cross-tabulate units or disciplines by the survey findings.

The exact form of the final survey report will depend on its purpose. If the data will be used to work on error-prone attitudes in small groups at all levels, the report should avoid inferences and conclusions. It should contain data grouped by unit, department, or division and be very clear, even to nonexperts. If senior managers and medical staff leaders will be using the data to formulate work culture improvement action plans, summary data and important findings may be more desirable. When preparing the final survey report, be sure to consider who will use it and for what purposes.

Source: Patrice Spath, *Patient Safety Improvement Guidebook*. Brown-Spath & Associates, 2000 (www.brownspath.com).

near misses and even smaller mistakes that may mean trouble
down the road.

- *"We're no worse than anyone else."* This implies an "acceptable" error range, Spath says, which dismisses improvement as
unnecessary. "If an airline said, 'We don't have any more plane
crashes than anyone else,' that would not be okay," Spath says.
"What we should have is zero tolerance. Even one error should
be prevented."

- *"There's nothing we could have done about it."* Spath says she
hears this statement most often. "If we continue to blame the
patient or the system, it keeps us from being proactive," she says.
Even though an error itself cannot be "taken back," it should not
prevent investigating how to keep it from happening again.

"These attitudes are something trustees can [look] for when they
[see] quality reports—they can read between the lines," she suggests.

"Generally, I find people want to have a safe environment," Spath
says. "We've got low morale in hospitals because caregivers know
where the problems are, but management isn't listening. If trustees
see a high employee turnover rate, it's a sign that [staff] are sick
and tired of trying to convince management that there is a problem.
Look at your turnover rates."

Other warning signs of a poorly constructed or non-existent safety
program include low attendance at quality-related meetings, particularly low physician attendance, or not having a specific individual
in charge of safety. Quality improvement projects that tend to focus
on business over clinical processes, such as reducing patient wait
times versus treating pain, are other signs of misplaced priorities.

How Intermountain Aims High

A health care system known for more than 20 years of making
safety a cutting-edge priority, Intermountain Health Care (IHC),
Salt Lake City, continually works on patient safety through clinical
quality improvement.

"Every employee at all 22 of our hospitals is aware that he or
she is responsible for clinical quality . . . and that a culture of safety
is part of a culture of clinical quality," says William Nelson, IHC's
president and CEO. As early as the 1970s, IHC's flagship, LDS

Hospital, innovated with its "Help System." Among many "prompts," this computerized medical data storage system combined lab data with patient information to flag contraindicated drugs on patient charts. It has since been replicated at the majority of IHC's other hospitals in Utah, Idaho and Nevada, and will soon expand into its second incarnation, "Help II," a more thorough patient care management system. This prompting system will give electronic recommendations, make clinical suggestions, and generally help clinicians provide optimal care and reduce error rates. IHC hopes to initiate a pilot Help II within the next two years.

LDS Hospital has continued to lead the field with a recent study on prophylactic antibiotic treatment published in a peer-reviewed journal. Staff researchers found that giving patients antibiotics between one to two hours before surgery was an optimal timeframe for preventing surgical infection. The procedure is now used in all system hospitals. Now IHC has stepped up its safety efforts.

"For the past two years, we've started focusing on specific patient safety goals as part of our annual strategic goals," Nelson says. In addition to its proven perioperative antibiotic initiative, which aims to be used on time in 90 percent of all IHC surgeries this year, the system has three other specific patient safety goals: eliminating adverse drug events (ADEs); preventing falls; and improving compliance for patient restraints.

The initiatives are led by a central operating group chaired by Nelson and divided into five geographic regions, three urban and two rural. In addition to a regional vice president leader from each region, this central group includes representatives from IHC's physician group, its health plan, human resources, legal counsel, and Greg Schwitzer, M.D., IHC's vice president of inpatient clinical programs and support services. The central group meets monthly and sets annual operations goals, which the IHC board must approve.

Standardized data gathered from all hospitals for each initiative are reported to a central operating group, which summarizes outcomes and sets patient safety objectives from the data gathered. Next, the system's professional standards committee, a system board subcommittee, reviews the central group's summarized findings and sends them quarterly to the full 27-member system board for review and approval.

Eleven Safety Practices Anyone Can Use

The Agency for Healthcare Research and Quality (AHRQ) recently issued an extensive report outlining several dozen health care practices that it endorses for improving patient safety. Of those recommendations, the following 11 procedures gave the strongest evidence supporting widespread implementation.

"No good system should fail to have these in place," says Brent James, M.D., vice president of research and education at Intermountain Health Care in Salt Lake City.

Safety practices are listed in order of proven efficacy and are geared toward care of the acutely ill.

1. Appropriate prophylaxis to prevent blood clots in at-risk patients
2. Preventive use of beta-blockers in cardiac patients before surgery to improve outcomes
3. Use of maximum sterile barriers while placing central intravenous catheters to prevent infections
4. Preventive use of antibiotics prior to surgery to avoid perioperative infections
5. Asking patients to recall and restate what they were told during the informed consent process
6. Continuous drainage of subglottic secretions to prevent ventilator-associated pneumonia
7. Use of pressure-relieving bedding materials to prevent pressure ulcers
8. Use of real-time ultrasound guidance to assist central line insertion to prevent complications
9. Appropriate outpatient self-management for warfarin (Coumadin) for effective anticoagulation without complications
10. Appropriate nutrition, particularly early enteral nutrition, in critically ill and surgical patients
11. Use of antibiotic-impregnated central venous catheters to prevent catheter-related infections

Source: Agency for Healthcare Research and Quality. Find the full report at www.ahrq.gov.

In his leadership position, Schwitzer takes prime responsibility for quality improvement and risk management for the system, monitoring patient safety goals and coordinating all IHC's patient safety initiatives systemwide.

"There's a high degree of variability among 22 hospitals, and it can vary within each hospital as well," Schwitzer says. IHC began all its initiatives with uniform definitions and baselines of where each hospital stood systemwide.

"It takes a multidisciplinary team of clinicians and administrators to set up the processes that will facilitate measurement and improvement," Schwitzer says. "There are four steps: define an area to pursue; make sure your definitions and measurements are commonly agreed upon; decide on your measurement tools; and get a baseline for the system."

He cautions that it takes six to eight months to find common measurement systems and definitions and tools, and six to eight more months to establish a baseline.

"You need at least two quarters of time or [ideally] a year to account for the seasonal variation of hospitals and establish a baseline," Schwitzer cautions. "Often analysis [estimates are] shot from the hip." He adds, "It's impossible to take a 'Big Bang' approach with patient safety. You have to evaluate and implement goals sequentially in a way that makes sense. What can you realistically do? Set a series of goals that can give you real benefit and are easily measured."

Resident Expert

Nelson acknowledges that one of the biggest reasons IHC has been ahead of the curve with patient safety was the foresight of its CEO in bringing Brent James, M.D., on board 15 years ago. Currently IHC's vice president of research and medical education, heading up clinical improvements, James was one of the authors of the groundbreaking 1999 Institute of Medicine report on medical errors. Consequently, he's quite familiar with how hospitals have handled safety problems historically.

Errors are typically reported in one of three ways, James explains. First, by voluntary reporting as injuries occur, which "tends to be underdetected," he says. Second, by detecting injuries through retrospective chart review of procedures with a high probability of injury.

"This is bad because it's expensive, the information is received well after any intervention opportunity has passed—and it misses a third of actual injuries," James says.

The final way of detecting medical error, and what James defines as "the gold standard," is through prospective expert review—or detecting potential errors "ahead of time." One key component of such a system is "data-based clinical trigger system responses," or tracking typical ways errors are fixed. This is what the Help System and Help II are designed to do.

For example, certain drugs are typically used to counteract overdoses of opiates, he says. A tracking system designed to flag orders for the antidote to that overdose would instantly question why it was ordered, potentially catching a near miss. The same clinical trigger principle in an error detection system could detect many other types of errors, both retrospectively, as in the above example, or prospectively, flagging such problems as a too-high drug dosage ordered for a patient's level of kidney function. Because 90 percent of injuries come from six events (adverse drug events, hospital-acquired infections, pressure sores, venous thromboembolisms, patient falls and injuries due to bed rails and restraints, and inappropriate blood product transfusions and reactions), James says that choosing what to watch becomes evident. IHC already tracks ADEs and hospital-acquired infections and is developing systems for the other areas.

Even with these systems, however, voluntary reporting still requires ongoing staff education. James sees IHC's culture of safety as being one where potential injuries are immediately regarded as system failures, not professional incompetence. This attitude eases fears of reporting mistakes, he says. But staff are reminded that they are expected to report errors, both for legal protection and to establish a professional ethic.

"You need to make it easy to report," James advises. "Look for where data bottleneck and target reporting there." He cites IHC's Pixus system, a central patient prescription dispensing system at a majority of nursing stations. The Pixus system identifies drugs ordered for treating injuries. The computer then automatically asks the orderer if that drug request is the result of an ADE. It is easy to answer yes or no, and no individual name is attached to the response. James says reporting has increased "100-fold" since IHC implemented the Pixus flag.

How Baptist Created Its Own Council

Another system ahead of its time, Baptist Memorial Health Care in Memphis, did a benchmark study with VHA (a national network of community-owned health care organizations and physicians) hospitals on medication usage and decided to make changes—a year before the IOM report came out. "After the benchmark study, the board set an [overall] patient safety mandate," explains Stephen Reynolds, Baptist's president and CEO. "We took the recommendations of those closest to the patient, and they told us that [to meet the board mandate] we needed a safety council." The three making the recommendation were William Poston, M.D., Baptist's chief medical officer; Nancy Nowak, vice president of nursing; and Jule Keegan, system director of pharmacy. They in turn chose the other 11 members of what became Baptist's Safety and Quality Council.

"Trying to make changes across the system [is an enormous task], but if we were trying to do best practices at the flagship (Baptist Memorial Hospital in Memphis), we had to do them at all hospitals," Nowak says. Baptist has 17 urban and rural hospitals across Mississippi, Arkansas and Tennessee.

Launched in April 2000, the council exists to provide organizational leadership for patient safety initiatives; establish a safety plan; oversee data collection and analysis; foster best practices implementation; and partner with patients and the community in care delivery.

In addition to Keegan, Poston and Nowak, who chairs the council, members include Baptist's system director of clinical services, chief information officer, risk management director and vice president of finance, among other leaders.

"These are the key decision makers across the system," Nowak says. "At this level, we can quickly bring information to senior leadership and make recommendations to systems operations and the board; it's easy to effect change quickly—there are key interconnections."

To get started, the council looked to national experts. "We looked at regulatory changes from the Joint Commission, the Health Care

Financing Administration, the Occupational Safety and Health Administration, and others to see where they were focusing their efforts [in patient safety], and we did the same . . . to see what initiatives were most important," Nowak says.

Baptist currently has nine active safety initiatives: medication system variance (now called the medication use safety team); use of restraints; pain management; in-house resuscitation; patient falls; needle safety; mandatory physician handwriting legibility guidelines; moderate sedation; and the clinical pharmacist practice model.

Each initiative has a representative safety council member and a system team. Each hospital has an equivalent team. Similarly, safety councils that mirror the system council have been implemented over the past year at each hospital.

Every facility has a data "grid" for each of the nine initiatives that it must fill out monthly for its system council. Each initiative asks for different types of data, but all hospitals fill out the same information for each. The chief nursing officer of each hospital is accountable for the reports. Nowak meets monthly with each of these nursing officers.

Just as system problems can be found this way, if an individual hospital finds an exceptional way of improving safety, its success can be shared systemwide.

Safety council structure is flexible within each hospital, depending on its size, but all include the chief nursing officer, a physician leader, and staff from medical records, risk management and quality assurance.

Nowak and Poston report safety council activity at all system board meetings. "The data allow us to take snapshots [of how the initiatives are progressing] and keep drilling down, asking continually, 'Are we doing our best? Could we do better?'" Nowak says. At the annual strategic planning and budget meeting, all initiatives are analyzed for what they have achieved and what new goals need to be added. Nowak calls it "a project in motion."

"It can be overwhelming. You have to tackle each initiative one at a time," she says. "But once you get rolling, it becomes a partnership versus 'What piece belongs to me?' The philosophy is that all of us take care of patients no matter what we do and if we're all asking the same questions, we'll come to the same outcomes."

To lead by example, Reynolds writes a letter to each system board member weekly, always including a note on patient safety, and he encourages every CEO in the system to do the same. All medical staff meetings include quality reports, and the topic is covered monthly in the employee newsletter.

Zeroing In on Medication Safety

To date, Baptist has spent the most time and effort on its medication safety initiative. For the past four years, the system's pharmacy team has collaborated with the VHA and 33 other hospitals to benchmark medication use. From this, best practices have emerged, and the Baptist system's director of pharmacy, Jule Keegan, has been able to effect innovative change.

"We check all the drugs in our formulary to look for potential confusions between them," Keegan explains. "If we determine we need both/all drugs that sound or look confusingly similar, we try to add additional information to separate them further from each other."

Beyond this, Keegan's department has focused on three high-risk medications—heparin, insulin and warfarin—and has significantly reduced associated ADEs. Preprinted physician orders are required for heparin, preventing handwriting problems. Nurses monitor the administration of all three drugs particularly closely, and additional lab tests are ordered to tightly track patient drug levels—a team effort.

"Health care teams have proven to have more positive outcomes than physicians alone," Keegan explains.

Similarly, Baptist's clinical pharmacy model safety initiative gives pharmacists more help—and more time to monitor drugs in patient units. A certified pharmacist assistant now performs the computer order entry of prescriptions, freeing clinical pharmacy specialists to make rounds, seeing patients for therapeutic drug monitoring, as well as getting more involved in patient education and discharge planning.

Like IHC, Baptist has gone to great lengths to make incident reporting and its perception more "blameless," starting with system-wide education for bedside staff. The clear message from the board on down is that the data collected will make care safer and that those filling out incident reports will not be held personally accountable.

Reports now have "action plans" on the back of them, where staff can address what they think would keep a problem from happening again. "It makes them feel more comfortable to be able to say, 'Here's how to fix it' and write it out," Keegan says. These changes

What's the Trustee's Role?

Beyond the data, models, and the teams in the field, trustees need to understand that the safety of their hospital is ultimately their responsibility.

"We approach the business of the hospital with the same degree of concern as we do our own personal business," says Watson Bell, trustee at Baptist Memorial Health Care. "You think of it as though you, or a member of your family, was receiving care." Bell also chairs Baptist's Joint Conference Committee, which meets quarterly with chiefs of staff at all the system's hospitals to review safety, among other clinical, operational and strategic goals related to patient care. They look at performance improvement reports, discussing their experiences and ways to improve safety.

"Trustees should demand accurate safety reports and ask appropriate questions of management, such as: 'Why do our data show this increase [in falls, for example]?' 'Are they the result of more reporting or a bigger problem?' 'Are we adequately resourcing patient safety?' 'What resources should be given?'" explains Greg Schwitzer, M.D., Intermountain Health Care's vice president of inpatient clinical programs and support services.

Asking these types of questions creates a "culture change" that lets the CEO know that the board expects safety to be a top priority, says Patrice Spath, president of health care quality consultants Brown-Spath & Associates.

"Boards need to realize that they have to [get involved in patient safety] whether they want to or not—there's a national push in that direction," says Brent James, M.D., IHC's vice president of research and medical education.

"We [trustees] bring a lay perspective to the board and sometimes [that] perspective is a breath of fresh air," Bell says. He knows from listening to local residents, for example, that a patient judges good nursing care by how quickly a call button is answered rather than more technical skills. "We feel, as trustees, the hospital reflects upon us . . . so we take it very personally," Bell adds. "Safety is part of our fiduciary responsibility."

—Laurie Larson

have increased the number of reports "by leaps and bounds," Nowak says, with more near misses versus incident reports. She says a follow-up survey is planned soon to determine if the staff now feels more comfortable with incident reporting.

Keeping Up with Change

Is patient safety in crisis? IHC's Schwitzer says that the acuity of patients has risen in hospitals—and it does make safety tougher. "[We] have a different kind of patient now," he says. "Historically, we had a large population of [relatively] healthy, alert inpatients. Now the majority is sicker, older, more disabled and more medicated"—and more prone to patient safety problems. Staff are also more stretched, with a higher volume of patients needing more resources just when staffing ratios are tightening. Technology figures in as well.

"Every time you increase technology to save people, the care environment becomes more complex," Schwitzer says. "But if we're going to improve [care], we have to have technology. Extensive training and setting goals and monitoring them for realistic improvement is the answer."

Ultimately, action may count the most. Spath points out that as of July 2001, the Joint Commission requires all hospitals to target at least one high-risk procedure for improvement, and if hospitals aren't sure where to start, the most common sentinel events are listed on the Joint Commission's Web site.

"Choose a high-risk process, go to the staff and ask them about it," Spath suggests. "Use their input to choose one to two projects. You don't have to spend so much time analyzing . . . just do something!"

Although other industries offer great models for safety improvement that health care can learn from, it is still a field unto itself in many ways.

"We do not have the luxury of stopping our work to fix things—and we [treat] people [when they are] most vulnerable and sensitive," Nowak says. "We have to keep doing the work while we fix it."

The solutions are being discovered, as IHC and Baptist, among many others, are proving. And as more of these models are found and followed, the axiom "practice makes perfect" becomes a foreseeable goal.

Patient Safety:
It Starts with the Board

By Shari Mycek

When it comes to the fundamentals,
patient safety tops the list.

I was in Paris interviewing airline pilots for a travel story when the Air France Concorde crashed just minutes after takeoff. The crash killed all 109 people on board as well as four more people on the ground. Reaction from the pilots was one of shock, numbness and disbelief. The Concorde, which flies at an altitude of 60,000 feet and crisscrosses the Atlantic in just three-and-a-half hours, had been considered among the world's safest planes. It had never been involved in an accident before. Immediately after the disaster, Air France grounded its five remaining Concordes until "passenger safety could be ensured."

In 1982, Johnson & Johnson quickly recalled 264,000 bottles of Extra Strength Tylenol from store shelves after seven Chicago-area residents died after taking the non-prescription pain medication. A probe revealed the product had been laced with cyanide, and the incident ultimately led to an FDA mandate that all over-the-counter pharmaceuticals must have tamper-resistant seals.

Shari Mycek is a writer based in Belle Mead, New Jersey.

But the "celebrated" cases are not reserved solely for the transportation or consumer industry.

In 1995, two tragic medication errors at the Dana-Farber Cancer Institute in Boston rocked the health care industry. One of the errors resulted in the death of a well-known *Boston Globe* reporter; the other triggered a significant medical intervention.

"Not only was the attention of the public and the media riveted on the events, so were the eyes of the entire health care field," wrote Jim Conway in his introduction to *Strategies for Leadership: Hospital Executives and Their Role in Patient Safety*, published recently by the American Hospital Association. Conway is the chief operations officer at Dana-Farber and now a board member of the National Patient Safety Foundation and the Massachusetts Coalition for the Prevention of Medical Error's steering committee. " 'What happened? Why? What can be done to be certain it doesn't happen again?' were questions we were asking ourselves," Conway adds.

Four years later, in 1999, health care leaders were once again troubled when the Institute of Medicine issued a groundbreaking report that as many as 98,000 Americans may die each year from medical errors. Although the IOM's most recent report, *Crossing the Quality Chasm: A New Health System for the 21st Century*, addresses quality problems inherent in the health care system as a whole and doesn't single out patient safety, Don Nielsen, M.D., the AHA's senior vice president for quality leadership, warns that health care leaders cannot relax. "The first report focused very much on medical errors; this one did not, but that doesn't mean there are fewer [errors]. Much work still needs to be done."

And that work starts with the board.

"Patient safety should be a standing item on the board agenda," says Nielsen. "It should not be an ancillary add-on item, but an item in which trustees should be asking questions of the organization's senior management as well as the clinical staff."

What exactly is patient safety? Kenneth Kizer, M.D., president and CEO of the National Forum for Health Care Quality and former head of the Veterans Administration, defines it as "continuously seeking to minimize hazards and patient harm. . . . [It is] shared responsibility for risk reduction . . . free and open communication . . . and facilitated reporting of errors . . . in a non-punitive environment."

Brock Nelson, CEO of Children's Hospitals & Health Clinics in Minneapolis, says his organization is working hard to create a patient-safe culture. Children's operates from two sites, employs 1,400 professional staff, 3,500 total employees, and serves the entire state of Minnesota. More than half of the hospitals' patients are critically ill.

In September 1999 (two months before the first IOM report was published), the Children's board endorsed an organizationwide patient safety initiative as part of its overall strategic plan.

"No specific incident—wrong-leg surgery or chemotherapy case— [inspired] this effort," says Nelson. "There was just an awareness [of the importance of patient safety]. We had a new chief operating officer at the time who was very much [concerned about the issue] of patient safety, and our board leadership was also very familiar [with the area] and supportive as well. The chair at the time had a child who had died—not the result of a medical accident or error, the child had cancer—but he saw a lot of opportunities, during the course of his child's treatment, for errors to occur. Another board member was in the transportation business and was well aware of [the significance of] safety."

Following the board's endorsement of a patient safety initiative, focus groups were conducted with hospital staff, physicians and parents, asking them what errors they had seen and what they believed could be a problem. As a result, patient safety courses have been conducted for staff, and a steering committee composed of physicians and parents has been established to oversee the patient safety program. Also, patient safety is now tied to compensation—for Brock, senior management, as well as departmental directors and clinical chairs throughout the organization. Board members receive dashboard-type key performance indicator reports, one quadrant of which covers patient safety.

"Now, [when] the board sees a financial report, it also sees a safety report," says Nelson. "Having a patient safety plan has made a big difference in terms of [getting] everybody's attention, but [ensuring patient safety] doesn't get easier; in fact, it gets harder."

For example, at this writing Nelson had just suspended a surgical program temporarily. Although he declined to elaborate on his reasons for doing so, he did note that no "incident" had prompted the measure but, rather, the potential for an error to occur.

"Physicians questioned my authority to suspend the program temporarily," says Nelson. "Why would I do that? We'd been doing [this procedure] forever—but it just came down to safety and whether or not we could guarantee it. A task force of physicians is now working on the issue, identifying what needs to be in place before we can resume—and we probably will resume [the program] in the very near future. Although their reaction [to the suspension] was negative, physicians are definitely part of the process—trying to figure out what needs to be done and making the necessary changes. And their buy-in is critical."

Indeed, physicians can make or break an organizationwide patient safety plan. According to Steven DeLashmutt, M.D., a trustee at St. Elizabeth Health Services in Baker City, Oregon, and chair of the AHA's Committee on Governance's patient safety committee, there are two partners in the "patient care business": the board/CEO and the medical staff. And the two must jointly commit to a patient safety plan "to successfully make the thing fly."

Certainly, that was one lesson learned at Dana-Farber. In the years following the high-profile medical errors there, COO Jim Conway has hit the lecture circuit, sharing with colleagues ways to guide their organization to a "culture of safety."

"Without voice, visibility and commitment from the top of an organization, little progress is possible," says Conway.

But obtaining buy-in from boards, CEOs and the medical staff is not as simple as it sounds.

"Most business partners try to work together because it benefits them both," says DeLashmutt. "But in a board-physician relationship, there's sometimes mixed direction. If the hospital does well, the board is happy. If the hospital does well, the physicians may or may not be happy. And so, if the business thrives, you have two partners—one of which will always be happy and the other who may or may not be—and that's a funny [kind of] partnership.

"The question comes down to: How can the board motivate physicians to participate in a patient safety plan? And the key is that physicians, 100 percent of the time, are geared to getting the best care for their patients. The way to get physicians on board is to [say], 'We can take better care of your patients by implementing a patient safety plan. At the other end, we'll come out with fewer errors, less harm to your patients, and they'll be safer in our institution. But you have to help us do that. You have to be an integral part, an architect, of the plan.' The reward comes for the physicians when they see, in actual fact, that things have changed, that their patients are being taken care of better. All this takes time, of course—six months to a year minimum."

Getting started is often the most difficult step. Once the board has committed itself to making patient safety fundamental to the organization's internal strategic initiative, a patient safety plan— crafted with input from physicians—should be put in writing (see "What Makes a Patient Safety Plan?" below).

"There is no magic formula for creating a culture of safety," says DeLashmutt. "And it's also impossible to peg a number and say the overall hospital error rate should be .001 or .00001, because every hospital is going to have a different goal—and a different culture.

What Makes a Patient Safety Plan?

Steven DeLashmutt, M.D., trustee of St. Elizabeth Health Services in Baker City, Oregon, and a member of the AHA's Committee on Governance, suggests the following elements be included in a patient safety plan:

- An outline of the patient safety officer position
- Quality improvement for patient safety
- Measurements to be monitored for patient safety (e.g., mortality and morbidity rates, length of stay, etc.)
- Details of error reporting and error assessment methods
- A comprehensive method for evaluating hospital and medical staff competency
- Outline of patients' and families' roles
- Qualifications of outside contractors
- Type and methods of ongoing education for all staff
- Type of data to be collected and to whom they will be reported internally
- How departments will collect and report data required by external organizations (e.g., the Joint Commission, the Institute for Safe Medical Practices)
- Brief description of the "culture of safety"
- How quality assurance will be built into the system
- Description of a "crisis team" comprising a cross-section of staff (e.g., social workers, nurses, physicians, etc.) and the training required for communicating with patients and families who have experienced a medical error
- Hospital's participation in patient safety research, if appropriate
- How often the plan will be updated, reviewed and critiqued

Our hospital, for example, is small and rural. We don't do cardiac catheterizations or chemotherapy. So our rate of error will be different from that of a hospital doing more complex procedures."

To determine where patient safety problems may exist within an organization, DeLashmutt suggests a study of quality indicators. "There will be a problem area," he says candidly. "There's not a hospital in the United States that doesn't have a problem someplace, so if you pull up the right indicators for your institution, it will put you on the right trail to figure out where your challenge lies."

Quality indicators may include death rate; length of stay; number and type of malpractice cases; number of patient falls; number and rate of errors made; number and type of sentinel events; number and type of near misses; policy changes as a result of error analyses; reports to the board by performance improvement teams involved in patient safety via the quality committee; reported hours spent in training staff in patient safety; and patient assessments of their perceived level of safety.

"An interesting piece of patient safety is patient satisfaction," says DeLashmutt. "If all the wheels are turning right in the patient safety arena, then patient satisfaction should also be high."

DeLashmutt also suggests tying CEO compensation to patient safety—as has recently been done in conjunction with healthy community initiatives. "Linking patient safety to compensation shows the CEO that the board is serious about its commitment. If the hospital's error rate drops by 15 or 20 or 30 percent, then there should be a bonus for the CEO or senior administration."

Like the AHA's Nielsen, DeLashmutt advocates making patient safety a topic at every board meeting.

"Trustees, persistently and doggedly, at every board meeting must ask, 'How many medical errors have [we made] in the past month? How many near misses have there been? And what is being done about them?' And you hope the answer isn't, 'Oh, we fired the dude who did this.' You don't want to hear that," he says. "By and large, it is not the person who's at fault but the system.

"I once read a classic account on how to ride a dead horse," DeLashmutt continues. "Many strategies were offered. You could change the rider, form a team to discuss how to ride the dead horse. But, in the end, the only thing that made sense was to call it a dead horse and get off; figure out a different—and better—way to get where you need to go."

Strategies for Leadership in Patient Safety

Complete?

Yes   No

Personal Education

☐   ☐   Read *To Err Is Human: Building a Safer Health System*, edited by L. T. Kohn, J. M. Corrigan, and M. S. Donaldson. Washington, D.C.: National Academy Press, 1999.

☐   ☐   Participate in external safety education programs, conferences, etc.

☐   ☐   Hold detailed conversations with in-house experts on our realities of practice.

☐   ☐   Walk my hospital with a human factors expert.

☐   ☐   Walk my hospital as a patient.

☐   ☐   Familiarize myself with enhanced Joint Commission Patient Safety Standards (see "Patient Safety and the Joint Commission: The Latest News," page 27, in the March 2001 *Trustee*).

☐   ☐   View Bridge Medical video "Beyond Blame" and Partnership for Patient Safety video "First Do No Harm."

Call to Action

☐   ☐   Speak publicly to the following audiences on the unacceptability of the current state of, and my commitment to, patient safety as a personal and corporate priority, as well as including a safety focus in hospital publications, strategic plans, etc.:
- board leaders
- patients/consumers
- media

☐   ☐   Implement a proactive effort on patient safety design, measurement, assessment, and improvement. Include direct care, administrative and clerical staff, and patients and family members in all aspects.

Continued →

Complete?

Yes	No	
☐	☐	Set the goal of establishing an environment of trust with a nonblaming, responsibility-based approach to the causation of incidents and errors; establish policy in this area.
☐	☐	Set the expectation for timely and interdisciplinary error and near-miss investigations with an emphasis on: patient/family affected by the error; the broader institutional implications of and learning from the error; and the support of staff closest to care.
☐	☐	Build quality improvement and patient safety policies into staff orientation and continuing education offerings.
☐	☐	Set the expectation for executive involvement in significant incident investigations.
☐	☐	Establish a policy to ensure patients/families are notified ASAP when an error affects a patient.
☐	☐	Establish effective grievance systems for patients/families who see themselves as "victims of error."
☐	☐	Establish mechanisms to train leadership and other experts in patient safety.

Practicing a Culture of Safety

Yes	No	
☐	☐	Openly engage with medical staff, nurses, and other leaders in patient safety planning.
☐	☐	Continuously articulate the business case for safety improvement.
☐	☐	Personally participate in a significant incident investigation/root-cause analysis.
☐	☐	Tell "my story" around incidents/errors that I have been involved with and the systems improvements that could have prevented them.
☐	☐	Routinely involve myself, all levels of our staff, and our patients and family members in direct ongoing communications around the patient safety work of our institution and areas for improvement.

Continued →

Complete? Yes	No	
☐	☐	Routinely probe staff perceptions of risk areas from existing or proposed systems and take immediate actions wherever possible.
☐	☐	Openly support staff involved in incidents and their root-cause analysis.
☐	☐	Ensure that there is ongoing prioritization and achievement of safety improvement objectives.
☐	☐	Ensure that articles on patient safety matters regularly appear in my organization's communication vehicles.
☐	☐	As part of annual budget approval, ensure resources are funded for priority safety areas.
☐	☐	Ensure self-assessments from the AHA and others are completed and used internally for quality improvement activities.
☐	☐	Cultivate media understanding of patient safety and my organization's efforts to improve safety.
☐	☐	Ensure effective systems are in place to assess individual accountability and competence.

Advancing the Field

☐	☐	Share my personal and the institution's patient safety learning outside of the organization.
☐	☐	Participate in local, regional, and national conferences, coalitions, and other efforts to improve patient safety.
☐	☐	Engage in initiatives to drive enhancements in regulatory, facility/professional licensing, and accreditation agencies that support safety improvement and cultural change in consort with the specific goals of the organization.

Source: Excerpted from *Strategies for Leadership: Hospital Executives and Their Role in Patient Safety*, by Jim Conway, formerly chief operations officer, Dana-Farber Cancer Institute, Boston. Reprinted with permission from the American Hospital Association, copyright 2001.

According to Nielsen, the journey must include a non-punitive reporting mechanism. He advises that "trustees must ask what kind of data and information are being collected in regard to safety and the care being provided. They must ask how opportunities for improvement are being identified and what actions have been or are being taken to improve/rectify the situation. But before they can do any of that, they must ensure that people are reporting what may potentially be unsafe practices or practices that have already caused unfortunate outcomes. Everyone has an obligation to report 'near misses' or events they think are leading to unsafe care. And trustees must ensure that the reporting mechanism be non-punitive and, at least at the beginning, confidential."

Unofficially and among themselves, physicians already do that. "Physicians are not hesitant to talk about mistakes [among themselves]," says DeLashmutt. "The idea is that if you can talk to somebody else and share what may have happened to you that was not good, it may prevent [your colleagues] from having a similar problem. But there's no systematic way to do that; there's no forum. Right now, it's just a matter of physicians bumping into one another and saying, 'Hey, guess what happened to me last week,' and sharing that experience."

But the trust necessary to share those experiences typically rests among physicians only.

It becomes a different story when another party, such as the board, enters the picture—to review competency, for example. On this issue, DeLashmutt humbly acknowledges he has limited advice.

"Part of any patient safety program has to include competency," he says. "You don't want people in the hospital who are incompetent taking care of patients. That's a no-brainer. But competency can be a dark can of worms. While the competency of hospital staff is relatively easy to corner and measure, [that of the] medical staff is very difficult to measure. Still, boards must address competency. And that's really tough. You go back to this strange [board-physicians] relationship where one partner [the board] is immune, but the other partner [physicians] has to go through some sort of competency evaluation, and that's a really funny business model. Hospital boards do—or should do—self-assessments every year on their effectiveness," DeLashmutt continues. "But that evaluation is a *self*-assessment. It is unusual for the board to have evaluations done by employees of the hospital or by the physicians. That's not to say it can't be done; it just isn't.

"The rules for physicians are different. While physicians also undergo an appointment/reappointment process that assesses their ability to practice medicine, new Joint Commission guidelines now demand a program where staff members and other physicians can refer a physician to be evaluated for illness or impairment.

"So far, the hospital board is immune from a system of hospital staff or physicians referring a board member for evaluation of illness or impairment," says DeLashmutt. "The 'partners in quality' [i.e., the board and physicians] do not receive equal treatment under the new Joint Commission guidelines.

"Plus, you have the egos of the physicians saying, 'What are you looking at me for? Obviously I'm an M.D. I've been practicing for years. So I'm competent. You don't need [to know] anything else but that.' The potential for tension is great."

Other stumbling blocks or "threats" to implementing a patient safety program do exist, according to DeLashmutt, but none of them "is a good enough reason not to implement an initiative."

Those threats may include:

- Board apathy
- A CEO who doesn't support a program
- A board that insists on starting a program before obtaining CEO buy-in
- Complexity of restructuring the reporting mechanism in order to channel patient safety data to the safety officer
- Public opinion and suspicion fueled by a lay press exposition of medical errors (e.g., the "celebrated" cases)
- The threat of litigation from discovery in an open, communicative environment
- Chronic history of denial by hospital administration, board and physicians that errors occur
- Lack of awareness by the board and/or administration that a problem exists (i.e., poor information reporting)
- A traditional medical culture of individual responsibility and blame
- Inadequate allocation of resources for quality improvement and error prevention

- Inadequate knowledge by the board and administration about the frequency, cause and impact of errors, as well as about effective methods for error prevention
- Belief that the current error rate is acceptable
- Notion that problems can be fixed as they happen (i.e., no proactive approach)
- The idea that patient safety is "a phase" that will pass if ignored long enough

CEO Brock Nelson, for one, begs to differ with this last impediment. "I've been around a long time," he says. "And, yes, a lot of things are fads that come and go. But patient safety isn't one of them. Those who view it as such are in denial."

And denial can be very costly—to an institution's reputation, to the hospital's bottom line and, most important, to patients' life.

Have You M.E.T. the Future of Better Patient Safety?

By Laurie Larson

How medical emergency teams work—
and how they can work for you.

A young nurse is in her second month on the floor. A housekeeper speaks little English, but knows all the patients by name. An anxious son has flown in from college and sits at his mother's bedside. Any one of them might notice a change in the woman's color or her breathing, but not be sure how serious it is or whether they should do something. The nurse is intimidated by the curt doctor on call and fears her judgment may be questioned if she calls him prematurely. The housekeeper knows she's not medically qualified. The son is simply overwhelmed. What very likely may happen is that the patient in Room 312 may "code," that is, stop breathing or go into cardiac arrest, before anything is done. It doesn't have to be that way.

A new "team approach" to inpatient safety is making its way across the country, with all the earmarks of a future standard for care. Medical emergency teams (METs), also called rapid response teams, are emerging gradually in the United States, but are up and running in close to half of all Australian hospitals, and supported in

---

Laurie Larson is *Trustee*'s senior editor.

the United Kingdom by the National Health Service in a surrogate form called "Critical Care Nursing Outreach."

According to Michael DeVita, M.D., associate medical director at the University of Pittsburgh Medical Center (UPMC) Presbyterian, widely acknowledged as a leading expert on METs in the United States, the teams provide a "pre-organized, standard, trained response of professionals and equipment to a patient in crisis"—in other words, an intensive care unit (ICU) brought to the bedside.

Ideally comprising two critical care physicians, two critical care nurses, two respiratory therapists and two staff members from the floor where the crisis happens (who could be nurses, therapists or physicians) all answering calls on a rotating schedule, METs are dispatched whenever anyone—whether a nurse, other hospital staff person or family member—observes deterioration in a patient's condition or is simply worried. The response is identical to that generated by respiratory or heart failure, but is enacted before those crises happen. "Everyone is sent who might help," DeVita says. "They are already at the hospital and on call." Both overhead pages and individual pages are repeated twice to on-call staff. Over a period of three to four years, all UPMC Presbyterian respiratory therapists have gone through MET training, all critical care nurse responders and all responding physicians.

The idea "arose simultaneously in a number of places," DeVita says, with UPMC leading the way in the United States in 1989, spurred by the sudden decline of the chief of surgery's wife while she was an inpatient at UPMC. The efforts and staff used to resuscitate her resulted in a new "Condition C" code (for "crisis"), a level of response used prior to a "Code Blue" or "Code A" for cardiac or respiratory arrest. Medical emergency teams are also called "Condition C teams."

Kenneth Hillman, M.D., professor of intensive care at the University of New South Wales in Sydney, Australia, first recognized the need for such a code in England and after implementing the procedure there, went to Australia to expand the system. There he began reporting his results in the mid-1990s, and UPMC started reporting its results in 2002, DeVita says. The two men met in 2004 and now work collaboratively.

"We felt there was a huge need, and we felt the idea was very important [to have] span the globe, if we did our homework," DeVita says. The two doctors set three major goals. First, they wrote a manual for creating METs with Rinaldo Bellomo, M.D., professor of medicine at the University of Melbourne in Australia. The manual is currently being printed. Second, they wanted to host an international conference, explaining and promoting METs. That meeting was held in Pittsburgh this past June, and more than 400 registrants came from around the world, DeVita says. Third, he and Hillman wanted to create a "consensus conference" to determine MET nomenclature and standardized procedures, simultaneously developing a research network. They were able to tag that conference onto the larger one last June.

Data tell—and sell—the story. In 2002, researchers in *The British Medical Journal* reported a 50 percent reduction in non-ICU cardiac arrests using METs, and in research published in the *Journal of Critical Care* in June 2003, DeVita and other researchers showed the comparative ineffectiveness of repeated STAT pages—the traditional way of responding to a patient in crisis—to METs. According to DeVita's research, the average time between first and last STAT pages is almost four minutes, while a Condition C call has an average response time of 90 seconds.

According to Carol Scholle, R.N., director of critical care services at UPMC Presbyterian who supervises all MET-responder nurses in the 567-bed hospital's nine critical care areas, the STAT method is "a piecemeal team, where there's always a delay because of the ambiguity of responsibility."

Since initiating METs, sequential STAT pages at UPMC have decreased by 5.7 percent and the number of Condition C calls has gone up by 19.2 percent. Concurrently, the number of fatal cardiac arrests decreased from 4.3 to 2.2 per 1,000 admissions over a three-year period, as DeVita and colleagues reported in the 2003 *Journal of Critical Care* article.

"It has changed the culture here," DeVita says. "There is now a flurry of activity before the crisis, as opposed to right before the patient dies." He adds, "Having the capability to bring more resources to the patient's bedside is very powerful over time—to see that it works."

The Institute for Healthcare Improvement (IHI), Cambridge, Massachusetts, has made METs part of its 100,000 Lives Campaign. (See "A Campaign for 100,000 Lives" in the Sept. 2005 issue of *Trustee*, page 12.) Kathy Duncan, R.N., is the self-described "point person" for IHI's Rapid Response Teams initiative, and she estimates 2,500 hospitals have signed up for the campaign. Of those, 60 percent have chosen to focus on METs. Until last May, she was the director of critical care services at Baptist Memorial Hospital, Memphis, Texas, and it was her enthusiasm for bringing such teams to her hospital that helped lead to her new position.

METs in Memphis

In 2003, Duncan found out what Australia was doing with METs relative to preventing cardiac arrest. Duncan was inspired by such a focused process, particularly because it tied in so directly to the way nurses approach their job. "Sometimes patients just look different . . . there are symptoms [of decline]," Duncan says. "Nurses know that, they develop a sense of reading patients." Duncan next talked to the administrative team at Baptist, including the medical director of critical care, and a three-day pilot was initiated the following summer. Following the symptoms Australian METs look for, Baptist critical care staff tracked their post Code Blue data to see what conditions led to them and how they were handled.

"You learn best by tracking the last 20 codes in a row in your [own] building," Duncan says. "You look back at heart rates, respiratory rates, mental status . . . the idea is to notice subtle changes and get there earlier." Ten codes were called during the pilot. Baptist's pilot team comprised one ICU nurse, a respiratory therapist and a physician intensivist. Even with a smaller team, improvements were obvious.

"The earlier we call the doctor the better, and when you have two people come in first [to co-determine an initial decision], it helps validate the call," Duncan says. She and her team next began educating staff on when to call a Condition C and rewarding them when they used the system. She says this "culture of calling" has developed over time and "no one is intimidated now" to make a call. "The bedside nurse is learning from the team as they [come to codes], which backs up the process even more," she says.

Baptist tracked patient outcomes for a year after implementing METs, or Rapid Response Teams, as they call them, both in the ICU and for non-intensive units. "As we have gotten better with our data, we have noticed the culture change," Duncan says. "It was important to get these data back to staff, important for them to know the impact of their calling on patients' living."

The METs system assumes human and/or system fallibility and prevents it. Teams know ahead of time who should do what—but all are trained to do everything in case all eight team members don't arrive at once.

"No matter what you are licensed to do, you learn all the responsibilities of all roles," Scholle explains. "You learn and understand the team goals and priorities. Even if eight people aren't there, you know what all eight are supposed to do. The overall [patient safety] goals are what matters." The result is an expanded group synergy. Scholle says that even though teams reconfigure for each Condition C call, all who have received MET training "gel" with each other, creating greater calm and organization on the call.

DeVita's training course uses computer-based human simulators and limits classes to eight people, the same size as a MET. Teams use the simulators in four emergency scenarios, changing roles for each one. Scenarios are chosen randomly, alternating between such crises as stroke, ventricular fibrillation, narcotic overdose and others. "The point of the exercise is to get the team to organize and the process is the same irrespective of the type of crisis that the team encounters," DeVita says. "If they set up and organize well, they can respond to any crisis."

The four chosen "codes" are videotaped with time stamps, and trainees can see how quickly and effectively they worked and learn how to improve. Scholle says typically the training team improves as it goes through the four scenarios. Now that all critical care physicians, nurses and respiratory therapists have been trained, Scholle says UPMC Presbyterian's non-ICU clinical nurse leaders are being trained to be MET members, with the eventual goal to train all staff.

Make It Concrete

This level of compliance and proficiency took a long time to truly take hold, however. Although UPMC initiated METs in 1989, eight years later, DeVita discovered that the old hesitancy and resistance to change still existed. "The rapid response was already in place, but it was resisted [at first]," DeVita says. "There were a number of surgeons who didn't want [other] people to take care of 'their' patients." He and his team applied process improvement thinking to the situation, leading to a more objective set of criteria for initiating a Condition C. DeVita and his colleagues found that a more concrete list of symptoms helped staff feel more certain they could recognize a crisis and more justified in making the call. The resulting criteria gives specific respiratory and heart rate change parameters, blood pressure change ratios and such other warning signs as change in color, sudden lethargy or agitation, seizure, sudden loss of movement, or chest pain complaints.

The criteria have been backed with hospitalwide education and marketing that included rewiring the hospital's emergency phone system to go to the MET number, with the slogan, "One phone call can save a life." Criteria are posted in each nursing station and pocket cards have been given to all staff.

Although anyone in the hospital can call the five-digit MET number posted on every hospital phone on a bright orange "Emergency" label, Scholle says UMPC Presbyterian has not educated patients or their families about METs. However, another of their campuses, UPMC Shadyside, has initiated a pilot program in one of its units, informing patients and their families about "Condition H" (for "Help"). Admitting nurses explain to patients and their families how to make an in-house call for a Condition H, not only if they have an emergency, but also if they don't understand their plan of care or if they believe their patient needs are not being met, Scholle explains. Brochures are also provided that explain Condition H. Even without informing the visiting public about METs, DeVita says that, since implementing the objective criteria for staff in 1996, they have seen their best results since 1999. Scholle adds that the more defined system has been great for patient safety.

"The objective criteria took the guesswork out of calling for help," Scholle says. "Under the old definitions, we waited until we saw a dramatic change, but now the objective criteria outline the subtle changes that are the precursors to more serious problems. We are able to roll back the clock . . . by catching things earlier, we are able to stop the downward slide."

As a smaller community hospital where physicians are more often on call than in the building, Duncan says Baptist has taken on an additional Condition C tool that allows nurses and all other staff to "talk to doctors in doctor terms." The tool is called "SBAR," which stands for "Situation, Background, Assessment, Recommendation." By telling physicians the same types of information in the same way every time a call is made, no basic questions are left unanswered and no assumptions are made on either end of the phone about what is happening to a patient.

Duncan explains that *situation* refers to what the staff person observed when he or she came into the patient's room; *background* describes why a patient is in the hospital; *assessment* refers to vital signs; and *recommendation* is what the staff person thinks the physician needs to do and what he or she thinks is happening to the patient. Such variations and improvements validate DeVita's stand that "all concepts are endorsed and supported that rapidly respond to patient needs . . . get it started however it works for your hospital . . . let it grow. Doing something is what matters."

"Rapid response teams teach staff four to five changes that are classic around the world," Duncan says. "It boils down to heart rate, respiratory rate, subtle changes . . . they give [staff] tools to act on their own." She adds that "a 100-bed hospital can still watch for the same things . . . you might not have eight people [on a team] . . . but a sharp ICU nurse, a recovery room nurse . . . can they assess the patient quickly? That's the main criteria. Most interventions are simple. The idea is to get there earlier."

What's the Price Tag?

A big question for the board: What does it cost? "There is zero cost for personnel," DeVita answers. "The code team just does more."

He says UPMC has not needed to ask for any additional full-time employees.

"Administration thinks it will cost a lot of money, but you've already got the people in the building—it's about rearranging priorities," Duncan says. She adds that IHI offers a how-to guide on its Web site (www.ihi.org) for starting METs, including advice on how to talk to administrators.

One possible exception for smaller hospitals might be the need for a full-time (24-hour) respiratory therapist. But Duncan encourages doing the math. "You can count on 10 calls a month per 100 beds, according to the research," Duncan says. "Perhaps [the added salary] could be justified if [the therapist] worked in the [emergency department] too, or some other position . . . it's an operational puzzle."

To get to a state-of-the-art MET system, however, DeVita strongly recommends standardizing hospital equipment, so that a team responding anywhere in the building knows how to use the tools at its disposal.

"Standardizing equipment is expensive, but I think it's extremely important to do," he says. As a prime example, there were nine different defibrillators formerly used at UPMC, which meant that all MET staff had to know how to use all of them. DeVita says he and the MET analysis committee he chairs, the Medical Emergency Response Improvement Team, or MERIT, made the case to the COO and the critical care director for standardization, pointing out that "failure rates were up during [emergency] events; there were different parts to keep up; equipment updates needed; nurse education to learn how to run all the different defibrillators. . . . We put all those costs together and showed it was cheaper and safer to have [only] one type of defibrillator."

As with all hospitalwide change, support from the top is needed, but in the case of METs, critical care physician and nurse leaders have to first be willing to become team members and to support their staff being on call. In turn, there have to be units that are willing to make Condition C calls.

"You need an agreement with management that this is a concept you [all] want to try," Duncan advises. Whoever pitches and directs the project has to be an "inside" person, she says, such as the ICU or ED manager or an ICU nurse, and he or she must "have a passion for trying this." She advises such a leader to "go to the administrator and give the data on what led to the last 20 codes—that's powerful." This should be followed by explaining the MET science and providing research data in the field.

Other important champions include the chief medical officer, the chief nursing officer, the COO and the critical care committee, but DeVita adds that follow-through is what matters most. "It doesn't matter who starts it, but if you don't have someone who wants it and is willing to work through all the logistics, it won't happen," he says.

What about the trustee champion? DeVita cautions that "the board cannot put pressure on clinicians. The medical leaders have to [do that] . . . talking to those who report to the board . . . such as the chief of medicine, CEO or COO." Putting himself in the trustee's shoes, however, he says he would say to his board chair or CEO, "Our hospital has to do this to be responsible to the community. We have to do it because of quality and because we want to compete." It boils down to a culture change, and Scholle says UPMC Presbyterian has had strong support from both physician and nursing leadership. The hospital's medical director has been an important champion, particularly by backing nurses if doctors contest a MET call.

"To have a young nurse be able to say 'I'm calling [a Condition C]' to a doctor is tough," Scholle says, and she sees nursing empowerment as one of the most important facets of MET. "Nurses love this—it's the best thing that has ever happened in the building," she says. "To give [myself as a nurse] a tool to call for help when I think I need it, when I can use my critical thinking and intuition from years of experience to get what I think my patient needs, that is huge." She adds, "Eighty percent [of nurses] will buy in if you say it will help patients, and the other 20 percent will buy in when you prove it can save time—METs can fix/change a patient's status in 30 minutes, and that frees nurses up to care for all patients."

The best argument for METs, particularly in view of their cost neutrality, may be simply that they make common sense.

"When you tell administrators you could have saved someone's life [by using METs], they're not going to argue or tell you to stop," Duncan says. "I think if you move things around to give patients better care, the money will follow. And you can do it with what you've got." Bottom line, she says, "If you teach people how to raise the red flag, fewer people will die."

25 Simple Steps to Save Patients' Lives

By Lee Ann Runy

Hospitals are in the business of saving lives. Yet, gaps in care continue to result in harm. According to a report last year by the National Commission on Quality Assurance, "1,000 Americans or more die each week because the health care system regularly fails to deliver appropriate care." An article in the June 2003 *New England Journal of Medicine* reported that clinicians failed to provide appropriate care in nearly half of all cases.

The good news is there are relatively inexpensive and simple steps that hospitals can undertake to reduce the number of avoidable deaths in their facilities. Although most of these practices have been around for years and have solid scientific backing, they are not being commonly used in many organizations.

"There's still a relative degree of complacency within health care organizations," says James Reinertsen, M.D., head of The Reinertsen Group, a health care consulting firm in Alta, Wyoming, and a senior fellow at the Institute for Healthcare Improvement (IHI), Cambridge, Massachusetts. "Many organizations are satisfied with being close to the benchmark in their practices. But, being close to the benchmark means there are still flaws in the system, often resulting in needless deaths."

Lee Ann Runy is a senior editor for *H&HN* magazine.

Part of the problem is that some errors occur so rarely that clinicians feel immune to them. "It's not until someone reputable makes an error that people start to see gaps in the system," says Paul Schyve, M.D., senior vice president of the Joint Commission, Oakbrook, Illinois. Another challenging issue is physician autonomy.

"We really honor autonomy and independent behaviors in health care," says Donald Berwick, M.D., president and CEO of IHI. As a result, hospital leaders worry about creating too many restrictions in clinical practice. "That concern is misaligned," he says, "because clinicians are looking to hospital executives and the board for direction."

Executives and boards can start by identifying physician and nurse champions to spearhead efforts to incorporate evidence-based practices in their work. And, they should present a clear case for change. For example, executives could show physicians overall mortality rates for acute myocardial infarction, as well as comparison data showing physicians how they rank against their peers.

Data collection is key, says Paul Keckley, M.D., executive director of the Vanderbilt Center for Evidence-Based Medicine, Nashville, Tennessee. "Hospitals must take a close look at their current practices. They will see there are substantially more lives to be saved."

Hospital leaders must realize that change will not occur without their direct involvement. Blair Sadler, president and CEO of San Diego Children's Hospital, estimates he spends 15 percent of his time directly involved in safety and quality issues. "A CEO in today's environment has to make a fundamental decision that supporting quality and safety is a core part of the job," he says. Sadler notes, "Ten years ago, I would have said, 'It's not my responsibility.'" He suggests that CEOs look at their calendars and see how they are spending their time. "It's a critical mind shift the CEO has to make to get from a project-to-project quality improvement process to organizationwide transformation."

Ultimately, it may take outside pressure to spur safer practices. "Currently, there isn't sufficient positive or negative consequences to push these practices in the direction of universal compliance," says Ken Kizer, M.D., president and CEO of the National Quality Forum, Washington, D.C. Adds Berwick, "Hospitals that fail to adopt these practices will find themselves out of alignment with payer organizations, accreditation bodies and the government."

Hospitals & Health Networks magazine asked the experts quoted here to identify 25 relatively simple practices that hospitals can implement to save lives. Their recommendations are presented below, in no particular order. This is by no means a comprehensive list. Many other steps have been identified by patient safety experts—and, perhaps, your organization has implemented still others. Visit www.hhnmag.com and click on the "Save Lives Now" button. You'll find links to the Web sites of organizations concerned with patient safety.

1. *Clean hands.* As many as 10 percent of hospitalized patients get an infection during their stay. Those can largely be traced back to the fact that clinicians do a poor job of washing their hands— some studies suggest that fewer than 50 percent of clinicians follow handwashing protocols. Hospitals should institute stringent policies requiring that hands be washed with either a hygienic hand rub or a disinfectant soap prior to and after direct contact with each patient.

2. *The right read.* Even the most basic things can be overlooked— for instance, putting the correct label on radiographs. Incorrect labeling can lead to clinicians misinterpreting an X-ray or CT scan. Establish simple policies such as marking "right" or "left" on every image so there's no confusion when it's put on the light box.

3. *Kidney alert.* Contrast media is regularly used during radiological procedures. Some patients can develop allergic reactions to those dyes, resulting in kidney failure. As many as one-third of all hospital-acquired renal failures are linked to intravenous contrast agents. Hospitals should develop evidence-based protocols to evaluate patients at risk of kidney damage due to contrast media.

4. *Right dose.* Nearly 40 percent of medication errors occur during drug administration, according to pharmacy industry reports. One way to cut the likelihood of errors is to store medications in unit-dose or unit-of-use packages, and, when feasible, in single-unit packages. Every unit dose should have a bar code. The Federal Drug Administration has mandated that pharmaceutical manufacturers put bar codes on unit dose packages of some drugs by 2006. Pharmacy industry estimates suggest that from 30 percent to 50 percent of current unit-dose packages currently have bar codes.

5. *Quick action.* Quick action can stop declining conditions. The chairman of surgery noticed a decline in his wife's condition and

ordered a nurse and respiratory therapist to her room. They saved the patient's life, and she was transported to the ICU. So began the use of "rapid response teams" at the University of Pittsburgh Medical Center (UPMC) Presbyterian Hospital in 1989. Initially, the teams were used to help transport seriously ill patients to critical care units.

Today, they can be summoned by anyone—including patients and families—when the patient's condition appears to be on the decline. The idea is to detect and treat as early as possible any changes in the patient's condition, such as blood pressure, level of consciousness, or respiratory rate, all of which can be early signs of cardiac arrest.

UPMC's medical emergency teams consist of a critical care physician, a medical fellow, two critical care nurses and two respiratory therapists. They replace "STAT" pages, which are time-consuming and erratic. A team can be summoned by placing one call; the response time is about 90 seconds.

"Crises happen in hospitals," says Michael DeVita, M.D., UPMC's associate medical director. "Planning how you will respond to a crisis will improve the way you respond."

Getting hospital staff to call the teams required a big cultural change, primarily because nurses were concerned that physicians would question their actions.

To address those concerns, the UPMC established a set of objective criteria to help health care professionals know when to call in a team. With the teams in place, incidents of cardiopulmonary arrests decreased by 17 percent between January 1996 and September 2002.

6. *Stay alert.* Long working hours are nothing new to health care. Interns regularly work 80-plus hours a week, and nurses often work long shifts, including overtime. Hospitals should teach staff to recognize the signs of fatigue, especially second- and third-shift workers, and work with employees on strategies to minimize fatigue.

7. *Clot watchers.* Nearly 2 million Americans suffer from deep vein thrombosis every year. As many as 600,000 of these patients develop pulmonary embolisms; 200,000 of them die. Clinicians should evaluate patients upon admission and during their stay for the risk of deep vein thrombosis. Each patient should be evaluated regularly for risk of aspiration.

8. *Sore spotters.* Between 7 percent and 25 percent of hospital and nursing home patients develop pressure ulcers. This delays recovery and increases morbidity. It also slows the availability of beds. Patients should be evaluated upon admission for risk of developing bedsores and reassessed regularly during their stay. Bedsore prevention plans should be documented in the patient's record.

9. *Speak up.* A high-profile death from a medication error involving a *Boston Globe* columnist in 1994 led the Dana-Farber Cancer Institute to transform patient care. Among the myriad changes implemented included involving patients and their families proactively in the care process.

"There's not a lot of scientific evidence to support the belief that patient and family involvement helps reduce the likelihood for errors," says Saul Weingart, M.D., vice president for patient safety at Dana-Farber. "However, clinicians believe it's true because everyone has a story about how a patient has made a statement that prevented an error or harm."

Additionally, patients participate on all safety committees. There are two voluntary patient-family councils—one for adults and one for pediatrics—that address safety concerns. Council members visit patients and their families to ask about safety issues and help identify potential problems.

Patients and family members are engaged in the medication administration process to avoid adverse drug events. Patients review their medication histories to ensure they are up to date. Medication errors are now rare—only about one error in every 800,000 outpatient doses has occurred since 1994.

"Our patients and their families hold us accountable to provide good care," says Weingart. "They don't let us get away with much, and that's a good thing."

10. *Risky medications.* Almost 6,000 people die every year because of medication errors. Five of the top seven drugs involved in errors are so-called high-alert drugs, according to U.S. Pharmacopeia. Lists of high-alert drugs should be made available to all staff. Orders should be double-checked by a clinician once they are filled. A multidisciplinary team should regularly review safeguards for all high-alert medications.

11. *Know the difference.* A large number of medications share similar names or look similar. Between January 2000 and March 2004,

approximately 31,932 reports were submitted to U.S. Pharmacopeia's medication errors reporting program that listed look-alike or sound-alike drug product names, packaging and/or labeling as a cause for the error.

Hospitals should maintain a list of look-alike and sound-alike drugs. Problem drugs should be stored in an alternate location from those that are similarly spelled. The purpose of the medication could also be written on the bottle. Policies should be instituted to ensure that verbal medication orders are read back to the physician.

12. Match the meds. Researchers say that 46 percent of all medication errors occur when the patient is moved from one care setting to another—during admission to, or discharge from, the hospital, for example, or when transferred between units.

A standardized protocol should be established requiring clinicians to do a side-by-side review of the patient's current medications with his or her new medication orders every time the patient moves to a new setting. This process is also known as medication reconciliation.

13. Catheter concerns. Researchers have estimated that 14,000 to 28,000 deaths a year are caused by central venous catheter-related bloodstream infections.

The Institute for Healthcare Improvement recommends a comprehensive five-step central line bundle approach to reducing catheter-related infections: conscientious hand hygiene, maximal barrier precautions, chlorhexidine skin antisepsis, appropriate catheter site and administration system care, and no routine line replacement.

14. Making marks to prevent wrong-site surgery. Although rare, wrong-site, wrong-person and wrong-implant surgeries can have devastating consequences. According to the Joint Commission, communication failures are the biggest cause of wrong-site surgeries, followed by insufficient orientation and training on hospital protocol.

The Veterans Health Administration's National Center for Patient Safety is at the forefront of developing safe surgery practices. A more comprehensive process tested late last year at the VA Houston Medical Center and modeled after the aviation industry's preflight checklist is being rolled out at VA facilities.

The process is used in consort with the VA's Ensuring Correct Surgery Directive, which requires that surgical sites are marked by the surgeon or a member of the operating team with their initials; the patient or family member reviews and signs off on a consent form that lists the procedure, correct side, and the name and reason for the procedure; patients are actively identified; and at least two members of the operating team review the images taken for the procedure.

"This is a very effective and inexpensive process to implement," says David Berger, M.D., operating care line executive at the VA's Houston facility. "It improves communication, and patient safety issues are covered before surgery." The checklist is reviewed in the operating room (OR) while the patient is still awake. The steps call for the surgery team to:

Step 1: Discuss with the patient the procedure and body part to be operated on.

Step 2: Review the patient's medication history.

Step 3: Review and administer appropriate prophylactic antibiotics to prevent surgical site infections.

Step 4: Ensure the proper positioning of the patient.

Step 5: Review special equipment, such as implants and blood products that will be required during surgery.

Step 6: Discuss potential anesthesia issues, such as changes in blood pressure that may prevent anesthesia from working properly.

Since the process was put in place at the Houston facility, at least two operations have been canceled. In one instance, a patient revealed prior to surgery that he had failed to stop taking an anticoagulant as directed. In another case, a patient's elevated blood pressure raised concerns and members of the operating team decided it was best to postpone the procedure.

Communication is also enhanced by use of a white board in the operating room that lists important factors related to the procedure and the first names of the surgical team. "The use of first names helps foster a team environment and encourages team members to speak up when they see a problem," says Beverly Rashad, R.N., operating care line nurse executive.

15. AMI prevention. About 1.1 million Americans experience an acute myocardial infarction (AMI) each year, and a third of them will die during the acute phase, according to the American College of Cardiology and the American Heart Association. Studies show that relatively simple interventions can significantly reduce the mortality rates.

In 2002, McLeod Regional Medical Center, Florence, South Carolina, established a physician-led, multidisciplinary team to review the literature and recommend changes in care. The team called for reducing wait time for reperfusion—the restoration of blood to the heart muscle—to 90 minutes. The best practice for reperfusion time was between 90 and 120 minutes. McLeod was averaging 176 minutes.

Other recommendations included administering aspirin at arrival and discharge, administering a beta-blocker at arrival and discharge, using ACE-inhibitors or angiotensin receptor blockers at discharge for patients with systolic dysfunction, and counseling smokers on how to quit.

Between January 2001 and November 2003, compliance with the AMI measures increased from 80 percent to 100 percent. As a result, the average inpatient mortality rate for AMI dropped to 4 percent from 8.6 percent. The compliance rate is consistently in the upper 90 percent range, says Daphne Heffler, associate vice president of McLeod Regional Medical Center. The wait time for reperfusion averaged 85 minutes in 2004.

"Communication and feedback is key to all of this," Heffler says. "And physician involvement also helped bring best practices into play."

16. Ventilator fallout. Ventilator-associated pneumonia (VAP) occurs in up to 15 percent of patients who receive mechanical ventilation, according to a 2001 article in the journal *Chest*. The hospital mortality rate for ventilator patients who develop VAP is 46 percent, compared with 32 percent of ventilator patients who do not develop VAP. The Institute for Healthcare Improvement calls for a five-step ventilator bundle: elevate the head to at least 30 degrees, give the patient daily "sedation vacations," assess if the patient is ready to be extubated daily, and provide preventive treatments to avoid peptic ulcer disease and deep vein thrombosis.

17. Shorthand rules. Between January 2000 and August 2004, nearly 19,000 medication errors at 498 health care facilities were attributed to misread abbreviations, according to U.S. Pharmacopeia's error reporting program. Hospitals should standardize drug abbreviations, and share a list of unacceptable abbreviations and symbols with all prescribers. Hospitals should also develop policies to ensure that medical staff refer to the abbreviation list and that they take steps to guarantee compliance.

18. ICU rounds. The opening of an expanded intensive care unit in 2002 inspired Baptist Memorial Hospital–DeSoto, Southaven, Mississippi, to find and adopt best practices in critical care. One result: The hospital established multidisciplinary rounds to improve care in its 28-bed ICU and stepdown unit.

Every morning, a care team of eight to 10 members spends about an hour visiting all ICU patients to discuss the plan of care and the patient's goals for the day.

The team comprises a physician, nurse, respiratory, physical and occupational therapists, a dietician, pharmacist, social worker and a case manager.

"By and large, this is an easy program to implement," says William Richards, M.D., medical director of Baptist Memorial's ICU. "It provides everyone an equal voice in the care of the patient. It helps us see where we've been and where we're going."

The hospital's quality indicators show that the undertaking is paying off. Average length of stay for ICU patients dropped to 4.5 days in 2004, down from 5.9 days in 2001.

Among other things, the process helped facilitate the adoption of bundles—sets of practices to address conditions—for ventilator-associated infections and central-line-associated bloodstream infections.

Despite initial concerns from clinicians that the rounds would increase workload, they now recognize the benefits.

"People like to be associated with good practices," Richards explains.

19. Prevent falls. Reducing patients' risk of injury due to falls is one of the Joint Commission's patient safety goals this year. While it's up to individual organizations to define what qualifies as a "fall," clinicians should routinely assess each patient's risk of falling, including noting his or her medication regimen. Bed alarms could also be installed. Fall prevention should be added to patient education programs.

20. *Flu shots.* Every winter, hospital emergency departments are hit with a wave of patients sick with the flu. Hospital staff are at risk of catching the illness from those who come in for treatment and passing it on to high-risk patients. Health care workers should be vaccinated against influenza, and hospitals should have explicit policies in place to ensure compliance.

21. *Say again?* Miscommunication is a frequent cause of errors in health care, one that could often be avoided if clinicians simply repeated verbal or phone orders to ensure accuracy. The Joint Commission recommends that the nurse or pharmacist write down the doctor's order and read it back, providing another level of certainty. Don't assume your clinicians are already doing this as a matter of course.

"Most hospitals will say this practice is in effect," says Ken Kizer, M.D., president and CEO of the National Quality Forum. "But, it's not done as much as we believe." The National Quality Forum recommends that hospitals develop clear policies and procedures regarding verbal orders, and to completely prohibit verbal orders for chemotherapy.

The big challenge is getting staff to change their behaviors, says Paul Schyve, M.D., senior vice president at the Joint Commission. Kizer additionally comments, "Obviously, McDonald's thinks this is important when it comes to ensuring that your hamburger order is correct."

22. *Stop the line.* Giving nurses and other clinicians the power to halt unsafe practices improves patient safety. In an all-too-common scenario, a nurse is berated by a physician because she questioned his orders. But the nurse doesn't take it quietly. She issues a patient safety alert, which instantly brings the treatment process to a halt. The physician's orders are examined, treatment is revised and a potential error is averted.

After hospital executives and the department head review the incident, the physician is required to take remedial training in the course of treatment in question as well as an anger management class.

At Virginia Mason Medical Center, Seattle, every member of the clinical staff is empowered to "stop the line"—stop or slow down practices they deem unsafe, ranging from potential medication errors to staff misconduct. The patient safety alert notifies senior executives and the appropriate staff members and managers. The incident is immediately reviewed and corrective action is taken to prevent recurrence.

Virginia Mason's patient safety alert system is modeled on Toyota's stop-the-line practice in which any employee can interrupt the production process to prevent a potential problem.

"Everyone has a responsibility to report safety issues," says Cathie Furman, the medical center's vice president of quality and compliance. "This process provides everyone a voice. It tells staff we want to know whatever happens that may get in the way of care."

Putting the process in place required no financial investment; it did, however, require a change in the organization's patient safety culture. Virginia Mason merged its risk management and quality departments to form a patient safety department. It also set out to develop a blame-free culture.

As that culture takes hold, the alert system is being used more frequently. In 2002, the first year of the program, the hospital averaged three alerts a month. In 2004, there was an average of 15 a month. Administrators set a goal of 800 alerts per year as a way of getting staff to pay attention and actually follow through on the policy.

23. Bundle protocols. About 500,000 surgical site infections occur annually, the Centers for Disease Control and Prevention (CDC) estimates. They can contribute to increased length of stay, higher costs of care and increased mortality. When surgical patients with nosocomial infections died, 77 percent of the deaths were related to that infection, according to the CDC's 1999 "Guideline for Prevention of Surgical Site Infection."

Mercy Health Center, Oklahoma City, joined the Centers for Medicare & Medicaid Service's National Surgical Site Infection Prevention Collaborative in 2002. Participants implemented a so-called "SSI bundle" consisting of three steps: follow guideline-based use of prophylactic antibiotics, do appropriate hair removal and use perioperative glucose control. With those steps in place, surgical site infections at Mercy Health Center plummeted 78 percent after one year.

Getting the bundle in place required a thorough, multidisciplinary review of practices. "We had to redefine our surgery processes," says Ronda Pasley-Shaw, manager of epidemiology and occupational therapy. For example, analysis revealed that medications found their way to the operating room in four official ways and about 15 unofficial ways.

"It differed between the time of the day, day of the week," she says. "Variability in a complex medical situation almost always guarantees an error."

The hospital established a standardized delivery system and developed a formulary for OR medications. The hospital also educated staff on the benefits of clipping hair compared with shaving the surgical site.

Prior to implementing the SSI bundle, Mercy Health averaged about one infection for every 101 procedures. As of early March, the hospital had performed more than 1,000 surgeries without an infection.

"We've been successful because we took the time to involve all of the stakeholders," says Pasley-Shaw. "Everyone understood where everyone was coming from and were able to reach a consensus."

24. Who's who? Improper patient identification remains a common source of medical errors. Hospital staff rely too heavily on room numbers as the main source for matching up patients with a service or treatment. The Joint Commission recommends that hospitals go a step further and find two additional and distinct identifiers. West Georgia Health System in LaGrange uses ID bands that list the patient's name and medical record number. Patients receiving blood products get an additional armband, and two nurses are required to verify the patient's identification before a product is administered; the same applies for high-alert medications.

25. Handling drugs. Improper labeling, packaging and storing of medications are frequently cited problems in hospitals. There's ample evidence proving that improvements in this area can dramatically reduce errors. The National Quality Forum and other patient safety groups suggest standardizing labeling, packaging and storing methods. Drug lot numbers, expiration dates and identification of persons preparing and checking the medication should all be documented.

The Top 10 Hospital Malpractice Claims— and How to Minimize Them

By Maureen Glabman

A preemie delivered at New York Infirmary/Beekman Downtown Hospital, New York City, suffers brain damage from oxygen deprivation because a resident delays care a few hours after birth. Plaintiff verdict against the hospital: $90.3 million.

Breast cancer spreads to the bones and liver of a 42-year-old woman because mammogram results from the University of Miami/ Jackson Memorial Health Center in Florida do not reach her in the mail. Plaintiff verdict against doctor and hospital: $8 million.

A nurse fails to administer a prescribed antibiotic to a 53-year-old man prior to surgery for an obstructed bowel at Botsford Hospital, Farmington Hills, Michigan. The patient develops gangrene and requires amputation of both of his legs below the knees. Plaintiff verdict against the hospital: $4.7 million.

These cases, plucked from the files of Horsham, Pennsylvaina-based Jury Verdict Research, exemplify three of the most common reasons plaintiffs win settlements or judgments against hospitals— delayed care, medication errors and diagnosis failures.

Precipitated by such costly lawsuits, the national spotlight began to shine on the nascent patient safety movement beginning with a

Maureen Glabman is a writer based in Miami.

1991 published Harvard University study of patient injuries in acute care hospitals in New York state, and came under the full glare of public scrutiny with the landmark 1999 Institute of Medicine report, *To Err Is Human.*

Medical literature now abounds with proven methods for reducing errors. Among them: evidence-based medicine, computerized physician order entry (CPOE) for medication orders, pharmaceutical bar coding and failure mode effects analysis, which is a way of predicting bad outcomes used by the military, aerospace and automotive industries.

Why isn't every hospital using these tried and tested methods? Many hospitals have adopted some of them, but others are expensive and difficult to put in place. Within the next 10 years, however, most hospitals will acquire new systems and technologies that will prevent injury and serve as "lawyer repellents," according to experts such as James Bagian, M.D., P.E., director of the VA National Center for Patient Safety, Ann Arbor, Michigan.

"You will never be able to eliminate all of what is considered medical malpractice," says Bill McDonough, senior vice president of New York City–based Marsh Inc., a medical malpractice insurance broker for approximately 2,000 U.S. hospitals and health systems. "Even when people are the best at what they do, unfortunately they make mistakes." Still, studies by Harvard researcher Lucian Leape, M.D., demonstrate that hospital injuries can be reduced by 20 to 70 percent.

Institutions that do not improve safety may continue to suffer financial and human losses. The average 250-bed hospital (or its malpractice insurance carriers) spends the equivalent of the cost of a new MRI unit—between $300,000 and $1 million—annually defending medical malpractice lawsuits, not including settlements and judgments, McDonough says. Lawsuits also jeopardize the ability of hospitals to retain physicians and nurses, exacerbating an already difficult nationwide problem. "It's a horrific thing for a clinician to go through, affecting their ability to continue working, their marriage and their families," McDonough says. Such losses do not even touch upon the additional loss of community confidence that springs from negative publicity.

The expense of court cases offers another pressing reason to avoid lawsuits. Juries are more likely to punish institutions than doctors because hospitals are perceived as faceless entities with large wallets. Hospitals pay claims in 50 percent of court cases brought, while doctors pay in 30 percent of claims. Median plaintiff awards against hospitals alone are $500,000, according to Jury Verdict Research.

Risk managers report that many cases spring from community doctors who make hospitals chronic co-defendants, dragged repeatedly into court solely because of that physician's troublesome behavior, combined with a "deep pockets" mentality on the part of patients and their lawyers.

Hospitals walk a fine line between doing everything possible to make community doctors welcome, and disciplining "outliers." But they can no longer afford doctors who might bring in considerable revenue but whose performance threatens a facility's financial health, according to National Quality Forum board member William Golden, M.D. Moreover, he adds, "The reputation of the institution is at stake since the collective behavior of the medical staff influences the public perception of the institution."

In truth, hospitals have always had a tool chest of medical malpractice fix-it devices to curb physician behavior that they have been reluctant to employ. Among the recommendations of Pamela Para, R.N., of the American Society for Healthcare Risk Management:

- Trustees could encourage malpractice insurers to reduce premiums for clinicians who take risk management/patient safety classes.
- Through medical staff bylaws, trustees could set medical malpractice policy limits based on whether or not physicians applying for privileges have been trained in risk management/patient safety.
- When physicians come up for recredentialing, hospital administration could mandate risk management/patient safety training.
- Trustees could make patient safety a priority. "Everyone will say it's a good idea but it needs board leadership to make it happen," National Quality Forum's Golden says.

Here, then, are the top 10 most common causes of medical malpractice lawsuits against hospitals, collected from Jury Verdict Research, Marsh Inc., and the Boston-based Risk Management Foundation. They are followed by a range of potential solutions suggested by some of the country's leading risk managers and patient safety experts.

The Truth Can Set You Free

"My experience has been that close to half of malpractice cases could have been avoided through disclosure and apology but instead were relegated to litigation," wrote Johns Hopkins researcher Albert Wu, M.D., in a 1999 *Annals of Internal Medicine* editorial, "Handling Hospital Errors: Is Disclosure the Best Defense?"

Take the case of seven-year-old Ben Kolb, who underwent surgery in 1995 for a routine ear problem at Martin Memorial Hospital in Stuart, Florida, and died the following day. Instead of lidocaine to anesthetize him, Kolb received a lethal dose of topical adrenaline, a drug that was supposed to be used later in the surgery. The medications, which both look like water, were taken out of their labeled bottles, emptied into cups and set beside each other prior to surgery.

According to a 2002 NBC *Dateline* transcript about the case, hospital officials walked courageously into the parents' lawyer's office and explained how the drugs had been mixed up prior to surgery. The hospital officials and Kolb's doctor accepted full responsibility and apologized. Instead of a lawsuit, the parents and hospital agreed on a settlement. The boy's father said, "We wanted to know what happened. We wanted the truth . . . revenge wasn't there for me."

In a Veterans Administration hospital in Lexington, Kentucky, where, since 1987, honest disclosure of errors has been the policy and where the hospital aids patients in filing claims, the tell-all policy has not caused an onslaught of litigation. "I suppose that, in some cases, revealing an error about which the patient was unaware could lead to a suit or a settlement. However, if the case were to come to light otherwise, the consequences would likely be worse for the hospital," Wu wrote in an e-mail.

As of July 2001, hospitals have been required by the Joint Commission to acknowledge patient errors. A 2002 survey of hospital risk managers published in the March 27, 2003, online issue of *Health Affairs* reveals one-third of hospitals had board-approved disclosure policies in place.

—Maureen Glabman

1. Problem: Medication Errors

Medication errors involve cases where patients allege they were given the wrong medication, the wrong dose, in the wrong form or place, at the wrong time, or not given their medication at all. Orders can be written incorrectly or illegibly by doctors, read incorrectly by nurses, filled incorrectly by pharmacists and administered to the wrong patient. This problem has received more attention than all other patient safety issues. Yet, the majority of prescriptions are still handwritten.

Solutions include CPOE, robots, bar coding, automated drug dispensing, and other non-technology-driven methods.

CPOE. Less than 10 percent of U.S. hospitals use CPOE technology, even though it has been proven to reduce prescribing errors by 55 to 88 percent, according to studies led by David Bates, M.D., chief of general medicine at Boston's Brigham and Women's Hospital and David Classen, M.D., assistant professor of medicine, University of Utah, Salt Lake City. Computerized physician order entry eliminates errors caused by misreading or misinterpreting hand-written instructions, intercepts orders that could result in adverse drug reactions, and highlights medication orders that deviate from standard protocols.

CPOE, however, is no panacea for medication errors. The software has to mesh with existing lab and hospital pharmacy information systems. And, there is still the human element—doctors can override the programs. What's more, resistant doctors sometimes perceive entering information into a computer as clerical work. And systems that cost millions of dollars take years to fully install. In published reports, a CPOE system at the 726-bed Brigham and Women's was estimated to cost $1.9 million, with annual maintenance of $500,000. Net savings, however, was between $5 million and $10 million annually when the avoided costs of patient injuries, admissions for drug errors, malpractice lawsuits and extra work generated by non-life-threatening medication errors were taken into account.

Robots. Robots perform repetitive, mundane tasks more accurately than humans. They can automate pharmacy storage, retrieval and medication dispensing. The estimated cost of installing a robot is $1 million to $2 million.

Bar coding. Bar coding for drugs, vaccines and blood products is implemented in the same way groceries are priced. Bar codes have been proven to reduce errors by 65 to 86 percent, but the Food and Drug Administration estimates it will cost U.S. hospitals and other organizations $7.2 billion to incorporate bar code readers and related technology into their systems. For nurses, bar codes represent a significant change in culture. Rather than keeping paper patient records, they will push around laptops on carts, checking patient wristbands to verify medication accuracy.

MedStation PYXIS, Omnicell, and others. These are automated drug dispensing systems at nursing stations that function like ATMs with PIN number/biometric access, delivering precise amounts of prescribed drugs. Estimated cost: up to $1 million over five years.

Non-technology. Smaller hospitals with tighter budgets can rely on several non-software methods for improving patient safety. Among them:

• Root-cause analysis—hospital employees analyze a variety of near-miss medication mistakes to learn what human factors create problems.
• Readback—originally an Air Force safety tool, where the recipient of telephone or verbal physician orders repeats the message back to the physician to ensure clarity and accuracy.
• Doublecheck—encourages prescribers and those who deliver medication to check and doublecheck—is it the right drug, the right dosage and the right patient?
• Pharmacy rounds—pharmacists in facility satellite offices go on patient rounds with physicians so that medication errors can be identified on the spot.
• Failure mode effects analysis—identifies and prevents failures before they occur. In 2001, the Joint Commission began requiring an annual proactive risk assessment for hospital accreditation.

2. Problem: Diagnosis Failure

Diagnosis failures are defined as instances where patients claim an incorrect diagnosis delayed their treatment and/or resulted in improper treatment. This is a common claim, particularly in cancer treatment. The problem often happens in emergency rooms, but it also occurs on med-surg floors and in radiology when reading fracture and mammography X-rays.

Solutions include evidence-based medicine, and coordination of care between clinicians and information technicians to provide reminders and avoid slip-ups. Requiring physicians to use published protocols—what doctors often call "cookbook medicine"—is an important defense tool. Specialty societies design these protocols; the Centers for Medicare & Medicaid Service (CMS) and the Joint Commission are developing them; but local hospital adaptation is critical if a protocol requires an expensive medication or piece of equipment that the hospital can't afford. For example, a treatment for heart problems may be an angiogram, which may not be readily available at a small, rural hospital. A child with eye problems may require a referral to a pediatric opthalmologist, who may be located hundreds of miles away.

3. Problem: Negligent Supervision

These involve cases where patients allege they were injured when their activities, or the activities of other patients, were not sufficiently monitored. This claim is most often lodged against teaching hospitals where medical students, residents and fellows are sometimes assumed to be stand-ins for absent attending physicians. Dangers arise when a rogue, overconfident trainee tries to resolve a problem without adequate supervision. To a lesser extent, this may involve nurse practitioners and physician assistants as well.

Solutions include standardizing how residency programs are managed; creating and enforcing more stringent guidelines in which supervision is well-defined and mandatory; and following CMS supervision rules.

4. Problem: Delayed Treatment

These are instances in which patients allege treatment was unnecessarily or unreasonably delayed. In some cases, patients claim the delay caused additional injury. Hospitals lose these cases at trial 39 percent of the time.

Solutions include failure mode effects analysis, proactive risk assessment and root-cause analysis. The purpose is to redesign how care is delivered. Examples include developing a tickler system to alert physicians to abnormal reports; following up to make sure faxes are received; and maintaining logs at both hospitals and private offices to track information exchanges between providers, ensuring that lab, X-ray, and procedure reports do not fall through the cracks. "The legal system will find ways to hold institutions accountable," Golden says. "But if the institution documents good-faith efforts, perhaps it will fare better if challenged."

5. Problem: Failure to Obtain Consent

These involve instances where patients contend they were not given adequate information to make an informed decision about their treatment. Hospital leaders have worked on correcting this problem for years, and find it surprising that the problem still persists. A typical example would involve a patient who dies from anesthesia, and his family claims no one spoke to them about risks. Patients win these cases at trial only 26 percent of the time, according to a 2002 Jury Verdict Research report, "Medical Malpractice Verdicts, Settlements and Statistical Analysis" (LRP Publications).

Solutions include videotapes, CD-ROMs and clear patient explanations. Hospital staff have patients watch a program at the facility explaining the risks involved in a procedure. After the program, patients sign a form attesting that they watched and understood what was presented.

6. Problem: Lack of Proper Credentialing or Technical Skill

This claim is made when doctors perform procedures or surgeries for which they have little experience or inadequate skill. A frequent outcome is organ perforation.

Solutions include mandating simulation programs where doctors repeatedly practice a procedure or surgery; requiring physicians to attend professional society refresher courses; creating a treatment standard, or asking physician specialty societies for their standards for performing a surgery or procedure. Even if a physician meets specialty guidelines, "there is no guarantee nothing bad will happen, but it decreases the probability," VA patient safety director Bagian says.

Some hospitals are already getting tough. McDonough relates, "One Chicago area general surgeon who wanted to expand his practice into bariatric surgery refused to provide documentation he had completed training and demonstrate he had practiced this type of surgery. His privileges were suspended."

7. Problem: Unexpected Death

Death is unavoidable, and interventions futile in certain instances as, for example, when patients do not know they will have an allergic reaction to medication. However, there are ways to prevent certain deaths.

Solutions include requiring the clinical staff to take thorough patient histories that include past medical treatments; herbal, over-the-counter and prescription drugs; and recent life events. For example, if a patient scheduled for a hernia operation mentions that he has been unable to climb two flights of stairs without experiencing tightness in his chest, it could indicate ischemic heart disease, which may not have been apparent on exam, Bagian says, and which could influence how the surgery is performed. Patients with complicated histories should bring all of their pill bottles to the hospital before an elective procedure, or, at the very least, a list of all their medications.

Doctors typically want to close the file on a bad outcome, but the patient file contains a wealth of information that could prevent the same outcome from occurring again. Hospital safety teams should examine the cases thoroughly to determine if early clues were ignored. Learn from errors and develop teaching abstracts from these cases.

8. Problem: Iatrogenic Injury, Nosocomial and Wound Infections, Fractures

The Centers for Disease Control and Prevention (CDC) estimates that two million U.S. patients acquire infections in hospitals each year, and about 90,000 of these patients die as a result. Infections also cause care complications. Additionally, patients frequently claim they were injured when they attempted to leave their beds without assistance, when they were allowed to move about while highly medicated, or when they were assaulted or otherwise injured by an unattended patient. Of all types of malpractice cases, patients have the highest chance—45 percent—of winning these cases at trial according to the 2002 Jury Verdict Research report.

Solutions to infections include the most basic and effective one—handwashing. Swiss and American studies have demonstrated that health care–acquired infections go down as adherence to hand hygiene goes up. Hospitals should enforce 2002 CDC Hand Hygiene guidelines requiring handwashing or use of alcohol-based hand rubs to reduce overall infection rates. Gloving should also be universally encouraged. For falls and other types of physical injuries, fall prevention programs teach how to predict which patients are likely to fall, and stipulate that orders be given specifying which patients may not be permitted to walk on their own. In addition, patients who are in danger of falling should be restrained.

9. Problem: Pain and Suffering, Emotional Distress

Patients sometimes come out of surgery or procedures with unrealistic expectations of what they will be able to accomplish when they return home. They could experience unexpected paralysis; they may not be able to resume normal activities such as driving; their relationships may be unexpectedly stressed.

Solutions include having physicians apprise patients prior to undergoing a procedure of the best and worst case scenarios following the procedure, including the possibility of death and disability if warranted. They should also explain how long patients should expect convalescence and rehabilitation to take. Some patients should be dissuaded from undergoing an elective surgery or procedures.

10. Problem: Lack of Teamwork, Communication

Particularly in surgical and obstetrical areas, when different staff members monitor patients over time, they may see worrisome signs and fail to let their team members know. This often happens in cases when hospitalized women are in labor or when surgical nurses, watching patients undergo long surgeries, notice warning signs of patient distress but are requested not to speak to surgeons who are concentrating. It is also common when patients are transferred from one doctor to another, or from one hospital floor to another.

Solutions include team training, such as MedTeam, an approach that draws lessons from military aviation. As applied to medicine, it improves patient safety, patient satisfaction and employee satisfaction. At least 16 U.S. hospitals use MedTeam, including Beaumont Royal Oak and UMichigan Health System in Michigan.

Also, electronic medical records enable notes, lab reports and studies to be accessible to entire hospital staffs, "so they don't have to thumb through a lot of scrawl," says the VA's Bagian.

Human errors that result in what lawyers call "medical malpractice" or what hospital administrators often term "bad outcomes" can be significantly reduced. By using proven techniques borrowed from the military and other industries to predict and prevent error, including failure mode effects analysis, root-cause analysis, readback and doublecheck, hospitals may reduce their exposure to lawsuits. Where does this culture of patient safety begin? With the board.

PART SEVEN

Physicians

The Hospital-Physician Relationship: Redefining the Rules of Engagement

By James E. Orlikoff and Mary K. Totten

How would you describe the relationship that exists today between your hospital and medical staff? Complex? Competitive? Paradoxical? Tense? Most likely, it's all of these.

Gone are the days when the traditional arrangements between hospitals and physicians mutually benefited both parties. Understanding how this relationship has changed and why new rules of engagement are necessary is critical for governing boards because they are ultimately accountable for the hospital's performance and mission, both of which depend on a productive hospital-physician partnership.

How to build and maintain such a partnership will differ among health care organizations depending on their structure and environment. Nevertheless, recognizing the need to re-examine what remains one of the most central relationships to the delivery of medical care should be a top priority for every board and begins with an appreciation of how this critical relationship has evolved.

James E. Orlikoff is president of Orlikoff & Associates, Inc., Chicago. Mary K. Totten is president of Totten & Associates, Oak Park, Illinois.

Once upon a Time

How the administration, the board and the medical staff work together for the good of the hospital is the basis of the time-honored "social contract"—a shared model of accountability and responsibility. Under this implicit contract, the governing board bears the ultimate accountability for organizational performance; it delegates day-to-day operational responsibility to hospital administration; and, as required by state regulations and accreditation, it delegates the responsibility for patient care (including clinical quality and patient safety) to the medical staff, which exists primarily to conduct physician credentialing and peer review.

According to a 2002 report, "Medical Staff Organizations: The Forgotten Covenant," based on research conducted by Irving, Texas–based VHA Inc.—published as part of VHA's 2002 Research Series—the social contract between hospitals and physicians:

> stems from an agreement struck between physicians and the hospital, usually at the time of the hospital's inception. The hospital, built with either community or investor resources, allows access to its facilities, supplies, equipment and staff without charge to the physicians for the care of their patients. In return, the physicians agree to abide by the bylaws of the medical staff organization and to participate in the medical staff organization as required. Typical requirements are attendance at meetings, taking emergency room call and accepting a certain number of no-pay patients.

This traditional agreement evolved during a time of plentiful resources. The market amply rewarded both hospitals and physicians without regard to their efficiency, and the "privilege" of being a member of a hospital medical staff ensured that physicians made a very good living. This privilege was so valuable that physicians agreed to be "on call" for patient care and participate in medical staff activities without compensation.

This "quid pro quo" arrangement worked reasonably well for both hospitals and physicians until rising health care costs led to initiatives such as the federal government's prospective payment system and managed care. Such cost-control efforts restricted payments to hospitals and physicians and linked financial rewards to more efficient behavior, changing the landscape for both parties.

VHA Recommendations

Based on its study findings, the VHA's 2002 research report recommended:

1. Health care organizations need alternatives to oversight of clinical performance and patient safety by the medical staff organization.

2. Health care organizations and physicians should invest in the behavior, hardware and content needed to assure effective communications and trust.

3. The medical staff and the health care organization need to make the necessary investment in developing physician leaders.

4. Medical staff organizations need to clearly articulate their goals, roles and responsibilities, as well as the value derived by all parties.

Source: "Medical Staff Organizations: The Forgotten Covenant," VHA Inc., Irving, Texas, 2002.

Today's hospital pressures include increasing costs to build needed infrastructure, declining reimbursement, increasing demands for inpatient and outpatient services that are straining existing capacity and resources, unfunded federal mandates, such as HIPAA compliance and growing demands from patients and payers for improved quality and safety.

As the VHA report suggests:

Improvements in patient care depend heavily on this "covenant" among the physicians and the hospital's board and administration. As pressure builds from all sides to address patient safety and clinical quality, boards are looking first to the administration to improve the quality of care and enhance patient safety. Ironically, administrators have neither the authority nor the responsibility to affect issues directly. While they can provide various levels of support and resources, changes in clinical processes rely on the wholehearted participation of the medical staff organization.

Jeff Goldsmith and Nathan Kaufman further observe in their article, "Between a Rock and a Hard Place: Physician Markets Create

New Strategic Problems for Hospitals" (published in the newsletter COR *Healthcare Market Strategist,* November 2004, a publication of COR Health, LLC), that changing economic incentives continue to play a central role in strained hospital-physician relationships.

Attempting to position themselves more favorably in the managed care marketplace in the late 1980s and 1990s, and in response to a growing number of physician practice management companies, hospitals crossed traditional boundaries and experimented with owning and managing physician group practices. These efforts strained hospital-physician relationships—and were economically unsuccessful as well. Today, most hospitals are unwinding these arrangements and minimizing their losses. They also are living with the lingering effects of the ill will generated by altering the traditional relationship—when hospitals and medical practices were separate—between hospitals and medical practices.

At the same time, physicians are seeing their incomes decline because the costs of operating a private practice keep increasing, even as shortages of specialists deepen. These income pressures are forcing a growing number of physicians to seek alternative sources of revenue, such as demanding payment for on-call coverage and other services that were traditionally provided without compensation under the social contract. Physicians are also investing in business ventures, such as imaging facilities and ambulatory care centers, which compete directly with hospitals.

Goldsmith and Kaufman describe the current catch-22 for hospitals this way:

> Hospitals are finding themselves caught between the Scylla of EMTALA—the federally mandated 24-hour physician coverage obligations related to emergency services—and the Charybdis of a depleted and angry cadre of specialty physicians, increasingly unwilling to provide call coverage without compensation. . . . Meanwhile, the balance of supply and demand in the physician services market has tilted decisively in the past three years toward a seller's market. Hospital-based specialty groups such as anesthesiologists and radiologists, as well as key hospital-focused specialists such as cardiologists and trauma surgeons, are having increasing difficulty filling their groups' vacancies and are turning to hospitals for increased subsidies and recruitment support.

The authors suggest two possible hospital responses: outsourcing needed specialty services or creating a salaried or closely affiliated "specialty care" division through which doctors who provide round-the-clock coverage are employed by the hospital. Obviously, both of these options are a far cry from the traditional social contract that still underlies most hospital-physician relationships.

Clearly the old social contract no longer serves either party well, and it is time to begin drafting a new one, with new sets of quid pro quos and new rules of engagement for a new day (see James E. Orlikoff's article, "Time for a New Social Contract," in the November 2003 issue of *Hospitals & Health Networks*).

Questions for Discussion

As part of a board meeting, leadership retreat or education session, board members and physician leaders should jointly consider the following questions:

1. What terms would we use to describe the current relationship between the hospital and the physicians? Do these describe the relationship we want?
2. How would we describe the traditional social contract that existed between the hospital and physicians?
3. In what ways has this contract been preserved?
4. How, if at all, are previous expectations changing?
5. Is it time to "rewrite" our social contract? If so, what should the new agreement be?

Where Do We Go from Here?

Understanding the changing landscape is an essential prerequisite to determining next steps for redefining the hospital-physician relationship. So is understanding how existing beliefs, structures and processes that underlie this relationship either assist or impede progress toward improving it.

In most medical staffs, as in any large group, it is often not the leaders or even the majority that most significantly affect the outcome of any decision or initiative, but rather, those who are the most vocal. Physicians who refuse to take emergency department call without pay, who take their profitable business outside of the hospital or who carry on a running feud with management get the attention and provoke a reaction from hospital executives and medical staff leaders. Rather than stepping back and redefining the hospital-physician relationship in ways that engage the support and influence of the medical staff majority, most hospitals and medical staff leaders choose to deal with the symptoms of physician discontent rather than its underlying causes.

VHA's research report, based on interviews with 87 chief medical officers or vice presidents of medical affairs of VHA member organizations as well as surveys of 418 physicians, provides useful insights into the hospital-physician relationship. The study concludes that:

- Physicians have forgotten their collective responsibility for patient safety and clinical care.
- Physicians increasingly are confining themselves to their office practices.
- Many of the traditional medical staff organization activities have been delegated to hospital employees such as chief medical officers.
- The relationship between hospital boards and medical staff organizations becomes strained in systems.
- Significant conflicts of interest arise as physicians become investors in ambulatory sites and health care organizations begin to purchase and operate physician practices.
- Physicians don't perceive that the medical staff organization provides strong leadership and believe that there is little effort by health care organizations to develop new leadership.
- Health care organizations are turning to other vehicles to assure quality and pursue non-clinical agendas.

Developing a New Social Contract

The rules of engagement between hospitals and physicians are beginning to change. In many organizations, both parties are negotiating the terms and conditions of joint ventures or other business partnerships, or they are working through the effects of head-to-head competition. On the other hand, some leading organizations, such as Virginia Mason Medical Center (VMMC) in Seattle, are taking a more comprehensive, long-term approach.

According to Gary Kaplan, M.D., VMMC's chairman and CEO, the organization held a retreat in 2000 for professional staff leaders and physicians in VMMC's group medical practice to talk about the expectations they all had about working together.

"At that time, we were facing several challenges as an organiza-tion, and it was clear that we needed to make significant changes to our culture and performance," Kaplan says. "Based on the retreat, we concluded that the old compact between hospitals and physicians was no longer working . . . because it was predicated on entitlement, rather than on a give-and-get relationship between both parties."

The retreat led to the formation of a committee comprising physi-cians, board members and human resources personnel that engaged in a yearlong process to develop the Virginia Mason Medical Center Physician Compact. (See "Virginia Mason Compact" on page 332.)

The compact works like a code of conduct and outlines the responsibilities for which both parties are held accountable. It is used in physician recruitment, orientation and performance review, and also is part of the job descriptions for physician leaders. VMMC also established a Compact College that helps educate everyone in the organization about the terms of the compact and provides examples of practical behaviors that support it.

"The compact has provided a lot of clarity for us about the expec-tations that the medical center and physicians have in their working relationship," Kaplan says. "This clarity and the improved communi-cation that has resulted from it have helped us all move forward."

Tips for Re-examining the Social Contract between Hospitals and Physicians

1. Schedule a specific time when board, executive and clinical lead-ers can discuss the expectations they have for working together and how today's expectations may differ from those that existed in the past.
2. Consider developing an explicit, written compact that defines the mutual expectations that the hospital and its physicians have for working together.
3. If your organization decides to develop an explicit hospital-physician compact, ensure that the needs of patients come first for all parties.
4. Include heavy involvement from front-line physicians, recommends Kaplan. The CEO should participate in, but not drive, the process.
5. Ensure that your organization devotes the resources necessary to build communication and trust with physicians.

Virginia Mason Compact

Organization's Responsibilities

Foster Excellence
- Recruit and retain superior physicians and staff
- Support career development and professional satisfaction
- Acknowledge contributions to patient care and the organization
- Create opportunities to participate in or support research

Listen and Communicate
- Share information regarding strategic intent, organizational priorities and business decisions
- Offer opportunities for constructive dialogue
- Provide regular, written evaluation and feedback

Educate
- Support and facilitate teaching: GME and CME
- Provide information and topics necessary to improve practice

Reward
- Provide clear compensation with internal and market consistency, aligned with organizational goals
- Create an environment that supports teams and individuals

Physician's Responsibilities

Focus on Patients
- Practice state-of-the-art, quality medicine
- Encourage patient involvement in care and treatment decisions
- Achieve and maintain optimal patient access
- Insist on seamless service

Collaborate on Care Delivery
- Include staff, physicians and management on teams
- Treat all members with respect
- Demonstrate the highest levels of ethical and professional conduct
- Behave in a manner consistent with group goals
- Participate in or support teaching

Listen and Communicate
- Communicate clinical information in a clear and timely manner
- Request information, resources needed to provide care consistent with VMMC goals
- Provide and accept feedback

Continued →

Take Ownership
- Implement VMMC-accepted clinical standards of care
- Participate in and support group decisions
- Focus on the economic aspects of our practice

Change
- Embrace innovation and continuous improvement
- Participate in necessary organizational change

Source: Virginia Mason Medical Center, Seattle. Reprinted, with permission, from Virginia Mason Medical Center Physician Compact, 2001.

6. Ensure that the hospital supports development of physician leaders.
7. Make sure that the purpose of the medical staff and its collective responsibility for quality, patient safety and peer review are addressed as part of recruitment, orientation and ongoing education for the medical staff, the board and executive leaders.
8. Provide adequate hospital resources and support for the medical staff to help it fulfill its purpose and responsibilities.

Based on the success of the initial VMMC physician compact, the organization has forged several other agreements. Virginial Mason has a compact for board members that defines the expectations they should have of each other and the full board and a leadership compact that defines expectations between leaders and the organizations. A staff compact is now under development as is a compact with the broader VMMC medical staff.

Conclusion

New challenges demand new solutions. The old social contract between hospitals and physicians is no longer viable, and the time has come for both parties to create new expectations for a more productive relationship. Boards can take the lead in bringing all parties together to examine current relationships and take the necessary steps to improve them. Better communication, deeper trust and clear roles and responsibilities between hospitals and physicians will lead to better working relationships. Ultimately, patients and communities will benefit.

Getting to Know You

By Shari Mycek

*An open dialogue between the board and physicians
will jump-start better relations.*

Popular culture has enthusiastically embraced the differences between men and women. By the time author John Gray's book *Men Are from Mars, Women Are from Venus* went into paperback, it had already sold more than 14 million copies. Wives purchased it for husbands, girlfriends for boyfriends—all hoping to learn how to build lasting, loving relationships; get what they want, without nagging or bullying; communicate difficult feelings; and, above all, understand their partner better than before.

Unfortunately, when it comes to helping physicians and hospital boards understand one another better, it doesn't appear that a new book on the topic will be hitting the bestseller list any time soon. So physicians and trustees are left on their own to sort it out. Is it hopeless? Are physicians and hospital trustees from different planets?

No, says Richard de Filippi, Ph.D., board chair of Cambridge (MA) Health Alliance. "Physicians are not different creatures," he says, but then pauses. "Physicians do have a very different kind of pressure on them, though. It's hard for most of us to really imagine the decisions and judgments that physicians have to make every

---

Shari Mycek is a writer based in Belle Mead, New Jersey.

single day. I'm not sure we realize just how difficult physicians' jobs are or how personally driven they are to do their jobs right."

The perfectionist M.D. attitude begins on day one of medical school, according to Joseph Bujack, M.D., vice president of Medical Affairs at Kootenai Medical Center in Coeur D'Alene, Idaho.

"From the onset, physicians are taught to never trust anyone but themselves," says Bujack. "If you're brought in on a case, you start from scratch. There's this expectation that doctors must be perfect, and nobody ascribes to that philosophy more than doctors themselves. Physicians hold themselves to the highest degree of accountability, and it makes sense, really. No matter how much a physician may want to share and delegate and play well with others, if anything goes wrong with a patient, guess who's ultimately responsible? The physician culture is a culture of personal accountability. Otherwise, how do they live with themselves?"

This autonomous "accountability factor" flies in the face, however, of board culture, which values collective responsibility and systems thinking.

Borrowing from his colleague David Eddy, M.D., who coined the term, Bujack refers to the accountability factor as "a difference of apostrophe."

"The role of doctors is to serve as a patient's advocate, while the role of the board (along with payers and legislators) is to serve as patients' advocate. Basically, physicians are taught to do all they can without doing harm, if it might benefit their patient," says Bujack. "This behavior is reinforced by all elements of society: patient and family expectations, legal expectations, personal perceptions of what equates with best care, colleague expectations of what ought to be done, societal expectations that we will live forever.

"But as resources have become limited, physicians are being asked to become the patients' advocate, to practice population-based medicine and to allocate resources to create the greatest good for the greatest number. The dilemma is that there exists a separate and equally valid set of ethics for operating within either paradigm. This conflict becomes pivotal when providers place themselves in a position of accepting actuarial risk. No physician can simultaneously work within each system. Being forced to do so creates considerable tension and internal conflict."

Bujack summarizes: "So this simple matter of punctuation explains why there's so much tension between boards and physicians. Boards don't understand what it's like to have such personal accountability. And doctors sure as hell don't understand the system perspective. When a physician is at a patient's bedside and needs to act, he doesn't give a damn about the system. He needs what he needs now—not to call a committee meeting."

Punctuation is, of course, not the only dividing line between hospital trustees and physicians. Fundamental economic issues are also at stake.

"In the traditional hospital-physician compact, hospitals provided physicians with a workshop of modern equipment and qualified staff, and, in return, physicians volunteered ED coverage, medical staff leadership and so on," writes governance expert Barry Bader of Potomac, Maryland. "But hospitals are becoming less important to many physicians. And today, hospitals are struggling to find specialists willing to provide emergency department coverage and accept traditional medical staff responsibilities to chair departments and serve on committees. Even specialists still reliant on [hospitals], such as neurosurgeons, are joining [additional] medical staffs to maintain their volumes and have less time to volunteer at one facility. And, of course, where hospitals used to stick to inpatient care and leave outpatient care (except for poor patients) to physicians in their offices, now hospitals and physicians compete on lucrative outpatient business. The 21st century is starting out as one of the worst periods in recent memory for hospital-physician relationships. Physicians are feeling underpaid and unloved."

A recent Kaiser Family Foundation survey confirms Bader's claim. According to the survey, 58 percent of physicians state their personal enthusiasm for practicing medicine has declined. Three out of four believe managed care has worsened medical care. Nearly half say they would not recommend a medical career today, blaming paperwork, loss of autonomy, less respect for the medical profession and inadequate financial rewards for their negative views.

So how is the gap between physicians—seeking autonomy and respect—and board members—striving for mission and unity—bridged?

For starters, by doing away with the "generic image of physicians," says Bujack. "Boards have a tendency to see doctors as this generic entity and are constantly asking questions conveying this bias. 'Tell me, what do the doctors think?' 'Well, I spoke to the chief of staff and he said. . . .' And what 'he said' suddenly becomes gospel—as if there's one answer, one opinion."

Bujack continues, "Governance strategy has, historically, been to build an ark that's going to the same place at the same speed and with the same purpose—and try to entice the doctors to board two by two. But physicians are not leaders. Nor are they followers. They are independents with opinions all their own. So to put all physicians into one ark to try and survive the flood is hopeless. You need a flotilla of boats: some to go fishing, others, deep-sea diving; one to go fast, another slow; one to go east, another west. The medical staff is not a singular entity, it is pluralistic. Boards have to let go of the bent that the medical staff is a single entity. They must stop dealing with *the* medical staff and start dealing with physicians in subsets, small groups of 15 or so physicians—radiologists here, family practitioners there—and create frequent and meaningful conversations."

In Provo, Utah, Intermountain Health Care (comprising three hospitals and many physician-based clinics) is doing just that.

On the day Robert Parsons, Ph.D., chair of Intermountain's Urban South Region and of the AHA's Committee on Governance, was interviewed for this article, he was going to a meeting with a small group of physicians. (See "Listening and Learning" on page 338.) These frequent physician-board exchanges started about a year ago.

While the Intermountain board had been giving a Distinguished Physician Award (nine to 10 annually) at every meeting, "we felt like we needed to get out of the boardroom more and see the physicians on their turf," says Parsons. Our goal is for the physicians in our community to see we are real people who care about them," he says.

"We haven't always had the best relationship with physicians," admits Parsons, who has served on Intermountain's board for 14 years and as chair for the last three. "I think the doctors would fairly say we didn't always respond in a timely way, and so they did things themselves. We're a major player in the market, and, to some of the doctors, we're seen as the 800-pound gorilla that didn't care about their needs. These one-on-one conversations are helping to change that."

> ## Listening and Learning
>
> Intermountain Health Care (IHC) System, based in Provo, Utah, is not a religion-based health care organization, but its board members do one thing religiously—get out of the boardroom and meet with small groups of local physicians. There's no agenda, at least on the board's part. "Our agenda is to show up, say 'thank you' for the work [physicians] are doing, and listen to what they have to say," says Robert Parsons, Ph.D., chair of Intermountain's Urban South Region.
>
> Physicians participating in these talks range wider than just IHC's own medical staff. Also included are doctors working in private practice in the community, and even physicians from niche hospitals that compete with the system. Responses from a recent conversation between eight IHC-employed physicians and the Urban South Region board yielded this feedback:
>
> "I now know we have a board of trustees. And really appreciate them coming here—to talk with us and create a dialogue."
>
> "I'm not sure they [board members] can solve the issues on the table now that they're aware of them. They listened to us. And that's a start."
>
> "When things aren't working well between physicians and administration, trustees may be able to serve as the facilitator."
>
> —Shari Mycek

Back in Massachusetts, Cambridge Health Alliance (comprising three hospitals, the Cambridge Public Health Department and more than 20 primary care practices, ranging from TB clinics to behavioral health centers) has had an easier time.

While Cambridge is, to much of the country, an upscale community that is home to Harvard University, the Alliance's immigrant population is huge. (To give some perspective, hospital and clinic signs are written in English, Spanish, Portuguese and Haitian Creole.) Only 25 percent of Alliance patients are covered by private insurers—the rest fall under Medicare, Medicaid and an uncompensated care pool.

"Our demographics alone put our board members and physicians on the same page in terms of mission (which is simply 'to improve the health of our communities')," says de Filippi. "The physicians who come to us really want to serve this [immigrant, uninsured] population. And by statute, Alliance board members must reside in the communities they serve. So we have doctors who really want to be here and board members who live here, so we start off with a good relationship."

But as in any good marriage, the love cannot be taken for granted. Communication must be constant and ongoing. And like Bujack and Parsons, de Filippi is also a strong advocate for building personal relationships.

"Again, I think for board members, it's about getting to understand better what a physician's life is like," says de Filippi. "When you see how our primary doctors are calling in interpreters [to translate for immigrant patients], how the IT system may not be functioning and really screwing up their day, or how much time they're spending doing administrative duties and answering the phone when all they really want to do is spend time with their patients—you have a much better understanding. Having a collaborative and successful relationship is really about developing dialogue."

Some of the best relationships de Filippi has with doctors—and subsequently, the relationships his board has—have come from talking, formally and informally.

As an example of an informal encounter, he says: "If you, as a board member, walk into the cafeteria (and yes, you should occasionally) and see a doctor who's just exhausted and more than a bit angry, you don't just avoid him or pass it off that he's having a bad day; you go over to him, you sit down and you start talking," advises de Filippi.

An example of a more formal relationship comes from the Alliance's CEO search a little over a year ago, a process that took about eight months and which de Filippi chaired.

"The search was a fascinating process in terms of communication," he says. "We [i.e., committee members] spent so much time talking, especially one-on-one without doctors. We're a teaching affiliate of Harvard Medical School (as well as Tufts School of Medicine) and one of our physicians called me to ask if we would sit down with the interns and hear what they had to say about the CEO search. This request was very important to this physician, so we did it. We spent two hours one morning going around the room of interns and hearing their thoughts about the ideal CEO. Dialogues of this kind have really helped board members and physicians get to know each other on a more personal basis."

As has actually using the health care system.

"You can't mandate that board members (or their families) use their own health care system, of course," says de Filippi. "But boy, what a vote of confidence it is to the doctors when you do. There's this thing called 'the mother test'—would you bring your own mother here? Well, I did. And she and I are totally happy. On a personal level, this decision said a lot to our doctors. I'm not going to take Mom over to Brigham and Women's. I'm keeping her right here because I trust you are going to give her the best care."

"There's no shortcut to creating trust or intimacy between board members and physicians," says Kootenai Medical Center's Bujack. "You have to start slowly, find out what each other's concerns are, and find the humanity—walk in each other's shoes. No one, whose story you know, can you hate."

So how does the "ideal" trustee-physician relationship look?

"I'm not so sure there is one single model to which everyone can conform and be happy," says governance consultant Mary Totten, president of Totten & Associates, Oak Park, Illinois. "I'm not sure there is an opportunity to create nirvana."

But there are stepping stones, according to everyone who was interviewed for this article. Among them:

- There should be frequent and meaningful conversations between trustees and physicians. "You go to lunch, find out what's important. You need to know them; they need to know you. Therefore there are no assumptions," says Bujack.
- Trustees need to stop viewing physicians pluralistically. As Bujack says, "There's no such thing as an opinion of *the* medical staff. Even though the medical staff chief may address the board regularly and two physicians may serve on the board, none of these doctors represents the entire medical staff."
- The board should not ask physicians to serve as both a patient's advocate and as patients' advocates.

- Physicians should come to board meetings and trustees should go to medical staff meetings.
- There needs to be mutual benefit: "Each party understands it still needs the other; that it isn't a one-way street," says Bujack.

"Overall, there [should be] open communication and constant interaction," he says. "Right now, in most health care systems, there is precious little interaction between boards and doctors. The doctors don't know the board members and the board members don't know the doctors."

Not so in Cambridge. Or Provo. But has either health care system (or any other, for that matter) created the ideal physician-board relationship?

"Ideal is a tough word," says de Filippi. "I'd hesitate to say we've mastered the ideal. But I can say we have an excellent physician-board relationship. Trustees admire and appreciate what our physicians have to do every single day, the decisions they have to make, how difficult their jobs are and how much personal drive they have to do their jobs right. I'd say that we [i.e., the board] have gotten to know our physicians on a personal level, one by one, and that they have gotten to know us better, too."

And neither is from Mars.

Physicians in Governance: The Board's New Challenge

By James E. Orlikoff and Mary K. Totten

In an era of challenged relationships between hospitals and physicians, where tension is routine and conflict erupts frequently, health care organizations are struggling to build positive physician relations, or at least trying to prevent them from deteriorating further. Placing physicians on the hospital or system board is a common approach to addressing these tensions and finding common ground. Having physicians on the board is a visible demonstration of a health care organization's commitment to involving them in the highest level of organizational leadership.

Including physicians on the governing board, however, is a structural solution to a functional challenge. It's important to remember that structural solutions alone rarely solve complex functional problems. In fact, many health care organizations have found that having physicians on their boards often exacerbates strained relations and even generates ineffective governance by potentially polarizing and paralyzing the board.

Physician membership on a health care board does promise several potential advantages: professional and clinical expertise; an insider's view of the organization, its patients and the communities it serves; a voice for a critical constituency; and demonstration of

James E. Orlikoff is president of Orlikoff & Associates, Chicago. Mary K. Totten is president of Totten & Associates, Oak Park, Illinois.

the organization's sincere commitment to involve key physician constituent groups at the highest level of the organization. (See "Center Voices," *Trustee,* July/August 2005, page 27.) Most health care boards also have physician members who are representatives of the organization's medical staff or other key physician groups, and they bring another perspective to the board. It is this representational issue that often presents unique challenges to the board.

Types of Physician Board Members

A physician trustee can fall into one of two categories: a board member, or a medical staff or physician group representative. Physician board members are just the same as any other member of the board—they are chosen through the board's nomination and selection process, they are subject to term limits and performance evaluations, and perhaps most importantly, they should not represent or serve any interests other than those that are best for the health care organization and its mission.

The medical staff or physician group representative, on the other hand, is very different because this individual is selected by the medical staff or physician group, typically as a leader of that group. If the interests of the medical staff are incompatible with those of the board and organization, the medical staff representative to the hospital board is expected to advance the interests of the medical staff and serves on the board as an ex-officio member.

Ex-officio members are those individuals who serve on the board by virtue of their office, job or position. They can either be voting or non-voting board members. Specific designations are generally included in the position title, either "ex-officio with vote" or "ex-officio without vote."

Established term limits do not apply to ex-officio board members as long as they are in the office or position that the board has designated for board representation. Usually the CEO, a physician leader (commonly the hospital's chief of staff or medical staff president), or other organizational "insider" is an ex-officio governing board member.

Thus, the primary loyalty of the medical staff representative on a hospital board tends to be first to the medical staff and not to the hospital or board.

Tips on Creating Effective Physician Participation in Hospital Governance

1. Clearly and explicitly distinguish the role and function of the medical staff (or other physician group) representative ("insider") on the board from that of the "outsider" physician trustee. Develop written job descriptions for each board position and use them as part of the recruitment process.

2. As a specific component of trustee orientation, educate each new trustee on the distinction between the roles of the insider physician trustee and the outsider physician trustee. Use the written job descriptions for both insider and outsider positions as the foundation for this part of the orientation. Make certain that every physician board member receives this orientation.

3. Routinely review this physician role and responsibility distinction with all board members during annual retreats and continuing education sessions.

4. Educate the entire medical staff about the distinction between the two types of physician governing board members.

5. Recruit physicians from outside your community, or who are not members of your medical staff, to serve on your board. Retired physicians who are truly independent-minded and removed from current medical staff politics and physician practice pressures may also be appropriate.

6. Develop concrete conflict-of-interest policies and procedures for physicians on the board. These policies should clearly define those situations where specific physicians are in conflicted situations, as well as outline the procedures to be followed when there is a conflict. Such procedures might include requiring a physician trustee to abstain from voting on an issue in which he or she has a conflict; requiring that the conflicted physician recuse himself while the issue is being discussed; and not including in the board agenda book any information relating to the situation or decision involving the conflict.

7. Ensure that all board members clearly understand the roles and responsibilities physician members play on the board.

Continued →

Reaching this understanding should be done by including an assessment of how physician trustees are fulfilling their roles as part of the full board and individual board member self-evaluation processes, determining if these roles are being properly discharged. Use the individual assessment process and the personal development plans that result from it as an opportunity to identify and address specific board needs and concerns.

8. Consider developing a physician leadership academy or providing other education and support to help physicians maximize their effectiveness as board members and organizational leaders.

Some argue that this trustee is on the board to express medical staff concerns, but when it comes time to vote, he or she is expected to vote in the best interests of the organization and the overall board, even if those interests are inconsistent with the interests of the medical staff. However, this rarely, if ever, happens in practice, especially in the current environment of strained relations and competition between hospitals and physicians.

In fact, it is quite common to see the reverse happen. Not only does the medical staff representative act first in the best interests of the medical staff, other physician board members (those who have been elected in the same manner as all the other trustees and who are not supposed to "represent" the medical staff) end up doing the same thing.

This dynamic frequently contributes to inefficient governance at best and dysfunctional governance at worst. When all physicians on the board make it their primary task to represent the best interests of the medical staff and physicians above those of the organization and its mission, a divided and awkward board dynamic ensues, which often paralyzes and polarizes the board. The cohesion of the board is disrupted, and the integrity of governance is compromised.

In short, the "physician faction" dynamic is inappropriate and antithetical to good governance. That's why it is so important for each board to address this issue by clearly and explicitly distinguishing the physician trustee's role from the medical staff (or other physician group) representative's role, as well as by other, more novel approaches described below.

Questions for Discussion

1. How many physicians serve on your hospital's governing board and what are their roles?
2. In what ways, if any, are the roles of physician trustees defined (e.g., job descriptions, orientation programs, printed material)?
3. Do physicians on your board tend to vote as a "bloc"?
4. Has your board experienced the "physician faction" dynamic and what influence, if any, has it had on governance effectiveness?

The Growing Challenge of "Insider" Board Members

Starting in 1993, the Internal Revenue Service (IRS) imposed a maximum limit of 20 percent physician membership on the board of a health care organization seeking Section 501(c)(3) tax-exempt status. In order to qualify for that tax-exempt status, a health care organization had to, among other things, demonstrate through its governing board bylaws that no more than 20 percent of the voting members of the board would be physicians having a direct or indirect financial interest in the organization. In addition, no physician representation was permitted on the board's compensation committee.

Recognizing the changing market and the need for hospitals and systems to forge new relationships with physicians and physician groups, in 1996 the IRS changed its rules to allow a not-for-profit, tax-exempt board to have up to 49 percent of its membership be "interested persons." In IRS terminology, *interested person* refers to any employee of the organization (such as the CEO), as well as any physicians who treat patients of the organization, or who conduct business with, or derive any financial benefit from, the organization. Thus, if a CEO is an ex-officio voting board member, that position counts as part of the 49 percent of interested persons allowed.

Also, the 49 percent interested persons rule only applies if certain requirements are met. These requirements are designed to ensure that the organization operates for the benefit of the community, and not in the interests of those on the board. The first requirement requires the board to have a strict conflict-of-interest policy. In addition to the policy itself, records must be maintained that demonstrate close adherence to it. Such records could include yearly signed acknowledgment of the conflict-of-interest policy by each board member.

The second requirement is that the organization conduct periodic reviews of all of its activities and operations, including those unrelated to its normal business, to ensure that it is conforming to its tax-exempt purposes. This review must also ensure that the organization is not engaged in activities that provide inurement or unwarranted private benefit to physicians or other interested persons on the board.

In addition to the IRS requirements, members of the medical staff (or related physician group) who serve on the board are considered non-independent board members under the Sarbanes-Oxley Act and similar emerging rules and standards relating to governance.

Although such regulations now apply only to public company boards, were they to become standard in health care, physician trustees who were on the medical staff or did business with the organization would be prohibited from serving on key board committees, such as the audit, CEO compensation and governance/nominations committees. These regulations would also make it difficult for an insider physician to become board chair.

Should such regulations become the norm, they would pose a significant challenge to a health care organization's claim that physician membership on the board demonstrates a commitment to involve physicians in the top leadership of the organization. This claim would be severely weakened by the prohibition against physicians serving on key board committees (audit, CEO compensation and governance) or serving as board chair.

Questions for Discussion

1. How many members of your board would be considered insiders?
2. Does your board have policies that designate which board committees are off-limits for insider membership? If yes, which committees?
3. Does your board have written policies that prohibit an insider from serving as board chair?

New Approaches to Physicians on the Board

Hospitals and health systems are beginning to adopt new approaches that address the challenges of physician membership on governing boards and that maximize the contributions they can make to organizational governance.

Recruiting "outsiders." A small but growing number of health care organizations are pursuing an effective approach to having physicians on the board while avoiding the problems of representational governance, conflicts of interest and regulatory challenge. Their solution is to seek physicians to serve as physician board members who are not members of the organization's medical staff (or physician group) and who live and work outside the communities served by the organization. Retired physicians who are truly independent-minded and removed from current medical staff politics and physician practice pressures may also fit the bill.

This approach allows a health care organization to gain the needed physician perspective on the board. Further, it enables the board to have physician members who can meaningfully participate in important governance functions such as audit, executive compensation and performance evaluation, as well as governance and nominations without concern about insider or conflict-of-interest scrutiny generated by current or future government regulations.

This approach would also allow an outsider physician to be board chair and to participate in all the normal and customary roles and functions of the governing board position without fear of running afoul of current IRS regulations or other Sarbanes-Oxley-like emerging standards.

There are other advantages to putting physicians on the board who do not live and work in the community or practice as a member of the hospital's medical staff. First, these physicians can bring a refreshing level of objectivity and honesty to the boardroom, in addition to providing an unbiased physician perspective. They can say what other physician trustees, or other lay board members, cannot (even pointing out when "the emperor has no clothes") because they are immune from social, economic and political pressures from local physicians and from members of the community at large.

These physicians are not members of the medical staff and do not depend on referrals from physicians who are; they are therefore free to speak their minds and vote their consciences without fear of peer pressure or economic reprisal. In addition, the board may recruit physicians who possess desired skills and experience that may not be available among members of their own medical staff.

Such physicians can bring the benefit of their specific background or expertise, as well as knowledge of relevant market trends and business acumen that may be critical to inform the board's strategic thinking and effective decision-making.

The idea of bringing in outsiders to serve on a health care organization board sometimes engenders resistance: "Why would someone from outside the community want to serve on the board? Wouldn't we have to pay someone to do that? How could they govern when they don't know us? We will be giving up community control."

For a few isolated, rural organizations, the first two questions may be valid concerns. For everyone else, they are simply excuses. Organizations that honestly look for the type of board members they need, find them. More importantly, bringing members from outside of the community onto the board can actually elevate the quality of governance by providing new insights and changing the dynamics of traditional board discussion and decision-making. Boards should start with one or two outside board members and evaluate the results.

Physician leadership academies. Some health care organizations that want to maximize the benefits of physician participation on the board are pursuing another strategy that focuses inward rather than outward. They are establishing leadership academies to provide education, skills assessment and other types of support to better prepare physicians to assume organizational governance and leadership roles.

Over 13 months, 25 physician leaders at Covenant Medical Center in Saginaw, Michigan (see the Viewpoint "Maximizing the Physician's Hospital Contribution," *Trustee,* June 2005, page 27), learn about industry developments, insurance and hospital finance, decision-making in large organizations and ways to enhance working relationships. The Covenant academy educates not only physician board members and current elected medical staff officers, but also younger leaders who are likely to become future medical staff officers and department chairs.

As part of the experience, academy participants can elect to undergo a 360-degree personal assessment that includes feedback from their elected medical staff leaders, physician colleagues and non-physician co-workers. Feedback focuses on communication skills, people skills, attitude and leadership. A professional facilitator provides confidential and objective interpretation of feedback data and helps the doctor develop a constructive improvement plan.

Physicians who have participated in the academy report they are highly satisfied with the experience and better understand how the hospital board and administration approach problem-solving and decision-making. They also gain leadership skills and information they can apply in their private practices.

A properly composed board can benefit from having insiders as members, including the CEO and physicians who are members of the medical staff, especially if their organizational knowledge and leadership skills have been honed through educational programs such as Covenant's academy.

However, care must be taken to avoid the very real risk that a board will be dominated by insider perspectives and interests. This risk generally springs from the contrast between the natural detachment of lay board members from the operations of the organization, and the intense involvement of insiders in the organization. This risk is magnified in the context of insider physician board members.

Considering the recruitment of outsider physicians to serve on the board promises physician perspective without the risks attendant to insider members while it enhances governance processes and practices. In addition, developing and supporting physicians to assume and discharge greater governance and leadership roles within a health care organization also builds the knowledge and skills necessary to improve leadership performance, accountability and value.

Conclusion

No other characteristic so directly and immediately affects the function of a board as its composition and its members' perspectives. Accordingly, physicians, as well as all other board members, should be chosen with great care, taking into account the needs of the board, its strengths and weaknesses, and the likely contributions of its members. The ability of a board to be creative in how it balances, blends and constantly fine-tunes its membership—including both insider and outsider physicians—is key to ongoing governance effectiveness.

Ten Questions for Building a Physician Relations Strategy

By David Miller and John Hill

Few relationships are more central to the success of the hospital than the one between the board and physicians. This relationship is becoming more important as physicians are increasingly deciding to compete with the hospital for patients in an effort to maintain their incomes.

What issues must the board address to build a strong, mutually beneficial relationship with physicians? Following are the 10 most important questions that the board should ask to cement that vital bond.

1. Is there trust among the physicians, the CEO and the board?
This does not mean you must have a love fest, but rather, that there should be mutual respect and a solid commitment that all parties will be straightforward and truthful with the other. If trust does not exist, trustees should determine why and focus management's attention on improving it. Also, the board can help identify physician leaders who can bridge the areas of distrust and encourage others to improve these relationships.

2. Is there a shared focus on quality care?
Everyone in health care says they are concerned about quality, but based on our experience, few are addressing the issue seriously. In

David Miller and John Hill are partners in Healthcare Strategy Group, LLC, Louisville, Kentucky.

those organizations that are, this shared focus can create a tighter bond among management, the board and physicians. Quality discussions can lead to useful communication among physician leaders, hospital executives and trustees, covering everything from medical staff credentials to the need for new and/or updated technology, and from physicians' treatment protocols to communication and working relationships among clinicians, pharmacists and technicians, including the speed and accuracy of hospital test reports.

In one organization, the hospital employs halftime physician executives to head six major clinical services. These physicians meet with management to set goals, create budgets, discuss quality improvement and deal with medical staff politics. Their cooperation with management lays a foundation for trust.

3. How and why do physicians make referrals, and how is that process changing?

Physicians make referrals to other physicians based on reputation, patient request, personal relationships, or simply who will take the patient. In some cases (more than you would expect), clerks in the referring physician's office choose a specialist based on the ease of making the referral.

This dynamic is changing in many markets with the advent of hospitalists who frequently assume the role formerly filled by primary care physicians (PCPs)—providing in-hospital care and making decisions about specialists. Combine this trend with the fact that PCPs can make more money providing office care, and it is not surprising that, in discussions with many family practitioners and internists, we have heard them say more than once, "I no longer need the hospital."

The result of these changes is that PCPs do not bond with specialists as their predecessors did, by meeting in the doctor's lounge or sharing care of a patient. Based on our interactions with physicians, many young PCPs have no idea to whom they can refer patients and simply depend on senior partners to direct them.

Through focused efforts, your hospital and medical staff can capture more business by asking PCPs and others for their referrals, handling the referral process and resulting patient interactions efficiently, and providing timely feedback about patients to the referring physicians.

4. Is the supply of physicians appropriate to meet the community's needs?

Faced with a physician shortage in many areas of the country, especially in certain specialties such as obstetrics, trustees should re-examine their role in building physician supply. Some trustees believe that ensuring an adequate number of physicians in the community is a core part of the hospital's mission and gladly use hospital resources to help meet that need. We have even seen a board set a policy that requires management to recruit doctors to meet the community's needs (thereby insulating management from dealing with their own medical staff's pressure to recruit physicians).

Others see this issue as falling squarely in the medical staff's domain. In a tight market, boards that relinquish this role are taking a big risk—one that could negatively affect the community's access to care and the hospital's ability to provide profitable services.

The board should direct the development of a plan to address deficiencies in physician supply. Doing so is complicated, as the federal government heavily regulates recruitment to avoid abuse of the Medicare and Medicaid programs. Because of legal complications, many organizations rely on outside, neutral consultants to determine both hospital and community needs. Others use internal resources and legal counsel, who can advise the board on the optimal approach for their organization, while ensuring compliance with various federal laws and regulations.

Either way, a thorough evaluation of the market and community needs will help the hospital through that minefield. And, planning far enough ahead will prevent the need to recruit physicians with questionable skills or capabilities.

5. Do you have a method for developing medical staff leaders?

This issue has never been tougher to address. As competition from specialists has grown, and PCPs increasingly abandon hospital practice, the interest in, and relevance of hospital leadership has declined.

On the other hand, these roles have never been more important to the hospital. Physician leadership in improving clinical quality will become crucial as Medicare and other payers demand accountability and begin to determine payment based on outcomes. Their management of utilization will also be critical as all payers come under increasing pressure to manage costs.

Unfortunately, few hospitals are addressing physician leadership aggressively. Succession planning for physician leaders should be approached in the same way that it is done for executives.

When the board considers this issue, trustees should ask four key questions: "What is the advantage for the doctors of assuming needed roles?" "Do specific management roles need to be defined?" "What skills should physician leaders have and how can the board help them acquire those skills?" And finally, "How should the hospital compensate physician leaders?"

6. Should the hospital have economic relationships that help drive common goals and expectations between it and key physicians?
Employment and joint ventures are the two primary economic models for hospital and physician integration. Despite losses suffered in the 1990s as organizations pursued integration strategies, we are still seeing a growing trend in physician employment by hospitals.

What's behind this trend? The first motivating factor is the demand for specialists. Organizations perceive that hiring them is the best way to ensure their availability in the community and in the emergency department as well.

The second integration model is the joint venture. An organization should first define under what, if any, circumstances it should consider such efforts—for all services, new services, services of strategic importance, or simply when the hospital is forced into it. The board must address the issue as part of the medical staff strategic planning processes.

7. Do you have attractive office space that will allow physicians to practice close to the hospital?
A physician's primary assets are knowledge and time. Convenient access, along with efficient use of his or her time, will increase both a physician's productivity and income. It is little wonder that close proximity to the hospital is a major determinant in where a physician practices.

8. Are physicians growing their own businesses aggressively, and how can the hospital help them?
In many cases, the hospital's business interests and those of its physicians complement each other, particularly if the physicians are loyal

to the hospital. Growth in the doctor's practice will translate into more admissions and outpatient procedures. So helping physicians grow is a good investment for the hospital. If, for example, existing demand indicates that physicians clearly need help, the hospital could help recruit new associates for the practice. That situation is relatively straightforward.

However, if there is no demand for additional physicians, the hospital can still help physicians' practices increase their market share in a couple of ways: A physician "finder" or referral service will help match patients in need with physicians who do not have a full patient load. A physician liaison service may help increase referrals from PCPs to specialists. Featuring physicians in hospital advertisements may help grow both businesses. And, by helping those physicians, you will undoubtedly increase their loyalty to the organization.

9. Do you have information systems that enhance clinical practice and increase physician satisfaction?

Increasingly, information technology is changing the practice of medicine. Hospitals are reporting results on their Web sites, spearheading development of communitywide medical records, allowing physicians to schedule hospital tests from their offices, and providing technology to help physicians make clinical decisions.

10. Do you have practice management resources that can be used to help key practices that are in crisis?

Some physician group practices are very well-managed, but others struggle with billing and collections, governance, staffing, financial reporting, compensation and productivity. When such problems afflict a group practice critical to the hospital's long-term success, the hospital is at risk.

For hospitals, the consequences of failed physician practices include lost revenue from admissions, poor access to care for the community, limited growth because the practice is not attractive to new recruits, and significant hospital expenditures to rebuild and solidify the situation. That's why the hospital should help prevent these problems rather than simply fix them.

An effective approach to helping physician practices thrive is to have management resources to work with strategically important groups. Core capabilities would include expertise in billing and collections, strategic planning and compensation systems. We have seen this approach used to merge groups, improve group performance, and focus group members on common goals.

The downside for many organizations will be perceived favoritism, as some groups are helped and others are not. That process has to be managed well, with some sensitivity to the political realities in which management operates. In any case, the board should anticipate this issue as it considers helping physicians.

Other trends will likely change but not diminish the doctor's role. The focus on quality outcomes and cost efficiency will create new pressures on physicians, although those who can best deal with the underlying problems of cost and quality will be stronger. The result is that physician relationships and a strong medical community have never been more important, and the organization's effectiveness will be closely tied to theirs.

Checklist for Physician Relations Strategy

This checklist is designed to help board members consider the organization's performance relative to physician relations and identify areas of potential concern. Not all issues are equally important to every organization, and issues requiring attention will vary by community and market. Setting priorities to improve that relationship is crucial if your executive team is to succeed in addressing deficiencies.

Check the items where you believe performance is appropriate. Items without checks represent poor performance. If you are not sure where the organization stands, use a question mark.

Trust
___ The CEO is trustworthy in dealing with physicians.
___ Physician leaders are trustworthy in dealing with the board and management.

Quality
___ The quality measurement and improvement program is very good.
___ Physicians are adequately engaged in the quality process.
___ Physicians and managers collaborate on quality initiatives.

Continued →

Referrals

___ Hospital executives and physician leaders understand the physician referral process.

___ Hospital executives and physician leaders understand the organization's competitive stance regarding referrals.

Physician Supply

___ An evaluation of the number of needed physicians has been completed in the last three years.

___ The organization has a policy on physician recruitment.

___ The organization is addressing the need for more physicians.

Development of Medical Staff Leadership

___ There is a succession plan in place for medical staff leaders.

___ Physicians' roles and required skills have been defined.

___ An education program for physician leaders has been developed.

Economic Relationships

___ The hospital has a policy on joint ventures.

___ The hospital has a policy relative to physicians who compete with the hospital.

Physician Offices

___ The hospital has evaluated the need for physician office space in the last three years.

___ Hospital executives understand how the organization rates compared with key competitors.

Marketing and Growth

___ The hospital has considered building physician practice volume as part of its overall marketing plan.

Information Systems and Technology

___ The hospital has evaluated physicians' IT needs.

___ The hospital understands its competitive position relative to other hospitals and niche providers.

___ The information technology plan addresses the hospital's competitive position.

Practice Management Capabilities

___ The hospital has considered developing resources to help strategically important groups who may be in crisis.

Physicians on the Board:
Inside or Outside?

By Karen Sandrick

If you ask Errol Biggs, Ph.D., which hospital in a two-hospital town would be more competitive, he'd pick the one with the most doctors on its board. Without knowing much else about the hospitals, Biggs would opt for the one with the most physician trustees because "physicians understand the product. They understand quality and the measurements that look at quality. They understand strategically how the hospital should compete and the services it could provide," says Biggs, director of programs in Health Administration at the University of Colorado, Denver.

There's little doubt that physicians are indispensable to hospital governance. Medical staff members who serve on a hospital's board have a real appreciation of the local challenges. "They know the marketplace, they know the competition, and they bring tremendous local insight into implementing what the board is hoping and wishing to do," agrees David Nash, M.D., chair of the Department of Health Policy at Jefferson Medical College, Philadelphia. "Local physicians have a good understanding of their peer group generally," he says, "so they can help the board communicate more effectively with other members of the medical staff and open up lines of communication that probably otherwise wouldn't even exist within the medical center."

Karen Sandrick is a Chicago-based writer who specializes in health care.

Physician trustees also serve as "tutors" for the lay members of the board on issues related to health care quality and safety. "The entire board needs to be concerned about quality, so we have to bring our lay leaders of the board up to at least some level of understanding," says Kathryn McDonagh, M.D., president and CEO of Christus Spohn Health System, Corpus Christi, Texas. "They will never have the perspective that the physicians or the administrator would have, but they have to have a working or talking knowledge of it. Where they learn a lot about it is in quality committees, from the physicians."

Nevertheless, over the last several years, as the health care market has contracted, physicians and hospitals often find that they are chasing the same patients and the same dollars. Seeking to preserve their autonomy and control, physicians are focusing on their own self-interest, says Joseph Bujack, M.D., vice president of medical affairs, Kootenai Medical Center, Coeur d'Alene, Idaho. "To hospitals, many physicians are saying, 'If you aren't going to make my work environment meet my needs, I'll go and create my own environment.' So they [transfer] much of what they do to their own offices or an extension of their offices and call it a surgery center, leaving the hospital lumbering behind," he says.

And, as physicians try to carve out niches for themselves by creating specialty hospitals, ancillary service clinics and ambulatory surgery centers in competitive markets, they may end up as rivals for patients with the very hospital on whose board they sit as trustees. "Physician board members are privy to strategic and recruiting and other issues that come before the hospital board of trustees, which may influence how those physicians operate their own practices or ventures or imaging centers or labs or whatever else might compete with the hospital," says Andy Clark, M.D., board member of Longview (Texas) Medical Center and a former member of the American Hospital Association's Committee on Governance.

Traditionally, most physicians on the board have represented the medical staff. In addition to the president of the medical staff, boards comprising an average of 10 members typically have one or two other physicians, says Biggs. Hospitals are essentially following the same governance model that worked well in the 1960s when there was less tension between medical staffs and hospitals. But this model is starting to show cracks and strains, says James E. Orlikoff, president of Orlikoff & Associates, Inc., Chicago, and senior consultant to the Center for Healthcare Governance.

"Physicians are far more competitive with hospitals than they used to be. They are far more competitive with each other as the market has become tighter," Orlikoff says. "Just because structural models . . . worked 20 or 30 years ago, doesn't mean those same models are going to work today because the economic relationships are different, the regulatory environment is different, the demand for effective governance is different, and hospitals are in much more difficult financial and competitive circumstances."

Many boards, therefore, are beginning to recruit physicians who are not members of their hospital's medical staff. Boards are looking for retired physicians who are removed from the economics and politics of the medical staff or for physicians who don't live or work in the community and therefore have no economic, social or political skin in the game and can truly be disinterested board members, while at the same time giving the physician perspective, Orlikoff explains.

Physicians who are not members of the medical staff are particularly effective on system boards where they can provide a national perspective. Catholic Healthcare Partners of Cincinnati, one of the largest religiously affiliated health systems in the country, has medical staff members serving as trustees on its regional boards and nonstaff members, such as Nash, on its corporate board. "At the local level, hospitals do need physician participation in all of the weighty issues the board must consider, most especially on measuring and improving the quality and safety of medical care," Nash says. "At the corporate board level, hospitals need more of a national perspective, which is unencumbered by local knowledge and can provide a policy perspective to the quality and safety issues."

Physicians outside the medical staff can offer a fresh viewpoint when evaluating a strategic move, says Biggs. McDonagh adds that physicians from other marketplaces provide insight about what goes on in other settings and how hospitals elsewhere may deal with similar issues. Moreover, physicians who are not members of the medical staff have no stake in board decisions.

"There are many boards that have to make tough decisions, and they realize that as they do, they will get a lot of political and economic pushback from friends, relatives and neighbors precisely because they live in the community," Orlikoff says. "It is getting increasingly difficult to find . . . members of the medical staff who can be resistant to the incredible social and economic pressures their colleagues will place on them."

Choosing a physician from outside the community can be tricky, however. "Just because a physician is on a hospital board doesn't mean he or she has the level of expertise, background or knowledge about quality and safety," Nash says. "Hospital boards are in danger of believing that as long as they have a physician board member, they are covering the quality question. But hospital boards need to make sure they have physicians who know about EMR [electronic medical records], the AHRQ [Agency for Healthcare Research and Quality], or the NQF [National Quality Forum]."

Hospital boards also should recognize generational differences in the physician community. As Bujack explains it, there are three generations of physicians walking the halls of hospitals today: traditionalists, who were born before 1945; baby boomers; and Gen-Xers. Yet most physician representatives on hospital boards come from the traditionalist generation.

"As such, you get an incredibly biased perspective that emanates out of their generation, and it's further cut by their own unique individual biases, assumptions and attitudes," Bujack says. "There is no simplistic, prescriptive way of trying to fashion strategies with physicians. Hospital boards may imagine that, because they sit around some hardwood table and talk to 'the' chief of staff or 'the' several members of the board who also happen to be physicians, they have an understanding of the collective identity of the physicians. They don't," he explains.

The Pressures on Medical Staff Members

For a variety of reasons, members of the medical staff who serve on hospital boards may have a difficult time taking action on behalf of the organization when a decision conflicts with the best interests of the medical staff. Medical staff members, such as the chief of staff, not only give voice to medical staff concerns, they also are supposed to represent the medical staff. "Legally, even though functional medical staff members on the board serve a representational role, their fiduciary duty is no different from that of any other board member: to fulfill their duty to the organization. This puts them at great stress," Orlikoff says.

Board decisions may place physicians in a difficult position with their colleagues on the medical staff. Clark recalls a time five years ago when anesthesiologists at his hospital split into two groups. Each was trying to build support among the medical staff, especially among the surgeons. It eventually became necessary for the board to resolve the problem by selecting one anesthesiology group over the other. The decision had direct personal ramifications for medical staff members who knew the anesthesiologists and often took care of their families. "One group was out, and one was in. We knew that the anesthesiologists [who were rejected by the board] would have to move somewhere else and uproot their lives," Clark says. "But when you go on a board, you have to be willing to make the tough and unpopular decisions, even though they may affect physician-to-physician and family-to-family relationships."

But hospitals can take steps to reduce the pressure on members of the medical staff and help them become more comfortable serving on the board. In this regard, education is key. Hospitals need to provide intensive orientation for all board members so they make sure physicians are not behaving as medical staff representatives in day-to-day board discussions and decisions. Hospitals also need to educate physician board members about the distinction between representing their medical staff and acting in the best interest of their health care institutions, Orlikoff says.

Most importantly, boards have to educate the medical staff as a whole. "Medical staff members will assume that any physicians on the board are their representatives, and they will put pressure on the physicians to support their interests because they are working with them and seeing them all the time," Orlikoff says. "So you have to educate the medical staff that just because there is a doctor on the board, that doesn't mean his or her job is to represent the medical staff."

It is also crucial to take particular care in selecting those medical staff members who might serve on the board. Physicians who will serve on the board should not be selected by the medical staff but by the board, based on identified characteristics of individuals who would make the best trustees. Boards should apply the same selection criteria they use to screen all board candidates—for example, a big-picture futuristic thinker, a person who is able to disagree without being disagreeable, someone who can keep matters confidential. And boards should look for specific skills sets, such as experience in direct ventures with hospitals, or a background in business or hospital administration, McDonagh recommends.

Further, to avoid any regulatory or compliance problems in these times of increased governance accountability, boards must erect firewalls against conflicts of interest, Orlikoff advises. "Any physicians on the board may be considered insiders because they do business with the organization, and they will have conflicts if you put them on the board," he says. "Many hospitals are ensuring that insider board members can't serve on certain committees, such as the audit or executive compensation committees, or maybe they can't be board chair."

Physician trustees must be willing to step down if they do not like the way the board votes or if they have a conflict of interest. "People who are willing to accept the responsibilities of [being] a trustee must recognize they are overseeing a huge community asset," Clark says. "Economically, health care is the leading provider of jobs in many communities. Hospitals are not only ancillary services around which physicians practice, they have a huge impact on their communities. Trustees have to be cognizant of the importance of the decisions they make and be sure they are living up to the expectations and obligations they accepted when they went on the board."

Outside Physicians

For those physician trustees who are not on the hospital's medical staff, service on a hospital board can be an attractive prospect. Board membership is a prestigious and rewarding experience, says Biggs. It allows physicians to apply and share the lessons they've learned practicing medicine while learning from business leaders who serve with them on the board. "Physicians obviously are not businessmen, so it's important to have people who are successful in business on the board," Clark adds. "But if you are successfully running a chemical company, you will not [necessarily] know anything about health care. We all bring different sets of perspectives to board meetings and learn from one another."

But how easy is it to find physicians who will take on a board position for a hospital that is not in their own back yard? It is probably easier to find physicians to serve on a large corporate or national board than on a community hospital board. Since the board's objective often is to tap the expertise of physicians who have wide-ranging policy experience or a national reputation, hospitals may seek out individuals who have published in the field of quality or safety or who regularly do consultant work. Or, physicians who have positions of responsibility at other health care systems in non-competitive markets may wish to draw on one another's expertise by participating in a board exchange, Nash suggests.

It may not be easy to find a local non-medical staff physician to serve on the board, unless he or she has some special cachet or skills, such as being a philanthropist, an expert in quality of care and patient safety, unique experience in the community, or having some "connectivity that would make sense at the local level," Nash adds.

Boards may have to seek these physicians from outside their communities, ask other hospital boards if they know of a physician who would be willing to serve or poll the physician community. "Once you start asking, you'll start getting interest from all over the place," Orlikoff maintains.

Whether physicians are on the medical staff or outsiders, boards need to be careful when choosing physician partners for the future. "You need to work backward from the outcome," Bujack says. "Think strategically and ask yourself, 'What are the critical ingredients to make that strategy successful?' 'What are the human capital needs?' 'Who are the players?' 'Who are the stakeholders?' 'Who needs to be part of what we want to do?' You need to figure out who you will make a match with, because it can't be with all the doctors. Otherwise your strategy will become so diluted it will be meaningless.

"This is incredibly hard work," Bujack continues, "and it can only be done in dialogue. You have to have conversations that find out what it is you care about, why it is important and what it means to the community."

Why Should You Develop a Medical Staff Plan?

By Nathan Kaufman

A hospital is only as good as its medical staff. Yet in recent years, the physician "supply" (to put it in the language of economics) of several clinical specialties—such as obstetricians, orthopedic surgeons, neurosurgeons, cardiologists—has not matched community "demand" (i.e., need), and hospitals have even been forced to divert patients from their emergency departments as a result. It is therefore critical that hospitals ensure they do not leave the supply of their most important resource to chance.

As hospitals' need for physicians increases and physicians' need for hospitals decreases, the relationship between the institution and its medical staff becomes more complex. For example:

- As a result of technological advances in imaging and surgery, many specialists who used to depend on hospital resources do not need to practice in a hospital to generate a decent living.
- In many cases, members of the medical staff have become major competitors to their hospital by developing free-standing centers and/or other types of specialty hospitals.
- Although hospitals are ultimately accountable for the quality of care provided in their facilities, many quality standards are directly related to physicians' decisions and performance.

Nathan Kaufman is managing director of Kaufman Strategic Advisors, LLC, San Diego.

- Although reimbursement for most inpatient services is now fixed by insurers, including Medicare and Medicaid, using case rates or per diems, the cost of care and, ultimately, the financial solvency of the health care institution are directly related to the practice patterns of its medical staff.

Hospitals generally do a good job planning for their future "hardware," such as facilities, diagnostic, clinical and information technology. However, most do not plan ahead for their "software"—for example, the number and mix of physicians on staff—to meet their patients' future needs.

Traditionally, administrators and the board have relied on the medical staff to recruit the physicians they think they need. That's why a medical staff development plan is so important, and why the board should insist that such a plan be in place and updated regularly. Medical staff development plans should focus on addressing the two key areas of leadership and supply.

Leadership. The chief medical officer (CMO) should have the ultimate responsibility for developing and monitoring compliance with clinical policies. However, CMOs cannot do this alone; they need a solid "bench," or backup in the form of other physician leaders.

At a minimum, the hospital needs physician directors of critical care, cardiology, surgery, radiology, laboratory, emergency medicine and other major departments. These should be paid positions as these directors are responsible for managing clinical care in their departments. The goal of physician leaders should be to ensure that the best medical science is being applied consistently and cost-effectively in each of their oversight areas.

Supply. The supply of physicians in a market cannot be left solely to the discretion of physicians practicing in a given specialty. The need to minimize competition, for example, may motivate some members of the medical staff to sway recruitment decisions for certain specialists more than meeting the community's needs.

Patients with unmet needs for care will ultimately leave the market to get it. That's why it is essential that physicians on staff be convinced of the need for the right mix of additional physicians.

In addition, the more physicians there are on staff, the less often any one doctor will have to be on call and the more opportunities there will be for physicians to share other responsibilities, such as committee assignments.

The issue of supply is further complicated by the fact that there is no standard methodology for determining the right number of physicians for a population. However, obtaining the following information may serve as guidelines:

- Assessment of the current supply of full-time equivalents (FTEs)— not all physicians on the current medical staff wish to have full practices. Keeping an accurate count of physicians in a given specialty should be based on estimating those who are FTEs, not just "bodies."
- Opinions from referring physicians (primary care doctors, for the most part, but could include almost all practicing physicians)— the subjective opinion of referring physicians is an important criterion for determining the need for more specialists.
- Tenure and capacity—the need for more physicians in a given specialty is indicated when there have not been any new physicians joining the staff for several years and current specialists are not accepting new patients.
- Age—anecdotal evidence suggests that physicians begin to wind down their practices after age 60. A succession plan needs to be developed for all physicians age 60 and older.
- Loss of market share—in many states, it is possible to measure market share by service line.

With that information, the hospital can tell if a disproportionate share of patients has left the market in search of a specific specialty. If that's the case, more specialists in that area may be needed.

Given the national shortage in many specialties and the many threats to physicians' incomes, such as declining Medicare reimbursement, hospitals that offer a range of options for recruiting and retaining physicians may have an advantage over those that don't.

Many hospitals offer physicians employment within a tightly structured, productivity-based, hospital-affiliated medical "division."

Alternatively, the hospital can offer an existing "host practice," providing incremental overhead support combined with an income guarantee for a new physician recruit.

Physician-to-Population Ratios*

Type of Practice	Physician Need per 100,000
Primary Care	
Family Practice	35.0
Internal Medicine	27.0
Obstetrics/Gynecology	13.0
Pediatrics	13.0
Subtotal Primary Care	**88.0**
Medical Specialties	
Allergy/Immunology	1.0
Cardiology	6.0
Dermatology	2.3
Endocrinology	0.9
Gastroenterology	1.7
Hematology/Oncology	2.5
Infectious Disease	2.5
Nephrology	0.9
Neurology	2.2
Physical/Occupational Medicine	1.3
Pulmonary Medicine	1.5
Rheumatology	0.8
Subtotal Medical Specialties	**23.5**
Surgical Specialties	
Cardiothoracic Surgery	1.1
General Surgery	7.0
Neurosurgery	1.3
Ophthalmology	3.3
Orthopedics	7.0
Otorhinolaryngology	3.2
Plastic Surgery	1.2
Urology	3.1
Vascular Surgery	0.7
Subtotal Surgical Specialties	**27.9**
Other Specialties	
Anesthesiology	5.5
Pathology	4.5
Psychiatry	10.0
Radiation Oncology	0.9
Radiology	8.0
Subtotal Other Specialties	**18.9**
Total All Specialties	**158.3**

*In 1990, the Graduate Medical Education National Advisory Committee published physician-to-population ratios by specialty.

Over the last 15 years, others (e.g., Saks, Solucient, Cjeka, etc.) have also published ratios. But many other recommended ratios have not been published. The ratios presented here have been culled from all of these sources.

—Nathan Kaufman

Working with their current physicians, hospitals and health systems should use both quantitative and subjective assessment tools to determine community need. Then they must develop plans to meet that need.

Governing boards that understand the need for, and key components of a medical staff development plan can help ensure their hospitals have the physicians required in place to help meet their communities' medical care needs today and into the future.

Hospital-Physician Gainsharing

By Rosemary Grandusky and Kathy Kronenberg

Hospitals are reconsidering gainsharing arrangements with physicians after the Office of Inspector General (OIG) issued several formal advisory opinions last year indicating that specific gainsharing practices would not violate federal law if properly administered.

In order to strengthen physician relations, improve loyalty and reduce costs, hospitals are making a proactive effort to align their own economic and financial interests with those of their medical staffs. Aligning these financial interests improves communication and trust between the two groups, who historically have tended to operate from an "us versus them" perspective.

Over the years, hospitals have shared savings with physicians by investing a portion of those savings in equipment purchases or continuing education seminars, or funding educational programs for nursing staff. While this may encourage physicians' support of the hospital, it is not gainsharing because the physicians do not receive a direct financial benefit from such programs.

What Is Gainsharing?

The OIG defines *gainsharing* as an arrangement by which hospitals and other health care organizations promote standardization and

---

Rosemary Grandusky and Kathy Kronenberg are directors at Navigant Consulting, Inc.

more efficient use of expensive supplies in order to cut costs; a percentage of the resulting cost savings is then distributed among the physicians who helped generate those savings.

From the supply chain perspective, reduced use of supplies—combined with the transition to standardized, less expensive, clinically equivalent devices—can save organizations a significant amount of money. Such changes are typically described as "quick wins" because of the immediate and favorable effect the adjustments can have on an organization's bottom line.

While hospitals are constantly looking for ways to reduce costs, especially supply costs (where, for instance, cardiac devices can cost thousands of dollars), physicians in the typical business model have no reason to choose less expensive devices. Physicians are paid on a fee schedule, whereas hospitals receive a fixed amount from Medicare and sometimes other payers for each patient regardless of the actual cost of treating that patient.

The ability to link financial reward to a more conscientious use of supplies translates into a mutually beneficial situation: hospitals save money, while physicians, responsible for those savings, reap a reward for their commitment to cost reduction. As Lewis Morris, chief counsel to the Inspector General in the U.S. Department of Health & Human Services, stated in his testimony to the House Committee on Ways and Means last October (2005), "By giving the physician a share of any reduction in the hospital's costs attributable to his or her efforts, hospitals anticipate that the physician will practice more effective medicine."

Why Is There a Renewed Focus on Gainsharing?

In February 2005, the OIG issued six advisory opinions addressing specific hospital-physician gainsharing arrangements. These opinions—targeting cardiology and cardiovascular services at four hospitals—made it possible for the hospitals to reward physicians financially for helping the organizations achieve cost reductions.

With respect to these six opinions, the OIG declared it would not impose administrative sanctions because of safeguards that were incorporated into the arrangements. The safeguards address concerns regarding gainsharing's potentially adverse impact on quality of patient care and potential payments to induce referrals.

Yet, the OIG had previously expressed significant concerns about the risks posed by gainsharing. In 1999, it issued a special advisory bulletin on gainsharing, warning that it violated the Civil Monetary Penalties statute prohibiting hospitals from offering payments to physicians that either directly or indirectly encouraged them to reduce or limit care for Medicaid/Medicare patients. This development summarily halted all gainsharing practices for the following two years.

By 2001, however, the OIG softened its position through its advisory opinion permitting a limited gainsharing arrangement under the Civil Monetary Penalties law and the antikickback law.

In its most recent advisory opinions, the OIG indicated that properly structured arrangements under which cost savings are shared can serve legitimate business and medical purposes. Lewis Morris' testimony indicated that the OIG remains concerned that such arrangements could limit patient care; lead to "cherry-picking" healthy patients and steering sicker, more expensive patients to other hospitals; result in payments in exchange for patient referrals; or lead to unfair competition among hospitals based on their gainsharing programs.

Still, the ruling is significant for not-for-profit hospitals as they have historically been limited by regulations governing fraud and physician self-referrals to hospitals, in addition to issues involving their not-for-profit status.

All six gainsharing arrangements approved by the OIG apply to acute care hospitals and to one or more physician groups (either cardiologists or cardiac surgeons). In each gainsharing arrangement, the participation of an outside independent "program administrator" to collect data and develop the one-year-long gainsharing programs was a feature that contributed to the success of the arrangement and helped address the OIG's concerns.

Under these arrangements, physicians can earn up to 50 percent of the cost savings achieved in a single year. To preclude any conflict of interest, the program administrator, who also monitors the program, is paid a fixed monthly fee not tied to any cost savings attributable to the program.

Successful Physician-Hospital Relationships

Traditionally, the challenge to find the "right" relationship between hospitals and physicians has been a constant struggle.

But when physicians have an economic interest, it is easier to get their attention, according to Jon Soderholm, president of Avera Heart Hospital, Sioux Falls, South Dakota. "There is a significant difference when physicians have 'skin in the game,'" he says. "In most [hospital] relationships, the physician isn't an equal partner. When a physician is an equal partner and has equal input into decisions being made, it is very powerful. In many hospitals, you only hear 'I need' from physicians; however, when the decision-making and influence are shared, then you begin to hear 'We need.'"

The 1999 report by the Institute of Medicine, *To Err Is Human,* as well as countless other research studies, point to standardization as the critical element in improving quality of care and cost reduction. Soderholm predicts, "The institutions that are going to be successful in the future are the institutions that are going to take the most variance out of the system. When you take variation out of the system, you drive your quality up and drive your costs down."

One way of eliminating variation in the system is to ensure that the hospital's interests and the physician's interests are aligned; gainsharing offers this opportunity.

Gainsharing Safeguards

However, the OIG has given only cautionary approval for specific gainsharing arrangements that it believes provide sufficient protection from abuse. (See "OIG-Approved Gainsharing Safeguards" on page 374.)

In the absence of such safeguards, the OIG has found that nearly all gainsharing cases violate the Civil Monetary Penalties statute and improperly induce physicians to reduce or limit items or services furnished to their Medicare and Medicaid patients. However, the proposed gainsharing arrangements in the advisory opinions contained sufficient safeguards to prevent the imposition of sanctions. "The most important thing to take from these new advisory opinions is that legal and effective gainsharing programs can be structured," says Tom Dutton, a partner with the international law firm Jones Day. "The key is to structure the program in a manner that tracks the safeguards that the OIG has described in the advisory opinions."

OIG-Approved Gainsharing Safeguards

1. Programs will be transparent, with clearly identified cost-saving actions and resulting savings that allow for public scrutiny and individual physician accountability.

2. The physicians will offer credible medical support for the position that the cost-saving recommendations would not adversely affect patient care.

3. Payments will be based on all procedures, regardless of payer, and savings that result from procedures related to federal health care programs are subject to a cap.

4. Procedures to which the cost-saving program applies will not be performed disproportionately on federal health care program beneficiaries or a generally healthier mix of patients.

5. Each cost-saving mechanism will be tracked separately to preclude shifting cost savings.

6. Objective historical and clinical measures will be used as benchmarks to protect against inappropriate service reductions.

7. After the arrangement is implemented, individual physicians will have discretionary judgment to select cardiac devices to use for specific patients.

8. The program is of a limited, one-year duration. (It is unclear as to whether the OIG will approve multiyear programs. In a footnote to the advisory opinions, the OIG indicated that "any renewal or extension of the Proposed Arrangement should incorporate updated base year costs.")

9. The hospital and the physician groups involved in the gainsharing program will provide written disclosures of their participation in the cost-saving measures about arrangements for patients whose care may be affected.

10. Financial incentives will be limited to a reasonable duration and monetary amount.

11. Participating physician groups will distribute their profits on a per capita basis, thus restricting the incentive for individual physicians to generate disproportionate cost savings through these programs.

The Board's Role in Developing a Gainsharing Program

The board's role in the process of developing a gainsharing program is to act as steward of the hospital, to ask the right questions and hold management responsible for implementing a solid gainsharing plan. Some of the questions a board member should ask include:

- What are the specific objectives for proceeding with this program? What are the clinical goals (e.g., to reduce length of stay, increase formulary compliance or product standardization)? What are the cost-savings goals?
- What other models are there for aligning hospital and physician interests? What are the pros and cons of each?
- What other hospitals or health systems have implemented gainsharing programs, and has someone from our organization talked to them about their experiences?
- Is there adequate physician representation and involvement in the process? Have all physicians signed a conflict-of-interest statement? Is there a process in place to update the conflict-of-interest statement annually?
- Is there an implementation plan in place with clearly defined action steps, accountabilities, costs and timeframes? Does the hospital have clear expectations of the physicians? What is the estimated cost of implementing a program?
- Who is providing legal counsel? (Make sure that approval by the OIG is also included in the time line, recognizing that sometimes OIG review can take up to a year and a half.)
- Will the hospital use a consultant to help with the process? (Hospitals often find it helpful to seek outside help to walk them through the process.)
- Who will provide the software to track costs? (Again, hospitals may find that it is easier to contract with an outside vendor to ensure complete objectivity and data integrity. This is also a way to gain physicians' confidence.)

While board members have a lot on their plates, they should expect to receive at least quarterly updates on the gainsharing program's development. Once the program is implemented, quarterly updates should be provided on its cost savings and the progress made in reaching the goals.

Gainsharing Practices

All of the 2005 OIG advisory opinions addressed arrangements to manage patient care and related costs between hospitals and either cardiac surgeons (with respect to cardiac surgery programs) or cardiologists (with respect to cardiac catheterization laboratory services). The cost-saving measures in the OIG-approved arrangements included:

1. Opening packaged items (e.g., surgical trays) only as needed during a procedure
2. Performing blood cross-matching only as needed
3. Substituting less costly items, such as a knee-high sequential compression device for items currently being used, such as a thigh-high sequential compression device, which provides the same level of effectiveness
4. Product standardization of certain cardiac devices where medically appropriate (e.g., stents)
5. Limiting the use of certain vascular closure devices to an "as needed" basis

Any gainsharing arrangement considered by the hospital should be reviewed by outside legal counsel. Additionally, the hospital should obtain an advisory opinion from the OIG before implementing a gainsharing program, since one court opinion has held that any gainsharing program will violate the Civil Monetary Penalties statute unless it has been approved by the OIG through the advisory opinion process. Larry Ellis, senior vice president for cardiovascular services for Sisters of Charity Providence Hospital, Columbia, South Carolina, says, "We would never have considered moving forward with a gainsharing program without first making sure we were in compliance with all state and federal laws and without the advisory letter from the OIG, which basically gave us approval to proceed."

Gainsharing Features to Avoid

Board members should also be aware that there are aspects of gainsharing programs to avoid. For instance, it is inappropriate to pay incentive rewards in the following cases:

- Where there is no direct, demonstrable connection between individual actions and any reduction in a hospital's out-of-pocket costs
- If individual actions would result in unspecified savings
- If there are insufficient safeguards against the risk that other actions, such as increases in patient volume or premature hospital discharges, might actually account for any savings
- If quality of care indicators are of questionable validity and statistical significance
- When there is no independent verification of cost savings, quality of care indicators or other essential aspects of the arrangement

The Future of Gainsharing

Although gainsharing agreements between physicians and hospitals are no longer strictly prohibited by the OIG, boards must nevertheless continue to approach the subject with caution. And while recent opinions indicate that the gainsharing door is opening, trustees should not assume that implementing a gainsharing program will be easy.

According to Dutton, "To date, there has been a lot of talk and very little action surrounding gainsharing programs." He says this is because, notwithstanding the recent OIG opinions, hospitals remain concerned about: potentially significant consulting, information systems and legal implementation costs; the uncertainty regarding re-basing cost targets in the second year, which could limit the hospital's anticipated cost reductions; and the long delay that the OIG advisory opinion process likely represents.

Even if the path is cleared, gainsharing still may not be the best solution for every organization. Says Ellis, "I think it is different for all facilities, and I don't know if gainsharing is going to work for every hospital." He adds, "Providence is more of a specialty cardiovascular facility. We have the largest open-heart program in South Carolina. Based on our volumes, gainsharing makes a lot of sense. But gainsharing may not make sense in a university setting, in a hospital where the physicians are employees, or in smaller facilities."

Boards are urged to stay informed for continued developments in gainsharing. Experience is very limited, since the OIG has only issued the six recent advisories and one previous advisory opinion in 2001; however, that number may rise as hospitals and physicians continue to seek options to align their interests for the future. When structured properly, gainsharing arrangements have the potential to decrease hospital and system supply costs and increase efficiency and quality.

Despite the obvious work involved and the long-term commitment hospitals must make to receive OIG approval, gainsharing does offer a unique set of rewards for hospitals and physicians willing to work together.

Dutton believes that possible pending legislation could have a significant effect on gainsharing. "Congress has recently become more aware of the merits of gainsharing from the Medicare Payment Advisory Commission report in March 2005.

"If Congress approves gainsharing," says Dutton, "then administratively it will become simpler to implement because you would not have to receive an advisory opinion from the OIG. And, it will become clearer what you can and cannot do with these programs. If this happens, gainsharing could really take off."

Case Study for Success:
Sisters of Charity Providence Health System

The Sisters of Charity Providence Hospital (SCPH), part of the Sisters of Charity of St. Augustine Health System (CSA), is a 322-bed acute care hospital in Columbia, South Carolina. The hospital is one of only four to have received the Office of Inspector General's (OIG) approval last year (2005) for its two gainsharing programs, one for cardiovascular surgery and one for cardiology.

The Sisters of Charity Providence Hospital was already successful in working with its medical staff on cost reductions. The organization had been benchmarking its performance against that of its peers and sharing this information with the board and medical staff. In the late 1980s and early 1990s, its physicians had worked closely with the hospital on numerous issues that had an impact on cost and quality, such as utilization and product selection. At the time, the hospital was struggling with new technology, such as cardiac

Continued →

stents, which allowed physicians to provide clinical innovation, but at a premium price. During the mid-1990s, as these demands continued to grow, SCPH began to talk with consultants about ways to move forward, but because of the legal ramifications of the Stark amendments, it was impossible to proceed. In addition, there was the question of how quality would be affected.

According to Larry Ellis, senior vice president for SCPH's cardiovascular services, in 2002 the hospital began working with Joane Goodroe, president and CEO of Goodroe Healthcare Solutions LLC, Atlanta. Goodroe had worked with St. Joseph's Hospital in Atlanta to help the organization achieve the first gainsharing approval from the OIG in 2001. Sisters of Charity management knew this model had worked and looked to St. Joseph's for advice. The board received regular updates, and the executive committee was deeply involved in several of the discussions. When the time came to make a decision, management and the board reviewed a list of pros and cons. The board knew the health care industry was struggling with the escalating cost of supplies and new technology. At the same time, it was important to make technology available to patients, strengthen quality of care and achieve desired outcomes. One of the safeguards favorably looked upon by the OIG is a system to monitor clinical outcomes for surgery. This software allowed SCPH to track a supply item from a patient, to a physician, and to an outcome. For example, if a cardiac catheter was substituted for one offered by a different manufacturer and was deemed therapeutically equivalent by the medical staff, then physicians could see the cost and efficacy data related to that change.

The gainsharing program began last year, involving 57 cardiologists on staff, and has already achieved several million dollars of savings. "What's important for boards to realize," says Ellis, "is that any time you can align a hospital and its physicians in the right direction, you are in a win-win situation. In our organization, we were able to lower our costs, and the patients, physicians and the hospital benefited from the effort." While Ellis concedes the organization may re-evaluate the program in the next several years as the health care marketplace changes, he says, "I'm very excited about what we are doing."

For Additional Reading

1. OIG Advisory Opinions Nos. 05-01-05-06. http://oig.hhs.gov/ fraud/advisoryopinions/opinions.html.

2. Testimony of Lewis Morris, Chief Counsel to the Inspector General, U.S. Department of Health & Human Services; House Committee on Ways and Means; Subcommittee on Health; Hearing Oct. 7, 2005. http://oig.hhs.gov/testimony/docs/2005/ Gainsharing10-07-05.pdf.

3. ABA Health eSource, November 2005, "The New Gainsharing— Has Anything Really Changed?" www.abanet.org/health/esource/ vol2no3/dean.html.

4. BNA's Health Care Fraud Report, June 8, 2005, "Gainsharing: Regulatory Breakthrough, but Challenges Remain."

PART EIGHT

Information Technology

The Role of the Board
in the IT Discussion

By John P. Glaser

Investments in information technology (IT) are a critical element of health care organizational strategies. Plans to advance patient safety, revenue cycles and operational efficiency usually include the acquisition of new and expensive information systems.

IT investments can place significant demands on the organization's capital and operating budgets. IT operating budgets often escalate faster than almost any other budget line items because of insatiable demand, contract price increases and the need for additional staff to manage a growing portfolio of applications.

Large IT capital demands may end up requiring that the board make difficult trade-offs with investments in other large capital projects, such as buildings and equipment.

Additionally, problems with IT security or the controls in financial systems pose a growing risk for organizations. Large IT projects that overrun budgets and timetables create major strategic and financial problems for the organization.

Despite these realizations, the board may be unsure how best to perform its responsibilities and assist the organization's management team. For most boards, IT is a new agenda item, and boards do not know what questions they should ask.

John P. Glaser is vice president and chief information officer, Partners HealthCare, Acton, Massachusetts.

Unlike other issues, such as finance or medical staff relationships, most trustees do not understand the critical issues that should frame their IT discussions. The board may look at its composition and find that no one has a background in or experience with IT.

Core Responsibilities

The board has five core IT responsibilities:

1. Ensuring that the IT strategy and plan have been well-developed and are tightly integrated with the organization's overall strategy and plan. IT is a tool. As such, it has no inherent value. The value of IT is determined by the degree to which it enables the organization to further its strategic goals and enhances operational and clinical performance.

   The board needs to ensure that there is a sound plan for IT investments and that these investments are clearly directed to furthering the organization's goals.
2. Making sure that major IT initiatives—for example, computerized physician order entry (CPOE)—are well-conceived and well-structured. Poor execution of such initiatives can significantly diminish the investment's value and can damage the organization's operations. That's why the board should ensure that plans for major initiatives are thoughtful and comprehensive.
3. Monitoring the organization's progress in implementing its overall strategy. To the extent that IT is a key component of organizational strategy, the board is responsible for monitoring the IT plan and implementation.
4. Ensuring that IT capital budget demands have been fully accounted for in the organization's multiyear capital plan. Because IT can consume 10 percent to 20 percent of a provider's capital budget, the board must appreciate the impact IT can have on its organization's bottom line.
5. Ensuring that risk factors tied to application systems and infrastructure have been addressed. Viruses and patient data theft pose big risks to the hospital.

   With increasing reliance on IT for day-to-day operations, an unreliable and poorly performing set of applications can paralyze major departments. Controls in financial applications must also be strong. The board must ensure that it is managing its IT risks.

Fulfilling IT Responsibilities

Trustees need not have any IT background or even be able to define a server to effectively discuss IT strategies and proposals.

Alignment with Organizational Strategy

The relationship between the IT strategic plan and the organization's overall strategy should be clear and convincing. For example, if there is a proposal to invest in an electronic medication administration record, it should be clear that this investment is tightly linked to overall organizational efforts to improve patient safety.

In discussing IT strategy, the board should ensure that:

- Each aspect of strategy has been addressed from an IT perspective, recognizing that not all aspects of strategy have an IT component, and not all components will be funded.
- The non-IT organizational initiatives needed to ensure a maximum leverage of the IT initiative are understood—for example, process re-engineering.
- The organization has not missed a strategic IT opportunity that might come from new technologies.

At the end of alignment and strategic planning discussions, an organization should have something that looks like a two-column table. The organization's strategies and plans should be listed in one column, and in the other column, in corresponding rows, should be a list of related IT investments.

As they discuss such a table, board members should be able to answer *yes* to each of the following questions:

- Is it clear how the IT plan advances the organization's strategy?
- Is it clear how care will improve, costs will be reduced or service will be improved as a result of the proposed IT investments?
- Are the measures of current performance and expected improvements well-researched and realistic?

- Have the related changes in operations, workflow, and overall organization been defined?
- Is senior leadership, whose areas are the focus of the IT plan, supportive? Could they present the plan?
- Are the resource requirements well-understood and convincingly presented to the board and to management? Have these requirements been compared with needs experienced by other organizations undertaking similar initiatives?
- Have investment risks been identified and addressed?

A *no*, a *maybe*, or an equivocal *yes* to any of these questions should indicate that the project has a greater risk of failing to deliver value.

Assessing Major Project Plans

Several cues will indicate that the plan is as solid as possible at the IT project's inception:

- The plan charter is clear and explicit. Fuzzy objectives and a vague understanding of resource needs indicate that the plan needs further development.
- Leaders of departments and functions that will be affected by the plan, or who need to devote resources to the plan, have reviewed the charter and plan. Their concerns have been heard and addressed and they have publicly committed to performing the work required in the plan.
- Project time lines have been reviewed by multiple parties to ensure they are reasonable and that they consider factors that will affect the plan. This might include temporarily losing those people who will have to stop working on the IT project in order to develop the annual budget, and the relative uncertainty that might exist for certain phases or tasks.
- The necessary resources have been committed, the budget approved and appropriate staff identified and approved by their managers to work on the project.
- The accountabilities for each phase of the plan and for each task are explicit.
- The project's risks have been comprehensively assessed in the plan's charter, which contains thoughtful approaches to addressing those

risks. An example of such a risk might include purchasing un-proven IT.

- The project incorporates a reasonable amount of flexibility to allow for inevitable problems and missed deadlines. For very complex projects, it is not unusual to see 20 percent to 25 percent of the budget allocated for contingencies such as these.

Tracking IT implementation, as with the monitoring of any organizational activity, should be conducted as a series of tasks and initiatives that are part of the organization's overall strategy.

The true measure of progress is whether the intended improvements in operational and clinical performance have been seen and, only tangentially, whether the initiatives are on time and on budget.

IT Capital Demands

Approving the IT strategic plan should lead to the approval of a multiyear IT capital budget. When determining this budget in the context of strategy and major IT projects, the board will have to resign itself to three unpleasant facts about IT capital budgets:

- IT is expensive.
- Infrastructure costs, such as servers and networks, are significant and recurring capital expenses.
- There may be no time at which the organization is "done." Boards sometimes assume that IT and buildings are similar financially. However, construction—while it often entails cost overruns and missed deadlines—does have an endpoint. IT, on the other hand, involves a series of continuous initiatives.

Managing IT Risk

Internal and external auditors are excellent resources for learning about IT risks and the steps that can be taken to mitigate it. There are three major areas of IT risk assessment that the board's audit committee (or full board) should discuss:

- Controls for the major financial information systems
- Security of the IT systems and mechanisms to protect patient privacy

- Appropriate management of the organization's applications and infrastructure—for example, is the organization up to date on major vendor releases and does the IT staff have the skills and tools necessary to provide day-to-day management of the computer systems?

Assessing the CIO

Most of the areas described above, and the questions to be asked, do not require that trustees be conversant with information technology. The IT strategy is either clearly linked to the overall organizational strategy, or it isn't. Project plans are either well-defined, or they aren't.

I Don't Understand the Jargon!

IT can bring a confusing set of jargon and terms. This new language invariably spans three areas:

1. Technology—for example, servers, networks and workstations
2. Management ideas—for example, "IT as a competitive advantage" and "IT portfolio management"
3. Applications—for example, computerized provider order entry (CPOE) and the electronic medical record (EMR)

How can a trustee become conversant in this language?

While there are books and articles that can explain most of these terms and jargon, trustees may not have time to become IT students. Moreover, the IT field is replete with innovation and the constant addition of new technologies, applications and management ideas, so it becomes very difficult to remain current. The solution—as for any other area—is to ask the experts.

If trustees are unfamiliar with language used in new Medicare regulations, they ask the chief financial officer to explain. If trustees have to decide whether to invest in a new imaging modality, they can ask the chief medical officer to discuss how patient care or physician productivity will be improved.

Similarly, the trustee should be able to ask the chief information officer to explain terms and jargon that are important for the board's discussion of the IT agenda. A good chief information officer should also be a good teacher.

Nonetheless, the organization's chief information officer (CIO) and the IT department are very important assets and the board usually relies on the CIO's skill, recommendations and knowledge. To make sure the board can trust the CIO and the IT department's judgment, how does it assess them?

Here are three questions the board should ask itself:

- Does our CIO communicate clearly and in business terms? If the chief information officer explains new technologies and application capabilities effectively to the board, then it is quite likely he or she was able to explain them to the management team and medical staff leadership. Hence, the organization's leadership is likely to have made informed decisions.
- Do we have a track record of success with the IT organization? The CIO (and CEO, chief operating officer and chief financial officer) ought to be able to elucidate the organization's IT successes and describe how they have assessed that success.

  If the CEO can describe such successes then it is likely that the business and clinical sides of the organization believe that they have received value from their IT investments and that the IT organization is competent at execution.
- Does our CIO have a good understanding of the health care IT industry and the efforts of similar institutions? Have these hospitals tried comparable IT implementations and if so, what were their results?

The CIO should be able to describe the status of the industry and any major forces that influence it. Examples could include the federal health care IT agenda and promising new technologies.

In addition, the CIO should be able to discuss the experiences of similar hospitals and health care systems with such technology as electronic medical records. No health care executive, including the CIO, can be effective if he or she is ignorant of the industry.

Board Oversight

The board has several options for establishing specific IT review methods:

- Appoint new board members who have IT backgrounds. These members could be current or former CIOs, executives from IT consultant or vendor organizations, or IT academics from a local business school.

- Establish a board IT subcommittee. This committee could comprise several trustees and outside members with IT experience. This committee would undertake the duties described under the core responsibilities listed above.

  Or the board may decide that IT capital discussions should occur within the finance committee, and IT risk factors should be addressed by the audit committee. A final option is that each board responsibility be addressed in joint committee meetings.

- Form an external advisory committee that would meet a couple of times a year, with several trustees and management, to comment on the organization's IT strategy and its progress.

- Request a regular update from the CIO on the status of the IT agenda and the performance of the IT department.

- Convene a special board meeting or a retreat dedicated to a discussion of IT strategy, plans and performance.

None of these steps is mutually exclusive. For example, the board may add members with IT backgrounds, request a regular update from the CIO and form an IT subcommittee.

There is no uniform approach to structuring IT-specific governance. For some organizations, IT is an important support function, but is not strategically critical. For these organizations, a board member with an IT background may be sufficient.

However, for those organizations that deem IT to be a major contributor to their strategy, an IT subcommittee will be important. Such a subcommittee may also be important for organizations that are in the process of turning around a poorly performing IT function.

Whichever governance mechanisms are chosen, they will need to address the critical responsibilities described earlier. As they fulfill these responsibilities, board members should be aware of two overarching concepts that are important to understanding how IT can improve organizational performance.

The first centers on those factors that contribute to organizational effectiveness in the application of IT. The second concept focuses on the nature of IT-enabled value.

Factors that Lead to Organizational IT Excellence

Trustees often focus on the specifics of an IT proposal or strategy and don't take the time to step back and ask, "Is the organization well-equipped for IT success?" If the answer is *no*, management and the board should focus on improving the following factors before significant IT investments are approved:

- *Individuals and leadership matter.* It's critical that the organization possess talented, skilled and experienced individuals. These individuals should occupy a variety of roles: CEO, CIO, IT staff and user middle management. They must be strong contributors.

  While such an observation may seem trite, too often, organizations, dazzled by the technology or the glorified experiences of others, embark upon technology crusades and substantive investments for which they have insufficient talent or leadership to achieve success.
- *Relationships are critical.* In addition to strong individual players, the team must be strong. The senior executive, IT executive and project team members must be highly competent and willing to build sound relationships among themselves.
- *Alignment among the elements of the IT strategy must be clearly linked to the overall organizational strategy.* The appearance of an elaborate planning methodology can be deceiving; the process of developing this alignment depends more on close working relationships between management and the medical staff, than on methodologies.
- *Evaluation of IT opportunities must be rigorous and thoughtful.* If this rigor is lacking overall, there is no reason to believe that the IT strategy development has been sufficiently thoughtful. While rigor needs to be applied to IT, high-performing organizations understand that a large element of vision, management instinct and "feel" often guides major decisions.
- *The IT organization is strong.* Strong IT staff, well-designed IT governance, well-crafted technology architecture and a superb CIO are critical to effectiveness.

If these factors are deficient, they can be corrected through management action.

The Nature of IT-Enabled Value

Achieving value from IT investments requires management effort. There is no computer genie that descends upon the organization once the system is "live" and waves its magic "value wand." The authors of a 2003 *Harvard Business Review* article made three significant observations about IT-enabled value:[1]

1. Extracting value from IT requires innovative business practices. All IT initiatives should be accompanied by efforts to materially improve or redesign the processes that the IT system is designed to support. If an organization "merely" computerizes existing processes without rectifying process problems, it may have only made process problems occur faster. In addition, those processes are now more expensive since there is a computer system to support.

Process change is difficult work. New processes must be designed, and administrative and clinical staff will need to change their workflow and behaviors. During process change, the organization's performance may dip. However, without process change, the value of an IT investment is diluted.

2. IT's economic impact comes from incremental innovations rather than "big bang" initiatives. Examples of such big bangs are the replacement of all systems related to the revenue cycle or the introduction of a new patient care system during the course of a few months.

Big bang implementations are very tricky and risky. It is exceptionally difficult to understand the ramifications of comprehensive change during the analysis and design stages that precede implementation. As a result, organizations risk material damage. Even if the organization grinds its way through the disruption, the resulting trauma may make it unwilling to engage in future ambitious IT initiatives.

On the other hand, IT implementation (and related process changes) that are more incremental and iterative reduce the risk of organizational damage and permit the organization to learn. The organization understands the value impact of Phase "N" and then can alter its course before it embarks upon Phase "N+1." Moreover, incremental change leads the organization's members to understand that change and realizing value are a continuous aspect of organizational life, rather than something to be endured every couple of years.

3. *The strategic impact of IT investments comes from the cumulative effect of sustained initiatives to innovate business practices in the near term.* If economic value is derived from a series of thoughtful, incremental steps, then the aggregate effect of those steps leads to a competitive advantage.

Most of the time, organizations that wind up dominating an industry do so through sustained incremental movement over the course of several years.

Conclusion

As it grapples with IT, perhaps the most important thing that a board can do is what it always does: Ask good questions and continue to ask them until it is satisfied with the answers. And make sure that the management team is strong and supported as necessary.

There are questions, mechanisms and techniques that the board can use during the IT discussion. These techniques are, in most ways, no different from the techniques used in any strategy discussion, review of major initiatives or evaluation of any large capital investments.

Persistent innovation by a talented team, over the course of years, will result in significant strategic gains—the organization will have learned how to improve itself, year in and year out. Strategic value is a long race that is run and won one mile at a time.

Reference

1. Brown, J. and Hagel, J. "Does IT matter?" *Harvard Business Review*, July 2003, 109–112.

Some of this content has been adapted with permission from: *Managing Health Care Information Systems: A Practical Approach for Health Care Executives* by Karen A. Wager, Frances Wickham Lee, and John P. Glaser. Jossey-Bass, May 2005.

Making a Commitment to IT

By Jan Greene

Investing in information technology
must be part of a long-term strategic plan.

Remember when cell phones and personal computers promised to revolutionize our lives? Supposedly, they'd be easy to install and function beyond our wildest dreams. But before long, the shine began to fade when the cell phone cut out during a crucial call, or software conflicts gave a computer the dreaded "blue screen of death," and we lost an important document to "cyberspace."

Most of us have experienced some unintended consequences of information technology (IT), and we've become more realistic about manufacturers' promises. As hospitals have invested in IT, they've run into such problems on a much bigger scale. The unfulfilled promises and unpredictable trouble spots have provided expensive lessons for many, and getting "wired" has been a slower process than originally predicted. Still, many health care organizations are making impressive progress in IT by planning carefully and strategically. And those tasks rest in large part with an active, informed board of trustees.

"This is one of the few things that will come before a board that will be make-or-break," says Lewis Redd, national practice leader for health at Capgemini, a technology consulting firm based in New York City. "A community hospital could spend $30 million or $50

Jan Greene is a writer based in Alameda, California.

million on this outlay, and the board needs to step up [to its strategic planning responsibilities]."

Creating an IT strategy is a pressing task for hospitals. Information technology contributes greatly to a safe, efficient, competitive future, and the time to start planning and investing in it is now—these are big-ticket items that will take years to pay for and implement. Meanwhile, the pressure is on from influential stakeholders. Payers and regulators increasingly see electronic patient records, computerized physician order entry (CPOE) and medication bar coding as standard technologies that every health care organization should be adopting or committing to now.

The Board's Role: Strategy

IT success doesn't require a board packed with senior vice presidents from computer companies. In fact, most trustees won't be asked to weigh the individual merits of a particular hardware or software package. Instead, hospital management is seeking trustees' vision and philosophy—the same fundamentals that drive the organization in other ways. Does your hospital leap to the front on new ideas or wait and learn from others' experience? What are your goals and priorities for the future, and for the capital budget? The board needs to give management direction on these big-picture questions to help guide their choices for IT planning.

"The board of directors and management have to have a basis from which to go forward or you become susceptible to every trend and every vendor's wish list," advises Gary Miller, senior vice president and chief financial officer of St. Alexius Medical Center in Bismarck, North Dakota. "It's easy to get lost in the IT wilderness." The 297-bed hospital was named one of the nation's 100 Most Wired hospitals and health systems in 2004 by *Hospitals & Health Networks* magazine, based on an annual survey of hospitals. (The Most Wired Survey and Benchmarking Study is a joint project of *Hospitals & Health Networks*, IDX Systems Corp., Capgemini and the College of Healthcare Information Management Executives.)

For hospital trustees, the way to respond to demands for better safety and quality of care through IT is the same way that all the most important board discussions should be approached: get educated, ask questions, be skeptical.

"Boards are getting more interested in making sure they have the competence to make good decisions," observes Manuel Lowenhaupt, M.D., a vice president of Capgemini. "Though they certainly trust their management team, for decisions of this size their governance responsibility requires them to take a more active role and make sure they're not just rubber-stamping a decision the management team has made."

At the same time, boards have to be careful not to get too involved in the operational side of things. While the board might have final approval on a big electronic medical record system, its evaluation of the project should center around such aspects as the stability of the vendor or the clinical staff's reaction to the proposal, rather than the specifics of the system's design.

What Boards Can Do

When considering all angles of big, expensive information technology (IT) purchases, here are four actions boards can take to reduce their hospital's risk:

1. *Invest for value.* While hospital managers and consultants talk about the proper percent of a capital or operating budget that should go into IT, the consultants see those numbers as unreliable. "It's not just what you're spending, it's the value you're getting," says Manuel Lowenhaupt, M.D., a vice president of Capgemini.
2. *Ask for the business case.* Start by asking questions such as "What are the financial and quality returns on the investment? How will this vendor meet those returns?"
3. *Have a multiyear plan.* Lowenhaupt recommends goals three, five, and 10 years out.
4. *Start implementation with something easy and popular.* "You want some early wins with high value and low cost, such as results reporting," Lowenhaupt advises. "Everybody loves [results reporting]. Then put in [digitized images, medical record tools and clinical documentation]. But save order entry and expert rules and decision support for later." They require more of a time investment from users.

—Jan Greene

"Board members don't want to get involved in which [computer] system is to be used," explains Chuck Reichert, incoming board chair at St. Alexius. "We set the strategic direction." When new projects come to the board level, "we ask whether this is getting us where we want to be. We've never been too shy about asking questions."

Adds Miller, the hospital's CFO, "On the administrative management side, you have to make sure you help educate your board on some of the complexities of providing cost-effective patient care at high quality. You've got to invest some time in your board, and your board has to be able to ask educated questions and hold people accountable."

Size Doesn't Matter

The board's responsibility is consistent, regardless of the hospital's size, according to trustees interviewed in a small sample of hospitals and systems designated as one of *Hospitals & Health Networks'* Most Wired hospitals for 2004. In each case—from a single 182-bed hospital in rural northeastern North Carolina to a huge Catholic system spanning seven states—governing board members described their role relative to IT as strategizing and overseeing the big picture.

At Albemarle Hospital in Elizabeth City, North Carolina, trustees and hospital administrators have developed an overall strategy for adopting new clinical IT that takes note of the sophisticated competition in nearby cities, but at the same time, doesn't let that pressure push the small regional hospital into unnecessary purchases. "We don't like technology just for the sake of technology," explains Chief Information Officer Ed Ricks. "If it doesn't solve some business problem, we'll stay away from it."

Albemarle CEO Sharon Tanner notes that the strategic plan sets out a process useful for any big capital purchase. "We look at the return on investment and quality implications and patient safety implications," she explains. "We have a team that looks at the whole matrix." Then there's review by physicians and the board.

It's not that different at Sisters of Mercy, a seven-state system based in St. Louis that includes 18 hospitals along with outpatient care, physician practices and a health plan. "We usually work with staff when they bring up an idea they're working on," says Marlon Priest, M.D., an emergency room physician who serves as chair of the Sisters of Mercy board quality committee. "The CEO brings up the idea and explains how it fits into the strategic imperatives we've agreed on. It's usually put on the table as a concept beginning to be fleshed out."

That's how it has worked with the Genesis Project, an ambitious effort to improve patient care through information technology approved by the Sisters of Mercy board in 2004. It is expected to cost about $226 million and encompass technology upgrades throughout the system in clinical, revenue, resource planning and supply chain areas.

Getting such a huge strategic plan going required two or three board meetings over a six- to nine-month period, says Priest. Well aware of the tremendous cost involved, the board acted carefully, asking questions about potential job losses from the new technology and how well doctors were likely to accept the changes in clinical systems. Much of a December board retreat was spent on fleshing out the original Genesis Project plan.

"Given the cost of this, when margins are 2 or 3 or 4 percent, that's a pretty scary proposition," Priest says. "We don't control the vendors and the technology and how it develops. We think a lot about how things could go wrong." At the same time, the Sisters of Mercy board doesn't see how it can ignore the electronic revolution, something of which health care has been slow to take advantage. "I firmly believe we cannot fulfill our safety and quality responsibilities unless we use technology as an enabler to improve our systems and individual clinicians," Priest says. "It's a risk like the ones taken by the early developers of cardiac surgery or antibiotics. We don't have any alternative but to take it and try to control it."

Different Hospitals, Different Strategies

Maimonides Medical Center in the Brooklyn borough of New York City is an example of a hospital that took control of its IT in a big way, making a long-term commitment to spend nearly half its yearly capital budget on IT purchases, well above the average hospital. For Maimonides, it's a matter of playing catch-up, but in a systematic way.

Ten years ago the aging facility was well behind the technology curve, explains long-time board chair Martin Payson. "We had no choice," he says. "The old systems had just broken down at that point. I had just become a new board leader, and we had a new administration, and our thinking was identical. We couldn't do it halfheartedly . . . we had to go into it wholeheartedly."

This meant investing early on in physician training on the new clinical systems. "We provided 24-hour, seven-day-a-week training for the doctors, available on their time, not ours, and that's expensive. But it turned out to be a very wise investment," Payson explains.

As a result, the 705-bed Maimonides is now one of the most wired hospitals around with its comprehensive electronic patient record and an order entry system that is used by nearly all its physicians. And the board of trustees was a key to getting it done. "We leapfrogged from virtually nowhere to a leading hospital," Payson says. "The board has been very supportive of computerizing every place that we can."

Similarly, at St. Alexius, the organization has been on a long journey of carrying out a strategy and building on it. More than a decade ago, the organization established a philosophy that it would base its systems on Linux or Unix, giving it the flexibility to buy the best hardware from any vendor. To that, it added a fiber optic backbone (see glossary on page 400) throughout the facility. "Once we had that infrastructure, it made it a lot easier for us to control the things that are being adopted to meet the board's strategic directive," says CFO Miller.

The board and the IT staff decided early on that even though the hospital was committed from the beginning to building its infrastructure, it would not try to be on the cutting edge of new technologies, such as CPOE. "We will not be an early adopter of that technology," Miller says. "We're going to let some of the software be tested and some of the implementation be sorted out before we invest significant dollars in that regard. That's a corporate strategy that surrounds our overall strategy."

It's not that the hospital lacks the technical expertise to pull it off. In fact, St. Alexius already has an order entry system in place that can be used by nurses at the bedside. And hospital leaders are acutely aware that the Leapfrog Group has set CPOE as one of its standards for hospitals to meet as a marker of quality and patient safety. But St. Alexius has chosen to bring CPOE along more slowly, planning for full use by 2007. "The major hang-up has not been

IT Glossary

1. **Backbone:** A high-capacity communications channel that carries data accumulated from smaller branches of a computer or telecommunications network.

2. **Bar coding:** A patient safety system that uses bar codes on medications, hospital patients' identification bands and nurses' identification badges that can be compared with the patient's medical record to ensure the correct dispensation of a drug.

3. **Clinical decision support:** The use of information to help a clinician diagnose and/or treat a patient's health problem, including information about the patient and information about the kind of health problem afflicting the patient and alternative tests and treatments for it.

4. **Clinical information system:** Hospital-based information system designed to collect and organize data related to the care given to a patient, rather than administrative data.

5. **Computer-based patient record (or electronic health record—EHR):** A compilation in digital form of all the clinical and administrative information related to the care of a single individual.

6. **Computerized physician order entry (CPOE):** An electronic prescribing system that intercepts errors when they most commonly occur— at the time medications are ordered. With CPOE, physicians enter orders into a computer rather than on paper. Orders are integrated with patient information, including laboratory and prescription data. The order is then automatically checked for potential errors or problems.

7. **Most Wired:** For the past six years, *Hospitals & Health Networks* magazine has named the Most Wired Hospitals and Health Systems. The list is based on the Most Wired Survey and Benchmarking Study, which is a joint project of *Hospitals & Health Networks,* IDX Systems Corp., Capgemini and the College of Healthcare Information Management Executives (CHIME). In 2004, 482 hospitals and health systems completed the survey, representing 1,298 hospitals.

8. **Picture archiving and communications system (PACS):** A computer-based system of storing and retrieving radiographic and other images in digital form.

9. **Rule-based expert system:** A decision support system based on large numbers of heuristics, or rules of thumb, derived from analysis of action patterns of experts or from published literature.

Sources: U.S. Congress, Office of Technology Assessment, "Bringing Health Care Online: The Role of Information Technologies," OTA-ITC-624 (Washington, D.C.: U.S. Government Printing Office, September 1995); Leapfrog Group; Institute for Safe Medication Practices; and Health Forum.

the technology, it's been the physician adoption and the capability of making it time-neutral for them," Miller explains. "We've got a 110-year culture where the physicians have been independent; they're good practitioners and we've got all kinds of quality awards showing we're in the top 5 percent of hospitals. We have to come to them with something that works."

Potential Pitfalls

With clinical systems, which are most closely related to the current push to improve patient safety, getting buy-in from physicians and nurses has been the biggest stumbling block for many organizations. Newspaper headlines across the country tell stories of hospitals that scrapped million-dollar computer systems because they simply didn't work in the real world. Every hospital wants to avoid that kind of waste of money, time, energy, and physician and employee good-will—and the board can help, Capgemini consultants Lowenhaupt and Redd say. Typical missteps they see often involve underestimating the size and cost of IT projects. "They typically take two-plus times as long" as expected, says Redd. Here are some of the specific pitfalls that can bedevil a hospital making a big IT investment:

Relying on Vendors for Implementation

"Some of the vendors of software are very good at writing software but not as good at implementing their own products in a large hospital," Lowenhaupt says. Be sure there's a realistic plan for implementation and that the internal information systems (IS) department can handle it with help from the vendor. Find out how previous "go-lives" have gone with the vendor's products.

Minimizing the Importance of Process Change

Technology is not the answer to a poorly designed process and could just make it worse. "You should . . . look at what type of process and workflow redesign is needed, early on," says Redd.

Allowing a Mishmash of Vendors' Products

Capgemini suggests a core vendor approach, where the system is based on one vendor's product, and further applications are added one at a time.

Accepting Unrealistic Promises from Vendors

"I get very anxious when I hear a vendor say, 'This will save your docs and nurses time,' or 'There will be zero downtime,'" Lowenhaupt says. Board members should probe what exactly is meant by those types of sweeping statements.

Ignoring Clinicians' Input

It's also unnerving, Lowenhaupt says, when the board is presented with a new system by the IT staff alone. "If there are some leading doctors and nurses in the room, I feel better," he says. And it's important to choose the right clinicians to lead the way. The chief of staff might not be as influential with other doctors as the hospital's busiest and best doctor—and this can cause some medical staffs "some real division," he says.

For example, at one hospital, a senior internal medicine physician said CPOE could be introduced into the hospital "over his dead body." "Considering that this organization is spending tens of millions of dollars, that came as . . . a disappointing conversation," Lowenhaupt says. "They [the board and administration] hadn't gone out to their front-line busy folks and run this by them."

He adds that purchasing and implementing IT to replace traditional clinical methods "is very complex stuff and reasonably high-risk, and there's a poor ability to predict an outcome. If you don't spend a lot of time mitigating the risk and investing with discipline and rigor, there's a reasonable likelihood that you will be disappointed. This is the time for you to do your homework as a board. Don't rush into these decisions without a lot of thought."

While it's important to rely on expert advice that you trust—possibly from an outside party—board members who are not hard-core techies shouldn't be intimidated by the technology. "Don't take a backseat and think this is a tech issue [and] let the tech guy handle it. It's not, it's a business issue and a large [risk] these community hospitals are going to take," warns Redd. "You don't have to be an expert to see that a good decision is made."

Sticking with the Commitment

While the rhetoric about information technology revolutionizing health care is probably overblown, at its core are some essential

Current IT Priorities (within next 12 months)

	2003 Respondents	2004 Respondents
Upgrade Security/HIPAA Compliant	47%	48%
Reduce Medical Errors/Promote Patient Safety	52%	47%
Replace/Upgrade Inpatient Clinical Systems	38%	44%
Implement Wireless Systems	20%	37%
Implement an Electronic Medical Record	30%	33%
Upgrade Network Infrastructure	34%	32%
Process/Workflow Redesign	16%	32%
Improvement of Information Systems (IS) Department	24%	29%

Source: 15th Annual HIMSS Leadership Survey (Feb. 23, 2004), sponsored by Superior Consultant Company. Reprinted with permission.

Projected IT Priorities (today vs. next two years)

	In Two Years	Today
Upgrade Security/HIPAA Compliant	25%	48%
Reduce Medical Errors/Promote Patient Safety	48%	47%
Replace/Upgrade Inpatient Clinical Systems	33%	44%
Implement Wireless Systems	23%	37%
Implement an Electronic Medical Record	43%	33%
Upgrade Network Infrastructure	21%	32%
Process/Workflow Redesign	27%	32%
Improvement of Information Systems (IS) Department	17%	29%

Source: 15th Annual HIMSS Leadership Survey (Feb. 23, 2004), sponsored by Superior Consultant Company. Reprinted with permission.

truths: Health care really will be safer with electronic systems backing up human decision-makers, and, ultimately, more efficient as both financial and clinical information are shared quickly and easily.

But because these systems involve such huge cultural change, implementation is often bumpy and unpredictable. Lowenhaupt sees a typical pattern where the organization first enjoys a peak of unreasonably high expectations, naively believing the system will solve all its patient safety and quality issues. "Then they drop to a valley of despair. They have to move to the point where they realize [technology] doesn't solve patient safety [problems], it's simply a tool we can use. One of the tasks the board [has] is to dampen that peak of unreasonable expectation and bring up that valley of despair."

The board can also help by sticking to its commitment as time goes on and competing priorities challenge the IT expansion plan. "The board has to have the will and the staying power to say this is important strategically to our organization," says Sisters of Mercy trustee Priest. "When margins are down a little or someone says they really want to build a new building, we have to say, 'We've said as an organization we are going to make a big investment in an information system, and it's going to improve patient care. This is our big commitment.'"

Physicians:
The Key to IT Success

By Sheree Geyer

Brent James, M.D., recalls the initial reluctance of a physician asked to participate in a technology pilot program at Intermountain Health Care (IHC) in Salt Lake City in 1999. James, executive director of the Institute of Health Care Delivery Research and vice president of medical research, spearheads clinical improvement efforts at IHC.

"We approached a general internist about buying a quarter of his time to help roll out a diabetes system. When we asked him to use our electronic medical record (EMR) tools as part of the project, he said, 'No way.' He'd seen the effects of testing these systems on other colleagues. They couldn't bill; couldn't operate a practice. It resulted in unhappy patients and unhappy staff," he explains.

James' story illustrates the challenges that hospitals face when trying to introduce new technology to physicians. Computer software fraught with "bugs" or information systems that crash regularly can have a negative impact on a physician's resolve to incorporate technology into his or her patient care and practice management scheme. As hospital trustees weigh the cost and patient safety issues of long-term planning and investment, physician acceptance and adoption of various computer technologies becomes a key element to their success.

Sheree Geyer is a writer based in Orland Park, Illinois.

405

Improving Physician Acceptance
of Hospital Technology

Hospitals increasingly rely on an array of technology to help streamline operations and improve patient care. A 2002 hospital executive report published by Cap Gemini Ernst & Young (CGE&Y),
McLean, Virginia, states that, "by standardizing and, where possible, automating internal processes and procedures, health care
organizations can reduce the amount of time it takes to move information internally, speed up the overall care process, utilize scarce
resources more efficiently, and enhance patient safety."

However, the October 2002 issue of "Healthcare Leadership and
Management Report," published by the American Governance &
Leadership Group, Bozeman, Montana, states that "Health system
leaders often lack a complete and concrete understanding of the
issues faced by physicians in their daily professional practice." The
report goes on to state that "To successfully engage physicians in
the adoption of clinical systems, physicians must be able to perceive
how a new system will influence three major activities that compete for their time throughout their professional day." Those three
activities are providing clinical care to patients; enhancing practice
management; and balancing personal and professional time.

James agrees, noting that "physicians are our primary customers, so
if technology doesn't work for them, it doesn't work for anybody.

"On a day-to-day basis, physicians are involved in competing
demands for their time. Any tool has to be immediately available
and beneficial to them. They have to perceive value," he asserts.

Daniel B. Hier, M.D., professor of neurology and rehabilitation,
University of Illinois at Chicago (UIC) Medical Center, agrees. He
says a health care system must be fast, smart and well-integrated
to enhance physician productivity, adding that "if it takes a doctor more time to do something on screen than by hand, you're not
going to have a happy doctor."

James believes that, to be accepted by physicians, information
technology (IT) must be blended into workflow and improve productivity. To do this, hospitals must first "build a foundation by
working with each staff member and integrating technology at each
step in the process." James, who says that, "each step should pay
its own way and lay the foundation for the next step," believes that
long-term planning ensures project success.

For example, he cites the building blocks required to install a hospital EMR system. These include billing and scheduling; a rich clinical data environment that includes lab and pharmacy information; an electronic filing cabinet that puts patient information in electronic form; and decision support tools to identify patient medical problems and help clinicians manage disease.

Computerized Physician Order Entry Systems

Computerized physician order entry (CPOE) systems are an important part of a hospital's technology arsenal. By digitizing prescriptions, CPOE helps prevent allergic reactions in patients and eliminates redundancies and errors resulting from misread handwritten orders. The Leapfrog Group, a Washington, D.C.–based consortium of public and private health care purchasers, advocates hospital adoption of these systems, noting in a fact sheet that "CPOE systems can be remarkably effective in reducing the rate of serious medication errors."

CPOE has reduced error rates by 55 percent at Brigham and Women's Hospital (BWH), a teaching facility affiliated with the Harvard Medical School in Boston. Brigham and Women's spent $1.9 million to initiate the system in 1993 and $500,000 a year on upgrades and maintenance, according to "First Do No Harm," published by BWH in spring 2003. The Leapfrog Group fact sheet estimates the hospital's "return on its initial investment has been between $5 million and $10 million in annual savings."

To work effectively, CPOE needs to reflect physician work practices, according to a report published in September 2002 by Gartner Inc., a technology research and advisory firm based in Stamford, Connecticut. The report, entitled "How to Gain Value from Physician Order Entry," encourages health care organizations to integrate CPOE seamlessly into clinical practices.

"Physicians won't use a [C]POE system if it seems clumsy or takes too much time. Accordingly, a good CPOE system will seem transparent to the physician and can be customized to suit individual preferences and the methods of the different medical specialties," the report states.

James also underscores the importance of building decision-making tools into the architecture of an order entry system. Without decision support, CPOE won't deliver the desired clinical results or cost savings to a hospital, he says.

Experts agree that CPOE represents one component of an overall system that should include advanced clinical information systems (CIS) and EMR. "Healthcare Leadership and Management Report" states that, while CIS and CPOE can be implemented independently, "real quality and financial opportunities" result when hospitals use CIS/CPOE as a lever to redesign processes." The Gartner report reiterates this point, stating that "all CPOE systems must be implemented as part of a comprehensive computer-based patient record strategy."

Kevin M. Fickenscher, M.D., partner and national director with CSC Consulting Group, an IT services company based in El Segundo, California, argues against the wholesale adoption of health care technology at the expense of clinical workers and processes and says hospitals should examine how they use information before installing a system.

"CPOE in use without the benefit of the other elements of health care information systems only does a limited amount of work. Information technology is as much about process as about application. The fundamental problem is a lack of attention to people, process and knowledge issues at the expense of technology," he explains.

Barriers to Physician Acceptance of Technology

"Healthcare Leadership and Management Report" states that "less than 20 percent of a given physician population is actively open to the adoption of new technologies, but another 60 percent can be persuaded to adopt over time." Experts offer their views on why doctors don't readily embrace technology.

Molly Coye, M.D., M.P.H., CEO of Health Technology Center (HealthTech) believes that systems that fail to live up to their claims, coupled with the pressures of running a practice, discourage many physicians from trying new technologies. HealthTech, a nonprofit research and education organization based in San Francisco, studies the impact of future technologies on health care organizations and delivery systems, according to its Web site.

"Doctors are under a great deal of stress with inadequate information and support. Their experience has been that new technologies that are supposed to support them and save time end up costing them time and money," Coye explains.

Suzanne Delbanco, the Leapfrog Group's executive director, speculates that doctors, like most people, instinctively resist change. CPOE systems, which electronically transmit orders, can disconcert those physicians accustomed to writing orders by hand or issuing them verbally.

Robert B. Williams, M.D., a principal with CGE&Y in Atlanta, says that to break through "the first barrier" of physicians' resistance to technology, a tool must demonstrate its worth, adding that "the physicians with whom I work are very engaged to influence change" in hospital processes and procedures.

Williams, who categorizes physicians as early, middle and late adopters of technology, advises hospitals "to recruit early adopters of technology as soon as possible and then have a strategy for those who are resistant. Because of their enthusiasm and foresight, [early adopters] need 'stroking' and support for their input and effort. They are key to serving as opinion leaders and becoming ambassadors for the project. Providing presentation skills and leadership training for them can be good quid pro quo for these physicians."

"Healthcare Leadership and Management Report" says that, in recruiting for leadership committees, hospitals usually seek "the majority of physicians who are in the middle of the adoption curve." It adds that "there is an increasingly enthusiastic group of early adopters ready to move faster than the rest of the organization. This group will require a strategy to manage and sustain their engagement."

Blackford Middleton, M.D., M.P.H., M.Sc., chairman of the Center for IT Leadership at the Partners HealthCare System, Boston, observes that physicians recently graduated from medical school tend to be early adopters of technology.

"There's a demonstrable shift in the attitude toward technology by young physicians who grew up with computers and had a PC since birth. They're more comfortable with technology. They all carry PDAs [personal digital assistants] and have e-mail," he observes.

Though young doctors appear to adopt technology more quickly than older colleagues, Williams says, "some of the best participants in the design process come from the over-50 crowd. Their contributions are superior because they know practice management so well."

Physician Stewardship of IT Projects

To ensure the effective integration of technology with clinical data, hospitals need doctors to sit on leadership or steering committees. Leadership committees, which oversee IT installation, allow physicians to provide clinical input during the early stages of design and development. "It is difficult to overstate the importance of creating the right leadership and participant group for a CPOE project," according to "Healthcare Leadership and Management Report."

Williams, who says that doctors possess a "keen understanding of workflow practices," endorses physician participation on steering committees, adding that "it's important for physicians to advocate the technology they need to use and use it well." To maximize the value of physicians' time and keep projects on track, he says that meetings must be structured.

"Work sessions have to be well-focused, well-planned and end on time. Doctors need to feel they've made a contribution and see the benefit to the activity," he explains.

CGE&Y developed a "Physician-Driven Design Framework" to encourage multiple groups of physicians to participate in the development of CIS projects, especially electronic order entry systems. The framework, which "keeps the benefits that physicians value front and center in the process," includes four activities: those that structure a technology project and encourage physicians to set expectations; those that structure decision-making; those that communicate issues and decisions; and those that encourage personal adoption of technology.

"Healthcare Leadership and Management Report" suggests that physician steering committees use a "key decision matrix" to organize work and track decisions. This tool minimizes time requirements for busy physicians and keeps participants up to date on pending issues and decisions. The report adds that most health care organizations reimburse physicians "at a fair market value" for consulting time served on steering committees. William L. Galanter, M.D., Ph.D., director of clinical decision support at the University of Illinois at Chicago, agrees with that assessment and believes that physician reimbursement should be factored into the overall cost of system integration, given the competing demands for doctors' time.

"Doctors are much less interested in volunteering their services as the market shrinks. Part of the cost of implementation is going to be paying doctors to participate," Galanter says.

Clinician Input and Training Keys to Success

Along with physicians, hospitals need to solicit input from other clinicians in the design and development of an IT system, including CPOE. Nurses, pharmacists and lab technicians need to be brought into the mix since they also use that technology. Williams says hospitals that exclude clinical workers from the design and development process lose valuable information and slow the system's adoption.

"The biggest mistake facilities make is focusing on the physicians [alone], which can diminish the important contributions of others. CPOE significantly impacts the workflow of nurses and pharmacists, which affects their services and adoption of the system," Williams says.

Hier, who served on the selection committee for UIC's EMR system, agrees. In his 2003 paper, "Resolving the Information Paradox: Why the Next Generation of Electronic Health Records Must Transform Workflow," he states that "process reengineering will require major investments in staff and training. This means investing time, money and attention toward training company staff."

Galanter says implementation of a hospital's IT system "will run more smoothly" when hospitals include staff members beyond physicians in the process. "They [clinicians] will use it more and be more positive about change if they're listened to in the process."

To speed the design process, James suggests a tiered approach to gathering clinical data that targets "nurses first, then your pharmacists, then your physicians." He says that physician input should come last when planning a major system installation since "nurses perform 80 percent of the work in a hospital."

Williams agrees that nurses should be trained to use technology first. This accelerates system adoption since nurses can train doctors while assisting them during patient care duties. He also emphasizes the need for one-on-one private training sessions to ensure a physician's comfort level with a new system.

412

Part Eight

"Invest in trainers who are elbow-to-elbow with users and get them up to speed soon. Getting doctors to look competent in front of other people is a critical part of the process," he says.

Trustees Need to Include Physicians

James predicts that major changes in hospital technology will occur in the next five to 10 years, driven primarily by "big hospitals and multi-specialty clinical groups of more than 10 physicians." Facilities that fail to invest in technology "will become so inefficient, they won't be able to compete, and they'll die," he says. Williams also forecasts dire consequences for institutions that don't make the leap to technology.

"Not making the investment can lead to loss of medical staff in some markets if competitors move ahead effectively; loss of patients in some markets; and reduced reimbursements," he predicts. Fickenscher says that senior management officials, including the CFO and CEO, need to be brought in on major technology projects, given their strategic importance to the health care organization. Additionally, because capital expenditures on information technology purchases, such as CPOE systems, represent a major investment that can cost hospitals millions of dollars, trustees must carefully assess their long-term goals, he adds.

"Lots of organizations are making investments that will last for decades, and there are strategic questions to face. Do they go with an open architecture or a tried-and-true platform? If they go with cutting-edge technology, is the environment totally stable or will the system be buggy? There's not a cookie cutter answer. It depends on the culture and structure of the organization," Fickenscher explains.

James believes that hospital trustees who approve spending for major technology systems need "to have a shared vision and a good strategy." Fickenscher adds that "when you move beyond the vision, support from people in the trenches becomes crucial. That's why you need a multidisciplinary team."

Williams outlines a series of steps to help hospital trustees analyze their information technology needs before embarking on a system installation. He says to first confirm the health care organization's business and clinical case; create a seven-year total cost of ownership analysis and readiness assessment; and engage physicians in the process from the beginning.

Information Technology
May Not Be "It"
for Patient Safety

By Jan Greene

Processes outweigh computers in improving quality.

Information technology is often touted as the panacea for many of the problems inherent in health care delivery—the best way to stamp out error and reinvigorate public confidence in the quality of hospital care.

Employers and payers across the country have adopted computerized physician order entry (CPOE) as the hallmark for hospital quality and IT legitimacy, as well as a prerequisite for enhanced reimbursement and performance bonuses. And so, hospitals by the hundreds have been putting up the big bucks to invest in clinical information systems. It may be a small percentage so far—just 4 percent have adopted CPOE systems, according to a recent study. But another 17 percent reported themselves well along the way, and experts say most hospitals are at least in the planning stages of adopting CPOE.

And yet, over the past six months, some distressing evidence has emerged about the lack of success of some CPOE implementations, indicating there's a much higher prevalence of unintended

---

Jan Greene is a writer based in Alameda, California.

consequences than was reported in the early, enthusiastic published reports about computerized order entry.

As an example, in Philadelphia, University of Pennsylvania researchers reported 22 different problems their new computerized order entry system actually created along the way to improving care. Clinicians at the Children's Hospital of Pittsburgh reported they saw an actual rise in mortality after installing their CPOE system among a group of seriously ill transfer patients.

In fact, IT projects in general are often unsuccessful, a commentary in the March 9, 2005, *Journal of the American Medical Association* argues, pointing to surveys showing that just 15 percent to 30 percent of IT projects are completed successfully—on time and on budget—and a third are abandoned midstream.

So what does this mean for IT, the so-called savior of the modern hospital? Is it time to stop the rush toward computerization? Or should boards go ahead and spend the millions needed to initially install a CPOE system and cross their fingers that all will go well? The bill for CPOE setup alone can range from $3 million to $10 million, with substantial continuing costs to keep it running. And many hospitals buy clinical systems as part of a bigger electronic health record initiative that can cost tens of millions over several years, adding in components such as bar code tracking of drugs and decision support alerts to help clinicians follow evidence-based guidelines for care.

The answer is neither of the above. There is now a decent body of evidence, order entry specialists say, to show that IT systems, properly installed, can reduce errors and improve quality. And there's plenty of information available on how to go about it. In fact, the researchers at University of Pennsylvania and Pittsburgh Children's have shared their own missteps from which others can learn. And even though trustees won't be in the trenches during the "go-live" stage, they still have a major role to play ensuring that their organizations are ready for clinical information systems and that the groundwork is laid properly before the big bucks get spent.

Prioritize Spending on Process Change

The main piece of advice experts give hospitals buying clinical information systems is to spend at least $2 to $3 on organizational

Slowly but Surely for CPOE

Despite the stories of rocky computerized physician order entry (CPOE) system starts, there are plenty of successes as well. One is Alamance Regional Medical Center in Burlington, South Carolina, a community hospital where long lead time and plenty of attention to process change led to significant CPOE use by community physicians over time. Even though using CPOE is voluntary, 85 percent of Alamance's doctors now do so. The hospital just won an award from Microsoft Corporation as the top hospital in the country using its technology.

"They started planning 10 years ahead of time and their planning process was superb and very inclusive," says Joan Ash, associate professor of medical informatics at the Oregon Health and Science University in Portland. "The clinicians were so used to the idea by the time CPOE came along, there were a few grumbly ones, but they all knew what it was about, upsides and downsides." The long lead time was a consequence of the merger of two hospitals that became the current Alamance Medical Center. After the merger, a new campus was built and the organization started from scratch, developing all new processes to replace two very different cultures.

"We were fortunate to have that exercise," says Ralph Holt, an Alamance board member since 1959 and its current chair. "We were also fortunate to have some very strong, capable medical staff leadership and our administrative team . . . that's been largely in place for 20 years."

Communicating with physicians has been a board priority. "We rotate our board meeting with the medical staff executive committee," Holt says. "You can't do enough to keep (physician input) on a high plane." Alamance implemented CPOE slowly—unit by unit—without requiring physicians to use it. "The reason we had success was that we didn't have any huge mandates," explains Marshall Anderson, M.D., hospital chief of staff. "We made our system a voluntary one and left it up to our physicians to see that this was a good thing for our patients."

Initially, he acknowledges, the system was somewhat slow and wasn't universally popular. But the IT staff kept making improvements, and, ultimately, the system gained adherents. The hospital has since begun careful efforts to adopt an electronic patient record to go along with order entry. "We've gone at this slowly to make the transition, and in some ways it's bad that it's not completely done," Anderson says. "But it's good in that it hasn't blown up in our faces."

—Jan Greene

process change for every $1 spent on the hardware and software. Some consultants say that the ratio should be even more lopsided— just 10 percent spent on the technology, the rest on organizational change and training. So what is organizational change?

As anyone who carries a cell phone knows, technology changes your daily life in fundamental ways, but sometimes introduces problems you couldn't have foreseen. For as wonderful as it is to be able to call home to say you're stuck in traffic and will be late, the device also requires you to remember to recharge it and turn it off when you go to the movies.

So it is in the hospital. When a clinical unit switches from paper charting to electronics, the whole care environment changes. Of course, there are obvious improvements, such as being able to enter an order immediately, so the information is instantly available to anyone on the system. And there's no confusion about what the prescriber meant by an illegible scrawl on paper. (See "Death by Handwriting" in *Trustee*'s October 2005 issue.)

On the flip side, however, at Pittsburgh Children's, inadequate bandwidth slowed the system to a crawl. Nurses and doctors found themselves spending precious time in front of computer screens instead of tending to critically ill patients.

Bottom line: Using IT requires a lot of thought about how it will change the way people do their jobs and how processes will change. This means planning, imagining and thinking ahead to how things will be different.

And because it's almost impossible to anticipate everything, it means making regular adjustments.

"In general, people still underestimate the cost and effort for a successful implementation," says Erica Drazen, vice president of emerging practices for First Consulting Group, a Boston IT consulting group. "And people underestimate the amount of change this takes in process. If you go back and dissect [failures], the problems are probably 20 percent system and 80 percent implementation."

CPOE Gone Wild

The early reports on CPOE, led by David Bates, M.D., and colleagues at Boston's Brigham and Women's Hospital in the late 1990s, suggested it could reduce adverse drug events by a dramatic

80 percent. A big problem here, however, was adapting the experience of these CPOE leaders—teaching hospitals that spent years designing their own unique clinical computer systems—to the typical community hospital.

The second wave of IT users has been buying off-the-shelf systems from vendors—with varied success. "Now hospitals are buying standard products, and the talent pool within hospitals is nowhere near what it was at Brigham and Women's or Regenstreif," two early innovators, Drazen says. (Regenstreif Institute in Indianapolis is a medical research institute associated with the Indiana University School of Medicine.)

The good news is, as the technology has evolved and matured, so has the published literature about how well it works. For instance, researchers at the University of Pennsylvania School of Medicine wrote in a March 2005 article in the *Journal of the American Medical Association* that their CPOE system actually introduced the opportunity for hospital employees to create 22 types of medication error risks.

As examples, it was easy for prescribers to mistake a list of medications stocked by the pharmacy for recommended dosages of those drugs; antibiotic renewal notices ended up on paper charts and were missed by doctors using electronic charts; and it was easy for doctors to choose the wrong patient name from the small-size type on crowded computer screens. Three-quarters of the house staff reported observing each of the 22 errors committed at least weekly. And this was in what would otherwise be considered a successful implementation.

An even more disturbing report came from an article in the December 2005 issue of *Pediatrics,* which described how physicians treating intensive care unit (ICU) patients at the Children's Hospital of Pittsburgh tracked the mortality rate of those patients transferred into the unit by ambulance and found it actually went up significantly after CPOE adoption. The article also listed a number of processes that were changed at the time of the transition from paper to computer, such as requiring drug orders to wait until the patient had arrived at the hospital rather than allowing an ICU fellow to order drugs while the patient was in transit.

CPOE specialists interpreting the study said it showed that the technology itself wasn't the problem; rather, a series of process changes gummed things up. "I do think there's very clear evidence there are all sorts of glitches that occur during the implementation [of CPOE]," says Robert Wachter, M.D., chief of the medical service at UC San Francisco Medical Center. "This is substantially harder than people thought it would be."

However, Children's Hospital administrators didn't agree with the ICU researchers' findings, who concluded that there was some connection between the elevated mortality rate and CPOE. The hospital's medical director defends the way their CPOE implementation was handled, saying that, overall, it was a success and followed many of the good, basic principles of getting an information system under way.

"Before we went live with CPOE, we spent more than a year in development, in which we had multidisciplinary teams work together" to personalize the vendor's system for the hospital, says Eugene Wiener, M.D. "It gave us an opportunity to do a lot of process redesign. Those process changes were more important than implementation of a CPOE system."

As for the unintended consequences documented in the ICU, Wiener says they were an inevitable part of any technology change and have been fixed.

"We learned you can never have too much planning, training and education," he says. "We think we did it well. You never can say something's perfect." There are natural rises and dips in mortality rates over time, Wiener notes, and overall mortality in the ICU has fallen since CPOE implementation two years ago. "We believe this is a small subset and a very narrow time line that caused this appearance of a rise in mortality," he says.

What to Look For

Once the decision is made to move forward, trustees can and should monitor their hospital's CPOE progress (or regress). That would include keeping tabs on the administration's continuing commitment to the project from start to finish. Specifically, consultant Drazen recommends that a senior executive outside of IT should take responsibility for its success.

From the outset, experts agree that part of a hospital's preparation for CPOE should involve a broad effort to develop "order sets"—that is, standard ways that clinicians at that hospital provide care, ideally based on evidence, but tweaked to fit with how a particular medical staff operates. These individualized standards of care are plugged into the automated system and are critical to its success.

Unfortunately, this is a process that's carried out hospital-by-hospital, and often, therefore, a great waste of resources, Bates contends. Some hospitals make the mistake of expecting these order sets to be provided by an IT vendor, but the vendors generally see them as a hospital responsibility.

"[Vendors] expect you to develop the knowledge and put it into the system," Bates says. "This points to the need for a national knowledge repository . . . something the federal government should support."

Once the CPOE system is up and running, trustees should be asking for outcome data indicating whether order entry is actually reducing errors and improving care. Boards can ask for measures such as the number of adverse drug events occurring during designated time periods, and how often certain medication alerts go off, such as drug-drug interactions. Other common measures, such as length of stay and mortality, should also be tracked before and after the IT implementation to check for unintended negative consequences and, ideally, to measure improvements.

"It should be possible to implement information technology without having negative impacts," Bates says, "and in some instances, having a substantial positive impact."

Care and Feeding of Legacy Systems

Another point to keep in mind is that clinical information systems are a long-term process rather than a one-time event. Not only do order entry, bar coding and decision support build on the electronic patient record—and one another—they each need to be maintained over time. But it's typical for legacy systems—those that have been in use for some time—to be neglected by an organization when it's focusing its attention on the bright shiny toy of the hour.

That's what's happened to some pharmacy medication management systems, according to research by the Institute for Safe Medication Practices, Huntingdon Valley, Pennsylvania. The institute asked 182 hospitals to run tests on their computerized pharmacy systems to check how well they could detect unsafe orders. Fewer than half were able to detect orders for medications that exceeded the safe maximum dose, and just four of the 182 systems were able to detect all unsafe orders.

Researchers from the Institute for Safe Medication Practices concluded that failure to update the systems' software could be partly to blame. More than half of the systems were more than five years old with no recent upgrades, and 38 percent of them were at least eight years old, without upgrades. "These systems need to be watered and fed, but that may not end up as a priority," explains Stuart Levine, an informatics specialist with the institute.

Are You Ready for "IT"?

Will it take your hospital 10 years to get ready for CPOE? Probably not, but it might take more than one.

Because the board has a big-picture, strategic planning role in the organization, deciding when to plunk down the big money on a clinical information system is an appropriate job for trustees.

One of the first things to know is whether there is a positive, trusting relationship between the administration and its physicians. That's bedrock for getting through a transition that will turn care giving upside down for a while.

"You need to have a way of judging the culture . . . and sensing whether there's trust there or not—that's the most important thing," says Joan Ash, associate professor of medical informatics at the Oregon Health and Science University in Portland.

Hospital staff responsible for quality assurance should formally evaluate processes that would be affected by computerized order entry and decide what changes need to be made. This should happen even before a vendor and a system are chosen. And once specific systems are under consideration, hospital representatives need to see them in action—not in alpha or beta testing, but in real-life use, advises Stuart Levine, informatics specialist for the

Continued →

Institute for Safe Medication Practices in Huntingdon Valley, Pennsylvania.

"It may be prudent for trustees to be part of that selection process, to actually go out and see what exists out there," he says. And take a look at all the options. "It amazes me that organizations decide to go with a certain vendor without having looked at other vendors in the market," Levine adds.

Choosing a vendor can be tough given the large number of clinical systems on the market, says David Bates, M.D., of Boston's Brigham and Women's Hospital. Soon, however, hospitals will be able to look at a certification process for IT vendors through a new organization called the Certification Commission for Healthcare IT. "There are way too many vendors in the marketplace now," Bates says. "This should help reduce some of the uncertainty." The certification process will tell potential buyers whether a particular vendor's product meets the commission's standards for functionality and interoperability.

Trustees should also find out whether the administration has an "informaticist" on staff or plans to hire a consultant for that crucial duty. Computerized physician order entry specialists were unanimous in recommending that someone be on hand who has been through a CPOE implementation before. Even better, that person should be a trained informaticist, a hybrid position between clinician and computer expert.

Informaticists tend to be doctors, nurses, pharmacists and other caregivers who are interested in IT and recognize that there's a huge need for someone who can bridge the clinical and computer worlds, two sides that often have a tough time communicating. "Neither group understands each other or their work," says Robert Wachter, M.D., chief of medical service at UC San Francisco Medical Center. "You also have to be very good politically—you're nobody's friend after a while on these jobs. Your CIO can't do this, the [chief medical officer] or [vice president of medical affairs] can't do it. It has to be someone whose job it is to do this. We [at UC San Francisco] came to believe our $100 million [IT] investment could hinge on having such a person." For a smaller institution, that person might be on the vendor's staff or it could just be someone in IT who knows enough to call in a consulting informatician at the right time.

—Jan Greene

Writing the Big Check

Ultimately, hospitals and health systems should not rely too much on a computer system to improve quality and patient safety. The hard work of making sure that processes of care are safe and effective is really what the quality movement is about.

"What trustees need to keep in mind is that CPOE is not a turn-key operation," Levine advises. "Just because you've decided to write the check for the application and its installation doesn't mean you're getting all the benefits of it."

It's that check-writing commitment that makes trustees understandably nervous about a technology that is still being tested. And yet, trustees face great pressure from payers to prove quality of care through markers such as adoption of clinical IT.

The fear of spending a lot of money on a system that doesn't work or is rejected by clinicians—which happened in a highly celebrated case at Cedars Sinai in Los Angeles—has a lot of hospitals on the fence about investing in CPOE, says UC San Francisco's Wachter.

And the recent spate of articles revealing some unattractive, unintended consequences of these systems could prompt more board and administration hand-wringing. Still, Wachter comments, "I'd hate to see this literature push ambivalent systems to not computerize."

Instead, hospital administrators and boards should be taking the opportunity to look closely at processes, clean them up, put the right teams in place, and design a plan for a slow and careful introduction of technology.

They should be sure there will be knowledgeable staff on hand to tweak things after they "go live" and catch the inevitable work-arounds that caregivers devise when the system puts unexpected roadblocks in their way, Wachter says.

"If you don't have the right horses in place, you're probably better off waiting," he advises. But IT's role in clinical care is inevitable.

"Delaying may be the right decision for next year," he says. "But not for 2010."

Index

(continued)